VICTORIAN GLASS

Opaque jade green Sandwich vase, with opaque white
Sawtooth bowl, of the 1840 period

VICTORIAN GLASS

SPECIALTIES
OF THE NINETEENTH CENTURY

BY RUTH WEBB LEE

PUBLISHED BY THE AUTHOR
FRAMINGHAM CENTRE , MASSACHUSETTS

ELEVENTH EDITION

ACKNOWLEDGMENTS

Victorian Glass has been in preparation for so many years that I am fearful credit may not be given to some good friend who may have lent me anything from a goblet to an item of valuable information. When this volume was first advertised as being "in preparation" it meant that the illustrations and notes were under way. The actual writing could not be accomplished until all the illustrations and notes pertaining to the glass were in order, because each chapter is related, one way or another, to the preceding or the succeeding one. All the photographs and line drawings were not completed until last fall, so the actual writing has been done during the spring and early summer of 1944. It was not thought it would require so long a time but wartime conditions imposed many delays and obstacles. Moreover, the average person does not have the faintest notion of how long a time is needed in the preparation of a highly specialized book, although it all appears so simple in printed form!

Practically all the illustrations of glass in the line drawings were taken directly from old trade catalogues in my possession, with the addition of a few pieces I purchased or borrowed to fill in. There are patterns included here which do not appear in any catalogues I have seen, such as the Fuchsia pattern, produced by the Boston & Sandwich Glass Co. I am indebted to the late Mrs. Bertha Garfield for that group. She collected the Sandwich Fuchsia for some years, as well as Morning Glory.

Miss J. Lindenberger of Washington, D. C., kindly lent me some dishes in patterns difficult to locate in New England, as did Mrs. Henry R. Gilliam. Mrs. F. H. Mann cheerfully sent me a picture of her novel "Shoe" lamp, and Mrs. Richard R. Kohrs came to my rescue when a missing dish was needed to complete a line in the Ball and Swirl pattern.

Some years ago Mr. Timothy Mojonnier sent me photographs of his late wife's collection of purple marble glass, in her memory. The pictures showed rarities, as well as massed effects from large groupings, so it is a pleasure to include them in this book. Mrs. Clara Edwards, who has specialized for some time in complete sets of pattern glass, kindly allowed me to use several of her groups, which will prove educational to those collectors unfamiliar with the possibilities of what may be accomplished with table sets. It may take a little time to find all the needed pieces, but there is always the joy of picking up a plate here or a creamer there from another unexpected source.

A special word should be said for the men in our armed services who have enjoyed hobbies that have now to be put aside. Many of them write to me and I find that the thought of their collections is one more thing that they cling to and it gives them pleasure to talk about them. There is Sergeant Robert Van Deventer, who sent me pictures of his collection of ducks a few years ago. They appear in the chapter devoted to animal dishes. Sergeant Van Deventer is in an engineering unit and is, I believe, overseas at present. Then there is S/Sgt. Richard Smith, who despite his busy days saw to it that I had some needed pieces in the Priscilla pattern for use in the line drawings. He helped considerably because his pattern is rarely found in New England. Lt. Clifton Blake furnished me with a list of his Bakewell Block, and lent me some of his pieces, which also appear among the line drawings. It is an early flint glass pattern which few collectors or dealers recognize because it is so scarce. Then there is Corporal Stutts, out in Texas, who is having a time finding the more unusual items in his Palmette pattern. Corporal Whipple, Sgt. Dale and Warrant Officer Bonica are others who find relaxation in "antiquing" excursions, when time and opportunity permit. All these men are looking forward to the day when they can return home and enjoy their hobbies once more.

Mr. and Mrs. R. E. Dougherty furnished me with pictures of their large collection of Coin glass, which is a scarce pattern.

Mrs. Maude Feld was very helpful in assisting me with the rare animal dishes.

There is nothing Mrs. Austin Chilson likes better than to discuss any phases of pattern glass. If I required an item to fill in a line of drawings she was always willing and helpful. She once wrote me of a dish I needed and said: "You can buy, borrow or steal it, whatever you like." Her sense of humor is never-failing.

Mrs. Lloyd Wilson of Washington, D. C., kindly gave me access to her collection of slippers, which was immensely helpful. It is of inestimable value for collectors to be able to *see,* because no printed words can convey impressions of slippers, boots and shoes in their myriad patterns. Mrs. Wilson has been an avid collector, so it is difficult to find anything in her line which she does not have.

Words cannot describe the kindly hospitality of Mr. and Mrs. Russell Neilson of Madison, N. J., who went to no end of trouble on my account that I might have a complete photographic group of their large and varied collection of vases. After all, it is upsetting to those who own large collections to have their house in a turmoil while a photographer spends two or three days rigging up all sorts of apparatus in order to picture all possible details.

Most helpful in many ways were Mr. and Mrs. Hobart Hollis of New York City, whose vast collection of glass hats is shown here. Mr. Hollis has a practical view of the hats and his knowledge is that of one well versed in the mechanics of glassmaking. He has left no stone unturned in gaining both knowledge and the history of the hats in his collection. I feel greatly indebted to both Mr. and Mrs. Hollis.

Others who contributed greatly by sending me lists of their glassware, which have added to the classifications, are Mr. Paul E. Zeeb, Mrs. Hayes Bigelow, Mrs. H. A. Fluharty, Mrs. George H. Fenno and Mr. Robert L. England. The *American Collector* also was helpful, and perhaps there are others whose names have been overlooked because of the length of time this book

Acknowledgments

has been in preparation. Without the assistance which was always promptly and cheerfully given by collectors and dealers, this book could not be so complete in detail. Friends lightened an intolerably heavy burden by sharing it with me.

RUTH WEBB LEE

INTRODUCTION

When my first book, *Early American Pressed Glass,* was presented to the public in December, 1931, it represented pioneer work and concerned the identification and classification of patterns of pressed glass tableware produced in this country during the 1840's through the 1880's. It had been said that no one could possibly hope to untangle the innumerable designs produced during such a highly commercialized era. Moreover, not so many years before, collectors of American blown glass did not deem worthy of mention the type of glassware which flooded our markets during the decades immediately preceding and following the Civil War. Sincere but uninformed lovers of antiques openly derided it as "Early Woolworth." We hear no more of that today.

During the years since the first edition of *Early American Pressed Glass* appeared, numerous patterns noted in that book became so popular that prices soared to fictitious values and the earliest and most sought-after patterns were almost entirely controlled by dealers or collectors. When that book was written, during 1929, 1930 and 1931, a staggering total of nearly three hundred designs and thousands of forms had been drawn, photographed, described and classified. Then I realized that it must be finished sometime, even though every available pattern was not represented. In 1933 I revised and enlarged it, after intense research work in the Pittsburgh area revealed a considerable amount of important historical data. No additional patterns were added, as the book was almost too heavy and bulky in its original form. The changes consisted of stating when and where a large percentage of the patterns were produced and additions were made to the classifications. The plate numbers were not changed, so as to benefit owners of the first and second editions. In 1934 I began what was planned to be a supplement to *Early*

American Pressed Glass, in an effort to carry on the patterns omitted in the first volume. The artist who did the line drawings had completed work on over one hundred goblets, when a book devoted to that specialty appeared. In the meantime, the tremendous popularity of old pressed glass tableware created a demand for sets of photographs, or, in other words, a small Handbook to carry about so that collectors could identify patterns without having to handle so heavy a volume as *Early American Pressed Glass,* with its 683 pages. In 1936 my *Handbook of Early American Pressed Glass Patterns* was published. It consisted of all the photographs and line drawings utilized in the large volume but not the text.

About this time it became apparent that the great demand for pattern glass by both dealers and collectors had made fraud profitable. A reproduction of the Horn of Plenty water tumbler appeared, followed by a copy of the Westward-Ho goblet. Between 1936 and 1938 fakers had taken advantage of the popular fad and were foisting imitations on eager but inexperienced buyers. To my regret, my "Supplement" had to be abandoned again for the time being, while *Antique Fakes and Reproductions* was being written. After that was completed, I wrote a column which appeared every month for four years, exposing each fake as quickly as it was brought to my attention. A new piece was always pictured alongside an old one, and the points of difference noted.

Once more it seemed advisable to delay the book that was started in 1934, in order to complete my last volume, *Sandwich Glass.*

Since 1940 an artist and various photographers have been working on the illustrations for the volume which in 1934 started out in life as a Supplement to *Early American Pressed Glass.* During the ensuing New Deal years there has been a definite change in the times and this in turn resulted in a difference in the trend of buying. My Supplement grew from a small Handbook consisting of between two and three hundred patterns not treated in my first book to a volume that includes many specialties which collectors indulge in today. The first few chapters of this book will be devoted to patterns and rarities of sufficient importance to demand particular attention. With some few exceptions, *Early American Pressed Glass* covers the earliest and most noteworthy patterns of old tableware collectible in sets, so it is deemed advisable to group the preponderance of the remaining patterns into chapters, particularly since most of them are of the same period. A great many of the drawings are reproduced from original old trade catalogues, thereby enabling me to state accurately where and approximately when they were produced. It must be remembered that not many of these catalogues are dated but it is as easy for one to judge styles and forms in glassware as it is for an expert in costume designing to judge periods in wearing apparel. We know, for instance, that hoop skirts were not being worn at the time of the Pan-American Exposition in Buffalo, N. Y., during President McKinley's administration.

Specialists in glass hats, slippers, vases, match holders and covered animal dishes will find much to check over against their own collections. The chatty volumes devoted to antiques in general and containing a chapter on this or that, which appeared along about 1916, were short-lived because collectors were fast approaching the point where authoritative, specialized knowledge was demanded. Today the "general" book is as outmoded as the horse and buggy.

A large part of my time during the past fifteen years has been devoted to pioneering in old glass. It has never been my policy to write about subjects on which others have written, unless important new historical data developed. A few scattered articles have appeared on wares discussed in this book, just as they did before *Sandwich Glass* came off the press, but apparently those articles did not completely satisfy collectors because persistent requests from correspondents have come in asking for more definite information. Most of the material in this volume was gathered in the Pittsburgh area in 1933, with the exception of a few specialties such as hats, slippers, vases and animal dishes. So, the Supplement which was started in 1934 has grown into a full-sized volume containing 264 pages of illustrations picturing thousands of forms, besides much important historical and technical data, to be designated in 1944 as *Victorian Glass.*

CONTENTS

ILLUSTRATIONS

Sandwich vase, opaque white and green. Period 1840

Frontispiece

PLATE   PAGE

142 Five threaded hats, probably produced by the Boston & Sandwich Glass Co. 372
143 Four case glass hats and two choice English hats, inscribed "To a good boy" 373
144 A group of case glass hats 374
145 A group of semi-opaque and milky-translucent white hats . 375
146 A group of varied shapes and colors in translucent glass . 376
147 A varied group of hats, including two in Spatter glass . . 377
148 A group of hats, all of which feature metal brims . . . 378
149 Four translucent hats, made at Baccarat, France, during the 1860's 383
150 A white frosted bonnet, an amber Hobnail hat, and another with a double crown 384
151 A varied group of hats, including a gold-iridescent; an opaque blue tumbler hat; a wine glass turned into a hat; a fedora and a bonnet 385
152 Three blown hats with double knob finials. Two tumbler hats, made from tumbler molds 386
153 Four hats, produced from a tumbler mold and a Cherry pattern hat, made from a goblet mold 387
154 A group of marked advertising and souvenir hats . . . 388
155 A group of advertising and souvenir hats 397
156 A varied group of hats 398
157 Pattern glass hats in Thousand Eye, Raindrop, Cube, Daisy and Button. Also a Jockey's and a Bandmaster's hat . 399
158 A variety of Daisy and Button hats with buttons decorated in color 400
159 Pattern glass hats. Two Diamond pattern with English Hobnail brim, one in Raindrop and others in Daisy and Button variations 401
160 Milk-white Fine Cut hat; Cube pattern. Horizontally ribbed hats 402
161 Varied group of hats 403
162 Varied group of hats, including two clown candle-snuffers, made in England 408
163 A group of cut and engraved hats. One bears the label of the Belgian factory of Val St. Lambert 409
164 Art glass hats of various types 410
165 A group of paperweight hats 411
166 Four hats, spattered or flecked in color. Two translucent colored hats 412
167 Group of choice Bristol and Bohemian hats 413
168 Cut, engraved, pressed and blown glass hats 414
169 Three unusual pitcher hats 415
170 Two pattern glass hats and two engraved styles . . . 424

VICTORIAN GLASS

Chapter I

VICTORIAN GLASS

It is now well over a century since little Victoria of England tripped down the stairs of an early morning, to be informed that she had become Queen of her Empire. By the time she actually came to the throne, the world's way of doing many things had begun to undergo a vast change. The industrial era was well under way, which meant that quantity production was becoming successful. Mass production in turn produced a great deal of new wealth. This added affluence gave the great middle class an opportunity to satisfy long-cherished dreams and they lost no time in fulfilling their desire for hitherto unknown luxuries. To these people, magnificence usually meant quantities of ornamental objects. The situation was a happy one for buyer and seller. Victorianism triumphed over conservatism!

What happened in England applied to America as well. Our great industrial era began just before the middle of the nineteenth century and thereafter gradually developed into the greatest period of prosperity in the history of this nation. The desire for decorative lavishness may well have been a strong reaction to the stern harshness of puritanism. "Victorian" is not really a set style, as were Hepplewhite and Sheraton and Chippendale. Its allurements are rather those of varied objects replete with color or ornamentation instead of the fine proportion and simplicity known to our forefathers. We responded capriciously to the veering winds of popular taste. This trend has never ended!

Queen Victoria was beloved for her admirable personal qualities. She regarded her royal authority as held in trust for the people and thus became a pattern of domestic virtue. Much progress was made by the Empire during her reign and, since it was such a long, happy one, it is little wonder that a century hence there should be in America a revival of interest in the Victorian style of furniture, glass, carpets, wallpapers and all sorts of decorative accessories.

Today there are still those critics who may be heard to speak with scorn of anything "Victorian," or that produced after the first two decades of the nineteenth century. These die-hards belong to the same category as those who scoffed at all pressed glass! Let them speak in whispers because this country of ours is filled with people who enjoy their hobbies and most of those hobbies are confined to collectibles which were produced within the confines of the Victorian era. Let it be understood that there are good and bad forms in all branches of antiques and this holds true of the period covered in this book—namely, from 1830 until the 1890's. Herein will be stressed those articles in glass which belong to the earlier period rather than the latter.

It is noticeable that the most caustic critics are usually those alleged amateurs who have never collected anything themselves. Where collectors are concerned, it is well to have an open mind. There is nothing the lover of primitive objects can do about Victorianism, because it has been developing more strongly year by year. Many collectors have been equipping their homes with Victorian furniture, filling their shelves with Victorian bric-a-brac and setting their tables with Victorian glass and china. There is a wholesome spirit about Victorianism, aside from the old-time shams and inhibitions—a spirit of honesty, a back-to-nature movement which may seem a homely virtue, but it has become the true heart's desire of the whole world during these perilous years.

Feeling that few people bother to read introductions in books, this digression is here in the hope that it will be read. Today there is a demand for "picture" books. In magazines this need has been met by *Life, Look* and many others. For several years people have been living under such a rapid-fire, hit-and-go nervous tension that few take time actually to read anything other than cookbooks, garden books and those which come under the heading of "escape" books. In a "specialist's" book, such as this one, pictures are necessary. Descriptions seldom prove adequate, even if collectors would take the time to read them. This being the case, nothing has been described in this book that is not pictured.

Of course, there is no intent to produce a picture book in *Victorian Glass.* Aside from the valuable collection of photographs and line drawings, which make identification of the various objects possible, students will discover a vast wealth of authoritative historical data. It is recorded here for their benefit, as well as to complete a record for future generations.

Reviews of any book devoted to a specialty requiring technical knowledge present a problem to magazine and newspaper editors. Their staff cannot carry the burden of experts in all fields, even if such persons were available. A book will stand or fall on its own merits. There are newspapers and magazines still left during these hectic days, which attempt to do an honest, fair bit of reporting and to those we owe a deep debt of gratitude.

Chapter II

RARITIES IN PATTERN GLASS

The acquisitive yearning which has been expressed by collectors in their efforts to acquire a table service of Ashburton, Bellflower, Tulip, or whatever the pattern, need not subside with the completing of the set. Though scoffers may insist that the pattern lacks the element of rarity, there is a vast satisfaction in discovering the twelfth item of a sought-for dozen. And if this emotion is less intense than that experienced in unearthing an individual piece so unusual as to be almost unique, pressed glass still affords good hunting.

In a number of the early patterns occur items apparently made in such limited quantity that few specimens are obtainable today. The need or demand for these particular items may have been insufficient to justify continuing their manufacture or they may have been speedily discontinued for technical or commercial reasons, such as a too complicated mold, or too high production costs, or lack of appeal to the buying public. Again, some desirable piece may have been made by a factory that did not remain long in business. Whatever the reason, all that collectors need realize is that pressed glass rarities exist and that they are worth searching for.

Probably the rarest pattern collectible in sets is the Morning Glory, illustrated on Plate 1, which was produced by the Boston & Sandwich Glass Co., of Sandwich, Mass., during the 1860's. The design has considerable merit, with its flowers and leaves in relief. It does seem as though present-day prices are somewhat artificial, if one considers value received, for it is the most expensive set one can acquire. In deciding on a table setting, there is not only the expense to consider, but relative rarity. Morning Glory is not easy to find, so apparently it was not ever

6

made in large quantities. Pictured are the goblet, champagne and egg cup. Besides these pieces there is a large compote on a high foot, a smaller compote on a low foot, sauce dishes, honey or preserve dishes (3½ inch), footed tumbler, creamer, sugar bowl and butter dish. The glass has a bell tone when tapped, though not so pronounced as in some of the earlier flint ware.

A pattern familiar to practically all collectors is Bellflower. The rarest pieces known would be, first, a hat; next, a cake plate on a standard. Then the octagonal covered sugar bowl shown on Plate 1. I know of two perfect specimens, from one of which the photograph was taken. A few others have been discovered, complete but imperfect. All were found in western states. We are justified in surmising that this exceptional bowl was either an experiment on the part of a short-lived factory or that the makers, finding that the round sugar bowl of the type usually found today was more easily and cheaply produced, discarded the eight-sided mold.

To a collector of Bellflower, the quest for an octagonal bowl will furnish a fresh aim in life. Next in order of rarity in the same early pattern are the footed tumblers (mistakenly termed rummers by some) and covered salts. The bases of the covered salts are found only in the type which has a beaded edge. The milk pitcher, which is a size larger than a creamer and smaller than the usual size water pitcher, is found only in the single vine and is ribbed almost to the end of the lip. The three-inch honey dish is another rarity. Remember, this is not the 3½-inch size. The three-inch dish always has the scallop and point edge. Egg cups and spoonholders in color are extremely rare. The colored egg cups and spoonholders were made by Deming Jarves at his Cape Cod Glass Works, which he built after he left the Boston & Sandwich Glass Co. in 1858. I suspect he produced the sapphire blue spoonholders and also the opalescent and deep-blue syrup jugs, since he was extremely fond of color and particularly blue. Many fragments in the earlier patterns in color were found at the site of his Cape Cod works.

The clear Bellflower cake plate is almost unobtainable today. The cologne bottles shown on Plate 2 I have always suspected of a foreign origin. The design is not the true *Ribbed Leaf,* as this pattern was termed originally, though it comes very close to that. These bottles, marked "Eau de Cologne" as well as unmarked, are to be found in more than one size, in opaque white, opaque jade green, and so on. The Ribbed Ivy celery vase, shown in the same illustration, is the only one I have seen to date.

The Horn of Plenty, so much in demand by collectors today, has rapidly become a scarce pattern. In this group the rarest piece is the cake plate on standard, of which I have seen or heard of but two, both being in a different size. The oval compote on a standard, illustrated on Plate 3, is one of the most elusive items, as well as the oblong covered honey dish, pictured above it. The compote is heavy, brilliant and rather suggests a large pickle dish! The standard has the thick loops at the base usually associated by collectors with Sandwich pieces. I strongly suspect that this compote may have come from the famous factory on the Cape. It should be noted that the disc design on the bowl is carried out in the base as well. So far only three of these dishes have come to my notice.

Next in rarity in this pattern is the oblong covered dish on Plate 3. I have owned one and know of two others. It is undoubtedly one of the earliest pieces in this pattern and, I might add, difficult to find in perfect condition. It is a reasonably large dish and not a covered salt size, as one collector suggested after seeing a picture. Horn of Plenty claret glasses are so seldom found as to challenge the persistence of any collector. Tall and slender, with a delicate, graceful bowl, they are desirable for more reasons than their extreme rarity. One is illustrated on Plate 1. Another noteworthy piece is the butter dish of which the cover knob is a head of Washington, queue and all. It may be found in clear yellow, and so may the six-inch plate. Look for either one if you specialize in what is hard to find. The Horn of Plenty spoonholder also may be obtained in clear yel·

low, in opaque white and in clear glass with an amber band about the edge. Six-inch compotes on a high standard, covered or open, were usually listed in the early catalogues as "sweetmeat dishes." They are rare in any early pattern and particularly so in Horn of Plenty.

The Lion pattern was produced by Gillinder & Sons of Philadelphia, Pa., in the 1870's and, though of a later date than the patterns previously mentioned, it does not lack its rarities. At this writing, one perfect lamp has been found, so it must be considered the rarest item in Lion, though not the most beautiful. After seeing it, one might judge that it was produced during the latter part of the period when this design was most popular. The lamp has a large, elongated, swirled, clear glass font, resting on a narrow collared base which is decorated with four paw feet, alternating with conventional scrolls. On two sides of the bowl is a frosted Lion head, in medallion form, similar to the finials on some of the covered dishes. It is 7¾ inches high to the top of the collar, and 5 inches across the widest part of the bowl. This Lion lamp is illustrated on Plate 90 in the 19th edition of *Early American Pressed Glass*. Of note are the cologne bottles, shown on Plate 2. I have known of exactly two pairs. There is a small powder jar, which presumably was a part of this set, not pictured. So far I have heard of three of these. The pair of oval salts pictured are also among the Lion rarities. Anyone collecting this pattern should be wary of reproductions because a large part of the set, including the goblets, has been reproduced and the market has been flooded with the copies. Fortunately the rarities described are not among them. The spurious pieces may be detected quite readily by those willing to spend a little time studying the differences between the old and the new.

Of the Centennial period, the Three Face pattern is well-known to collectors. It was made by George Duncan & Sons of Pittsburgh, Pa., during the 1870's. After *Early American Pressed Glass* came out, a woman wrote to me from Washington, Pa., whose mother, still living, was the model used for the

PLATE 1—RARITIES IN PATTERN GLASS
Group of Morning Glory pattern.
Bellflower octagonal sugar bowl.   Horn of Plenty claret glass.

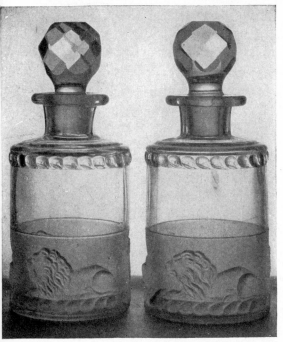

PLATE 2—RARITIES IN PATTERN GLASS
Opaque cologne bottles, not true Bellflower. Ivy celery vase.
Rare Lion cologne bottles and pair of Lion salts.

PLATE 3—RARITIES IN PATTERN GLASS

Horn of Plenty rectangular covered honey dish.
Horn of Plenty oval compote. Both probably Sandwich.

PLATE 4—RARITIES IN PATTERN GLASS

Covered egg cups in opaque glass. Left, Cable; right, Bull's Eye and Bar
Three Face Saucer champagne (left) and another with hollow stem—
an unusual feature in pressed glass.

Three Face pattern by her father, John E. Miller, who was designer for the Duncans. She sent me a profile view of her mother, then ninety-two years of age, so that I could see the likeness, which was still apparent. Her father was associated with the glass business for seventy-six years and died in 1931 at the age of ninety-one. She sent me numerous newspaper clippings to bear out her stories, so I gave this interesting account at a lecture at the Early American Glass Club of Boston, Mass., in 1935.

Among the unusual pieces of Three Face are the saucer champagnes and hollow-stem champagnes, as pictured on Plate 4. Nearly all of the glasses of the early pressed period that are five or five and a half inches in height are listed in the old catalogues in my possession as "champagnes," and had solid glass stems. The pressed champagne glass with a hollow stem was apparently a later innovation. Another rarity in the Three Face design, in partly frosted and partly clear glass, is the tall, ribbed, covered biscuit jar, shown on Plate 7.

In Three Face, as in Lion, a good many reproductions are now being foisted on eager but often careless buyers. The first new items to appear in the Three Face were the goblets and footed sauce dishes. Then a champagne with a deep bowl, similar to the one pictured in the Morning Glory pattern, came out. Something drastic should have been done long ago to stop the perpetration of these frauds on collectors.

From time to time other rarities may be added to this list. Once a sapphire blue Comet goblet was brought to me. It is the only one in this color I have ever seen. Not long ago an odd piece was discovered in Bull's Eye and Fleur de Lys, which appeared to be an ale glass. Lately someone wrote me about a Lion cake plate on a standard, which up to this time has been unknown. I did not see it so can only report on it. Offhand pieces produced by glassworkers, such as hats made from whisky tumbler molds, are heard about now and then. Two have been seen in Ribbed Ivy. We know such items were never a commercial product but were a whim of some workman, usually to present to a friend or relative as a gift.

One remarkably interesting collection may be formed of those small objects originally termed "egg glasses." They were made in nearly all the patterns collectible in sets of tableware, as well as exceptional specimens that sometimes are found not only in color but covered. Two of the latter, both in opaque white, are shown on Plate 4. One is the Cable pattern and the other is known as Bull's Eye and Bar. An old glassworker once informed me that the covers were designed to keep the eggs warm as they were served. Covers were, however, gradually abandoned, perhaps because they broke so easily as to prove a liability instead of an asset. Thereafter egg cups came sans covers. A collection of these dainty cups is not only charming but well worth study. It might be well to add that many pieces of early glass served several purposes. In my collection is an opaque covered blue Diamond Point egg cup, bearing an original paper label, part of which reads "Floral perfumery." The name of the firm who handled these in New York is not legible.

Many interesting items in milk-white glass, both early and late, are available to collectors. A pair of opal six-inch sweetmeat dishes in the Prism pattern are rare pieces. They were probably made by M'Kee Bros. of Pittsburgh during the 1850's and possibly in the 1840's. The Liberty Bell cup in milk-white with the serpent handle was produced on the grounds of the Centennial Exposition in Philadelphia in 1876, by Gillinder & Sons, in plain sight of the visitors. One of the rarest and most decorative of the dense white pieces of that period is the large swan dish with uplifted wings. It is impossible to enumerate and describe all the rarities in the large number of interesting patterns. Let it be remembered that any dish in an early Sandwich pattern may be found in color, though previously unreported. It is the joy of finding any rare and unexpected piece in any form of early collectible that creates the lure of the antique.

Chapter III

THE MOST POPULAR PATTERNS

One point that has impressed me about our American collectors is that not enough individuality has been shown in collecting, until it has become a matter of necessity either to specialize or to seek little-known designs because the most popular patterns in pressed glass became, in a scant decade, not only next to impossible to find but very expensive. It is a sad fact that we have not shown much tendency toward becoming real antiquarians but are content to amass. Most of us are quantitative instead of qualitative.

If you will stop to think of it, collectors at first *did* all want the same designs largely because their neighbor had them, until a point was reached where dealers could scarcely find a piece in any one of the ten most popular patterns and when they did find any they were priced so high that there was no room for profit. The long-continued years of the depression, coupled with higher and higher taxes, brought a collection on the market now and then, and therein lies about the only hope of buying any considerable number of items in those most-wanted pieces. The same thing happened in Europe, where the rarest antiques were obtained at auctions of famous collections.

The ten most popular patterns, as I listed them years ago, were: Bellflower; Horn of Plenty; Rose in Snow; Wildflower; Thousand Eye; Three Face; Lion; Westward-Ho; milk-white Blackberry, and Daisy and Button. Of course, Daisy and Button is still plentiful in some forms. It is a fairly late pattern produced by practically every factory making tableware and so it has been widely reproduced. Try to find *old* goblets today, in either clear or colors! All the ten patterns noted are illus-

16

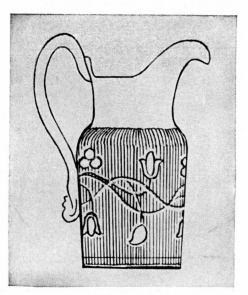

PLATE 5

Upper, Bellflower water pitcher.
Lower, Horn of Plenty water pitcher.
Both patterns of the late 1850's.

PLATE 6

Upper: Wildflower pattern as taken from page in original catalogue of the producers, Adams & Co. of Pittsburgh.

Lower: Extremely rare milk white Blackberry water pitcher.

PLATE 7
Westward-Ho butter dish.
Three Face biscuit jar.

PLATE 8
Rose in Snow goblet.
Lion oval compote.

PLATE 9
Thousand Eye goblet
Daisy and Button water pitcher.

trated in Plates 5, 6, 7, 8 and 9, some pictures being taken from the original old trade catalogues.

Out of 268 outstanding patterns listed in *Early American Pressed Glass* those ten came into prominence the quickest. In the twelve years after my book was written, they became so scarce and high-priced that collectors were practically compelled to select other designs. As a result, thirty other patterns became exceedingly popular. For the benefit of those who are just beginning to collect, I shall list them. They include: Tulip; Beaded Grape, both in emerald green and in crystal; Panelled Grape; Excelsior; Thumbprint; Princess Feather; Bull's Eye and Diamond Point; New England Pineapple; Bull's Eye; Comet; Ribbon; Hobnail; Dahlia; Stippled Forget-me-not; Panelled Daisy; Roman Rosette; Bleeding Heart; purple Marble glass; Red Block; Ruby Thumbprint; Deer and Pine Tree; Wheat and Barley in clear or colors; Shell and Tassel; Classic; Baltimore Pear; Diamond Quilted; Jacob's Ladder; Sawtooth, and Diamond Point. It is now difficult to find good pieces in any of these patterns.

I have mentioned the ten most popular patterns plus thirty others selected at random, which came into prominence during the past twelve years, making forty exceedingly popular patterns out of 268 listed in *Early American Pressed Glass*. Of course, there are many other popular patterns but they are in demand to a more limited degree, sometimes because they were produced in such small quantities originally that they have always been difficult to find. Such a pattern is the Morning Glory, illustrated in the chapter on rarities.

There are 228 collectible patterns in which prices have not soared out of sight. It is my belief that many collectors have been discouraged both by the scarcity of the most popular patterns and by high prices. So, why not look a little further? Besides the 228 mentioned, there are in addition between two and three hundred collectible patterns, shown in this book, and numerous specialties, also illustrated and described. There is nothing like a hobby as a means of relaxing your mind.

Chapter IV

THE TREE OF LIFE

Before World War I, popular interest was largely confined to what may be called the more romantic varieties of American craftsmanship. The inveterate Stiegelite regarded the Sandwich hunter much as the devotee of Philadelphia Chippendale looked upon him who garnered the carved grapes of the mid-Victorian era. Thirty years ago few would have admitted that an old whisky bottle bearing John Quincy Adams's bust was as justly an "ultimate antique" as a silver porringer initialed by Paul Revere. Today, however, nobody at all familiar with the antiques business during the depression would dream of denying that the overwhelming majority of the customers who made it possible for hundreds of small dealers to live sought and bought chiefly pattern glass. Inexpensive goblets paid the rent of shops where aristocratic highboys halted.

The amazing growth of interest in pattern glass has created a demand for authentic information concerning the source of various patterns. Moribund myths are finding fewer believers. Collectors who once accepted easy trade ascriptions now demand birth certificates. But, alas, not all. An army of buyers still insist upon being misinformed. The persistence of "Sandwich" as a convenient generic designation for all kinds of pattern glass is not to be wondered at so long as tourists will buy any so-called Sandwich glass in Sandwich and, while they remain within the sacred precincts of Cape Cod, will decline anything offered as Pittsburgh. The authenticity of a piece bought at a shop within a few minutes' drive from the old factory is accepted without question. There are the ruins to prove all claims! A pilgrimage to Pittsburgh on a midsummer holiday is

23

unthinkable. So, all glass in Sandwich just *must* be Sandwich glass no matter how devious the route by which it may have arrived there.

Two decades ago only a veteran Pittsburgh glass manufacturer could laugh when he found glass offered as "genuine Sandwich" that he recognized as the product of his own plant, made long after the Sandwich factory had ceased operations. At that time, too, all fine blown glass acquired in the middle West was baptized "Stiegel." Years passed before proud owners consented to call it "Ohio Stiegel." Eastern collectors may yet decide to rechristen some of their treasures "Pittsburgh Sandwich."

The pattern so well known as Tree of Life was apparently designed originally by William O. Davis at Portland, Maine. He became associated with the Portland Glass Co. as superintendent in 1865, succeeding Enoch Egginton. Mr. Davis's full history is not known, beyond the fact that he was for a time connected with the O'Hara Glass Co., one of the earliest in the Pittsburgh glass district, during the 1850's. That he designed some patterns for the Portland Glass Co., besides being superintendent, is fully supported by a copy of the patent taken out by Mr. Davis in Portland, Maine, dated May 11, 1869, on the pattern now known as Loop and Dart with round ornaments. This design was fully illustrated in my *Early American Pressed Glass* but the copy of the patent had not been discovered when that book was written. A photograph of the original patent is pictured in Plate 10. As may be noted, his patent is No. 3494 but no name is given to the design. Part of the wording of the patent will be of interest because it is addressed "To all whom it may concern: Be it known that I, William O. Davis of Portland, in the county of Cumberland, and State of Maine, have originated and invented a new and useful Design for glass-ware; and I hereby declare the following to be a full, clear, and exact description thereof, which will enable others to make and use the same, reference being had to the accompanying drawings forming part of the specification, in which is shown a side view of a goblet or glass with my design illustrated thereon.

"My invention relates to designs for the exterior of glass vessels of any kind, and is composed of the following forms and figures, and the arrangement thereof . . ." etc., etc.

Under the heading "Design for glassware" it further stated: "the schedule referred to in these Letters patent and making part of the same."

The Portland Glass Co. was founded in Portland, Maine, in November of 1863 and was in operation a brief ten years, closing in 1873. Among the patterns created there was the Tree of Life, several pieces of which are pictured on Plate 11. Any of the items shown may be found with "P.G.Co. Patent" embossed either underneath or on top of the base and they may also be found without this mark of identification. The accompanying illustrations of the Tree of Life motif will show that many true examples have a narrow clear band surrounding the knob of the goblet stem, and a similar device about the knob of the covered pieces. Compotes, epergnes and vases would not necessarily show this clear band; in fact, many did not have it.

Enthusiastic collectors particularly treasure specimens that have the name *Davis* interwoven in the complicated vinelike tracery, usually discovered in the bowls of compotes or epergnes. Such pieces must be attributed to the designer, William O. Davis. A correspondent once wrote me that she owns an epergne revealing not only the name of *Davis* but likewise the date of *1875*. Since the Portland enterprise closed in 1873, it would appear unlikely that a piece thus marked can be "genuine Portland." If the collector was not mistaken about the 1875 date, then we must assume that Mr. Davis continued to make his wares elsewhere. Whether or not the Portland molds were sold to him, or to others, is another matter.

Variations of the Tree of Life pattern were widely carried on, presumably after the Portland factory closed in 1873. Panelled or fluted specimens in a similar design, such as those illustrated in Plate 11, are pictured in a catalogue of George Duncan & Sons of Pittsburgh under date of 1884 though they may well have been produced before the catalogue was issued. I have never seen or heard of any of these fluted pieces carrying the Portland mark. It is reasonable to assume that all of the latter type came from factories in the Pittsburgh district. The design resembles that of the Portland product, but may be easily distinguished from it. In these variants the knobs of the covers and of the stems have a hand carrying a ball and they occur either in clear or in the frosted, satin finish. The Pittsburgh version of the Tree of Life pattern may be found in colors as well as in clear glass. Finger bowls in amber and a fairly deep blue are not uncommon. The only marked Portland pieces I have seen in color were a rather remarkable pair of tall vases in canary yellow. Another similar pair has been reported in light green.

Still another Pittsburgh variation is found in an open compote form, the stem supporting the bowl being in the shape of a hand which may be in clear glass or with a frosted finish.

The Hobbs Glass Co. of Wheeling, W. Va., illustrate two Tree of Life finger bowls, one with a plain edge and one having a melon-shaped bowl. They also pictured gas globes in the same pattern.

On Plate 12 is shown another Tree of Life variation, a goblet and a footed piece, which may have been intended either as a spoonholder or a footed tumbler. Almost invariably a spoonholder carries a scalloped edge instead of a plain rim. In these two pieces, fragments of which have been found at the site of the Sandwich factory, the design resembles the Portland version at first glance, though on close examination the branches are deeply incised instead of salient and the intermediate facetings are less clearly and neatly defined. Apparently the Sandwich product was not built up into a large line of tableware, since little of it is found today.

The other two pieces on the upper row of Plate 12 are also a Sandwich product known as "Overshot" glass. Though faintly

N.̣ **3494**

W. O. DAVIS

Design For Glass Ware

PATENTED
MAY 11 1869

Witness _Inventor_

M. Franklin Leavy W. O Davis

Henry C Houston Per W H Clifford atty

PLATE 10.
Copy of original Davis patent.

PLATE 11
1. Portland Glass Co. Tree of Life pattern.
2. Pittsburgh varieties of Tree of Life.

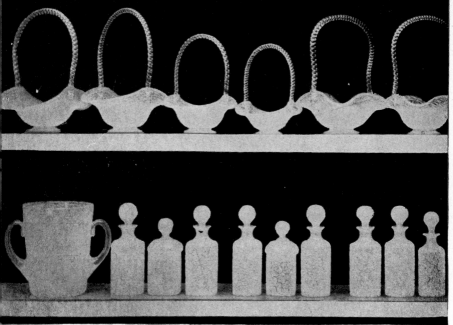

PLATE 12

Goblet and footed glass are Sandwich versions of the Tree of Life. Plate and water tumbler are Sandwich "Overshot" glass.

Baskets and bottles as taken from an original Boston & Sandwich Glass Co. catalogue.

PLATE 13
Sandwich Overshot glass, from a Boston & Sandwich Glass Co. catalogue

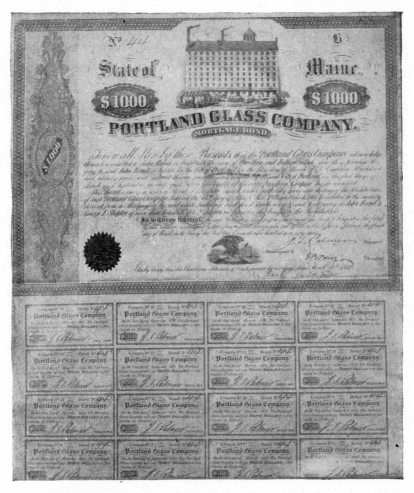

PLATE 14

Copy of original Portland Glass Co. Mortgage Bond, No. 44 of a series issued on
March 15, 1867.

suggesting the Tree of Life, it represents a very different type. A Boston & Sandwich Glass Co. catalogue in my collection displays a wide line of this ware, which has a rough, almost sharp surface. Photographs of the Overshot glass taken from the Sandwich catalogue are shown on Plates 12 and 13. Eggnog sets, consisting of a large covered jar with an open space for the ladle in the cover, a spacious tray to fit, and handled cups, may be found, as well as baskets in various sizes and shapes. A piece treasured by one collector was a rose-pink water pitcher, striped about the lip and handle in gold. Colored items in the Overshot glass are rarely encountered. Oval dishes, such as those shown in the lower row of Plate 13, were originally termed *nappies*.

Of all the Tree of Life interpretations, I consider the Portland at once the earliest and the best in quality. It is unfortunate that more is not known of William O. Davis but the future may bring to light more details of his history. If, as may be assumed from the patent No. 3494 (Loop and Dart, with round ornaments) taken out in Portland, Maine, he originated the pattern that embodies his name—and perhaps cut the mold —the recurrence of his device on glass made in the Pittsburgh district subsequent to 1873 would be readily explained. But this hypothesis must remain conjectural until reliable information concerning Mr. Davis is found. It is entirely possible that he may have gone on to Sandwich for a time after the Portland factory closed, or trekked back westward to the Pittsburgh area, where he was so well-known, when local means of support became invisible.

A list of patterns made by the Portland Glass Co., as listed by a professional snooper in the 1860's, are as follows:

Portland; Leaf; National; sc. Flute; and Altered Grecian. These are original trade names, so in most instances they do not identify the pattern. We might conjecture that the leaf pattern referred to may be my favorite design, now known as Frosted Leaf. That it was first produced at Portland there seems little doubt. The Altered Grecian may well be the Roman Key as the quality of glass is similar to the Frosted Leaf. A Loop

pattern may also have been produced at **Portland**. It was originally designed at the O'Hara Glass Co. and was known as the
O'Hara pattern in the trade, but several factories made it with
slight variations. Since Mr. Davis apparently went to work at
the Portland Glass Co. after leaving Pittsburgh it seems reasonably certain that he may be responsible for one of the Loop
designs. Some patterns ascribed to the Portland Glass Co. by
wishful thinkers can easily be disproved; on the other hand,
there are doubtless many good patterns which were produced
at Portland that do not have proper credit because the factories' records were all destroyed in a disastrous fire.

A list of the Tree of Life forms which collectors may find, is
given below:

Portland:

1. Butter dish, marked and unmarked (P.T. patent)
2. Champagne
3. Cordials; sizes vary
4. Creamer, marked and unmarked
5. Celery vase, marked and unmarked
6. Cake plate on standard, two sizes; marked "Davis"
7. Compote, two sizes; may be found with or without patent mark, or "Davis"
8. Epergne, marked and unmarked
9. Epergne, with figure of child in standard; bowl is often marked "Davis"
10. Finger bowl
11. Goblet, marked and unmarked
12. Pickle dish, oval
13. Plate, 6 inch
14. Sugar bowl, marked and unmarked
15. Sauce dish, two sizes, marked
16. Honey dish, 3½ inch, unmarked
17. Tumbler, footed, marked and unmarked
18. Wine
19. Water pitcher

Rarities: Wineglass with applied handle. Colored pieces with patent mark or "Davis." Vases, tall, round foot, scalloped top. These bear patent mark. Yellow, light green.

Pittsburgh types:
1. Berry bowl, 8 inch
2. Celery vase; stem has hand clasping ball, clear or frosted
3. Compote, covered, to match celery vase
4. Compote, large, open, on high foot; standard is form of full hand, clear or frosted
5. Creamer, with hand clasping ball, to match table set
6. Finger bowls, fluted, in amber, blue, yellow and apple green
7. Honey dish, 3½ inch
8. Ice cream sets; oblong tray with handles and dessert dishes in form of a leaf (not footed) ; two sizes, clear and colors
9. Plates, 6 inch
10. Salts
11. Sauce dishes, several sizes and forms
12. Toothpick or match holder, footed; green, blue, amber crystal and cranberry

Chapter V

THE COIN PATTERN

Students of our American pressed glass are aware that the popularity of clear glass, with the design partly frosted, began during the 1870's. Mr. James Gillinder, a grandson of the founder of Gillinder & Sons of Philadelphia, told me that his grandfather came here from England in 1854, and among his possessions carried with him a small bottle of "white acid" with which to experiment in what we know today as the frosted, or satin, finish. He had been in the glass business prior to his journey to this country and he continued his line of endeavor here. The experiment of the Gillinder père bore fruit, for it was the Gillinders who gave us several of the best of these frosted and clear glass patterns, such as Westward-Ho (which they termed "Pioneer"), Lion and Classic. Whether they ever made any of the Coin pattern is not known at present. Probably most of it was produced by the Central Glass Co. of Wheeling. W. Va., who illustrate many pieces in one of their catalogues. Other factories may have been responsible for some of it, too.

Coin glass was made showing both American and foreign money. Knowing that the most popular Centennial patterns often carried the frosted, or satin, finish, it is not surprising to find a water tumbler having a frosted American coin dated 1878 in the base. A side view and the base picturing the coin are illustrated on Plate 15. Above the tumbler is a covered compote which utilizes United States coins of 1892. Indeed, more coin pieces may be encountered with the 1892 date than any other. Included in this chapter will be a list of one hundred and fifty pieces of this date, which are in the collection of Mr. Paul Zeeb of Greenville, Ill. The illustrations are from

35

PLATE 15
Coin pattern, showing tumbler with American glass coin dated 1878, and a compote.

Collection of Mr. and Mrs. R. E. Dougherty

PLATE 16

Coin pattern, consisting of "table set" (sugar bowl, creamer, spoonholder and butter dish) all with American coins of 1892.

PLATE 17

Coin water pitcher, epergne, goblet and wine, with coins of 1892.

PLATE 18

Coin beer mug, compote and celery vase.

the collection of Mr. and Mrs. R. E. Dougherty of Washington, Iowa.

It should be noted that some of this pattern is found in all clear glass, some with the coins gilded, and toothpick holders are known with the coin in red. Generally, the coins are frosted.

A story has often been repeated to me here in the East, where coin pieces are seldom seen, to the effect that little of this glass was ever produced because a law was passed years ago prohibiting the reproduction of our money. I have been informed that a law to this effect exists, and presumably that is the reason the production of this pattern was soon stopped. It is unfortunate because the glass copies of the money could do no possible harm and the design is both novel and interesting.

All I have ever found in these parts have been match or toothpick holders, bearing a foreign coin, a celery vase with a Spanish coin, and one really good, large open compote with flaring sides, having United States coins. Collectors will find that such pieces as the wine glasses have dimes, while some of the large dishes bear dollars, usually of the 1892 date. Of course, coins of various denominations were utilized, according to the size of the article.

Listed below are the forms which may be found, for which I am indebted to Mr. Paul Zeeb. Nearly all are of the 1892 date.

1. Berry bowl, 6, 8 and 9 inch
2. Beer mug
3. Bread tray, oblong
4. Butter dish
5. Candlesticks
6. Cake plate on standard
7. Celery vase
8. Compotes, open, flared edge. 7, 8, 8½ and 10 inch
   a. Compote, covered, 6, 7 and 8 inch
   b. Covered compote on low foot: 20-cent coin on bowl, 25-cent coin on cover
9. Creamer

10. Dish, candy or jelly
11. Epergne
12. Finger bowl
13. Goblet with dimes
    a. Goblet with half dollars, flared top
14. Lamps, 4 types with square fonts (some with gold coins on font and stem)
    a. 4 types with round fonts, coins only on stem
    b. One type with 20-cent pieces on base: "Night Light"
15. Pickle dish
16. Sauce dishes, footed, small
    a. Footed sauce with scalloped edge
    b. Small flat sauce dish
    c. Large flat sauce dish
17. Salt and pepper shakers
18. Spoonholder
19. Sugar bowl
20. Syrup pitcher
21. Toothpick holder
    a. Red, with frosted coins
22. Tumblers, with dimes
23. Water pitcher; two sizes, large and small
24. Water tray, round
25. Wines; two sizes, small and large

Chapter VI

PATTERN GLASS

The succeeding nine chapters are devoted to patterns which could not be included in *Early American Pressed Glass* because that volume is already bulky enough. Practically all of the material contained herein was gathered during a trip to Pittsburgh, Pa., in 1933. It is my purpose to list all of these in an orderly manner, telling when and where the glass was made, when such information has been available, and naming as many forms as possible. In some cases, no records are available to state what items were produced. No one person can ever hope to see every piece of American pressed glass. Many factories were in operation from 1840 to the 1890's, turning out tons of glassware. It is not possible to list, classify and identify every odd water set, fruit set, child's mug, etc., because descriptions are inadequate and the expense of attempting to illustrate all these odd pieces would make the cost of such a book prohibitive. At that, no one could ever be sure that his work was all-inclusive. Moreover, while many of the odd pieces are interesting, as a whole they do not represent enough importance to attempt a book about them. There are collections of individual pieces, such as early flint glass compotes, which are well worthy of consideration, but at this time cannot be included in this volume. Other collectors' specialties, such as glass hats, slippers, match holders, vases, covered animal dishes and Victorian novelties, will follow the additional patterns which have come into prominence since the publication of *Early American Pressed Glass.*

It is my belief that practically every pattern of any importance produced in sets of tableware during the Victorian period, which are not treated in *Early American Pressed Glass,* is included here. Since my collection of old trade catalogues and other historical data is such as to make it possible for me to state when and where a goodly share of the patterns and novelties were made, this should prove to be valuable historical data for future generations.

It must be remembered that old glass houses issued cata-logues of their wares at irregular intervals, so that one catalogue would not necessarily illustrate or name every item in any one particular design. Lines of tableware were often built up, if they proved to be popular, so that additional pieces were added from year to year. I feel fortunate to own so many old glass catalogues, because they are extremely difficult to find. Many of them were burned up in factory fires. At the time they were in use, they were not considered of any more importance than we regard our daily newspapers today. So if one could perform such a miracle as to be able to name every form ever made in all the patterns, it would be necessary to have a complete file of all the trade catalogues ever issued by all the glass manufacturers in America. Needless to say, that will never be possible; but illustrating some of the lesser known patterns, in which few pieces have been noted, may bring to light more valuable information.

In discussing our glassware of the earlier days with a work-man who made some of the patterns, I learned some facts which I have not seen in print. He said that one of the reasons why the first table glass was so heavy was not alone because of the taste or fashion of the day but rather because the old-time workers did not know as much about the flow of the glass as did the later makers. For one thing, they wanted quick action without thinking of quality. Like their successors, they were anxious to obtain quantity, so they sacrificed thinness to speed. An expert glass worker can notice a certain "feel" to glass in the molten stage. Their glass (or "metal," as the workers termed it) was often not hot enough when they began to work it. Today pressed glass can be made almost as thin as blown glass and that has always been one of their aims. In other words, they attempted to make pressed glass look like the earlier blown wares.

Another point which the glassworker mentioned was that the early makers did not know how to construct the molds so that the glass could flow as easily as it might have, so that the workman could feel his way and help the mold turn out the right kind of products. Today the glass metal is made softer by the use of certain ingredients and the iron of the molds is better. Porous iron in the molds gave the glass rough surfaces, so the finer-grained the iron the better the surface.

The old-timers reckoned tonnage by the weight, so making goblets heavier did not hurt their feelings. When they spoke of a three, two and one batch, they meant three parts sand, two soda and one lead.

Barrel shapes were used in what was called "hotel" goblets. They were made in a barrel shape, or curved in at the top, so that the rims would not touch against each other and thereby chip so easily as they did in the regular straight-sided goblets and tumblers. Today the modern trade name is "No-nick" goblets. The barrel goblets were made in the mold the same as the others but the shape was changed by the glass finisher. They were made entirely for hotels and restaurants. The barrel-shape tumblers came later, after the goblets.

In the old days they used to have Christmas tables for the employees, where they could buy cup-foot goblets, which were more expensive than the flat-foot, for $1.75 per dozen.

For years, Hobbs was the only mass production concern that worked in color. The New England factories could not meet midwestern competition, so the twenty or more factories in the Pittsburgh glass district flourished. Some of the factories were located just over the Pennsylvania state line but they were all near-by.

The Penn Glass Co. was incorporated in 1875 and expired in 1877. They made one of the Liberty Bell plates and other Centennial specialties.

A chapter concerning figured glassware, or what we call pattern glass, will be of more interest to readers after studying the following pages of Victorian designs. Therefore, it will appear at the conclusion of this section of the book.

Eighteen old glass factories were absorbed by the United States Glass Co. in July, 1891, when most of them were meeting financial difficulties. After the merger, the United States Glass Co. referred to patterns they carried on by the letter which represented the factory, according to the following chart, copied exactly as it appears in the old catalogues:

	Now Known as Factory
Adams & Co., Pittsburgh, Pa.	"A"
Bryce Bros., Pittsburgh, Pa.	"B"
Challinor, Taylor & Co., Tarentum, Pa.	"C"
Geo. Duncan & Sons, Pittsburgh, Pa.	"D"
Richards & Hartley, Tarentum, Pa.	"E"
Ripley & Co., Pittsburgh, Pa.	"F"
Gillinder & Sons, Greensburg, Pa.	"G"
Hobbs Glass Co., Wheeling, W. Va.	"H"
Columbia Glass Co., Findlay, Ohio	"J"
King Glass Co., Pittsburgh, Pa.	"K"
O'Hara Glass Co., Pittsburgh, Pa.	"L"
Bellaire Goblet Co., Findlay, Ohio	"M"
Nickel Plate Glass Co., Fostoria, Ohio	"N"
Central Glass Co., Wheeling, W. Va.	"O"
Doyle & Co., Pittsburgh, Pa.	"P"
A. J. Beatty & Sons, Tiffin, Ohio	"R"
A. J. Beatty & Sons, Steubenville, Ohio	"S"
Novelty Glass Co., Fostoria, Ohio (Leased)	"T"
New Factory, at Gas City, Ind.	"U"

SHOW ROOMS

Main Office, 9th & Bingham Sts., S.S. Pittsburgh, Pa.
New York, 29 Murray St.
Philadelphia, 715, 717, 719 Arch St.
Baltimore, 18 South Charles St.
San Francisco, Calif., 18 Sutter St.

PLATE 19

1. WEDDING RING goblet, decanter, water tumbler.
2. FLOWERED OVAL goblet, creamer, egg cup.
3. CROWFOOT goblet, spoonholder, sauce dish.
4. CHRYSANTHEMUM LEAF butter dish, sherbet cup, syrup jug.

PLATE 20

1. SEASHELL butter dish, sugar bowl, creamer.
2. CHICKEN sugar bowl, butter dish.
3. PRISM AND CRESCENT goblet, lemonade, champagne.
4. DIAMOND POINT WITH PANELS spoonholder, salt, champagne.

PLATE 21

1. FLAT DIAMOND AND PANEL egg cup, decanter, covered egg cup, goblet.
2. ROSETTE AND PALMS goblet, compote, wine.
3. DIVIDED HEART goblet, lamp, salt, egg cup.
4. SCALLOPED LINES goblet, butter dish, wine.

PLATE 22

1. BRADFORD BLACKBERRY goblet, creamer, sugar bowl.
2. RIPPLE goblet, sauce dish, creamer, salt.
3. STIPPLED CHAIN goblet, oval pickle dish, salt.
4. DRAPERY VARIANT goblet, pickle dish, spoonholder.

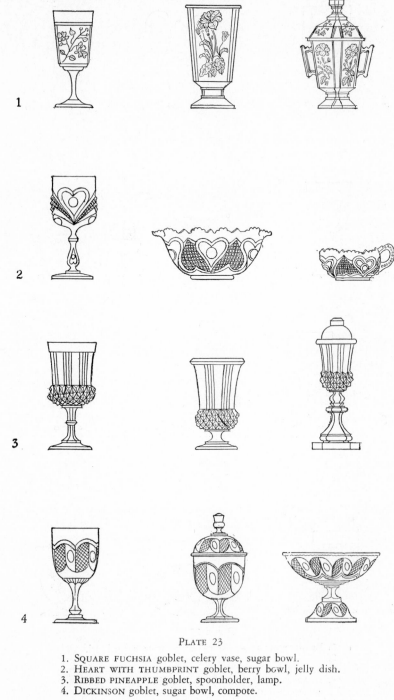

PLATE 23

1. SQUARE FUCHSIA goblet, celery vase, sugar bowl.
2. HEART WITH THUMBPRINT goblet, berry bowl, jelly dish.
3. RIBBED PINEAPPLE goblet, spoonholder, lamp.
4. DICKINSON goblet, sugar bowl, compote.

PATTERN GLASS COLLECTIBLE IN SETS—I

PLATE 19

1. WEDDING RING. An attractive heavy, brilliant flint glass pattern is known today as Wedding Ring. It should not be confused with a later variant known as "Single Wedding Ring." No record of where it was made has been found. It is of the early 1860's and so far it has been noted only in clear glass. While a large line of tableware was not produced, it is collectible in enough pieces to make an interesting set.

1. Champagne
2. Decanter
3. Creamer
4. Goblet
5. Water tumbler
6. Wine

2. FLOWERED OVAL. This pattern was produced by the Boston & Sandwich Glass Co. Judging from the quality of the glass and the forms, it dates from the early 1860's. It was apparrently made only in clear glass and not in a large quantity, because it is seldom found today, even in New England. My classification is based on those items I have seen. Collectors will undoubtedly find other pieces.

1. Creamer, applied handle
2. Egg cup
3. Goblet

3. CROWFOOT. Crowfoot was probably produced after the Moon and Star design, to which it bears some resemblance. It was made by the M'Kee Glass Co. of the old Pittsburgh glass district and was originally known as the Yale pattern. It is

51

familiar to most collectors, as pieces may be seen in various sections of the country, so it must have been widely distributed. It presumably dates from the 1890's and is not a flint glass. Quite a wide variety of pieces was made in this tableware. It has been known by several names, but Dr. Millard designated it as "Crowfoot" in his book on goblets.

1. Butter dish
2. Compotes, open, on high foot
    a. Compotes, covered, on high foot
3. Creamer
4. Goblet
5. Pickle dish
6. Sauce dish, footed
    a. Sauce dish, flat; two sizes
7. Spoonholder
8. Sugar bowl
9. Tumbler
10. Water pitcher

4. CHRYSANTHEMUM LEAF. An old resident of Sandwich, Mass., told me that this was the last pattern made by the Boston & Sandwich Glass Co. in sets of tableware, before the plant closed down. Certainly it could not have been produced in large quantities because it is rarely seen, even in its home town. It would date close to 1888. So far as I can learn, there are no pieces in color. There must be many more forms than I can list.

1. Butter dish
2. Creamer
3. Sherbet cup
4. Syrup jug

PLATE 20

1. SEASHELL. The Seashell was made both plain and engraved, probably by some midwestern factory. If the purchaser wanted his glass engraved, he was usually given a choice of patterns from a book of designs, kept by the company. It was

produced in clear glass, with the knobs of the covers in the form of a heavily stippled seashell. The stems of goblets and other pieces are quite ornate. It appears to date in the 1870's and 1880's. This design should prove to be an attractive one for those having summer homes at the shore, particularly since it is not well known.

1. Butter dish
2. Creamer
3. Goblet
4. Spoonholder
5. Sugar bowl

2. CHICKEN. It is difficult to imagine what name was bestowed on this pattern by the factory that produced it. Generally it is seen in clear glass, with the knobs to the covers frosted. The knobs to all the covered pieces are in the form of a chicken emerging from a shell. It is rarely that one encounters this design with the knobs in clear glass but a few such pieces have been found. To date there is no record as to where it was made but it is probably midwestern, of the 1870's. I have seen only the following pieces but hope collectors may add to my list:

1. Butter dish
2. Compote
3. Goblet
4. Sugar bowl

3. PRISM AND CRESCENT. This design is a heavy flint glass which has a fine bell tone when tapped. It was produced by the Boston & Sandwich Glass Co., apparently in a limited quantity because it is rarely found today. Other forms than those I list probably exist but they are scarce. The pattern appears to date in the late 1850's and early 1860's. No pieces have been found in color, so far as I can learn.

1. Champagne
2. Goblet

3. Handled mug
4. Whisky tumblers
5. Water tumblers

4. DIAMOND POINT WITH PANELS. The original name of this pattern is unknown. It was produced by the New England Glass Co. and possibly carried on by the Boston & Sandwich Glass Co. It is a good quality of flint glass. A limited number of pieces have been noted to date but doubtless there are others. It is found in clear glass and appears to date in the late 1850's and early 1860's.

1. Celery vase
2. Champagne
3. Creamer
4. Goblet
5. Salt, footed
6. Spoonholder or spillholder
7. Sugar bowl

PLATE 21

1. FLAT DIAMOND AND PANEL. This choice pattern is credited to the Boston & Sandwich Glass Co. It was produced in crystal in flint glass, as well as in several shades of color in opaque glass. Covered egg cups are rare and may be found in translucent white, as well as in opaque blue, jade green, lime green and other shades. There is no limit to Sandwich colors, so that one never knows what unexpected piece or color may come to light next. This pattern probably dates in the late 1850's and 1860's.

1. Champagne
2. Creamer
3. Decanter, quart and pint sizes
4. Goblet
5. Egg cup
6. Egg cups, covered
7. Wine

2. Rosette and Palms. An interesting midwestern pattern of the 1880's has been christened Rosette and Palms. So far as I know, it appears only in clear glass. There are probably a great many forms which I have not seen but the illustrations will serve to identify the design.

1. Butter dish
2. Celery vase
3. Compote
4. Creamer
5. Goblet
6. Plates, 8 and 10 inch
7. Pickle dish
8. Spoonholder
9. Sugar bowl
10. Water pitcher
11. Wine

3. Divided Heart. The Boston & Sandwich Glass Co. produced this pattern, probably during the early 1860's. It may be presumed that there is a full line of tableware but any of it is rather difficult to find today, even in its home State. I have seen the following pieces, in clear glass:

1. Butter dish
2. Compote
3. Creamer
4. Egg cup
5. Goblet
6. Lamp, with marble base
7. Salt, footed
8. Sugar bowl

4. Scalloped Lines. It has been established by fragment findings, that this design was made by the Boston & Sandwich Glass Co. It is not so fine a quality of glass as either the Flat Diamond and Panel or the Divided Heart. Probably it was made during the late 1860's and 1870's. My listing of forms

is not complete as there are undoubtedly other pieces such as the celery vase, compote, etc.

1. Butter dish
2. Creamer
3. Egg cup
4. Goblet
5. Pickle dish, oval
6. Plate, 6 inch
7. Sugar bowl

PLATE 22

1. BRADFORD BLACKBERRY. This design was named by the late Emma Fitts Bradford, who first called it to my attention. It is a clear, brilliant, heavy flint glass. Fragments of this pattern were unearthed at Sandwich, so that is probably its place of origin. It appears to date in the early 1860's. Collectors may be able to add to the list of pieces I have seen.

1. Champagne
2. Cordial
3. Creamer
4. Goblet
5. Sugar bowl.
6. Tumbler

2. RIPPLE. The Boston & Sandwich Glass Co. produced the Ripple in an effort to meet midwestern competition during the 1870's. Pieces in color have not been seen to date. There is no record of the original name for this pattern, which is not flint glass.

1. Butter dish
2. Champagne
3. Cordial
4. Compote, covered
5. Creamer
6. Dishes, oval
7. Egg cup
8. Goblet

9. Lamp
10. Plate, 6 inch
11. Salt, footed
   a. Oval, flat, with cane design in base
12. Sauce dish
13. Spoonholder
14. Sugar bowl

3. STIPPLED CHAIN. The Stippled Chain is illustrated in a footed salt, on Plate 190 of *Early American Pressed Glass*. At the time that book went to press not enough of the pattern had been found to describe or picture it adequately. It was produced by Gillinder & Sons of Philadelphia, Pa. It is not strange, therefore, that one finds this design most readily in Philadelphia. Gillinder made a wide variety of this tableware during the 1870's. The glass itself is brilliant, and the clear chain is looped against a stippled background.

1. Butter dish
2. Compotes
3. Creamer
4. Dishes, flat, oval, several sizes
5. Goblet
6. Salt, footed
7. Sauce dish, flat, 4 inch
8. Spoonholder
9. Sugar bowl

4. DRAPERY VARIANT. The design in this pattern stands in fairly high relief, against a lightly stippled background. So far no record has been found as to where it was made, but it appears to be midwestern, of the 1870's. No colored pieces are known at this time. Other forms than those listed must exist.

1. Dishes, oval
2. Goblet
3. Sauce dish
4. Spoonholder

PLATE 23

1. SQUARE FUCHSIA. This pattern has been designated as Square Fuchsia so that it may not be confused with an earlier Stippled Fuchsia or still a different Fuchsia produced by the Boston & Sandwich Glass Co. There is another style goblet which matches the design better than the one pictured but it is exceedingly scarce. Covers are found that fit some of the sauce dishes, thus making small covered dishes. This glass is probably midwestern, of the late 1870's and 1880's. It is usually found in clear glass though there is some amber and possibly other colors.

1. Bowl, flat, 6x9 inches, no handles
2. Bowl, flat, 5½x8 inches, no handles
3. Bowl, flat, 5¼x8 inches, 2 handles
4. Butter dish, 2 handles
5. Cake plate on standard
6. Celery vase
7. Creamer, handle on corner
8. Compote on standard: 7½ inches across, 10½ inches high
9. Compote on standard: 5 inches across, 6¾ inches high
10. Jelly compote, open or covered
11. Goblet, 2 styles
12. Jam jar, covered, 5½ inch
13. Pickle jar, covered, 6¼ inch
14. Square plates, clear glass and amber
15. Sauce dish, footed, 4 inch, 2 handles
16. Sauce dish, flat, 4 inch, 2 handles
17. Sauce dish, flat, 4 inch, no handles
18. Sauce dish, footed, 3½ inch, no handles
19. Sauce dish, flat, 3½ inch, no handles
20. Sauce or honey dish, footed, 2¼ inches high
21. Spoonholder
22. Sugar bowl
23. Salt and pepper shakers
24. Water pitcher

2. HEART WITH THUMBPRINT (Millard's Bull's Eye in Heart). Little is known of this glass at present. By the forms one can judge that it was made at the turn of this century. Like many late patterns the surface has a brilliant sheen.

1. Berry bowl, 9 inch
2. Bowl, 6 inch
3. Butter dish
4. Cordials
5. Creamer, small
6. Cruet
7. Goblet
8. Jelly dish, handled
9. Plates, two sizes, 6 and 10 inches
10. Salt and pepper shakers
11. Sauce dish
12. Sugar bowl
13. Syrup jug
14. Vase, tall
15. Water pitcher
16. Water tumblers
17. Wines

3. RIBBED PINEAPPLE. This is an early flint glass pattern, of the 1850's or possibly earlier. It is most frequently found in New England, so it was doubtless produced by one of the local factories. It is usually seen in clear glass but a colored spillholder (made for holding the tapers to light whale oil lamps, often to match the lamp bowl) may be found in color or in clear glass with amber or some other shade "flashed," or applied, to the piece. Very often the spillholders did service for spoons and even cigars! Other items may be found but any pieces are scarce.

1. Goblet
2. Lamp
3. Spoonholder or spillholder

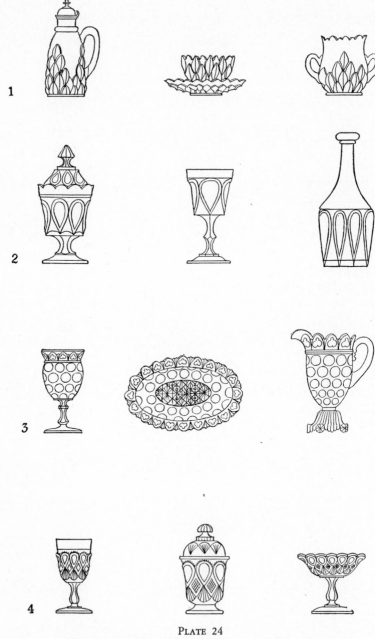

PLATE 24

1. FROSTED ARTICHOKE syrup jug, plate and finger bowl, spoonholder.
2. LEE sugar bowl, goblet, decanter.
3. ORION THUMBPRINT goblet, oval platter, creamer.
4. LOOP AND FAN goblet, sugar bowl, 6 inch compote.

1

2

3

4

PLATE 25

1. Four campaign tumblers.
2. Four campaign tumblers.
3. EXCELSIOR VARIANT champagne. TONG compote and spillholder.
4. SMOCKING spoonholder, compote, sugar bowl.

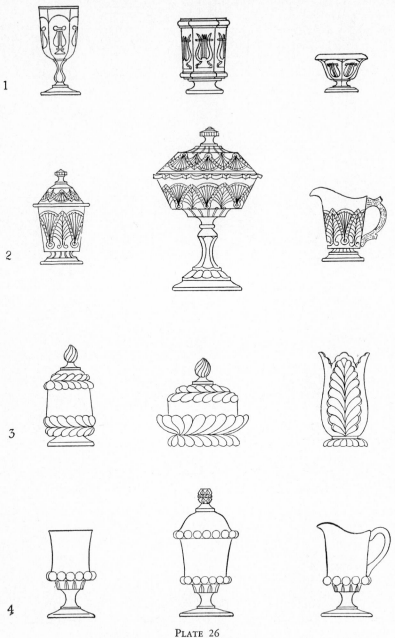

PLATE 26

1. HARP goblet, spillholder, salt.
2. ANDERSON sugar bowl, compote, creamer.
3. PLUME sugar bowl, butter dish, celery vase.
4. ATLAS goblet, sugar bowl, creamer.

PLATE 27

1. LOOP AND JEWEL open sugar bowl, sauce dish, salt.
2. BALL AND SWIRL creamer, goblet, butter dish.
3. BUTTERFLY creamer, base to sugar bowl, pickle dish.
4. TEXAS goblet, match holder, oval relish dish.

PLATE 28

1. SCROLL WITH STAR cup and saucer, plate, sauce dish.
2. LATE BUTTERFLY butter dish, water pitcher, berry bowl.
3. MOON AND STAR VARIATION goblet, compote, sauce dish.
4. LOOP AND JEWEL sugar bowl, butter dish, spoonholder.

4. DICKINSON. This also is a flint glass pattern, and it was produced by the Boston & Sandwich Glass Co., probably during the 1860's. Other forms than those listed must exist. It has been found only in clear glass.

1. Butter dish
2. Compote
3. Creamer
4. Goblet
5. Sauce dish
6. Spoonholder
7. Sugar bowl
8. Water pitcher

PLATE 24

1. FROSTED ARTICHOKE. There are three variations of this design. I: Petals frosted, clear portion plain. II: Petals in both frosted and clear sections, very brilliant. III: All clear glass, without satin finish on petals.

Variation Number One:
1. Bowls, flat and shallow
2. Butter dish
3. Cake stand
4. Celery vase
5. Compote, $6\frac{1}{2}$ inch. Also larger sizes, footed
6. Creamer
7. Cruet
8. Fruit bowls, footed, 6 inches tall, 10 inches diameter
9. Lamps, large and small; night lamp with glass shade
10. Rose bowl
11. Sauce dish, 2 styles, footed and flat
12. Spoonholder
13. Sugar bowl
14. Syrup pitcher
15. Water pitcher, 2 styles, tall tankard pitcher and bulbous shaped pitcher

16. Water tumblers
17. Water tray, large, round, with small rim

Variation Number Two:

1. Berry bowl, 10 inch
2. Finger bowls, 4 inch
3. Plates, 6 inch
4. Vase, tall and large
   Finger bowl and plate are pictured together

Variation Number Three would follow most of the forms listed in Number One. The origin of this pattern is unknown. It is probably midwestern, as it is seldom seen in the East. Most of it is found in Illinois, Wisconsin, Ohio and Indiana. It probably dates in the 1880's and 1890's.

2. LEE. This is an early flint glass pattern of excellent quality. Since any pieces are rare, it must have been produced in a limited quantity. All items illustrated were found in Massachusetts; therefore, it was probably made by a local factory. It is a more attractive pattern than it appears to be in the line drawings. Dr. Millard named it after this author when he did his book devoted to goblets.

Other items than those listed may exist but they are scarce. So far it is not known except in crystal. It appears to date in the 1850's or possibly the early 1860's.

1. Cordial
2. Decanter
3. Goblet
4. Sugar bowl

3. ORION THUMBPRINT. An unusual pattern produced by the Canton Glass Works in Indiana, about 1893, is now known as Orion Thumbprint. It may be found in clear glass, blue, amber, and yellow. Some items were made in opaque blue, milk white, and black glass. My classification is not complete but the illustrations will serve to identify the design.

1. Berry bowl
2. Butter dish
3. Celery vase
4. Compote, on high foot
5. Creamer
6. Finger bowl
7. Goblet
8. Platter, oval
9. Plates, two sizes (opaque, without Daisy and Button center)
10. Spoonholder
11. Sugar bowl

4. LOOP AND FAN. Collectors will find that the Loop and Fan, like some other late patterns, varies in the quality of the glass. Some is clear but most of it reflects a carelessness in manufacture. It was produced during the late 1890's by the United States Glass Co. of Pittsburgh. Unless one has a sentimental reason for collecting it, there is little to recommend this design. There is a wide range of pieces to choose from but my catalogue is incomplete, so I cannot name them all.

1. Celery
2. Compote
3. Creamer
4. Goblet
5. Pickle dish
6. Sauce dish
7. Spoonholder
8. Sugar bowl
9. Water pitcher

PLATE 25

CAMPAIGN TUMBLERS AND PATTERN GLASS

1. Tall tumbler showing cannon, cannon balls and flag on one side; reverse, an eagle with sword crossing a flag. Second

tumbler has a large American flag. Third glass is half-pint size with a shield and stars surmounted by conventional ornament.

2. Tumbler lettered "Yankee Doodle" with decorated scene showing drummer, flagbearer, etc. Next tumbler has a large eagle perched on two flags, lettered "Remember the Maine." Both were produced by the United States Glass Co. of Pittsburgh in the 1890's. Third glass carries portrait head of Garfield and is marked "Garfield." The fourth tumbler has a bust of Hancock and is lettered with his name. These last two were made by A. J. Beatty & Sons of Tiffin, Ohio, in the 1880's. They produced many campaign tumblers, such as Cleveland, Blaine and others. There are many interesting campaign tumblers to be found, some of the earliest having silver busts inset in the base, of such celebrities as Lafayette, Henry Clay, etc. The process of inserting these medallions is covered in a patent taken out by Apsley Pellatt and listed in the English *Dictionary of National Biography*. To quote: "In 1819 he [Pellatt] took out a patent for crystallo-ceramie or glass incrustation which consisted in enclosing medallions and ornaments of pottery ware, metal or refractory material in glass." A collection of tumblers having historical interest is well worth while. The A. J. Beatty Co. made other novelty tumblers, such as "Third Pint Bar" glasses having a different flower inset in the base of each.

3. EXCELSIOR VARIATION. A charming early flint glass pattern, of which other forms exist, is now known as Excelsior Variation. Note the hourglass-shaped ornament in the illustration, which alternates with a large diamond-shaped figure enclosing a smaller diamond. The two knobs in the stem form another unusual feature. The design is similar to the well-known Excelsior and yet so different that there should be no confusion between them. This variation is of a fine quality of lead flint glass which has a bell tone when tapped. The producer is unknown but the style would indicate the 1850's. There are doubtless many more forms than I can list.

1. Champagnes
2. Cordials
3. Goblets
4. Spoonholder
5. Sugar bowl

3. TONG. Pictured next to the Excelsior Variation is another early flint glass design, known to a few collectors as Tong. The covered compote with the interesting finial on the cover is a splendid example of this pattern. It will be noted that the hourglass motif is not so large in the covered dish and the diamond ornament encloses a round thumbprint or "punty." Doubtless there are many forms which I have not seen, as the Tong is seldom found in this locality. Pictured is the covered compote and a spillholder or spoonholder. In the early days such glasses served several purposes. This pattern probably dates in the 1840's and 1850's and so far is known only in crystal.

1. Compote, covered, on high foot
2. Spoonholder or spillholder

4. SMOCKING. Some of the pieces in this early flint pattern have round bases, while others are scalloped. The goblets are exceedingly scarce. It is possible that more than one factory produced Smocking, though it is found in such a limited number of pieces that it appears to be of only New England ancestry. Some fragments were unearthed at the site of the Boston & Sandwich Glass Co. It appears to be of the 1840's and 1850's and is known only in crystal.

1. Compote
2. Creamer
3. Goblet
4. Lamp
5. Spillholder
6. Spoonholder
7. Sugar bowl

PLATE 26

1. HARP. This pattern is being illustrated because the goblets are so very rare. The one pictured was sent to me from the South. Another type has a bowl with a distinct flare at the top. Lamps, salts and spillholders (made to hold tapers for lighting the early whale oil lamps) are frequently seen in New England but the goblets are extremely rare. Most of the pieces are fairly crude, indicating an early date of manufacture. They are of a heavy flint glass and aside from the goblets are seldom found in perfect condition. The goblet has six panels in the bowl, all carrying the Harp motif. Harp appears only in clear glass and is evidently of the 1840–1850 era.

2. ANDERSON. The O'Hara Glass Co., one of the earliest factories in the Pittsburgh glass district, was the original producer of this design. According to their old trade catalogue, it was simply known as "No. 82 pattern." Pieces listed in the classification are according to their catalogue, which may not be complete as other forms were often added, from year to year, when a pattern continued to sell well. It is known only in clear glass and appears to be of the 1870's.

1. Butter dish, flange rim
2. Butter dish, footed
3. Butter dish, flat
4. Creamer
5. Compote, covered, on high foot, 7, 8 and 9 inch
     a. Open, on high foot, 8, 9 and 10 inch
6. Goblet
7. Plate, 7 inch
8. Sauce dish, flat, 3½ and 4 inch
     a. Footed, 3½ and 4 inch
9. Spoonholder
10. Sugar bowl
11. Water pitcher

3. PLUME. Adams & Co. of Pittsburgh, Pa., produced the Plume pattern during the 1880's. Since it was sold plain or engraved, pieces may be found today either way. This design was originated by the Boston & Sandwich Glass Co. in flint glass but not in a full line of tableware. No goblets were made by them but there were bowls, often with stippling, as on their earlier lacy glass, sauce dishes, compotes and a few odd pieces. Some of the Sandwich dishes may be found in a beautiful opal, as well as amber, but any colored pieces are rare. The Adams' Plume was not flint glass, as it belonged to a later period.

1. Berry bowl, feather pattern around top edge, 8 inch
   a. Berry dish, oblong, 5 inch
2. Butter dish, collared base
3. Cake plate on standard, 9 and 10 inch
4. Celery vase, two styles
5. Creamer
6. Compotes, open, flared, 6, 7 and 8 inch
   a. Open, crimped, 7, 8 and 9 inch
   b. Fruit compotes, 8, 9 and 10 inch
   c. Covered, on collared base, 6, 7 and 8 inch
   d. Compotes on high foot, crimped edge to bowl, 7, 8 and 9 inch
   e. Open, on high foot, plain edge, 8, 9 and 10 inch
   f. Covered compotes on high foot, 6, 7 and 8 inch
   g. Open compotes, with flared bowls on collared base, 6, 7 and 8 inch
7. Finger bowl
8. Goblet
9. Lemonade or cider set, consisting of ½-gallon pitcher, tumblers and tray
10. Pickle dish
11. Sauce dish, footed, 4 inch
    a. Flared sauce, 4 inch
12. Spoonholder
13. Sugar bowl
14. Tumbler
15. Water set with pitcher and bowl
    a. Tray, large and round, with upturned brim, 12½ inch

16. Water pitcher, ½ gallon
17. Water tray

4. ATLAS. This design was produced by Bryce Bros. of Pittsburgh, Pa., during the 1880's and their original trade name was Atlas. When the United States Glass Co. absorbed eighteen of the older factories in 1891 they carried on some of the other factories' earlier patterns, and among them was Atlas. This pattern should not be confused with the glassware known as Cannon Ball, or with the Ball and Swirl. The United States Glass Co. has one sheet of its catalogue marked "Set red, engraved," so we know that they followed the popular trend at the time of the World's Fair in 1893 and produced this line in a combination of clear and red. There were many more forms than my catalogue lists, some footed and others with flat bases.

1. Cake plates on standard, 8, 9 and 10 inch
2. Bowl, flat, covered, 5, 6, 7 and 8 inch
3. Butter dish
4. Creamer
5. Goblet
6. Sauce dish, footed, 4 inch
7. Spoonholder
8. Sugar bowl
9. Tankard pitcher
10. Water pitcher

PLATE 27

1. LOOP AND JEWEL. So far I have not encountered either tumbler or goblet in this pattern, though doubtless they were made. No record of where this design was produced has been found to date. It appears to be midwestern, of the 1880's, and is found in clear glass. Some of the covered pieces carry the design on the lid while others are plain.

1. Bowls, round, several sizes
2. Butter dish
3. Creamer

4. Pickle dish, 8½ long, 4½ wide
5. Plates, square, 5½ inch
6. Salt, footed
   a. Salt shakers
7. Sauce dish
8. Sherbet cups
9. Spoonholder
10. Sugar bowl
11. Water pitcher

2. BALL AND SWIRL. Since the Ball and Swirl is a midwestern pattern, it is difficult to find in the East. Many forms were probably produced but so far I have been unable to learn who made it or obtain an adequate classification. It is listed here as a means of identification. Its forms indicate the 1880's. I have seen it only in clear glass.

1. Butter dish
2. Cake plate on standard
3. Creamer
4. Goblet

3. BUTTERFLY. Very little of this pattern has been seen in antique shops wherever I have traveled. The first pieces encountered were in central New York State. Probably the pattern is midwestern and was made in limited quantities. If a new "line" did not prove popular, it was soon discontinued.

The bands about the creamer and the base of the sugar bowl in the illustration are frosted and the balance of the glass is clear. The creamer has an open butterfly handle, while all other pieces I have seen have had closed handles. It is found also in clear glass without any satin, or frosted, finish. It appears to date in the 1890's.

1. Creamer
2. Pickle dish
3. Salt and pepper shakers
4. Sugar bowl

4. TEXAS. This is one of the latest patterns illustrated, but is pictured because a number of people collect it and it is not difficult to find. It was produced by the United States Glass Co. of Pittsburgh, Pa., and they christened it *Texas*. Despite the fact that it is not so early as most of the other designs, it makes an attractive table setting. I have listed only those pieces I have seen; there are probably many other forms. It is found in clear glass, in clear flashed in ruby, and in clear with a gold stripe on the edges. It is probably of the early 1900's.

1. Butter dish
2. Creamer
2A. Dish, oval, $11\frac{1}{2}$ x $4\frac{3}{4}$
3. Goblet
4. Pickle dish, oval
5. Salt, footed
6. Sauce dish
7. Spoonholder
8. Toothpick or match holder
9. Water pitcher
10. Wine

PLATE 28

1. SCROLL WITH STAR. Challinor, Taylor & Co. of Tarentum, Pa., produced this design and referred to it as "No. 310 ware." Many patterns went by factory line numbers in the old days, rather than by descriptive titles such as we have given them today, as a means of identification. It is illustrated here because the three sizes in plates and the cup and saucer would complement such patterns as the Wedding Ring, in which these useful items were not made. So far Scroll with Star is known only in clear glass and appears to be of the late 1880's and 1890's.

1. Berry bowl, 8 inch
2. Cup and saucer
3. Plates, 6, 8 and 10 inch
4. Sauce dish, 4 inch

2. BUTTERFLY (LATE). Some collectors have been buying this type of pressed glass, though it is only one of two or three patterns in imitation of cut glass shown in this book. No record has been discovered as to where it was produced but it may be reasonably assumed to be from the Pittsburgh area. I have seen it only in clear glass and the forms and style would indicate the early 1900's.

1. Berry bowl
2. Butter dish
3. Creamer
4. Sauce dish
5. Water pitcher

3. MOON AND STAR VARIATION. The variation of the Moon and Star is elaborate in detail and is a heavy, brilliant glass. Little is known about it except that it is midwestern. There are probably more forms than are listed here but it is seldom seen; therefore, it is certain that it was not produced in quantity, like the Moon and Star. It dates in the 1880's or early 1890's and so far I have seen it only in clear glass.

1. Berry bowl
2. Compote, on high foot
3. Goblet
4. Sauce dish

4. LOOP AND JEWEL. These represent more forms of the pattern illustrated in Plate 27. The classification is with the first listing.

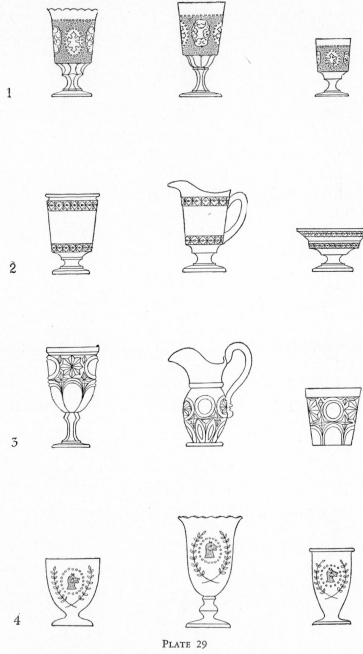

Plate 29

1. STIPPLED MEDALLION spoonholder, goblet, egg cup.
2. SPIREA BAND spoonholder, creamer, sauce dish.
3. BULL'S EYE AND ROSETTE goblet, creamer, tumbler.
4. HORSE-HEAD MEDALLION open sugar bowl, celery vase, spoonholder.

PLATE 30

1. DIAMONDS goblet, sauce dish, spoonholder.
2. JEWEL BAND egg cup, plate, footed sauce dish.
3. BEADED OVALS goblet, creamer, sugar bowl.
4. PANELLED OVAL spoonholder, sugar bowl, goblet.

Plate 31

1. SANDWICH LOOP goblet, wine with knob stem, creamer, sugar bowl.
2. DIAMOND MEDALLION goblet, celery vase, sauce dish.
3. MITRED DIAMOND sauce dish, celery vase, cordial.
4. CANDLEWICK compote, plate, wine.

PLATE 32

1. FAN goblet, sugar bowl, sauce dish.
2. PANELLED GRAPE BAND goblet, pickle dish, sauce dish.
3. BRYCE creamer, compote, wine.
4. FLAT DIAMOND creamer, goblet, celery vase.

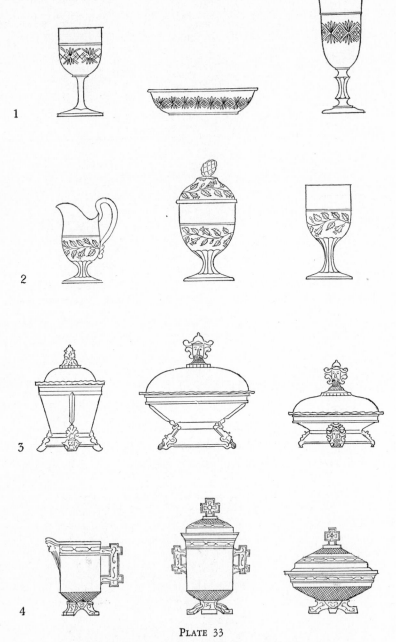

PLATE 33

1. Diamond sunburst (variation) goblet, relish dish, celery vase.
2. Fuchsia creamer, sugar bowl, goblet.
3. Viking sugar bowl, compote, butter dish.
4. Bearded man creamer, sugar bowl, butter dish.

Chapter VII

PATTERN GLASS COLLECTIBLE IN SETS—II

PLATE 29

1. STIPPLED MEDALLION. Since the egg cup and spoonholder are illustrated here, as well as the goblet, one may feel certain that other pieces, such as the creamer, sugar bowl, butter dish, may also be found. It is an interesting design but difficult to find. It is of clear glass with stippled background. Practically all of this stippled glass was made during the end of the 1860's and in the 1870's.

1. Butter dish
2. Egg cup
3. Goblet
4. Spoonholder

2. SPIREA BAND. This is a popular midwestern pattern because it is collectible in colors as well as in clear glass and makes an attractive table setting. It was probably made in the 1870's and 1880's and may be found in blue and amber besides clear glass. The blue is scarce and is seen in two shades. The amber also comes in light or dark shades, and I have been told of some pieces in apple green. One collector reported an oval platter in amethyst.

1. Butter dish
1A. Celery vase
2. Compotes, on high foot, open or covered
    a. Compote, 6 inch, covered
3. Cordial
4. Creamer
5. Goblet
6. Platter, oval
7. Sauce dishes, footed or flat; several sizes

   8. Spoonholder
   9. Sugar bowl
10. Tumbler
11. Water pitcher
12. Wines

3. BULL'S EYE AND ROSETTE. A rare early flint glass design, which is seldom seen and so far is known only in a limited number of forms, is now known as Bull's Eye and Rosette. All the pieces I have found were in New England, so probably it was made by one of the local companies. It might date in the 1840's and certainly in the 1850's. So far, it has been reported only in clear glass.

1. Creamer
2. Goblet
3. Spillholder or spoonholder
4. Tumbler

4. HORSE-HEAD MEDALLION. Certain characteristics of this design indicate that it may have been produced by the Portland Glass Co. of Portland, Maine, who were in business between 1863 and 1873. The celery vase has a stem similar to those in the Tree of Life pattern, meaning the type with a narrow clear band about the stem. Not many forms have been found, which is regrettable as the design has considerable appeal. It appears to date in the late 1860's or early 1870's and is collectible in milk-white as well as clear glass. A few pieces have been found · in fiery opalescent. It is difficult to find the sugar bowls, complete with the covers.

1. Celery vase
2. Compote
3. Creamer
4. Egg cup, small
5. Spoonholder
6. Sugar bowl

PLATE 30

1. DIAMONDS. Since there are sauce dishes as well as the other pieces illustrated, there must be a more complete line of this attractive pattern. It is a fairly heavy, brilliant glass. The few items pictured were found in New York State. At this time there is no record of where it was made. So far as I have been able to learn, it was produced only in clear glass. The forms would indicate that it was a product of the late 1870's or 1880's.

1. Goblet
2. Sauce dish, footed
3. Spoonholder

2. JEWEL BAND. Doubtless there is a full line of tableware in this design but the pieces listed are the only ones I have seen, and they were in clear glass. It is probably a midwestern pattern. Judging by the forms, it is of the 1870's and 1880's.

1. Creamer
2. Egg cup
3. Plate
4. Salt
5. Sauce dish

3. BEADED OVALS. This design is so attractive that it is illustrated as a means of identification for collectors. When a goblet and other table pieces come to light, such as the sugar bowl, creamer, spoonholder or butter dish, then it may be quite safely assumed that a fairly complete table setting may be acquired. It has been reported only in clear glass and appears to date in the 1870's.

1. Creamer
2. Goblet
3. Spoonholder
4. Sugar bowl

4. PANELLED OVAL. Though this pattern is found most frequently in New England, there is no record of who produced it, and it is scarce. Egg cups are seen more often than the other pieces. Doubtless there are many other forms than those I can list. It is a clear flint glass of good quality and was probably made in the early 1860's.

1. Creamer
2. Egg cup
3. Goblet
4. Spoonholder
5. Sugar bowl

PLATE 31

1. SANDWICH LOOP. A small "finger loop" is quite different from all the other varied loop designs found in pressed tableware. This variety, having an acorn knob on the covered pieces, is definitely a product of the Boston & Sandwich Glass Co. The creamer has an applied handle. Many of the articles display evidence of early manufacture, as they are quite crude. This pattern is seen most often in New England, in a milk white, generally quite opalescent in coloring. Many of the dishes have a clear bell tone when tapped. Unfortunately, it is difficult to find the opalescent goblets free of dirty streaks and curiously, too, the goblets show this tendency more than any of the other pieces. The footed salts with scalloped edge are usually found nicked on the rim. Even so, it is possible to assemble an interesting set of this unusual glass. It is also found in a brilliant clear flint glass, though less often. It can be reasonably assumed that the Sandwich Loop is of the late 1840's and 1850's.

1. Butter dish
2. Compote on low foot
3. Compote on high standard
4. Celery vase
5. Champagne

6. Creamer
7. Egg cup
8. Goblet, two styles, one with knob stem
9. Spoonholder
10. Sugar bowl
11. Salt, footed

2. DIAMOND MEDALLION. Little is known of this pattern, which is frequently found in New England, though thought to have a midwestern ancestry. Some of the pieces have plain rims and others are scalloped. So far I have never seen any of it in color. It appears to be of the late 1870's and 1880's.

1. Butter dish
1A. Cake plate on standard, 10 inches
2. Celery vase
2A. Compote on low foot, covered, 8¼ inches
3. Creamer
4. Goblets
5. Plates
6. Sauce dish, footed, scalloped rim
7. Sauce dish, plain rim
8. Spoonholder
9. Sugar bowl, elaborately scalloped rim
10. Sugar bowl, smaller size, plain rim
11. Water pitcher
12. Wines

3. MITRED DIAMOND. This is a midwestern design and may be found in clear glass and in color. I have never seen much of it, though it may be more abundant in localities I have not visited. It is pictured here as a means of identification. The fact that it is not so well known as most patterns that occur in color should make its purchase possible at a reasonable price. It is seen in amber, blue, and clear glass. Patterns of this type usually date in the 1880's and 1890's.

1. Celery vase
2. Compote, collared base

3. Cordial
4. Goblet
5. Pickle dish, oblong
6. Sauce dish, collared base

4. CANDLEWICK. The name "Candlewick" has been generally adopted for this popular pattern. It is my belief that it
may be found in a wide range of pieces but I am listing only
those I have actually seen. No record has been found so far
as to where this glass was produced. It appears in clear glass,
milk white, opaque blue, and amber. It probably came out first
during the 1880's.

1. Compotes, open and covered, several sizes
2. Cups and saucers
3. Creamer
4. Goblets
5. Plates, 9 x 8 inches and 8½ x 7½ inches
6. Sauce, flat, round
7. Wines

PLATE 32

1. FAN. It is possible that there may be another goblet which
will follow more closely the details shown in the sugar bowl
illustrated here, but if there is one I have not seen it. The motifs
in all the pieces in my possession vary according to the size of
the article. It will be noted that the conventional band is the
same about the base of both goblet and sugar bowl, as well as
the ribbing underneath and the shape of the stems. The designer evidently intended to create an Oriental atmosphere!
The sugar bowl has a palm leaf fan, inverted, on each side of
the bowl. One fan is plain and the other has a duck swimming
across it. There are bamboo shoots cavorting along a conventional band, and long-stemmed leaves somewhat like those of a
calla lily. There are other patterns somewhat similar but I have
not seen enough pieces to warrant showing them here. There
may be a full line of tableware in the Fan, but only the pieces

I have seen are listed, and these were in clear glass. The pattern appears to date in the 1880's.

1. Creamer
2. Goblet
2A. Platter, or bread tray
3. Sauce dish, footed
4. Spoonholder
5. Sugar bowl

2. PANELLED GRAPE BAND. This is a design of merit, though the pattern was apparently not produced in large quantities; it is rarely found. I can list only the pieces I have seen though it is quite likely that other forms exist. It appears to be of the 1870's and so far has been noted only in clear glass.

1. Goblet
2. Dish, oval
3. Sauce dish

3. BRYCE. The Bryce pattern was produced originally by Bryce Bros. of Pittsburgh, Pa., and later carried on by the United States Glass Co. where it was known as "Pattern No. 15010." My old trade catalogue of the U. S. Glass Co. names only the pieces I have listed but they may have added to their line at another time. By some few collectors and dealers this design is known as "Ribbon Candy." It is usually found in clear glass and the forms indicate the 1880's.

1. Berry bowl, 8 inch
    a. Covered bowls on low foot, 5, 6, 7 and 8 inch
2. Butter dish; two styles, flat and footed
3. Cake plate on standard, 8, 9 and 10 inch
4. Celery
5. Claret
6. Cordial
7. Compotes, open, on high foot, 5, 6, 7 and 8 inch
    a. Open, on low foot, 5, 6, 7 and 8 inch
    b. Covered, on high foot, 5, 6, 7 and 8 inch
8. Custard cup and saucer

9. Creamer
10. Cruet
11. Dish, oval, 8 inch
12. Goblet
13. Honey dish, square, covered
14. Pickle dish
15. Plates, 6, 7, 8, 9 and 10 inch, round
16. Salt and pepper shakers
17. Sauce dish, footed, 3½ and 4 inch
     a. Flat, 3½, 4 and 4½ inch
18. Spoonholder
19. Sugar bowl
20. Syrup pitcher
21. Tumbler
22. Water pitcher, quart and ½ gallon
23. Wine

4. FLAT DIAMOND. Little is known about the Flat Diamond design. There is an early flint glass goblet which resembles it closely except that the diamonds are pointed instead of being flat. Among the pictures of goblets in a catalogue issued by the United States Glass Co. after they absorbed eighteen of the earlier glass companies in 1891, is a Flat Diamond (with a panel) goblet, marked "Old No. E" which would be Richards & Hartley, of Tarentum, Pa., and their name for the design was Pillar. In the same catalogue is still another goblet along the same lines, except that it has a knob in the stem, called "Old No. K," which would be the King Glass Co. of Pittsburgh. The Richards & Hartley goblet more nearly matches the pieces illustrated on Plate 32. The diamond pattern in the panels, which alternate with those in clear glass, are flat. Usually a diamond pattern is either quilted, so that it is concave, or else pointed, and therefore convex. Flat Diamond appears to be of the 1870's and is not a lead flint glass. It is attractive and so I hope someone may write me and list many more pieces than those shown here.

1. Celery vase
2. Creamer
3. Goblet
4. Sauce dish, flat
5. Spoonholder
6. Sugar bowl

PLATE 33

1. DIAMOND SUNBURST (VARIATION). This is another of the rather confusing number of Sunburst patterns. It is not related to the Sunburst design shown on Plate 12 of *Early American Pressed Glass* or to the Diamond Sunburst shown on Plate 78 of that same volume, though it is more nearly like the latter.

I find the goblet of the Diamond Sunburst Variation, as shown on Plate 33, in a catalogue of the United States Glass Co. issued after 1891. Of course, practically all of the goblets they picture are patterns carried over from former years but I have never seen any pressed glass Sunburst variation that would be of an earlier period than the late 1870's. Applied handles do not date glass as they are being used today on some modern blown glassware. Some few pressed glass patterns did carry in their line what were referred to in the 1890's as "butter chips," meaning individual butter plates, and some novices have mistaken these for the earlier cup plates. If one tries to approximate the age of glassware by weight, he can encounter plenty of difficulties because the heaviest pattern ever produced in pressed glass is the Moon and Star, which came out in 1888, made by Adams & Co. of Pittsburgh, Pa., as their Palace pattern. An old-time glassworker told me that the Palace was finally discontinued because the customers complained of the high freight rates, due to the weight.

It will be noted here that there are three petals, both above and below the connecting diamond-shaped ornaments, whereas in the design shown on Plate 78 of *Early American Pressed Glass* there is a wider fanlike design between the diamonds. This goblet has a plain stem (U. S. Glass Co. No. 77) while the Diamond Sunburst has a knob stem.

1. Celery vase
2. Goblet
3. Pickle dish
4. Sauce dish

2. FUCHSIA. The Fuchsia illustrated on Plate 33 should not be confused with that type having a stippled background (in which I have found only goblets), or of the Square Fuchsia illustrated on Plate 23. It is a brilliant glass and the flowers and leaves stand out in heavy relief. It was made by the Boston & Sandwich Glass Co., probably during the 1860's, or about the same period as the Morning Glory. A set of this pattern makes a highly satisfactory table setting. It appears only in clear glass.

1. Butter dish
2. Compote, open, on low foot
3. Creamer
4. Goblet
5. Spoonholder
6. Sugar bowl

3. VIKING. Probably more people have written to me to know the name of this pattern than any other since *Early American Pressed Glass* was published. It is curious that this should be the case, when there are so many more attractive patterns collectible in sets.

The quality of the glass is bright and clear and the faces in the design are well-modelled. The bases of the dishes are collared, as in the well-known Lion. Three and sometimes four of the heads serve as pedestals for some of the pieces. So far no documentary evidence has been found to shed any light as to what glass factory produced it but it is fairly safe to assume that it is a midwestern pattern of the late 1870's or 1880's. It has been known in different sections of the country by a variety of names, such as "Old Man of the Mountain," "Prophet," "Bearded Man," "Viking," and so on, but in order to spare future confusion, it is being christened by the name I have found to be in the most general use. I have never heard of any piece in color. The forms vary, as they do in many of the old patterns. One creamer has a straight edge and has four heads on the base. Another has a different shape, the edge is scalloped, and it rests on three heads.

On Plate 79 may be seen a sauce dish which corresponds almost exactly with the Viking, except in place of the man's face there is a goat's! I have searched in vain for other pieces to match. It may be that only fruit sets were made, composed of a berry bowl and sauce dishes. Any pieces in the Goat pattern are scarce.

1. Bowls, covered and open
2. Butter dish
3. Celery vase
4. Compotes, covered
5. Creamer
6. Goblet
7. Pickle dish
8. Platter
9. Salt, large
10. Sauce dish, 2 sizes
11. Spoonholder
12. Sugar bowl
13. Water pitcher

4. BEARDED MAN. It is quite probable that other pieces besides those enumerated may be found in this pattern but I am listing those I have seen. Some designs were made only in "table sets" consisting of the four pieces named. If the pattern proved popular, then it was built up into a larger line. This set is pictured as a means of identification, with the thought that other pieces may exist. The knobs of all the covered pieces carry a Maltese cross, and the lid and base of the bowl are

adorned with a band of small sharp diamonds. On the bowl
the diamonds are on the outside but the lid carries the band on
the inside. The spout of the pitcher is embellished with the
head of a bearded man, hence the title. Since it is not a New
England pattern it was probably produced in the midwest; the
style would denote the 1880's.

1. Butter dish
2. Creamer
3. Spoonholder
4. Sugar bowl

PLATE 34

1. DAISY AND BUTTON WITH NARCISSUS. This is a familiar
pattern, but I did not come across it until a short time after
Early American Pressed Glass was written. The illustration
shown here was done in 1934. A few years later a collector
wrote and thanked me for not including it in my first book as
she felt that its omission had enabled her to assemble a set very
cheaply! I have seen the design only in clear glass. A collector
from Richmond, Va., was able to augment my rather incomplete
listing and I am indebted to her for her kindness. No record
has been found of where this glass was produced. It is not seen
in New England but is prevalent in the South. The collector
who sent me her list of pieces said that much of it came from
the West.

1. Bowls, open
    a. Round, flat, 7¼ and 8¼ inch
2. Butter dish
3. Celery vase
4. Compotes, open
    a. Large fruit compote
    b. Jelly compote, 5 inch
5. Creamer
6. Decanter, quart, with stopper

PLATE 34

1. DAISY AND BUTTON WITH NARCISSUS sugar bowl, water pitcher, creamer.
2. FROSTED FRUIT berry bowl, water pitcher, dessert dish.
3. PANEL AND FLUTE tumbler, water pitcher, cup and saucer.
4. BEADED CIRCLE goblet, creamer, handled mug.

PLATE 35

1. HUMMINGBIRD goblet, water pitcher, butter dish.
2. PERT sugar bowl, spoonholder, butter dish, creamer.
3. MAIDEN'S BLUSH goblet, creamer, open sugar bowl.
4. SHRINE sugar bowl, goblet, sauce dish.

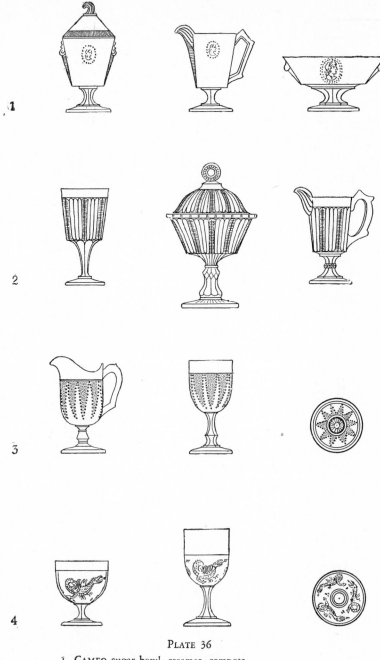

PLATE 36

1. CAMEO sugar bowl, creamer, compote.
2. ZIPPER goblet, compote, creamer.
3. DEWDROP IN POINTS creamer, goblet, sauce dish.
4. DRAGON open sugar (lid missing) goblet, sauce dish.

PLATE 37

1. OHIO spoonholder, sugar bowl (engraved), creamer (plain).
2. MARYLAND spoonholder, sugar bowl, creamer.
3. RIVERSIDE goblet, water pitcher, tumbler.
4. CARMEN spoonholder, sugar bowl, creamer.

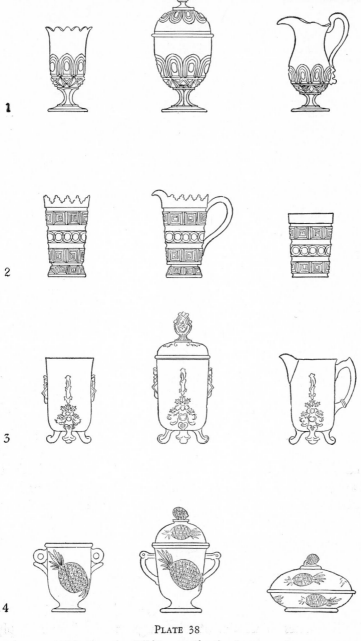

PLATE 38

1. MELTON spoonholder, sugar bowl, creamer.
2. DOUBLE GREEK KEY spoonholder, creamer, tumbler.
3. GRASSHOPPER spoonholder, sugar bowl, creamer.
4. PINEAPPLE spoonholder, sugar bowl, butter dish.

7. Goblet
8. Pickle dish, oblong, 9 inch
9. Salt and pepper shakers
10. Sauce dishes
    a. Flat, 4 inch, 4¾ inch
    b. Footed, 4 inch
11. Sherbet cups
12. Spoonholder
13. Sugar bowl
14. Trays, round
    a. Scalloped edge, 10¼ inch diameter
    b. Clear glass rim, 10¼ inch.
15. Tumblers, two sizes
16. Water pitcher
17. Wines

2. FROSTED FRUIT. Not many forms have been located in this attractive pattern. It has been named Frosted Fruit because the glass has a cool frosted appearance without actually being stippled or having a satin finish. About the top of the pitcher is a limb of an oak tree, with oak leaves and acorns in relief against a background of such finely drawn lines that a soft frosted glow is the result. The base of the bowl is in a basket weave pattern, so that the fruit which stands out in heavy relief appears to be a basket of luscious-looking grapes, pears, berries, peaches, cherries and apples. The handle of the pitcher looks like a log or limb, similar to the stem of the Maple Leaf goblet. No record has been found of this design and it has not been found in color. It is probably midwestern, of the 1880's. Doubtless some other forms exist.

1. Berry bowl, large and deep
2. Sauce dish
3. Water pitcher

3. PANEL AND FLUTE. This glass was produced by the United States Glass Co. of Pittsburgh, where it was simply known as "Pattern No. 15022." It is a brilliant, heavy glass

which apparently was not made in a large quantity, because it is seldom seen today. The factory catalogue is undated but this design appears to be of the 1890's or 1900's. It is quite possible that other forms exist.

1. Custard cup
2. Custard cup and saucer
3. Finger bowl
4. Tumbler
5. Water bottle
6. Water pitcher

4. BEADED CIRCLE. In New England this pattern is quite well known because it was made by the Boston & Sandwich Glass Co. It is fairly scarce, even in its home territory. I do not know of anyone who collects it, so can only list the pieces I have seen.

The Beaded Circle would date in the late 1860's and early 1870's. So far I have not heard of any pieces in color.

1. Butter dish
2. Celery vase
3. Compote
4. Creamer
5. Egg cup
6. Goblet
7. Mug, handled
8. Spoonholder
9. Whisky tumbler

PLATE 35

1. HUMMINGBIRD. Some collectors know this pattern as Hummingbird and Fern and others as Bird and Fern, but it seems advisable to shorten titles wherever possible. This glass has a great appeal for table use in country homes and also for bird lovers. It is especially attractive in color. So far no record has been located as to where it was produced but it appears

to be a midwestern pattern of the 1870's or 1880's. It is known in blue, amber and in clear glass.

1. Butter dish
2. Celery vase
3. Creamer
4. Finger bowl
5. Goblet
6. Sauce dish, footed
7. Spoonholder
8. Sugar bowl
9. Tray, for water set
10. Tumbler
11. Water pitcher

2. PERT. So far as I know this pattern was made only in table sets, by a midwestern factory. By table set is meant a sugar bowl, spoonholder, butter dish and creamer. The four pieces are illustrated. They are smaller than the usual size but still not toy pieces.

3. MAIDEN'S BLUSH. An elderly glassworker in the Pittsburgh glass district once told me that this pattern was originally decorated with "Maiden's Blush" so it seemed like a better name for the pattern than "No. 15071" by which it was known at the Bryce Bros. factory, in Pittsburgh, where it was made. It is a late glass, probably dating in the early 1900's. Nevertheless, it makes an effective table setting in the crystal with rose-pink color flashing. The pieces edged in gold are less appealing. Some sets were made in crystal, some in crystal with pink coloring below the diamond band, and it is possible other sets may have been produced with still a different color. It seems to me that I have seen it in green and crystal. My listing of pieces is according to the items named in a Bryce Bros. catalogue.

1. Berry bowls, two styles, 6, 7 and 8 inch
    a. Covered bowls, 6, 7 and 8 inch
    b. Flared bowls, 7½, 8½ and 9½ inch
2. Bonbon dish, 5½ inch

3. Boudoir set on 11-inch oval tray; set includes candlesticks, 2 pomade jars, 2 cologne bottles, puff box and ring stand
4. Butter dish
5. Candlesticks, 9 inch
6. Celery vase
7. Celery trays, two styles, boat shape and straight
8. Compotes, covered, on high foot, 6, 7 and 8 inch
    a. Open, on high foot, 6, 7 and 8 inch
    b. Punch bowl, with solid glass foot, 15 inch
    c. Punch bowl, without foot, 13 inch
    d. Footed sweetmeat dish, covered, 7 inch
    e. Open, with flared bowl, on high foot, 6, 7 and 8 inch
9. Creamers
    a. Larger size, 6 oz.
    b. Small oval creamer
10. Cruet
11. Custard or lemonade cup
12. Decanter with handle
13. Dishes, oval, 6, $7\frac{1}{2}$, 9, $10\frac{1}{2}$ and $12\frac{1}{2}$ inches
    a. Boat-shaped olive dish
14. Finger bowl
15. Goblet
16. Match holder
17. Marmalade dish, with cover, footed, $4\frac{1}{2}$ inch
18. Pickle dish
19. Punch bowl with solid foot, 15 inch
    a. Punch bowl without foot, 13 inch
20. Salt and pepper shakers, two styles
21. Sardine box, oblong
22. Sauce dish, oval, $4\frac{1}{2}$ inch
    a. Straight side, 4 inch
    b. Flared bowl, 4 inch
    c. Square sauce dish, 4 inch
23. Spoonholder
24. Sugar bowl
    a. Sugar bowl, oval, small
    b. Sugar bowl, for powdered sugar
25. Sugar shaker

26. Syrup pitcher
27. Sweetmeat dish, footed, covered, 7 inch
28. Tankard pitcher, ½ gallon
29. Tumbler
30. Vases, 6 and 9 inch
31. Water pitcher

4. SHRINE. This partly stippled pattern is of unknown origin but would appear to be of the late 1880's. Since there were some twenty glass factories operating in or near Pittsburgh, it is quite reasonable to assume that many designs of which no record has been found were produced in Pennsylvania, Indiana, Ohio and West Virginia. The shape of the sugar bowl, which is not footed, would denote a later period of manufacture than most of the designs having stippling. No piece of Shrine has ever been called to my attention in color, so probably it was made only in crystal. There are doubtless many more pieces in this set than I can give in the classification.

1. Berry Bowl
2. Creamer
3. Butter dish
4. Goblet
5. Platter
6. Sauce dish
7. Sugar bowl
8. Tumbler

PLATE 36

1. CAMEO. The Cameo, which should not be mistaken for the Actress pattern or for a fine type of English overlay cut glass, may be found in a wide number of pieces but unfortunately my notes covering all of them have been lost. The glass is of good quality, even though it is not flint, and has a bright sheen to it. The faces in the cameolike medallion are similar and do not vary as they do in the Actress, though they appear

somewhat different in the larger pieces, such as compotes, because of the increased size. There is no record of the pattern among my old trade catalogues but it appears to date in the 1870's or 1880's.

1. Butter dish
2. Celery vase
3. Compotes
   a. Open, low foot
   b. Covered, high foot
4. Creamer
5. Goblet
6. Sauce dish, footed
7. Spoonholder
8. Sugar bowl
9. Water pitcher

2. ZIPPER. Since *Early American Pressed Glass* appeared, a number of collectors have written to ask me for information about this design. It is a brilliant clear glass but has no bell tone when tapped because it is not flint glass. It was produced by Richards & Hartley of Tarentum, Pa., during the 1880's. No pieces have been seen in color, so far as I know. Their original name for it was Cobb.

1. Butter dish
2. Celery vase
3. Compote, covered, on high foot
4. Creamer
5. Goblet
6. Spoonholder
7. Sugar bowl
8. Water pitcher, two sizes, quart and ½ gallon

3. DEWDROP IN POINTS. The plate in this design was shown in *Early American Pressed Glass.* Since that book was written I have seen so many additional pieces that I decided it should be more fully illustrated. Besides the few items shown on Plate 36, a portion of a table setting is pictured on Plate 87.

These pieces were assembled by Mrs. Clara Edwards, who has specialized in complete sets. One or two dishes of any pattern do not give anyone an idea of the beauty that may be attained by a massed effect. No pieces have been found in color. This design is in clear glass, with the points stippled and outlined in a heavier beading.

Dewdrop in Points was produced by the Greensburg Glass Co. of Greensburg, Pa., during the 1870's and 1880's.

1. Butter dish
2. Cake plate on standard, 10½ inch
3. Compotes, open, on high foot, 7 and 8 inch
4. Creamer
5. Goblet
6. Pickle dish, oval
7. Plates
8. Sauce dishes
   a. Footed, 4½ inch
   b. Flat
9. Spoonholder
10. Sugar bowl

4. DRAGON. Almost nothing is known about the Dragon design, so it is being shown here as a means of identification. The only pieces I have seen came from Illinois and New York State and they were in clear glass. Perhaps one of my readers may be able to throw additional light on this interesting design.

1. Creamer
2. Goblet
3. Sauce dish, flat
4. Sugar bowl, minus lid

PLATE 37

1. OHIO. During the 1890's, the United States Glass Co. of Pittsburgh, Pa., produced a series of six patterns named after battleships. These six were the Ohio, Kentucky, Maryland, Pennsylvania, Michigan and Illinois. The Ohio pattern came

out in 1897 and was made both plain and engraved, as shown in the illustration on Plate 37. Generally factories carried a series of designs for etching or engraving and the purchaser could make his own selection. My old trade catalogue lists only the table set in clear glass, meaning the sugar bowl, creamer, spoonholder and butter dish, but it is quite likely the Ohio was produced in many other forms.

2. MARYLAND. This is another in the series of battleship patterns produced by the United States Glass Co. in 1897. The glass is fairly heavy and the design is in rather high relief.

1. Butter dish
2. Celery vase
3. Creamer
4. Goblet
5. Nappies or bowls, in various sizes
6. Pickle dish
7. Spoonholder
8. Sugar bowl
9. Toothpick or match holder
10. Water pitcher

3. RIVERSIDE. The Riverside is named after the factory that produced it, since the catalogue in which it was illustrated did not even give it a line number. It was made by the Riverside Glass Works, of Wellsburg, W. Va. Apparently it was not produced in large quantities, since little of it is seen today. The following classification is taken from the catalogue, which listed it only in clear glass:

1. Compote, covered, on high foot
     a. Square-faced open compote, on high foot
2. Creamer
3. Goblet
4. Spoonholder
5. Sugar bowl
6. Tumbler
7. Water pitcher

4. CARMEN. Little is known about this design except that it was produced by the Fostoria Glass Co. of Moundsville, W. Va., probably in the late 1890's. The catalogue listed only the table set, consisting of sugar bowl, creamer, spoonholder and butter dish. Doubtless other forms exist. It is shown here as a means of identification for collectors who may own pieces of it.

PLATE 38

1. MELTON. Only a few pieces of this attractive design have been found in New England. Doubtless the reason for this is because it was made by Gillinder & Sons of Philadelphia, Pa. Generally speaking, patterns from the Philadelphia and Pittsburgh areas were dispersed throughout the South, midwest and Canada. Any of the Melton is scarce, so it probably was not made in large quantities. A goblet appears in a Gillinder catalogue of the early 1870's. So far, this glass has not been seen in color.

1. Butter dish
2. Creamer
3. Goblet
4. Sauce dish
5. Spoonholder
6. Sugar bowl

2. DOUBLE GREEK KEY. The first pieces in this set to come to my attention were sent to me from Illinois. This glass is practically never seen in New York State or New England, though distribution as a means of attributing patterns to any one section has been greatly upset in recent years because of the carting of glass from state to state by those antique dealers who follow the Antiques Fairs or Exhibits. In the case of the Double Greek Key, it seems certain that it was produced in or near the State of Illinois. It may be found in opalescent as well as clear glass. It probably dates in the 1880's.

1. Butter dish
2. Creamer

3. Sauce dish
4. Spoonholder
5. Sugar bowl
6. Water pitcher
7. Tumbler

3. GRASSHOPPER. This is an engaging pattern as we seldom find glass adorned with animals or insects. It is difficult to show the grasshoppers in an illustration but they stand out in rather high relief, above the somewhat conventional design of foliage. This same pattern may be found *with* the foliage and *minus* the grasshoppers. No record of where it was produced has been discovered but it probably dates in the 1870's or 1880's. Perhaps some collector may be able to add many more pieces to my classification:

1. Butter dish
2. Creamer
3. Goblet
4. Spoonholder
5. Sauce dish
6. Sugar bowl

4. PINEAPPLE. The Pineapple is an attractive design which would be particularly apropos in certain localities of the country. The sugar bowl has a large pineapple in heavy relief on each side, with the leaves heavily stippled. The knob to the covered dishes is also in the shape of a small pineapple. So far I have been unable to locate many pieces and have known of only one person who collects it. This may be due to the fact that the pattern has not been identified before. There is as yet no record of where it was produced but it appears to be a design of the 1880's. It is in clear glass. A few pieces are known in milk-white.

1. Butter dish
2. Creamer
3. Spoonholder
4. Sugar bowl
5. Tumbler

PLATE 39

1. WESTON tumbler, water pitcher, syrup pitcher.
2. IVANHOE butter dish, water pitcher, sugar bowl.
3. INDIANA butter dish, sugar bowl, creamer.
4. KENTUCKY butter dish, water pitcher, celery vase.

PLATE 40

1. CUT BLOCK spoonholder, water pitcher, creamer.
2. FANDANGO spoonholder, water pitcher, creamer.
3. BLOSSOM spoonholder, water pitcher, butter dish.
4. ESTHER tumbler, water pitcher, goblet.

PLATE 41

1. BEADED SWIRL spoonholder, sugar bowl, creamer.
2. BLOCK spoonholder, sugar bowl, creamer.
3. BLOCK WITH FAN BORDER goblet, compote, compote on low foot.
4. BARRED OVAL goblet, relish dish, plate.

PLATE 42

1. AMAZON tumbler, sugar bowl, creamer.
2. MILLARD goblet, cake plate on standard, celery vase.
3. HARTLEY goblet, compote, berry bowl.
4. MASCOTTE (ENGRAVED) goblet, sugar bowl, creamer.

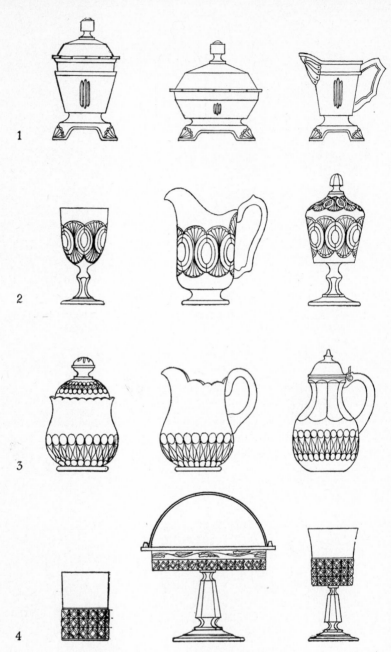

PLATE 43

1. PENTAGON sugar bowl, butter dish, creamer.
2. ROMAN goblet, water pitcher, sugar bowl.
3. MARIO sugar bowl, water pitcher, syrup jug.
4. MASCOTTE (PLAIN) tumbler, cake basket, goblet.

Chapter VIII

PATTERN GLASS COLLECTIBLE IN SETS—III

PLATE 39

1. WESTON. This design was known simply as "Pattern No. 123" by the manufacturers, who were the Robinson Glass Co. of Zanesville, Ohio. The company made a full line of this tableware but I can list only the few pieces they pictured, for the benefit of those who desire to identify their own sets. It is a heavy glass and, judging by the other items illustrated in the undated catalogue, was made in the 1890's.

1. Syrup pitcher
2. Tumbler
3. Water pitcher

2. IVANHOE. The Ivanhoe was listed under that name in an old catalogue, by Dalzell, Gilmore & Leighton Co. of Findlay, Ohio. It was produced about 1897. Probably a full line of tableware was produced but I can list only the following, all in clear glass:

1. Butter dish
2. Creamer
3. Spoonholder
4. Sugar bowl
5. Water pitcher

3. INDIANA. The Indiana pattern was produced by the United States Glass Co. of Pittsburgh. Though it is named for a state, it is not included among their "Battleship" series. They produced it in 1897 at their plant at Gas City, Ind., and not in Pittsburgh. The only pieces of this set I have seen were in clear glass. I presume some collectors may have many more items

in Indiana than are listed here but I can vouch for only the following:

1. Butter dish
2. Creamer
3. Spoonholder
4. Sugar bowl

4. KENTUCKY. The Kentucky was made by the United States Glass Co. of Pittsburgh in 1897. It was one of their "Battleship" series. It appears to be very like the Teasel pattern illustrated in *Early American Pressed Glass.* The catalogue shows only the table set but probably a full line of tableware was made. There is no record so far of any colored pieces.

1. Butter dish
2. Creamer
3. Spoonholder
4. Sugar bowl

PLATE 40

1. CUT BLOCK. The Cut Block had to be christened, as it bore only a line number in the old catalogue where it was pictured. It was produced in a full line of tableware by the Central Glass Co., of Wheeling, W. Va., probably in the late 1890's. The items noted are in clear glass:

1. Butter dish
2. Creamer
3. Spoonholder
4. Sugar bowl
5. Tumbler
6. Water pitcher, tankard style

2. FANDANGO. This elaborate pattern pictured in Plate 40 was produced by A. H. Heisey & Co. of Newark, Ohio, and was there known by the line number 1201. It was made in a full set of tableware in clear glass. Never having seen much of it,

I can list only the items I know to exist, even though the cata-logue stipulated a full line in this design.

1. Berry bowl, 9 inch
2. Bowl, 8 inch
3. Butter dish
4. Creamer, 2 sizes
5. Spoonholder
6. Sugar bowl, 2 sizes
7. Water pitcher
8. Tumbler

3. BLOSSOM. The United States Glass Co. of Pittsburgh, Pa., made the Blossom pattern under the line No. 15045. It is an attractive enamelled glass of the 1890's. My classification is limited to the items listed in the old trade catalogue, which does not state whether it was produced in a full set of tableware or not.

1. Butter dish
2. Creamer
3. Lemonade set, tankard pitcher (quart) and handled cups
4. Rose bowl
5. Spoonholder
6. Sugar bowl
7. Tankard pitcher, ½ gallon
8. Toothpick or match holder
9. Tumblers

4. ESTHER. Very little is known about the Esther pattern beyond the fact that this is the original name given it by the Riverside Glass Works, of Wellsburg, W. Va., who made it. The only items I have seen were in clear glass. It was produced in 1896. I trust collectors will be able to add to my classifi-cation:

1. Compote
2. Creamer
3. Goblet

4. Tumbler
5. Water pitcher

PLATE 41

1. BEADED SWIRL. This pattern was produced by George Duncan & Sons. My catalogue is undated but the quality of the glass and style of the pattern would suggest the 1890's. It was listed by the firm as their No. 335 set. It came in two styles, one with rather attractive scrolled feet and the other with flat bases. The catalogue lists the latter as "low shape."

The style having scrolled feet is not collectible in so many forms as the low shape. I have not seen a goblet in this pattern but one has been reported to me, so if it exists, then it could be used with the Beaded Swirl having the scrolled feet, as illustrated, or with the flat base type. The footed forms are as follows:

1. Butter dish
2. Compotes
3. Creamer
4. Cruets
5. Goblet
6. Sauce dishes
7. Spoonholder
8. Sugar bowl
9. Water pitcher
   Color: clear glass; clear glass with beading gilded; milk-white

Beaded Swirl—Low Shape:
1. Bowls, 7, 8 and 9 inch
2. Butter dish
3. Celery vase
4. Compotes, covered, 7 and 8 inch
   a. Open, 7, 8 and 9 inch
   b. Oval, footed, 9 inch; rare

5. Creamer
6. Cruet
7. Dishes, oval, flat, 7, 8, 9 and 10 inch
8. Finger bowl
9. Goblet
10. Lamp
11. Pickle dish
12. Salt and pepper shakers
13. Sauce dishes, footed, 4 and $4\frac{1}{2}$ inch
    a. Flat, 4 and $4\frac{1}{2}$ inch.
14. Sherbet cup
15. Sherbet cup and plate
16. Spoonholder
17. Sugar bowl
18. Sugar shaker
19. Syrup pitcher
20. Tankard pitcher
21. Tumbler
22. Water pitcher, $\frac{1}{2}$ gallon

2. BLOCK. George Duncan & Sons made the Block pattern pictured in Plate 41 in two forms, flat and footed. The footed style, which has a plain collared base, is somewhat more attractive. So far as I know, this was produced only in clear glass. My catalogue is not complete, so probably there are a few more forms than given in my classification. The pattern ran as line "No. 308" and "No. 309." In 308 there are listed the following:

1. Butter dish, flanged edge
2. Creamer
3. Spoonholder
4. Sugar bowl

In 309, with the collared base, the classification seems fairly complete. No goblets or tumblers are noted but one or both must have been made.

1. Basket, 9 inch

2. Butter dish
3. Celery, large
4. Celery boat
5. Cheese plate with cover
6. Creamer
7. Egg cup
8. Gas globes
9. Ice cream tray
10. Ice cream tray, handled
11. Ice cream dish, 5 inch
12. Pickle boat
13. Spoonholder
14. Sugar bowl
15. Water pitcher, two styles $\frac{1}{4}$ and $\frac{1}{2}$ gallon

3. BLOCK WITH FAN BORDER. The large round bread plate in this pattern was pictured in *Early American Pressed Glass*. At that time I had not seen a complete set and did not know that it was produced in a full line by Richards & Hartley of Tarentum, Pa. An original old trade catalogue in my possession makes possible a sizable listing in this attractive pattern, which was originally known as "No. 544 pattern." The use of line numbers is not nearly so effective as descriptive titles, which often enables a collector to identify a pattern. Original names, when they were utilized by a factory, were lost for so many years that there is no alternative for us today except to christen the various designs to the best of our ability. The Block with Fan Border appears to be of the 1880's and is usually seen in clear glass. The table set is not pictured, but probably exists.

1. Butter dish
2. Bowls, 6, 8 and 10 inch
3. Celery vase
4. Compotes
    a. Collared base, 7 and 8 inch
    b. On high foot, open, 7 and 8 inch
5. Creamer

6. Goblet
7. Pickle dish, oblong
8. Sauce dish
   a. Footed, 4 inch
   b. Flat, 4 and 5 inch
9. Spoonholder
10. Sugar bowl
11. Sugar shaker
12. Plate, large
13. Tumbler
14. Waterpitcher
15. Wine

Goblets and wines have been found with the blocks and fans flashed in red.

4. BARRED OVAL. This pattern was produced originally by George Duncan & Sons and later carried on by the United States Glass Co. of Pittsburgh, where it was known as "Pattern No. 15004." It is more attractive in the pictures than in the line drawings on Plate 41. My catalogue is not complete, so I can list only those pieces pictured or that I have seen. Doubtless many other forms exist. Earlier forms, such as compotes, exist in flint glass, though the number of bars across the ovals vary.

1. Celery boat
2. Goblet
3. Oblong deep dishes in three sizes: 7, 8 and 9 inch
4. Plate; appears to be 6 or 7 inch size
5. Sauce dish, 4½ inch

PLATE 42

1. AMAZON. The Amazon pattern was first made by Bryce Bros., glass manufacturers of Pittsburgh, Pa., and may have been carried on later by the United States Glass Co. It is a variation of the earlier Sawtooth pattern. My catalogue is undated but this design appears to have been produced during the 1870's and 1880's. So far it has been noted only in clear glass.

1. Bowls, open, flared, 4, 4½, 5, 6, 7 and 8 inch
   a. Covered, 5, 6, 7 and 8 inch
   b. Flat, scalloped, 4, 4½, 5, 6, 7 and 8 inch
2. Butter dish
3. Cake plate on standard, 8, 9 and 10 inch
4. Celery vase, footed
   a. Flat base
5. Champagne
6. Claret
7. Compotes, open, on high foot, 8, 9 and 10 inch
   a. Scalloped edges to bowls, on high foot, 5, 6, 7 and 8 inch
   b. Same, on high foot, with flared bowls, 5, 6, 7 and 8 inch
   c. Covered, on high foot, sometimes engraved, 5, 6, 7 and 8 inch
8. Cordial
9. Creamer
10. Flower vase
11. Goblet
12. Jelly compote, footed, 4½ inch
    a. Covered jelly compote, footed, 4½ inch
    b. Flat, round-handled jelly dish, 4½ and 6 inch
13. Salt and pepper shakers
    a. Large, heavy salt
    b. Individual salts
14. Sauce dish, footed, 4 inch
    a. Flat, flared bowl, 4 and 4½ inch
15. Spoonholder
16. Sugar bowl
17. Syrup jug
18. Tumbler
19. Water pitcher, ½ gallon
20. Wine

2. MILLARD. This attractive glass was produced by the United States Glass Co. of Pittsburgh, as their "Pattern 15016." They also called one colored version "Ruby Engraved" in a catalogue. It was made in clear glass and in clear with amber flashing, instead of the ruby, which also comes engraved. Certainly the crystal and ruby combination provides a beautiful

table setting and, fortunately, it was made in a wide enough variety of pieces to delight any collector. My catalogue is in color, showing the fluted portion in crystal and the plain panel in red, with a fern leaf engraved through the color. The catalogue is undated but the forms indicate the early 1890's. The following pieces are illustrated:

1. Berry or fruit bowls, 7, 8 and 9 inch
2. Butter dish
3. Cake plate on standard, 9 and 10 inch
4. Celery vase
5. Celery trays, flat, oblong; medium and large
6. Compotes, all open, on high standard, 6, 7, 8 and 9 inch
7. Creamer
8. Cruet
9. Custard cup
10. Dishes, oblong, 7, 8, 9 and 10 inch
11. Goblet
12. Plates, 7, 9 and 10 inch
13. Salt shaker
14. Sauce dishes, flat, 4 and 4½ inch
    a. Ice cream dish, 5 inch
    b. Footed sauce dish, 4 inch
15. Spoonholder
16. Sugar bowl
17. Syrup jug
18. Tumbler
19. Water pitcher
20. Wine

3. HARTLEY. Richards & Hartley of Tarentum, Pa., made this rather elaborate pattern, under the name of "No. 900 pattern." Glassmaking at that period was not a romantic enterprise but rather a highly competitive business. We might wish now that all tableware had been given suitable names instead of the unalluring line numbers.

The Hartley design was made plain or engraved, the purchaser using his own pleasure in the matter. Certainly the glass would cost more with the additional labor of engraving it, but it was much more attractive. The page in my catalogue enumerates "No. 86 engraving," so this must have been the number of the leaf design appearing in the plain panel. Colors are listed as amber, blue, yellow and clear glass. My catalogue displays the following pieces though doubtless others exist:

1. Berry bowl, 8 inch
2. Butter dish
3. Bread plate
4. Celery vase
5. Compotes with deep bowls, on high foot, 7 and 8 inch
6. Creamer
7. Dish, round, 6 inch
8. Goblet
9. Sauce dish, flat, 4 inch
10. Spoonholder
11. Sugar bowl
12. Water pitchers, quart and ½ gallon
13. Wine

4. MASCOTTE. The Mascotte pattern was made both plain and engraved, according to the desire of the purchaser. On Plate 42 this design is shown engraved. It was produced and named by Ripley & Co., of Pittsburgh, Pa. The Maude S. butter dish listed in the classification is in the shape of a horseshoe and, though not related to the design, is pictured with it. Undoubtedly it was named after the famous and popular trotting horse. The Maude S. butter dish is illustrated in this book among a number of odd butter dishes, on Plate 77.

My catalogue is undated but this glass appears to be a product of the 1870's and 1880's. The number of blocks in the design vary, according to the shape and size of the piece. It will be noted that the cake basket has one row, the celery vase carries four, the water pitcher seven, but the average piece, such as the goblet, sugar bowl and creamer, has three. I have never seen this pattern except in clear glass, though colors may exist.

1. Bowls, covered, with straight sides, 5, 6, 7, 8 and 9 inch
   a. Open, with straight or flared bowls, 5, 6, 7, 8 and 9 inch
2. Butter dishes, two styles, one referred to as "Maude S."
   a. Individual butters
3. Cake plate on standard, nickel-plated handle, 8, 9, 10 and 12 inch
4. Celery vase
5. Cheese plate and cover
6. Compote with shallow flared bowl on high foot, 6, 7, 8, 9 and 10 inch
   a. Straight bowl on high foot, 5, 6, 7, 8 and 9 inch
   b. Covered compote on high foot, 5, 6, 7, 8 and 9 inch
7. Creamer
8. Goblet
9. Platter, oval
10. Salt and pepper shakers
    a. Large salt
    b. Individual salt
11. Sauce dish, footed, 4 inch
    a. Flat, 3½ and 4 inch
12. Spoonholder
13. Sugar bowl
14. Tumbler
15. Water set with tray and bowl
16. Wine

PLATE 43

1. PENTAGON. George Duncan & Sons of the old Pittsburgh glass district produced the rather simple Pentagon pattern, under the trade name of "No. 100 Pattern." It is seldom seen, but, since it was made in sets of tableware, it is included here as a means of identification. Probably it was not a great commercial success and was soon discontinued. I have not heard of it except in clear glass. Judging by the other patterns included in the same catalogue in which it is illustrated, it is a pattern of the late 1870's or 1880's.

1. Butter dish

2. Compotes, on low foot, with deep bowl, 7 and 8 inch
   a. On low foot, shallow bowl, 8 and 9 inch
3. Creamer
4. Goblet
5. Sauce dish, footed, 4 inch
6. Spoonholder
7. Sponge cup (footed like sauces, but turned in at edge)
8. Spoonholder
9. Sugar bowl

2. ROMAN. This was the original name of the pattern illustrated on Plate 43, which was produced by George Duncan & Sons, probably during the late 1870's or the 1880's. They made an amazing number of compotes, both open and covered. Many of the pieces listed in the classification are taken directly from Duncan's old trade catalogue.

1. Compotes, covered, on high foot, 7, 8 and 9 inch
   a. Compotes, open, on high foot, 7, 8 and 9 inch
   b. Compotes, open, on low collared base, 7, 9 and 10 inch
   c. Compotes, open, on low collared base, with deep bowls, 6, 7 and 8 inch
2. Dishes, oval, for olives, celery, etc., 8 and 9 inch
3. Goblet
4. Jelly dish, flat, 6-inch bowl
5. Sauce dishes, flat, 3½ and 4 inch
6. Spoonholder
7. Sugar bowl
8. Sweetmeat dish, 6-inch compote on high foot
9. Water pitcher

3. MARIO. Names for patterns seem preferable to line numbers, so this George Duncan & Sons design has been christened Mario. They called it "341 ware." It is so rarely encountered that not much of it could have been produced. It appears to date in the 1890's and, so far as I can learn, was made only in clear glass. The pieces listed I can vouch for.

1. Butter dish
2. Creamer

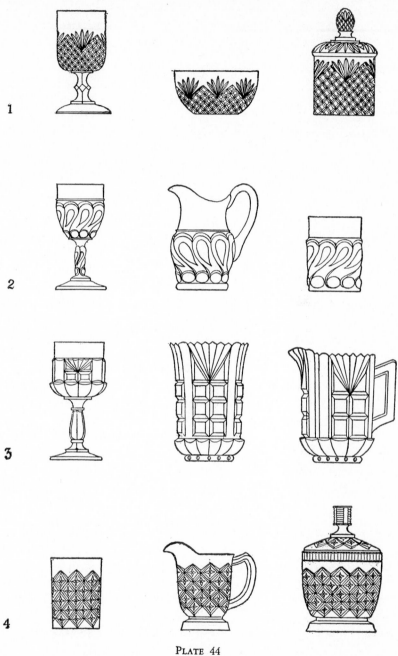

PLATE 44

1. CUBE WITH FAN goblet, finger bowl, piccalilli jar.
2. OVAL LOOP goblet, water pitcher, tumbler.
3. OREGON goblet, celery vase, water pitcher.
4. STAR tumbler, creamer, sugar bowl.

PLATE 45

1. ADAMS goblet, finger bowl, sherbet cup.
2. ART spoonholder, sugar bowl, creamer.
3. TREMONT sugar bowl, creamer, footed sauce dish.
4. BERKELEY goblet, cup and saucer, cruet.

PLATE 46

1. CLIO spoonholder, sugar bowl, creamer.
2. ROANOKE spoonholder, butter dish, creamer.
3. COMPACT goblet (engraved), covered bowl, sauce dish.
4. PANEL AND RIB waste bowl, goblet, water pitcher.

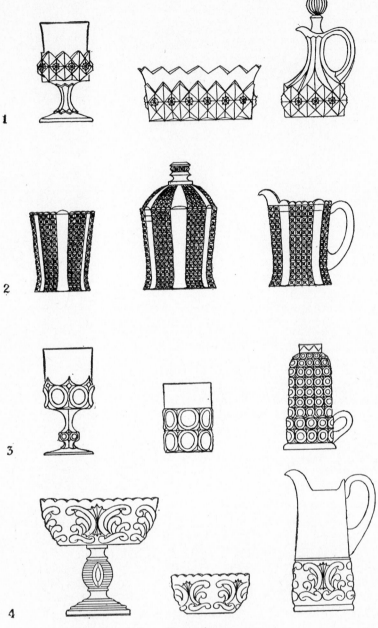

PLATE 47

1. SAWTOOTH AND STAR goblet, berry bowl, cruet.
2. PANELLED STRAWBERRY CUT spoonholder, sugar bowl, creamer.
3. BULL'S EYE (VARIATION) goblet, tumbler, night lamp.
4. OPAQUE SCROLL compote, sauce dish, tankard pitcher.

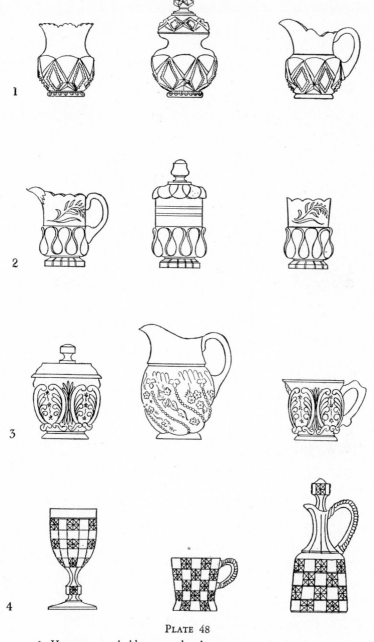

PLATE 48

1. HELENE spoonholder, sugar bowl, creamer.
2. CRYSTAL WEDDING creamer, sugar bowl, spoonholder.
3. SCROLL AND FLOWER sugar bowl, water pitcher (odd), creamer
4. CUBE AND DIAMOND goblet, mug, cruet.

3. Salt shakers
4. Spoonholder
5. Sugar bowl
6. Syrup jug, two sizes, ½ and 1 pint

4. MASCOTTE. This pattern was illustrated and described on Plate 42.

PLATE 44

1. CUBE WITH FAN. This fairly late pattern was produced by the United States Glass Co. of Pittsburgh, Pa., as "No. 15041 pattern." It is pressed in imitation of cut glass and was probably made in the early 1900's. So far as I know, it is not found in colors. My catalogue pictures the following pieces:

1. Celery vase (not footed)
2. Dishes, for pickles, jelly, etc., 5 and 6 inch
3. Finger bowl
4. Goblet
5. Pickle jar, covered
6. Piccalilli jar, covered (larger size)
7. Sugar bowl
8. Tumbler
9. Water bottle

2. OVAL LOOP. In his book devoted to goblets, Dr. Millard calls this design "Question Mark" but it seems to me the loops are at quite an angle for such a purpose! It was produced by Richards & Hartley of Tarentum, Pa., under the unglamorous title "No. 55 pattern." Probably more forms exist than I can name from the original catalogue dated 1888, as a previous one might have additional items. So far as I know, the Oval Loop exists only in clear glass.

1. Bowls on collared base, 7 and 8 inch
    a. Bowls, 4, 5, 6 and 8 inch
2. Butter dish

3. Celery vase
4. Compotes, open, on high foot, 7 and 8 inch
   a. Covered, on high foot, 7 and 8 inch
5. Creamer
6. Dishes, deep oblong, 7, 8, 9 and 10 inch
7. Goblet
8. Salt and pepper shakers
9. Sauce dish, footed, 4 inch
10. Spoonholder
11. Sugar bowl
12. Sugar shaker
13. Tankard style pitchers, quart and ½ gallon
14. Tumbler
15. Water pitchers, quart and ½ gallon
16. Wine

3. OREGON. This is the original designation for this design, made by Richards & Hartley of Tarentum, Pa., in 1888 and possibly earlier. While I have seen it only in clear glass, a collector has informed me that she has found some of the items, including the tumblers, with the blocks flashed in ruby red. The classification is taken from the old catalogue.

1. Bowls, 5, 6 and 8 inch
2. Butter dish
3. Celery vase
4. Compotes, open, on low foot, 7 and 8 inch
   a. Covered, on high foot, 7 and 8 inch
5. Creamer
6. Dishes, oblong, 7, 8 and 9 inch
   a. Olive dish
7. Goblet
8. Salt and pepper shakers
9. Sauce dish, footed, 4 inch
10. Spoonholder
11. Sugar bowl
12. Tankard style pitcher, ½ gallon
13. Tumbler

14. Water pitchers, quart and ½ gallon
15. Wine

4. STAR. Challinor, Taylor & Co. of Tarentum, Pa., made the Star, though in their factory it was known as "No. 9 ware." Probably they produced a full line of tableware but I am listing only the items they illustrate. The forms would appear to make it a ware of the late 1880's. It is quite possible that this pattern was not built up into an extensive line, since it is so seldom seen.

1. Berry bowls, on collared base, 7, 8 and 9 inch
2. Butter dish
3. Compotes, on high foot, 7, 8 and 9 inch
4. Creamer
5. Spoonholder
6. Sugar bowl
7. Tumbler
8. Water set with tray and bowl

PLATE 45

1. ADAMS. Since this pattern was made by Adams & Co. of Pittsburgh and not named by them beyond calling it "No. 29 pattern," it seems that it should fare better, so it is now called Adams. It was produced in a wide variety of table pieces and is more attractive than it appears in the drawings. It may be found in more items than can be enumerated because my catalogue is incomplete. So far as can be learned, it appears only in clear glass and dates in the late 1870's or the 1880's.

1. Berry bowl, deep, 7 inch
2. Custard cup
3. Finger bowl
4. Goblet
5. Water pitcher
6. Water tray, to accommodate pitcher, 2 goblets and bowl
7. Tumbler
8. Wines

2. ART. The Art pattern also was produced by Adams & Co. of Pittsburgh. It is similar to the Moon and Star, which is a heavy design that came out as the Palace pattern in 1888. An old glassworker in Pittsburgh told me that some of these extra-heavy patterns were discontinued because of their weight, which made transportation expenses too high for the customers. My catalogue probably states accurately all the pieces produced. It was made in a large variety of tableware, in clear glass, so there may be later additions not listed here.

1. Basket, for fruit, 10 inch
2. Berry dish, round
   a. Berry bowl, 8 inch
   b. Berry or "dessert set," pointed style

3. Butter dish
4. Cake plate on standard, 9 and 10 inch
5. Celery vase
6. Cracker jar
7. Creamer
8. Cruet
9. Compotes, covered, on high foot, 6, 7 and 8 inch
   a. Open, on high foot, 6, 7 and 8 inch
   b. Covered, different style, 6, 7 and 8 inch
   c. Fruit bowl, high foot, flared bowl, 8, 9 and 10 inch

10. Dish, oblong preserve, 8 inch
11. Dessert set
12. Goblet
13. Pickle dish
14. Sauce dishes, 4 and 4½ inch, flat
    a. Footed sauce, 4 and 4½ inch

15. Spoonholder
16. Sugar bowl
17. Tumbler
18. Vinegar jug
    a. 3-pint and 2½-quart squat jugs
    b. ½-pint jug
19. Water pitcher, ½ gallon

3. TREMONT. The Tremont was so named by Richards & Hartley, of Tarentum, Pa., who produced it. It is a most attractive glass, with more delicate detail to it than is associated with some of the Daisy and Button variations. My catalogue does not state whether it was produced in color or not. It appears to date in the 1870's.

1. Butter dish
2. Compote, on low foot, two sizes, 7 and 8 inch
3. Creamer
4. Goblet
5. Pickle dish, referred to as "Shell pickle"
6. Plates, with clear scalloped rims, 4, 5, 6 and 7 inch
    a. Large 10-inch plate, to match
7. Sauce dish, footed, 4 inch
8. Spoonholder
9. Sugar bowl

4. BERKELEY. The Berkeley was made by the United States Glass Co. of Pittsburgh, Pa., and referred to by them as "Pattern No. 15020." Doubtless it was produced in many more pieces than I can list. It is difficult to tell when it was first made because many patterns that were popular were carried on over a period of years but it was still on the market in 1895, when it was apparently being closed out. I have not seen it except in clear glass, though some water tumblers have been reported, partly frosted.

1. Cruet
2. Custard cup and saucer
3. Finger bowl
4. Goblet
5. Salt shakers, two sizes, large and small
6. Syrup jug
7. Tumblers
8. Wines

PLATE 46

1. CLIO ware was the original name of the pattern illustrated in the first line of Plate 46. It was produced by Challinor,
Taylor & Co. of Tarentum, Pa., probably during the late 1870's.
My catalogue is undated but it lists a wide variety of tableware
in clear glass, blue, yellow and a color they term "old gold,"
which is very likely a honey amber.

Illustrated on one of the same pages with the Clio ware is
shown a Daisy and Button round plate with scalloped edge,
which they list in the seven-inch and ten-inch sizes, "made in
crystal and colors." The ten-inch size was reproduced a few
years ago and many of them in blue found their way into collections. Some buyers were skeptical enough of the fakes, so that
a few were sent to me to pass upon. It is not difficult to detect
the reproductions if one devotes a little time to studying the
differences between the old and the new. None of the Clio
ware has been copied.

The Challinor, Taylor & Co. catalogue lists the following
pieces:

1. Berry bowl, and matching 4½ inch footed sauce
2. Bowl (nappy), 6 inch
3. Bowls, covered, on collared base, 7 and 8 inch
4. Butter dish, two sizes
5. Celery dish
6. Compotes, covered, on high foot, 7 and 8 inch
7. Creamer
8. Plate, plain Daisy with imprinted button, 7 and 10 inch
   a. Cheese plate, 7 inch
9. Sauce dish, collared base, 4½ inch
   a. Sauce, flat, 4½ inch
   b. Sauce, with fan corners, 5 inch
10. Spoonholder
11. Sugar bowl

2. ROANOKE. The Roanoke pattern was made by **Ripley &
Co.** of Pittsburgh, Pa., and this was their original name for it.

It is a later adaptation of the Sawtooth design, though the Roanoke is not of flint glass. It was probably carried on by the United States Glass Co. after they absorbed some eighteen earlier factories in 1891, when they were all undergoing a financial crisis. The catalogue lists this pattern only in clear glass.

1. Butter dish
2. Cake plate on standard, 9 and 10 inch
3. Creamer
4. Goblet
5. Pitcher, tankard style, ½ gallon
6. Rose bowl
7. Spoonholder
8. Sugar bowl
9. Tumbler
10. Wine

3. COMPACT. Doyle & Co. of Pittsburgh, Pa., produced this pattern under the name of "Pattern No. 360." There is not much to be done about unknown designs which went by line numbers, except to christen them. The United States Glass Co. carried on the Compact, in both plain and engraved styles, and they are illustrated on Plate 46, both ways. My list is from a catalogue that may be presumed to be quite complete.

1. Bowls, 7, 8 and 9 inch
   a. Flared bowls, 7, 8 and 9 inch
   b. Flared, with covers, 7 and 8 inch
2. Butter dish
3. Cake plate on standard, 9 and 10 inch
4. Celery
5. Cheese dish and cover
6. Cruet
7. Creamer, two sizes, one individual
8. Custard or sherbet cup
9. Finger bowl
10. Fruit basket, 9 and 10 inch

11. Goblet
12. Jelly compote on high foot, 9 and 10 inch
13. Jug, ½ gallon
14. Plates, 6 and 7 inch
15. Rose bowls, 3, 5, 6 and 7 inch
16. Salt and pepper shakers
17. Spoonholder
18. Sugar bowl, two sizes, one individual
19. Sugar shaker
20. Syrup jug
21. Tumbler
22. Water pitcher, five sizes (some of these may have been different shapes), 1 pint, 1½ pint, quart, ¼ gallon and ½ gallon

4. PANEL AND RIB. This design is pictured in a catalogue of Young, Keiper & Co., No. 215 North Third St., Philadelphia, Pa., as "No. 99 ware." It would appear that this firm might be wholesale merchants, so it is not possible to say who made the pattern originally. Since no colors are mentioned, it must be assumed that it was produced only in clear glass. It appears to date in the 1880's. There may be other items than those listed as my catalogue is not complete.

1. Butter dish, two styles, flat and footed
2. Compotes, covered, on high foot, 7 and 8 inch
3. Creamer
4. Dish, covered flat oblong, 7 inch
5. Dishes, oblong, handled, 7, 8 and 9 inch
6. Goblet
7. Pickle jar, covered
8. Salt, oblong on rounded feet
9. Sauce dish, flat, 4 inch
10. Spoonholder
11. Sugar bowl
12. Water tray, oblong, with handles
13. Waste bowl or finger bowl

PLATE 47

1. SAWTOOTH AND STAR. This rather attractive pattern was introduced by the old O'Hara Glass Co. of Pittsburgh, Pa., during the 1880's. It was carried on by the United States Glass Co. of Pittsburgh as "Pattern No. 15001." So far as I know, it was made only in clear glass though someone has told me that he has seen pieces flashed in ruby red. There are probably many more forms, since my catalogue states that there is a full line of tableware.

1. Bowls (nappies), 5, 6, 7 and 8 inch
2. Butter dish
3. Claret
4. Cruet
5. Creamer
6. Cup and saucer
7. Goblet
8. Jelly compote
9. Honey or preserve dish, 3½ inch
10. Plate
11. Sauce dish, 4 inch
12. Spoonholder
13. Sugar bowl
14. Sugar shaker
15. Syrup pitcher
16. Wine

2. PANELLED DIAMOND. There would be more romance to the old glassware for us today if the producers had not grown weak on names and resorted to line numbers. This glass was produced by Doyle & Co. of Pittsburgh, Pa., under the title of "No. 100 pattern." They illustrate the following pieces, which appear to date close to 1900:

1. Berry bowl, oval, 9 inch
2. Butter dish
3. Creamer

4. Goblet
5. Spoonholder
6. Sugar bowl
7. Sauce dishes, 4 and 5 inch
8. Water pitcher

3. BULL'S EYE (VARIATION). This pattern was produced by the United States Glass Co. of Pittsburgh, Pa., as their "Pattern No. 151." The goblet was named "Bull's Eye and Spearhead" by Dr. Millard in his book devoted to goblets, but it is my endeavor to shorten titles whenever possible, because I believe that will make collecting easier.

Apparently this Bull's Eye Variation is not very old, judging by the forms, unless it was carried earlier by another company. My catalogue lists the following forms, in clear glass:

1. Brandy bottle with ground stopper, tall and narrow in shape, 22 oz., 16 oz., 12 oz.
2. Claret jug (tankard shape)
3. Goblet
4. Night lamp
5. Tumbler
6. Vases, tall and narrow, 7, 8 and 9 inch
7. Wine

4. OPAQUE SCROLL. Challinor, Taylor & Co. of Tarentum, Pa., produced the pattern illustrated in line 4 of Plate 46, as their "No. 314 ware" in crystal, opal, turquoise and olive. Translated in our terms today, these colors would be clear glass, milk-white, opaque blue and opaque green. In examining glass for some twenty-five years I have never yet seen or heard of this pattern in crystal though it must exist, since the Challinor catalogue specifies it. It is often seen in opaque blue or green. While it was not made in many forms, some of those we do find are decorative and colorful. My catalogue is undated but the pieces appear to date in the late 1890's or early 1900's. Even though they are late, they are popular with collectors who like useful articles and need a spot of color.

1. Berry bowl, round, 8 and 9 inch
    a. Hexagonal bowl, 8 inch
2. Butter dish, square
3. Compote on high foot, hexagonal bowl, 8 inch
    a. Round, on high foot, 8 inch
4. Creamer
5. Sauce dish, round, 4 inch
6. Spoonholder
7. Sugar bowl
8. Tankard pitcher, ½ gallon
9. Tumbler

PLATE 48

1. HELENE. During the eleven years since this book was begun, and through all the interruptions caused by the publication of my other books, which seemed more timely, this is another of the few patterns about which I have lost my notes. To the best of my recollection, it was produced by the Heisey Co. during the early 1900's and went by a line number rather than a name. At any rate, it is pictured here and given a name for the purpose of identification. It is a heavy imitation of cut glass. Illustrated are the spoonholder, sugar bowl and creamer of the set.

2. CRYSTAL WEDDING. This is the original name of the pattern produced by Adams & Co. of Pittsburgh, Pa. The catalogue states "Fancy Engraving" and shows a creamer embellished with an old-fashioned rose, a sugar bowl having a bird very much on the alert on one side and a rose on another. The spoonholder has a crane amidst some cattails, and the top of the butter dish is decorated with leaves, such as is shown in the illustration on Plate 48. Another page in the catalogue advertises the Crystal Wedding as "square shape, plain, banded, frosted or engraved." Unfortunately I do not have a complete list of the tableware, but my notes state that there is a large line of this ware.

1. Berry bowl
2. Butter dish
3. Cake plate on standard
4. Celery vase
5. Compotes on high foot, covered
   a. Open, on high foot
   b. Covered, on low foot
   c. Open, on low foot
6. Creamer
7. Goblet
8. Lamp
9. Salt and pepper shakers
10. Sauce dishes
11. Spoonholder
12. Sugar bowl
13. Tankard pitchers
14. Tumblers
15. Water pitcher

3. SCROLL AND FLOWER. This pattern is usually found in opaque but it may have been produced in crystal as well. It was made by the United States Glass Co. of Pittsburgh. My catalogue is undated, so I can only suggest that the forms indicate the late 1890's and possibly early 1900's. The forms are square, with the scroll raised in heavy relief and the flower decoration painted on. The odd water pitcher in the center of line 3 on Plate 48 is pictured on the same page with the Scroll and Flower in my catalogue. Some collectors specialize in pitchers, so it seemed an attractive piece to illustrate. In design it is similar to the Beaded Swirl. Originally, different flower patterns were frequently used to decorate the panels, and sometimes a flower spray appears underneath the spout of the pitcher.

In the Scroll and Flower, I have seen the following pieces:

1. Butter dish
2. Creamer
3. Spoonholder
4. Sugar bowl

5. Tumbler
6. Water pitcher.

4. CUBE AND DIAMOND. The United States Glass Co. of Pittsburgh, Pa., made this design and their original designation for it was "Pattern No. 373." Doubtless it was produced in a wide variety of pieces but I can list only those pictured on the two pages of the catalogue in my possession. The most unusual item is listed as a "spice tray" though it is quite a complicated arrangement and looks more like a caster set, minus the bottles. The top portion is open, somewhat like an epergne.

1. Claret
2. Cordial
3. Cruets, three sizes, 8 oz., 5¾ oz., 3½ oz.
4. Goblet
5. Mug, handled, four sizes
6. Mustard pot
7. Oil set tray: glass holder, with cruet, and salt and pepper shakers; very unusual
8. Salt shaker
9. Spice tray; rare
10. Wine

PLATE 49

1. WESTMORELAND spoonholder, sugar bowl, creamer.
2. BARRED STAR sugar bowl, creamer, butter dish.
3. BANDED DIAMOND POINT spoonholder, sugar bowl, creamer.
4. HIDALGO creamer, sugar bowl, goblet.

PLATE 50

1. LEAF AND FLOWER celery vase, butter dish, syrup jug.
2. TAUNTON goblet, cake plate on standard, tankard pitcher.
3. HOLLIS tumbler, berry bowl, sugar shaker.
4. SCALLOPED DIAMOND POINT sugar bowl, creamer, pickle dish.

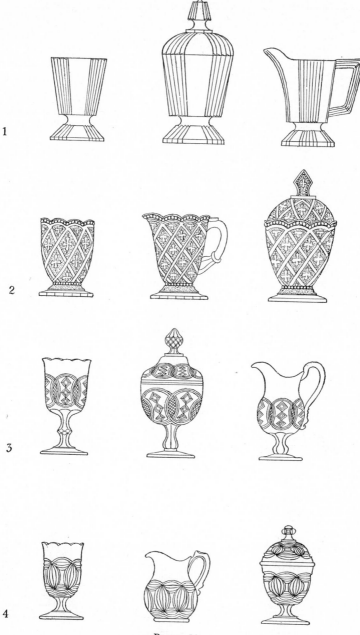

PLATE 51

1. FLAT PANEL spoonholder, sugar bowl, creamer.
2. NONPAREIL spoonholder, creamer, sugar bowl.
3. CENTENNIAL spoonholder, sugar bowl, creamer.
4. MELLOR spoonholder, creamer, sugar bowl.

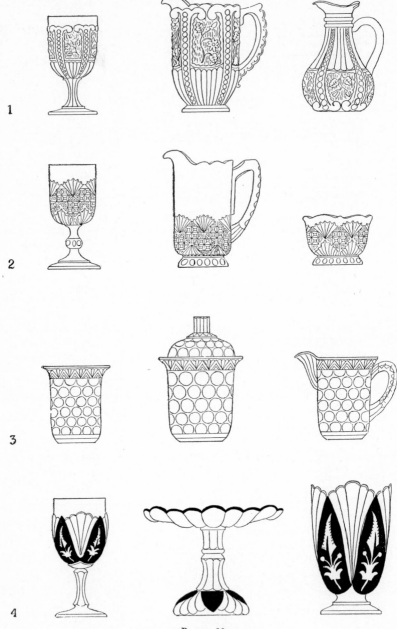

PLATE 52

1. MAINE goblet, water pitcher, syrup jug.
2. CUBE WITH FAN, goblet, water pitcher, finger bowl.
3. DOT spoonholder, sugar bowl, creamer.
4. MILLARD variation (ruby) goblet, cake plate, celery vase.

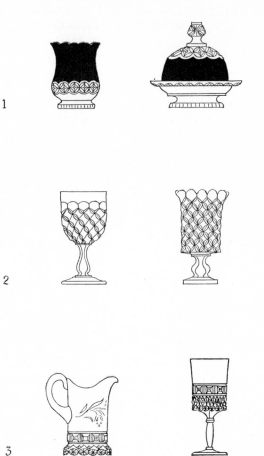

1

2

3

4

PLATE 53

1. RUBY ROSETTE spoonholder, butter dish, creamer.
2. BAKEWELL BLOCK goblet, spoonholder, tumbler.
3. DAISY BAND creamer, goblet, sauce dish.
4. CUT LOG jelly compote, wine, mug.

Chapter IX

PATTERN GLASS COLLECTIBLE IN SETS—IV

PLATE 49

1. WESTMORELAND. It seems strange that Gillinder & Sons, of Philadelphia, Pa., should have produced a pattern named "Westmoreland" when there was a Westmoreland Specialty Co. of Grapeville, Pa., founded by one Mr. West of Pittsburgh, who was a large producer of glass. In fact, the Westmoreland Glass Co. is still in operation though under entirely different management. They have been intensely active during recent years, in making up reproductions of old-time patterns.

Apparently Gillinder's Westmoreland pattern enjoyed a wide sale for years. In my collection is an original catalogue, nearly half of which is devoted to this design. The following classification is long but is taken entirely from the illustrations, so they may be depended upon. It probably dates in the late 1890's or early 1900's.

1. Berry bowls, sizes 6, 7, 8 and 9 inch
    a. Oval, 7, 8 and 9 inch
    b. Punch or lemonade bowls: No. 1, 14 inch; No. 2, flared to 15 inch
    c. Hexagonal bowl, 9 inch
    d. "Hat dish," odd-shaped bowl, 9 inch
    e. Rose bowl, 10 inch
    f. Rose bowls, 3, 4, 5, 6 and 7 inch
    g. Finger bowl
2. Butter dish
3. Butter dish, individual
4. Caster bottles: pepper, mustard, vinegar
5. Celery, tall
    a. Boat shape

148

6. Champagne
7. Cheese dish, covered
8. Cologne bottles, five sizes, round, with stoppers, from 1 oz. to 12 oz.
9. Cracker jars, covered, 5, 6 and 7 inch
10. Compote, open, on high foot, 6, 7, 8 and 9 inch
    a. Covered compotes, 6, 7, 8 and 9 inch
    b. Open, on high foot, flared bowl, 7, 8, 9 and 10 inch
11. Creamer, scalloped edge, round bowl, 1/4 pt. and 1/2 pt.
    a. Scalloped edge, straight sides, tankard style, 1/4 pt. and 1/2 pt.; largest size termed "Pompeian Cream"
    b. Small, individual creamer
12. Cruet, 1, 2, 4 and 6 oz.
13. Dish, square, 7, 8 and 9 inch
    a, Oval, 7, 8, 9, 10 and 11 inch
    b. Olive dish, round, with handle
14. Egg cup
15. Goblet
16. Ice tub
17. Jars, Marmalade, with stopper
    a. Pickle jar, with stopper
    b. Pickle jar, with flat cover
    c. Honey jar with cover
18. Lamp, night type with shade
    a. Hand lamp
19. Mug, handled, lemonade, to go with punch bowl
20. Pitcher, squat, plain edge, quart, 1/2 gallon
    a. Scalloped edge, 1/4 pt., 1/2 pt., 3/4 gallon
21. Plate, 6 inch
    a. Bread plate, round, with scalloped edge
22. Salt and pepper shakers
    a. Individual salts, two sizes
23. Sauce dishes, scalloped edge, 4, 4 1/2 and 5 inch
    a. Plain edge, 4, 4 1/2, 5 inch
24. Scent or pungent bottles, 4 styles: curved; straight; round; cross-shaped
25. Spoonholder

26. Sugar bowl
    a. Sugar basket, square
    b. Sugar basket, round
    c. Sugar sifter
    d. Small covered individual sugar bowl
27. Tray, 13 inch
28. Tumbler, two sizes
    a. Toy tumbler
29. Water bottle
30. Wine

2. BARRED STAR. This design was originally termed "No. 414 pattern," but as I have only one page from a catalogue I cannot tell whether or not more of it was made than is pictured. It was produced by Gillinder & Sons of Philadelphia, probably in the late 1870's. The pattern is seldom seen, so probably was not produced in a large quantity.

1. Bowl, 8 inch
2. Butter dish
3. Creamer
4. Lamp fonts
5. Goblet
6. Sauce dish, 4 inch
7. Spoonholder
8. Sugar bowl
9. Tumbler

3. BANDED DIAMOND POINT. Very little of this design is shown in the old trade catalogue of Gillinder & Sons, Philadelphia, so it probably was not carried on into a complete set of tableware. A goblet, champagne and wine glass in a "diamond" pattern are shown on another page, though it cannot be certain whether they were intended to be used with the Banded Diamond Point, which is not so coarse. Of course, they would combine nicely. The catalogue illustrates the following pieces:

1. Berry bowl, 8 inch
2. Butter dish

3. Creamer
4. Sauce dish, footed, 4 inch
5. Spoonholder
6. Sugar bowl

4. HIDALGO. The Hidalgo pattern was made both plain and engraved, as suited the purchaser. We find many times that designs having large panels or open spaces were decorated.

Hidalgo was produced by Adams & Co. of Pittsburgh, Pa., and was apparently popular, as a large line of tableware was developed. I have a dozen of the goblets, engraved as in the illustration, which I use frequently. The catalogue lists the pattern only in clear glass, plain or engraved. One odd piece is listed as a "Bread Boat." The pattern probably dates in the 1880's.

1. Berry set, with 9-inch square dish and 5-inch handled dishes to match
2. Bowl, salad, 11 inch
   a. Bowls, 6, 7, 8 and 9 inch
3. Butter dish
4. Celery
5. Compotes, covered, with collared base, 6, 7 and 8 inch
   a. Open, on high foot, with flared bowl, 10 and 11 inch
   b. Covered compotes on high foot, 6, 7 and 8 inch
6. Custard cup and saucer
7. Goblet
8. Olive dish
9. Pickle dish
10. Salt and pepper shakers
    a. Open salts
11. Sauce dish, footed, 4 inch
    a. Flat, 4 inch
    b. Handled dish, 5 inch
12. Spoonholder
13. Sugar bowl
14. Sugar shaker
15. Syrup pitcher

16. Tumbler
17. Vinegar jar
    a. Jugs, quart and ½ gallon
18. Water set with tray and bowl

PLATE 50

1. LEAF AND FLOWER. Hobbs, Brocunier & Co. of Wheeling, W. Va., are responsible for this flower pattern, which may be found in clear glass or flashed in color in combination with crystal. In fact, I believe it was produced as a novelty ware in various styles. I have seen it in clear glass, partly amber, and the original catalogue lists ruby bottles. Some collectors have mistaken this pattern for the New England Pomona, but the two designs and methods of production are utterly unlike.

The Leaf and Flower was probably produced during the 1890's and quite possibly into the early 1900's. A water set is pictured on Plate 75.

1. Berry bowl, tops cupped in at edge, 7 and 8 inch
    a. Bowls, flaring edge, 7, 8 and 9 inch
2. Butter dish
3. Caster set: leaf with handle, holding mustard, oil bottle, and two shaker bottles; bottles listed in ruby; no design on the sides
4. Celery vase
    a. Long tray with handle, termed "Basket Celery"
5. Creamer
6. Finger bowl
7. Salt and pepper shaker
8. Sauce dish, flat, 4½ and 5 inch
9. Spoonholder
10. Sugar bowl
11. Syrup pitcher
12. Tankard pitcher
13. Tumbler

14. Water set with metal tray: tankard pitcher and six tumblers

15. Water set with metal tray: tankard pitcher, two tumblers and waste bowl

2. TAUNTON. This design was originally known as "Scroll" pattern. I have a page from the original catalogue and find it was produced by the O'Hara Glass Co. of Pittsburgh. Scroll is a more appropriate title for this glass, but since there is in *Early American Pressed Glass* a design well known by that name, this is being rechristened so as to spare confusion.

Taunton was not made in a wide variety of forms but all the needed pieces are available. It appears to be a pattern of the late 1880's or 1890's.

1. Bowls, 6, 7 and 8 inch
2. Butter dish
3. Cake plate on standard, 10 inch
4. Celery vase
5. Compotes on low foot, covered; all of bowl is swirled; 6, 7 and 8 inch
   a. Covered, on high foot, 6, 7 and 8 inch
   b. Open, on high foot, 6, 7 and 8 inch
6. Creamer
7. Goblet
8. Sauce dish, footed, 4 inch
   a. Sauce dish, flat, 4 inch
9. Salt and pepper shakers
10. Spoonholder
11. Sugar bowl
12. Tankard pitcher
13. Tumbler
14. Water pitcher, round bowl, quart and ½ gallon

3. HOLLIS. The Hollis design was originally known as "No. 750 pattern" but the makers are unknown. There may be many more forms than those I list but the illustrations in my catalogue of "No. 750" are limited to a few items. The pattern

looks different in the catalogue than in the line drawings. It appears to be a heavy glass, with large diamond-shaped blocks and a pointed diamond at each intersection. This is the only line drawing of a pattern in the book that seems to be confusing.

1. Berry bowl, large and deep
2. Bonbon dish
3. Orange bowl, footed, deep bowl, similar to a punch bowl
4. Sauce dish, 5 inch
5. Sugar shaker
6. Water bottle
7. Tumbler

4. SCALLOPED DIAMOND POINT. There are so many variations of the Diamond Point pattern that it is necessary to give descriptive titles in order to avoid confusion. The earliest Diamond Point pattern, which is flint glass, is shown in *Early American Pressed Glass*. Almost every factory producing tableware in later years made variations of both the Sawtooth and the Diamond Point, with minor differences, so as to avoid plagiarism. It will be noted that the Banded Diamond Point on Plate 49 is quite different from the one having a scalloped border on Plate 50. The Diamond Point with scalloped edge was made by the Central Glass Co. of Wheeling, W. Va., under the title of "No. 439 pattern." The Central Glass Co. was one of the eighteen companies later absorbed by the United States Glass Co. of Pittsburgh. Some of the old patterns were carried on by the new branch of the U. S. Glass Co., which was referred to as "Factory U" and was located at Gas City, Ind. Collectors will note the large number of plates in this pattern, which is unusual.

So far as I know, this particular Diamond Point was not produced in colors. It probably dates in the 1880's.

1. Cake plate on standard, 8, 9, 10, 11 and 12 inch
2. Bowls, oval, 6, 7, 8 and 9 inch
   a. Bowls, round, 5, 7, 8 and 9 inch
3. Butter dish

4. Cheese dish, covered, 8 inch
5. Creamer
6. Goblet
7. Pickle dish
8. Plates, 5, 6, 7, 8 and 9 inch; all have star centers
9. Sauce dish, footed, 4 inch
    a. Sauce, flat, 4 inch
10. Spoonholder
11. Sugar bowl

PLATE 51

1. FLAT PANEL. Bryce Bros., who were absorbed by the United States Glass Co. of Pittsburgh in July of 1891, made this design originally. It was carried on by the United States Glass Co. where it was known as "Pattern No. 15003." The catalogue states "Factory B," which means that this glass was made by Bryce Bros. but was probably continued at the United States Glass Co.'s plant at Gas City, Ind. A wide variety of pieces were made but, unfortunately, my list is incomplete.

1. Bowls, covered, 6 and 7 inch
2. Butter dish
3. Creamer
4. Goblet
5. Spoonholder
6. Sugar bowl

2. NONPAREIL. This is the original name of the pattern illustrated in line 2 of Plate 51. It was produced by A. J. Beatty & Sons of Tiffin, Ohio. It is an attractive pattern, with scallops about the edge of the footed pieces. Doubtless a complete table setting was produced but I can list only the following pieces:

1. Butter dish
2. Creamer
3. Spoonholder
4. Sugar bowl

3. CENTENNIAL. Though the Liberty Bell pattern was a Philadelphia Centennial pattern of 1876, so apparently was the design of Gillinder & Sons of Philadelphia, which they named "Centennial." Many were the specialties put out at that time for our souvenir-loving public, and it seems unfortunate that two glass patterns should have carried the same name at the same time. However, Liberty Bell is well-established and this Centennial is hardly known at all. It was produced in quite a wide variety of pieces, including three oval platters, which are listed as bread plates. One is marked "Independence Hall" and has a replica of the building in the center of the plate, and the lettering "The Nation's Birthplace, Independence Hall." A second platter or bread plate has the same border and handles, with Carpenters Hall in the center, lettered "The Continental Congress, First Assembled in Carpenters Hall, Sept. 5, 1776." All three platters have handles in the form of bears' paws, and each is marked "Centennial, 1776–1876." The third platter has a bust of Washington in the center and is lettered "First in War, First in Peace, First in the hearts of his Countrymen." It was called the "Washington Bread Plate." A miniature platter was made like the others in all details except for a plain star center. It is small and was termed "Centennial pickle." Any one of these platters would constitute a rarity for a collector. So far as I can learn, this design was made only in clear glass. There may be other items than those listed, as my catalogue is not complete. The platters may be found in color.

1. Bowls, solid stem
2. Butter dish
3. Cake plates on standard, 7, 8 and 9 inch
4. Celery vase
5. Champagne
6. Compotes, covered, on high foot, deep bowl, 7, 8 and 9 inch
    a. Open, on high foot, shallow bowl, 7, 8 and 9 inch
    b. Open, on high foot, deep bowl, 7, 8 and 9 inch
    c. Sweetmeat, 6-inch covered compote on low foot

7. Dishes, oval, plain edge, 7, 8 and 9 inch
8. Egg cup
9. Goblet
10. Pickle dish, same style as platters
11. Platters; three styles, all with bear paw handles
    1. Washington
    2. Independence Hall
    3. Carpenters Hall
12. Salt, oval
13. Sauce dishes, 4, 4½ and 5 inch
14. Spoonholder
15. Sugar bowl
16. Water pitcher, two sizes
17. Wine

4. MELLOR. At one time there was a Mr. Thomas W. Mellor associated with Gillinder & Sons, either at their factory in Philadelphia or in Greensburg, Pa., or possibly both, and this pattern was named after him. At any rate, it is the original designation for this glass. Mr. Mellor was artistic, so perhaps he designed it. It appears in a Gillinder catalogue, along with their Centennial patterns and other such specialties. It was probably produced only in clear glass.

1. Beer mug
2. Butter dish
3. Celery vase
4. Compote, 6-inch covered sweetmeat, on collared base
    a. Open, on high foot, deep bowls, 7, 8 and 9 inch
    b. Open, on high foot, flaring bowl, 7, 8 and 9 inch
5. Creamer
6. Dishes, oval, with scalloped edge, 7, 8 and 9 inch
7. Goblet
8. Sauce dish, flat, 4 inch
9. Spoonholder
10. Sugar bowl
11. Tumbler
12. Water pitcher, two sizes

PLATE 52

1. MAINE. There hardly seems any good reason for the United States Glass Co. of Pittsburgh, Pa., to name this lovely stippled flower pattern the "Maine," but possibly the designer came from that State. Of course, Maine has much to recommend it but I never noticed that the flowers grew any more prolifically there than elsewhere. The catalogue also calls it "No. 15066 pattern" and states that it is "also made decorated." The latter must mean that the flowers may be painted in natural colors. I never happened across any of the decorated types, though I did find a lovely pair of oval dishes in a nice shade of emerald green. There is a wide variety of pieces in this set. The classification has been taken from the items illustrated in the company catalogue.

1. Bowls, 6, 7 and 8 inch
1A. Oval, 8 x 6 inches
2. Bread plate, oval, 10 x 7½ inches
3. Butter dish
3A. Celery vase
4. Cake plate on standard, 8, 9, 10 and 11 inch
5. Compotes, open, on high foot, deep bowl, 6, 7 and 8 inch
    a. Compotes, open, on high foot, flaring bowl, 8, 9 and 10 inch
6. Creamer
7. Cruet
8. Goblet
9. Jelly compote, open, on high foot, 5 inch
    a. Same as above, covered
10. Mug, handled
11. Pickle dish
12. Preserve dish, 8 inch
13. Salt and pepper shakers
14. Spoonholder
14A. Sauce dish, 4 inch
15. Sugar bowl
16. Syrup jug
17. Toothpick or match holder

18. Tumbler
19. Water pitcher, two sizes
20. Wine

2. CUBE WITH FAN. Originally the Cube with Fan was known as the "Shell" pattern by Doyle & Co. of Pittsburgh who made it, but I am changing the name to avoid confusion with other known Shell pieces. Apparently this design was produced during the 1880's because in 1891 Doyle & Co. became a part of the United States Glass Co. So far, I have not seen any of this glass in color, though it is entirely possible it was made.

1. Bowl, round, 6 inch
2. Butter dish
3. Creamer
4. Dishes, deep, oblong, 8, 9 and 10 inch
5. Finger bowl
6. Goblet
7. Mug
8. Salt and pepper shakers
9. Sauce dishes, 4 and 5 inch
    a. Square, 5 inch
10. Spoonholder
11. Sugar bowl
12. Tankard pitcher, ½ gallon
13. Water set with tray

3. DOT. This pattern with its enlarged "dots," or raindrops, on the exterior of the glass, was produced by Doyle & Co. of Pittsburgh, who were later absorbed by the United States Glass Co. There is not much that can be told about the design at present, as my catalogue illustrates only one page of this ware. The forms would suggest the late 1880's or 1890's.

1. Butter dish
2. Creamer
3. Spoonholder
4. Sugar bowl

4. Millard Variation. On Plate 42 the Millard pattern is illustrated in clear glass and the description states that this design was also made with part of the pattern flashed in color, the colored section being either plain or engraved. Line 2 of Plate 42 pictures the Millard pattern in what the factory referred to as "Pattern No. 15016," or in the plain, clear form. Another catalogue illustrates the same design fully under the title of "Ruby Engraved." In line 4 of Plate 52 is the latter style. Certainly this would provide a most attractive table setting, for those who enjoy red in their scheme of decoration. This variation was also produced in an amber and clear combination, both plain and engraved.

1. Berry or fruit bowls, 7, 8 and 9 inch
2. Butter dish
3. Cake plate on standard, 9 and 10 inch
4. Celery vase
5. Celery trays, flat, oblong, medium and large
6. Compotes, all open, on high standards, 6, 7, 8 and 9 inch
7. Creamer
8. Cruet
9. Custard cup
10. Dishes, oblong, 7, 8, 9 and 10 inch
11. Goblet
12. Plates, 7, 9 and 10 inch
13. Salt shaker
14. Sauce dishes, flat, 4 and 4½ inch
    a. Ice cream dish, 5 inch
    b. Footed sauce dish, 4 inch
15. Spoonholder
16. Sugar bowl
17. Syrup jug
18. Tumbler
19. Water pitcher
20. Wine

PLATE 53

1. RUBY ROSETTE. Not much is known about this pattern at present, beyond the fact that its forms indicate the 1890's. Combinations of ruby and clear glass were at the height of their popularity during the period of the World's Fair in 1893. In the illustrations on Plate 53, the dark part of the glass indicates a ruby coloring. It is a heavy ware and the red part is nicely done, being in a rich clear color, indicating good workmanship. I have found the following pieces:

1. Butter dish
2. Creamer, two sizes, one being small
3. Spoonholder
4. Sugar bowl, two sizes, one being open and small
5. Toothpick or match holder
6. Tumbler

2. BAKEWELL BLOCK. This early pattern was not christened by me but was called to my attention by a collector who assured me that he felt certain it was a product of the old Bakewell, Pears & Co. firm of Pittsburgh, makers of some of the finest flint glass ever produced in America. Deming Jarves, founder of the Boston & Sandwich Glass Co., visited their factory before starting operations in the Sandwich, Mass., plant with which he was associated from 1825 to 1858. He paid the highest tribute to the Bakewell Co., for the quality of workmanship displayed in their merchandise.

Bakewell Block is an exceptionally heavy flint glass, with large knob stems on the footed pieces. This pattern is seldom encountered but is well worth searching for. Any items are rare, so apparently the set was not produced in quantity.

1. Celery vase
2. Compote, open, on low foot
3. Cordials
4. Creamer
5. Champagne

6. Decanter, quart, footed
7. Goblet
8. Mugs (whisky tumblers with applied handles)
9. Spoonholder
10. Sugar bowl
11. Tumbler
12. Tumbler with solid glass foot
13. Whisky tumbler

3. DAISY BAND. The Daisy Band is a fairly heavy clear glass and may be found either plain or engraved. Many illustrations of it appear in the catalogue of a wholesale house but they do not state when or where the design was made. The catalogue is dated 1886 but many of the patterns pictured are carried over from the 1870's. This glass is not plentiful, so it undoubtedly was not produced in as large quantities as were many others, perhaps owing to the fact that it did not have so much popular appeal, or else the factory making it may have come to an untimely end, as often happened. In my catalogue this is listed as the "Beauty" pattern, but wholesalers often adopted names of their own. The wholesale price of the cake plate was fifty cents.

1. Butter dish
2. Cake plate on standard, 9 inch
3. Celery vase
4. Compote, covered, on high foot, 8 inch
    a. Jelly compote
5. Creamer
6. Sauce dish
7. Spoonholder
8. Sugar bowl
9. Water pitcher, ½ gallon

4. CUT LOG. This pattern is so generally known as the Cut Log that it would only cause more confusion to change it. It is as good a descriptive title as any other, but should not be confused with the Broken Column.

It apparently came out during the 1880's, as it appears in a Butler Bros. catalogue under date of 1890. A collector kindly sent me a list of the pieces in her collection, which was of great assistance, since none of my old glass trade catalogues show it. She has the pieces listed and I have added the four mentioned in the wholesale store's catalogue.

1. Butter dish
2. Cake plate on standard
3. Celery vase
4. Compotes, open, on high foot; two styles, scalloped edge and plain edge
    a. Compote, covered, 6 inch
    b. Compote, sides tilted for banana dish
    c. Covered compote, odd shape, like candy jar, short stem
5. Creamer, scalloped edge; two sizes, 3 and 5 inch
6. Cruet
7. Dish, covered, with short stem and handles, large size
8. Goblet
9. Honey dish, square
10. Mustard jar, 3 inch
11. Mugs
12. Olive dish, round, with handle
13. Pickle dish, boat shape
14. Relish dish, large, narrow, rectangular
15. Salt shaker
16. Sauce dishes; two styles, scalloped edge and plain edge
17. Tumbler
18. Water pitcher, wide band of pattern, ½ gallon; some have applied handle
19. Wine

PLATE 54

1. TRILBY. The Trilby pattern must have been inspired by the fond hope of some moldmaker for a ladylove. The face enclosed within the heart-shaped motif was probably someone known to him, just as the wife of the designer for George

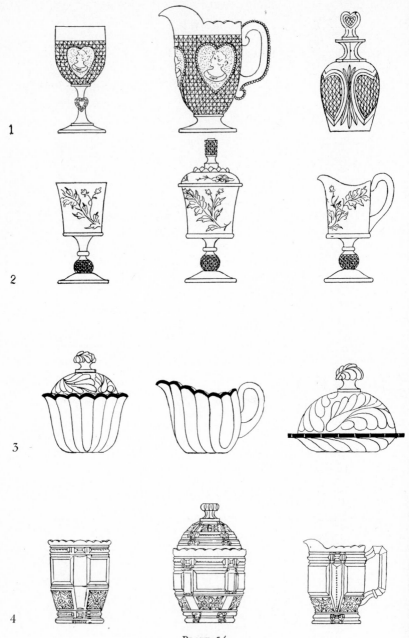

PLATE 54

1. TRILBY goblet, water pitcher, cologne bottle.
2. PAVONIA goblet, sugar bowl, creamer.
3. CRYSTALINA sugar bowl, creamer, butter dish.
4. HANOVER spoonholder, sugar bowl, creamer.

PLATE 55

1. LOOP AND BLOCK celery vase, wine, creamer, butter dish.
2. BEADED CHAIN spoonholder, open sugar bowl, plate.
3. SHERATON goblet, platter, footed sauce dish.
4. LAMP spillholder, odd goblet, cat goblet, Scarab goblet.

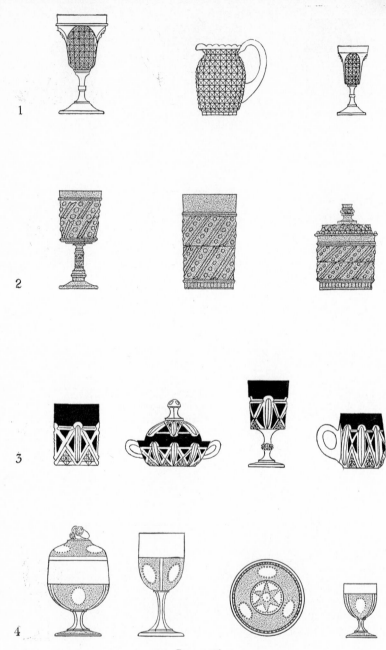

PLATE 56

1. HOURGLASS goblet, creamer, wine.
2. BARRED HOBNAIL goblet, celery vase, sugar bowl
3. TRIPLE TRIANGLE tumbler, butter dish, goblet, sherbet cup.
4. BEADED MIRROR sugar bowl, goblet, plate, egg cup.

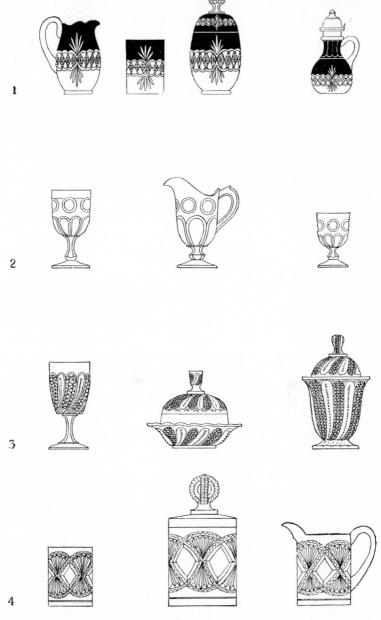

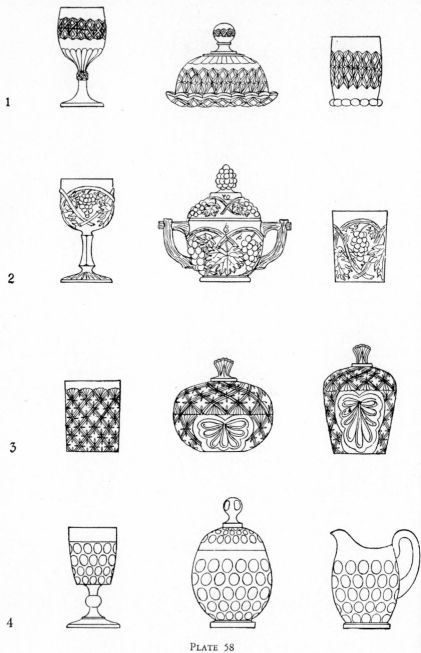

PLATE 58

1. PATRICIA goblet, butter dish, tumbler.
2. PALM BEACH goblet, sugar bowl, tumbler.
3. SUNBURST AND BAR tumbler, butter dish, sugar bowl.
4. CHALLINOR THUMBPRINT goblet, sugar bowl, creamer.

Duncan & Sons was his inspiration for the Three Face pattern, which is among the first ten most popular patterns today.

Trilby was produced in a limited number of pieces, by the United States Glass Co. of Pittsburgh, Pa. While there may be other items which I have not seen, I can be sure of the following:

1. Butter dish, heart shape, with cross as knob to cover
2. Cologne bottle
3. Goblet
4. Match safe
5. Water pitcher, ½ gallon
6. Toothpick holder, wall pocket

2. PAVONIA. The Pavonia pattern was made by the United States Glass Co. of Pittsburgh, Pa., both plain and engraved. In line 2 on Plate 54 all the pieces are engraved and they are much more attractive this way. The catalogue is undated but the forms in the glassware would indicate the late 1870's and 1880's. No pieces in color have been reported to date.

1. Bowls, 5, 6, 7 and 8 inch
2. Butter dish
3. Cake plate on standard
4. Compotes on high foot, open, 5, 6, 7, 8, 9 and 10 inch
     a. Compotes on high foot, covered, 5, 6, 7, 8, 9 and 10 inch
5. Creamer
6. Goblet
7. Sauce dishes, 3½, 4 and 4½ inch
8. Spoonholder
9. Sugar bowl
10. Tumbler
11. Water pitcher

3. CRYSTALINA. This attractive glassware with ruby-colored edge was made by the Hobbs Glass Co. of Pittsburgh and later carried on by the United States Glass Co. It must have appeared in the late 1880's. Many of the forms are unlike earlier pat-

terns, so probably it enjoyed its widest sale during the 1890's, as did all the ruby and clear combinations.

My catalogue is not complete, and though it lists quite a few forms, there is neither a goblet nor a tumbler. I am sure one or the other must exist. This pattern would make a most interesting table setting. It is particularly appealing to collectors because there are plates, which are missing in so many sets. If one chooses, a ruby goblet or one in crystal would combine nicely.

1. Berry bowl, square, 8 inch
2. Butter dish
3. Creamer; two sizes, one being individual, with a very short handle
4. Plate, round, 9 and 10 inch
    a. Plate in shape of palm leaf, 7 inch
5. Sauce dish, square, 4½ inch
    a. Round, with short handle, 4½ inch
6. Sherbet cup and 4 inch plate; cup has short handle
7. Spoonholder
8. Sugar bowl, covered
    a. "Berry sugar," open

4. HANOVER. Hanover is the original name of this pattern, which was made by Richards & Hartley of Tarentum, Pa., in 1888 and possibly earlier. It was produced in a wide variety of pieces, the classification given here being taken directly from one of their old catalogues. It is the type of pattern often made in colors but the pages of the catalogue do not mention any.

1. Berry bowl, 10 inch
    a. Berry dish, 5 inch
2. Butter dish
3. Cake plate on standard, 10 inch
4. Celery
5. Cheese plate and cover
6. Compotes, open, on collared base, 7 and 8 inch
    a. Compotes on high foot, open, 7 and 8 inch

7. Creamer
8. Dishes, deeper than saucers, 4 and 6 inch
9. Goblet
10. Ketchup bottles, small and large
11. Mugs, two sizes
12. Plate, bread
    a. Plate, 10 inch
13. Puff box
14. Sauce dish, footed, 4 inch
15. Spoonholder
16. Sugar bowl
17. Tumbler
18. Water pitcher; two sizes, quart and ½ gallon

PLATE 55

1. LOOP AND BLOCK. To date I have been unable to learn where this pattern was made. It is very similar to the Red Block shown in *Early American Pressed Glass* except that the design is more elaborate. Moreover, the quality of the metal also is better, as pieces are practically never seen with the red worn or scratched. The glass itself has a nice sheen and the red is a deep, rich ruby shade. It undoubtedly dates in the early 1890's.

1. Butter dish
2. Celery vase
3. Creamer
4. Goblet
5. Spoonholder
6. Sugar bowl
7. Tumbler
8. Water pitcher

2. BEADED CHAIN. This pattern is seldom seen in New England but is found frequently throughout the midwest. That fact would indicate that it was probably produced by one of the many factories in the Pittsburgh area, and the forms would sug-

gest the 1870's. So far as I can learn, it has been seen only in clear glass, partly stippled.

1. Butter dish
2. Creamer
3. Goblet
4. Plate, 6 inch
5. Sauce dish, flat
6. Spoonholder
7. Sugar bowl

3. SHERATON. This design was named by Dr. Millard in his book devoted to goblets. It is a midwestern pattern, probably of the late 1870's and 1880's, and it may be found in blue and amber, as well as in clear glass. A mail-order house illustrates the design and mentions it in blue and amber but I do not know any collector who has found the Sheraton in any other color. It is not pictured in any of my old trade catalogues of glass companies.

1. Butter dish
2. Creamer
3. Dish, open, round, 6 inch
   a. Panelled, eight-sided dish
4. Goblet
5. Platter, oblong, with eight panels
6. Sauce dish, footed
7. Spoonholder
8. Sugar bowl
9. Water pitcher
10. Wine

4. This line of odd pieces was started in 1933 and, since three of the items are unusual or scarce, it was decided to leave them in for the benefit of collectors. Number one in line four is a spillholder. It has all the appearance of a lamp which has been ground off at the top, but examination would convince anyone that this is not the case. It probably started off in life as a lamp and an inexperienced workman may have bungled

the top of the bowl and so decided to finish it to suit himself. The edge is rolled and has been fired. It remains a curiosity, with which experienced collectors are quite familiar because such odd items come to light now and then.

The second item is an unusual goblet. I have never seen another like it. The third piece is a goblet that would delight children. It has a horse, a cat and a rabbit about the bowl. Apparently not many were made because it is rarely seen today. The last goblet is an early flint pattern, of New England ancestry. It was probably made during the early 1860's. In his book devoted entirely to goblets, Dr. Millard has named this one "Scarab."

PLATE 56

1. HOURGLASS. The goblet and wine glass on Plate 56 are the only pieces I have seen in this particular "fine cut" pattern, with flattened sides or panels. Doubtless there are many other items, but they have escaped me. Because collectors have asked about the goblets and wines, they are shown here as a means of identification. The pitcher in the center of the line combines nicely with the stemware and may be found in a variety of pieces, as well as in color. I have found no record of where any of them were made. There are several pressed patterns having a similar fine cut design, which may puzzle collectors, so I have selected those most commonly encountered and, by illustrating and naming them, hope it will be easier to identify them in the future. On Plate 70 is shown the Pressed Diamond pattern, which also combines well with the Hourglass goblets and wines. It may be quite safely assumed that these patterns are all midwestern, of the late 1870's and 1880's. They may be found in clear glass, amber, yellow and blue, in such pieces as large orange bowls, large round sauce dishes, water sets, composed of an oblong tray and water pitcher; odd-shaped bowls, and so on.

2. BARRED HOBNAIL. The pieces illustrated on Plate 56 all have the frosted, or satin, finish. This pattern may be found to

a limited extent in clear glass. It would not surprise me to learn that it may be found in colors, or in combinations such as a frosted bowl with an amber band about the edge. It is listed and pictured in a mail-order catalogue of the 1890's. Collectors will find that pieces such as the spoonholder and sugar bowl, which have flat bases instead of being footed, belong to this later era.

1. Berry bowl, 7 inch
2. Butter dish
3. Celery vase
4. Creamer
5. Goblet
6. Spoonholder
7. Sugar bowl

3. TRIPLE TRIANGLE. This attractive ruby and clear glass pattern was produced by Doyle & Co. of Pittsburgh, Pa., before their merger with the United States Glass Co. It was simply called "No. 76 Set" by them. Collectors find descriptive titles much more useful than line numbers, which mean nothing.

My classification is not complete, but I can vouch for enough pieces to make an interesting table setting. This glass dates in the 1890's, as do most all of the ruby and clear combinations. Some pieces may be found without the ruby coloring.

1. Butter dish
2. Creamer
3. Goblet
3A. Mug, handled
4. Sherbet or punch cup
5. Spoonholder
6. Sugar bowl
7. Tumbler
8. Water pitcher
9. Wine

4. BEADED MIRROR. This pattern was produced by the Boston & Sandwich Glass Co. during the 1870's. It will be noted

that many of the Sandwich patterns have acorns as knobs to the covered pieces. It was undoubtedly a favored motif. The rarest decanter stopper known is one made during the early days at Sandwich, in Blown Molded glass, or that which some misguided person erroneously termed "three mold"—a title which lasted for quite a time.

Beaded Mirror was made in quite a wide variety of table pieces. My list is incomplete. There are probably compotes, footed salts, sauce dishes, and other items which I have not seen.

1. Butter dish
2. **Creamer**
3. Egg cup
4. Goblet
5. Plate, 6 inch
6. Spoonholder
7. Sugar bowl

PLATE 57

1. ROYAL CRYSTAL. Dr. Millard named this pattern in his book devoted to goblets. It makes a striking table set in ruby and crystal but is not quite so outstanding in all clear glass. Most of the Royal Crystal found in this area is in the ruby and clear combination. It was produced in a wide variety of pieces, but I do not have a catalogue recording it so cannot say where it was made or name all the forms. It would date in the early 1890's.

1. **Butter dish**
2. **Celery vase**
3. Creamer
4. Goblet
5. Sauce dish
6. **Spoonholder**
7. **Sugar bowl**
8. Syrup jug
9. Tumbler

10. Water pitcher
11. Wine

2. BULL'S EYE AND LOOP. This is another pattern I did not christen. It is rather well-known under its present name, so there is no use causing further confusion by attempting to change it. It is flint glass, some pieces having a much better bell tone, when tapped, than others. I have been unable to find a record of where it was produced and I do not know anyone who collects it, so my classification is limited. Little of this glass is seen, so apparently it was produced in limited quantities.

1. Butter dish
1A.Champagne
2. Creamer
3. Egg cup
4. Goblet
5. Spoonholder
6. Sugar bowl

3. FEATHER. The original name for this pattern was Doric and it was probably made in Indiana. It is a late pattern and that is the reason it was not included in *Early American Pressed Glass.* Some of the Feather is rather brilliant and glossy; other pieces are in a decidedly poor quality of metal. Collectors will find some items with a light-greenish cast to the glass and others faintly amethystine. This is caused by carelessness in the mixture.

Feather has been known by several names in various sections of the country, such as Indiana Swirl, Swirl and Feather, Feather and Quill, etc. Establishing a common nomenclature by which all patterns can be known simplifies matters for both dealers and collectors.

There are two variations in this pattern, one having a more distinct swirl than the other and there are other minor variations in detail. It will be noted that those dishes having a medallion in the base are a better quality of glass and more brilliant than those with the rayed bases. Besides clear glass, it is found in a fairly deep green.

1. Berry bowl
2. Butter dish; two styles, one having a wide flange where the cover joins
3. Cake plate on standard
4. Celery vase
5. Cordial
6. Creamer
7. Dish, large oval vegetable
8. Goblet
9. Jelly compote
10. Plate, 10 inch
11. Sauce dish, flat
    a. Sauce, footed
    b. Small honey or preserve dish
12. Spoonholder
13. Sugar bowl, two sizes
14. Tumbler
15. Water pitcher, two sizes
16. Wine

4. DOUBLE FAN. Challinor, Taylor & Co. of Tarentum, Pa., were the producers of this pattern, which their catalogue refers to as "No. 305 ware." Since it was not a popular pattern at the time it was made, the available forms are few and scarce. It is a pattern of the late 1880's and, so far as I can learn, is not found in color. Probably many other items exist than are listed.

1. Berry bowl, 7 inch
2. Butter dish
3. Compote on high standard, open, 7 inch
4. Creamer
5. Spoonholder
6. Sugar bowl
7. Tumbler
8. Water pitcher

PLATE 58

1. PATRICIA. The United States Glass Co. of Pittsburgh, Pa., produced the Patricia design under the title of "No. 15025 pattern." I have never seen much of this glass but it is shown here as a means of identification for some collectors who may have a full set of it. I can vouch for only the following pieces:

1. Cake plate on standard, 9 and 10 inch
2. Goblet
3. Honey dish, square, covered
4. Tumbler
5. Water pitcher
6. Wine

2. PALM BEACH. This is the original name of the glass pictured in line 2 on Plate 58, which was made by the United States Glass Co. of Pittsburgh, Pa. As usual, they also had a line number, which was 15119.

A very satisfying number of pieces may be had in this set, as will be noted by the classification. It is a late glass, dating close to 1900.

1. Berry bowl, flared style, 5, 6, 7 and 8 inch
2. Bowls, deep, without flaring sides, $5\frac{1}{2}$, 6 and 7 inch
3. Butter dish
4. Celery vase
5. Compotes, small, for jelly, $4\frac{1}{2}$ inch, footed, with deep bowl
    a. Same, with flared bowl, 5 inch
6. Creamer
7. Cruet
8. Goblet
9. Olive dish, handled
10. Pickle dish, oval
11. Plate, 8 inch
12. Salt and pepper shaker
13. Sauce dish, $4\frac{1}{2}$ inch flat
    a. Footed

14. Spoonholder
15. Sugar bowl
16. Tumbler
17. Water pitcher, ½ gallon
18. Wine

3. SUNBURST AND BAR. Hobbs, Brocunier & Co. of Wheeling, W. Va., were the originators of this rather elaborate pattern. They referred to it as "102 pattern" with "decoration No. 9." The catalogue is undated but the style of the pieces would indicate the 1880's. The Hobbs, Brocunier & Co. pictures of this pattern show the fan edges in a different shade, which must have indicated color and would account for the "decoration No. 9." It was also listed as being made in crystal (clear glass), old gold (honey amber), sapphire, and yellow.

1. Bowls, round, 8 and 9 inch
   a. Square, 8 and 9 inch
2. Butter dish
3. Celery vase
4. Creamer
5. Dishes, oval, 7, 8 and 9 inch
6. Finger bowl
7. Pickle dish, oval
8. Sauce dishes, 4 and 4½ inch
9. Spoonholder
10. Sugar bowl
11. Tumbler
12. Water pitcher; two sizes, quart and ½ gallon

4. CHALLINOR THUMBPRINT. As nearly as it has been possible to learn, Bakewell, Pears & Co. of Pittsburgh produced the earliest and best Thumbprint pattern collectible in sets of tableware. Theirs was a heavy flint glass that is greatly admired by all collectors today. It proved to be so popular that almost every factory making tableware copied it, with slight variations. The largest percentage of patterns in this book are not flint glass and the Challinor product is no exception. The forms

produced by Challinor, Taylor & Co. of Tarentum, Pa., vary greatly from the earlier Bakewell product, because this variety shown on Plate 58 dates in the 1880's. My catalogue lists the following pieces:

1. Bowls, shallow, 6 and 8 inch
   a. Berry bowls, 7 and 8 inch
2. Butter dish
3. Creamer
4. Goblet
5. Pickle dish, oblong
6. Salt and pepper shakers
7. Spoonholder
8. Sauce dishes, round, 4 and 4½ inch
9. Sugar bowl
10. Tumbler
11. Water bottle

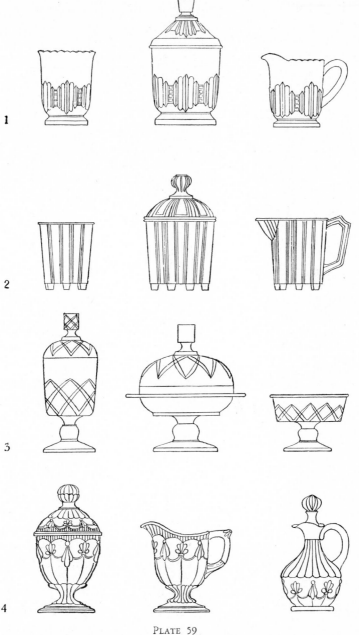

PLATE 59

1. TRIPLE BAR spoonholder, sugar bowl, creamer.
2. PANELLED RIB spoonholder, sugar bowl, creamer.
3. CROSSBAR sugar bowl, butter dish, footed sauce dish.
4. FLEUR-DE-LIS AND DRAPE sugar bowl, creamer, cruet.

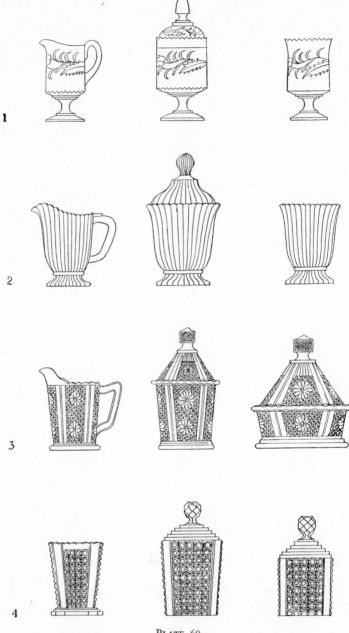

PLATE 60

1. SAXON ENGRAVED creamer, sugar bowl, spoonholder.
2. RIBBED WARE creamer, sugar bowl, spoonholder.
3. FLOWER AND PANEL creamer, sugar bowl, butter dish.
4. BLOCK AND PANEL spoonholder, pickle jar, puff box.

PLATE 61

1. RICHMOND spoonholder, sugar bowl, creamer.
2. PANEL AND STAR spoonholder, sugar bowl, creamer.
3. CANE AND ROSETTE goblet, sugar bowl, butter dish.
4. FEATHER AND BLOCK spoonholder, butter dish, creamer.

PLATE 62

1. VERA tumbler, creamer, sauce dish.
2. SANBORN sugar bowl, butter dish, creamer.
3. APOLLO goblet, sugar bowl, creamer.
4. BAR AND DIAMOND goblet, finger bowl, tankard pitcher.

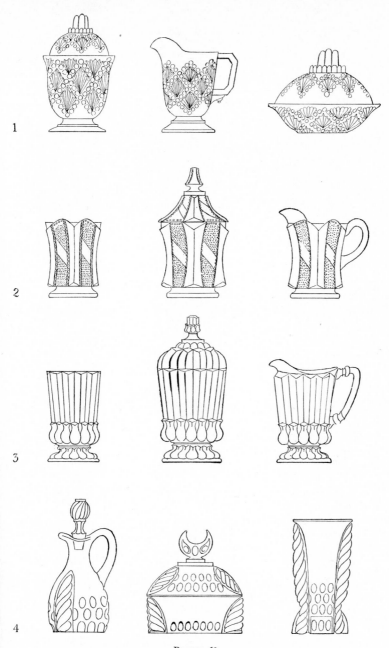

PLATE 63

1. DEWDROP AND FAN sugar bowl, creamer, butter dish.
2. STIPPLED BAR spoonholder, sugar bowl, creamer
3. PITTSBURGH spoonholder, sugar bowl, creamer.
4. SWIRL AND DOT cruet, covered dish, celery vase.

Chapter X

PATTERN GLASS COLLECTIBLE IN SETS—V

PLATE 59

1. TRIPLE BAR. This design was made by Doyle & Co. of Pittsburgh, Pa., under the term of "No. 84 set." Very little can be learned about it at present as my catalogue is incomplete and the pattern is rarely encountered. So far, it has been recorded only in clear glass. Judging by the forms, it must have been made in the late 1880's or 1890's.

1. Butter dish
2. Creamer
3. Spoonholder
4. Sugar bowl
5. Tumbler

2. PANELLED RIB. The Panelled Rib is very difficult to portray in line drawings. The wide division between the ribs is convex and all the flat ware has small round feet, or what has been described as "table rests," when used on cup plates. Many of our early oblong salts also rested on round feet. The Panelled Rib was made by Challinor, Taylor & Co. where it was known as "No. 308 set." Like the Triple Bar, little is known about it because apparently not much of this glass was made. It is illustrated here as a means of identification. Possibly many more forms exist.

1. Butter dish
2. Creamer
3. Spoonholder
4. Sugar bowl
5. Tumbler

3. CROSSBAR. Challinor, Taylor & Co. of Tarentum, Pa., made this design, where it was known as "No. 311 ware." It is an attractive glass, and was produced in a large line of tableware, as one may see after examining the classification. This list of pieces has been taken from an original Challinor catalogue. It appears to date in the early 1880's and so far as I can learn, may be found only in clear glass.

1. Bowls, shallow, 6 and 8 inch
    a. Deep bowls, 7, 8 and 9 inch
    b. Nut bowls, 6½, 7½ and 8½ inch
2. Butter dish
3. Celery vase
4. Creamer
5. Cruets, for oil or vinegar, in six sizes, with round or straight sides
6. Dishes, oblong, 7, 8 and 9 inch
7. Finger bowl
8. Goblet
9. Salt and pepper shakers
10. Sauce dish, footed, 4 inch
    a. Flat, 4 and 4½ inch
11. Spoonholder
12. Sugar bowl
13. Tumbler
14. Water pitcher, ½ gallon
    a. Squat pitcher, ½ gallon

4. FLEUR-DE-LIS AND DRAPE. Such long names to patterns are objectionable but there is an early flint glass Bull's Eye and Fleur-de-lis design, and so it is necessary to avoid confusion by adding to the descriptive title.

The Fleur-de-lis and Drape was produced first by Adams & Co. of Pittsburgh and then carried on for some years by the United States Glass Co. after Adams was absorbed by them. It was made in clear glass and in deep emerald green. There are not many patterns to be had in deep green, and this one makes a most distinctive and sophisticated table setting. It was made in a wide enough variety of forms to suit the most fastidious buyers.

1. Butter dish; two styles, one footed and one flat
2. Celery vase
3. Celery tray, oblong
4. Compotes
5. Cup and saucers
6. Creamer
7. Cruet
8. Goblet
9. Mustard jar with cover
10. Plates
11. Salt and pepper shakers
12. Sauce dish
13. Spoonholder
14. Sugar bowl
15. Water pitcher

PLATE 60

1. SAXON ENGRAVED. A fairly early trade catalogue of Bakewell, Pears & Co. of Pittsburgh, Pa., pictures a Saxon pattern that is entirely different from that shown in line 1 of Plate 60 in this book. However, Adams & Co. of Pittsburgh display this one as "Saxon pattern, plain or engraved." Since the design shown here is not known by any name, it seems advisable to retain its original one, adding the "engraved" to the title in order to differentiate it from the earlier ware.

This glass would not be attractive without the addition of the flower and leaf pattern, so in all probability little of it was sold plain. It apparently belongs to the 1880's and presumably was not made in quantity, because little of it is seen today. There is no record of any of it except in clear glass and in milk-white. A wide variety of pieces was produced but my catalogue is incomplete.

1. Bowls, several sizes
2. Butter dish
3. Claret
4. Compotes, covered, on high foot, several sizes
   a. Compotes, open, on high foot
5. Creamer
6. Goblet
7. Sauce dish
8. Spoonholder
9. Sugar bowl
10. Water pitcher
11. Wine

2. RIBBED WARE. This pattern was produced by Gillinder & Sons at their Greensburg, Pa., plant. Little is known about it because it is seldom seen in shops or collections. Apparently it was not carried on into a large line of tableware. I have seen the following pieces:

1. Butter dish
2. Creamer
3. Spoonholder
4. Sugar bowl

3. FLOWER AND PANEL. Challinor, Taylor & Co. of Tarentum Pa., produced this glass as their "Ware No. 23. Made in colors and mosaic." It is extremely popular in "mosaic," by which Challinors meant that type of glassware known as "marble glass" in *Early American Pressed Glass* because of its marbelized effect, and to many collectors by the uninteresting term "slag." Judging by the research work I have done in the field of American pressed glass, Challinor, Taylor & Co. made more of the mosaic ware than any other one factory in this country.

My experience has been that the Flower and Panel may be found most frequently in the purple marble glass, rarely in opaque blue or milk-white, and scarcely ever in clear glass. The last-named is not so attractive as the colored pieces, so rarity in this case should offer no special inducement to collectors. There may be other items than those I have seen or are listed in my catalogue of Challinor, Taylor & Co.

1. Butter dish
2. Creamer
3. Spoonholder
4. Sugar bowl
5. Water pitcher; two sizes, quart and ½ gallon

4. BLOCK AND PANEL. This pattern is not well known though a piece of it can be seen now and then in the larger antique shops where any amount of pattern glass is carried. I find it listed as "No. 90 pattern" and it was produced by the O'Hara Glass Co. of Pittsburgh, Pa. The catalogue is not complete, so my classification will not be large. There is pictured an unusual footed butter dish that has a wide flange where the cover joins the base. Another unusual feature of the design is a number of square footed sections, such as on the base of a pitcher or the cover of a jar. A description is inadequate but the illustrations on Plate 60 will show better what I have attempted to express in words. So far I have not heard of any pieces in color but they may exist. A goblet that seems to match the pattern quite well appears among some pages devoted exclusively to goblets and lists it as "old No. M." This "M" is a reference to one of the eighteen older factories absorbed by the United States Glass Co. on July 1, 1891. "M" was the Bellaire Goblet Co. of Findlay, Ohio.

1. Berry bowl, 10 inch
2. Butter dish
3. Creamer
4. Goblet
5. Jelly dish, 6 inch
6. Pickle jar
7. Puff box
8. Salt and pepper shakers
9. Sauce dish, 4 and 5 inch
    a. Footed, 5 inch

10. Spoonholder
11. Sugar bowl
12. Toilet bottles, 5 sizes, from 1 oz. to 16 oz.
13. Tankard jug
14. Water pitcher, ½ gallon

PLATE 61

1. RICHMOND. The Richmond pattern was so named by the makers, Richards & Hartley of Tarentum, Pa. It was produced in a wide number of table pieces, so I am listing those pictured in their old trade catalogue. It appears to be a pattern of the 1880's and so far as I know at this time was produced in clear glass only.

1. Berry bowl, 9 inch
2. Butter dish
3. Celery vase
4. Creamer
5. Compotes, open, on high foot, 7 and 8 inch
6. Cruet
7. Goblet
8. Salt and pepper shakers
9. Spoonholder
10. Sauce dish, 5 inch
11. Sugar bowl
12. Sugar shaker
13. Tumbler
14. Water pitcher; two sizes, quart and ½ gallon
15. Wine

2. PANEL AND STAR. The O'Hara Glass Co. of Pittsburgh, Pa., probably the oldest in the Pittsburgh glass district, produced the Panel and Star, under the title "No. 500 pattern." While the majority of the pieces in this set were plain, a large number were made either cut or engraved in the long panel on the side of each bowl. Some had an eight-pointed star cut in

this panel, and others were engraved with leaves. Whichever way one encounters this glass, it is an attractive pattern. Panel and Star, plain, cut or engraved, may be found in the following pieces:

1. Butter dish
2. Cake plate on standard
3. Celery vase
4. Cologne bottles
5. Compote, covered, on collared base, 6½, 7½ and 8½ inch
    a. Covered, on high foot, 6½, 7½ and 8½ inch
    b. Open, on collared base, 5½, 6½, 7½ and 8½ inch
6. Creamer
    a. Milk pitcher, pint size
7. Cruet
8. Pickle jar
9. Salad bowl
10. Salt and pepper shakers
11. Sauce dish, footed, 5 inch
12. Spoonholder
13. Sugar bowl
14. Tumbler
15. Water set, with tray, pitcher and two tumblers

3. CANE AND ROSETTE. This pattern was originally known as "No. 125 pattern." While I have two pages of the original catalogue of the producers of this glass, there is no way to identify the particular factory that made it. There is an unusually large variety of pieces of tableware which will delight collectors looking for large sets. Apparently this is a midwestern pattern of the 1870's and was probably made in colors, as well as clear glass.

1. Butter dish; two styles, flat base and footed
2. Cake plate on standard, 9, 10 and 11 inch
3. Celery vase
4. Champagne
5. Claret

6. Cordial
7. Compotes, covered, on high foot, 6, 7, 8 and 9 inch
     a. Open, on high foot, plain edge, 6, 7, 8 and 9 inch
     b. Open, on high foot, scalloped edge; deep bowl, 6, 7, 8 and 9 inch
     c. Open, on high foot, scalloped edge; shallow bowl, 7, 8 and 9 inch
     d. Covered, on low foot; rare type, 6 inch
8. Creamer
9. Dish, octagonal, flat base, covered, 7, 8 and 9 inch
     a. Octagonal, covered, on collared base, 7, 8 and 9 inch
     b. Octagonal, open dishes, flat base, 7, 8 and 9 inch
     c. Round, open bowl, flat base, 6 inch
10. Egg cup
11. Goblet
12. Salt dish, footed
13. Sauce dish, collared base, 4 inch
     a. Footed, 4 inch
     b. Flat base, 4 and $4\frac{1}{2}$ inches
14. Spoonholder
15. Sugar bowl
16. Water pitcher, $\frac{1}{2}$ gallon
17. Wine

4. FEATHER AND BLOCK. Richards & Hartley of Tarentum, Pa., produced this pattern during the 1880's as their "No. 189 ware" before they merged with the United States Glass Co. of Pittsburgh. It is an attractive design and, though it was not made in as many forms as some others, still there is a satisfying table set. Their catalogue does not mention it except in clear glass, so if any colors were made they must have been brought out later.

1. Berry bowl, on collared base, 7 and 8 inch
2. Butter dish
3. Celery vase
4. Creamer
5. Goblet
6. Sauce dish, collared base, 4 inch

7. Spoonholder
8. Sugar bowl
9. Tumbler
10. Water pitcher; two sizes, ¼ gallon and ½ gallon
11. Water tray

PLATE 62

1. VERA. This pattern is heavy and brilliant, partly frosted and partly clear. The frosted, or satin, finish is indicated in the illustration by the gray coloring. All that I have ever found in this design was in Washington, D. C., and in Cincinnati, Ohio, so it is probably of midwestern origin. There are probably many more forms than I can list but this will serve to identify it for interested collectors. By the forms it would appear that this ware dates in the late 1880's and 1890's.

1. Berry bowl
2. Butter dish
3. Compote, open, on high foot
4. Creamer
5. Sauce dish
6. Spoonholder
7. Sugar bowl
8. Tumbler

2. SANBORN. Challinor, Taylor & Co. of Tarentum, Pa., produced this design, under the trade term "No. 83 ware." It is doubtful whether many forms were produced as the design is seldom encountered. Certainly it could not have been made in large quantities. I find no record of colored pieces, though they may exist. I can vouch for the following forms:

1. Bowls, covered, on four feet, 7 and 8 inch
2. Butter dish
3. Creamer
4. Spoonholder
5. Sugar bowl

3. APOLLO. Adams & Co. of Pittsburgh were the makers of the Apollo pattern "plain or engraved" and this was their original name for it. It is a rather elaborate design, probably of the middle or late 1870's. There was a wide and varied number of pieces produced, in enough forms to suit the taste of the most avid collector. So far as I can learn, it was made only in clear glass.

1. Bowls, flared, 3½, 4, 5, 6, 7 and 8 inch
2. Butter dish
3. Cake plate on standard, 10 and 12 inch
4. Celery vase
5. Compotes, open, on high foot, 5, 6, 7 and 8 inch
    a. Open compotes, on low foot, 6 and 8 inch
6. Creamer
7. Goblet
8. Pickle dish
9. Sauce dish, footed, 5 inch
    a. Flat sauce, 3½ and 4 inch
10. Spoonholder
11. Sugar bowl
12. Tray, for water set
13. Tumbler
14. Water pitcher

In addition, pieces not illustrated are listed as Dessert bowl, Salad bowl and Fruit bowl.

4. BAR AND DIAMOND. This pattern, which was made by Richards & Hartley of Tarentum, Pa., was sold plain or engraved. It was known as "No. 190 pattern." If the purchaser desired to have the glass engraved, he was usually given his choice from a book of designs kept by the company. I have never discovered any list of prices for this additional work, though I have seen pages of patterns from which the buyer could choose.

The Bar and Diamond appears to be of the late 1880's. I

have not heard of any pieces in color. The items listed are taken from an original old catalogue.

1. Bowls, covered, on collared base, 5, 6, 7 and 8 inch
   a. Bowls, open on collared base, 6, 7 and 8 inch
   b. Bowls, 6, 7 and 8 inch
2. Butter dish; two styles, footed and flat
3. Celery vase
4. Compotes, open, on high foot, 5, 6, 7 and 8 inch
   a. Covered compotes, on high foot, 5, 6, 7 and 8 inch
5. Condiment set with oval dish
6. Creamer
7. Cruet
8. Decanter
9. Dishes, oblong, 7, 8, 9 and 10 inch
10. Finger bowl
11. Goblet
12. Hand lamp
13. Pickle dish, oval
14. Plate, for bread, oblong, with rim
15. Salt and pepper shakers
16. Sauce dish, footed, 4 and 5 inch
    a. Flat, 4 and 5 inch
17. Spoonholder
18. Sugar bowl
19. Sugar shaker
20. Syrup jug
21. Tankard pitcher; two sizes, $\frac{1}{2}$ pint and quart
22. Tray
23. Tumbler
24. Water pitcher, rounded bowl, quart and $\frac{1}{2}$ gallon
25. Wine
26. Wine set, with jug and tray

PLATE 63

1. DEWDROP AND FAN. Unfortunately, there is little I can tell about this pattern except that it was orginally termed "No.

50 set" by the United States Glass Co. of Pittsburgh, Pa. It is pictured on a page showing the well-known Roman Rosette design. There may have been a full line of tableware but I have been unable to find any items beyond those listed. It is illustrated here as a means of identification for collectors who may have other forms.

1. Butter dish
2. Creamer
3. Spoonholder
4. Sugar bowl

2. STIPPLED BAR. Originally the Stippled Bar was known as "No. 15044 set" by the United States Glass Co. of Pittsburgh, Pa., who produced it. The stippling is indicated in the illustration by the gray coloring. My catalogue is not complete, so I can list only the pieces shown. It is quite possible many other forms were made, though sometimes factories did not build up their lines and only made what were known as "table sets." A table set consisted of the following pieces:

1. Butter dish
2. Creamer
3. Spoonholder
4. Sugar bowl

3. PITTSBURGH. The Pittsburgh pattern was produced by Bryce Bros. of Pittsburgh, Pa., and this was their original name for it. Unfortunately, it is another of those few patterns of which I have only the table set to list. The butter dish is footed and has a flange where the cover joins. The Pittsburgh pattern probably dates during the 1880's. It appears to be a fairly heavy, brilliant glass and it was carried on by the United States Glass Co. after their merger in 1891. A goblet has been noted as this goes to press.

1. Butter dish
2. Creamer
3. Goblet

4. Spoonholder
5. Sugar bowl

4. SWIRL AND DOT. The Central Glass Co. of Wheeling, W. Va., made the Swirl and Dot, under the term "No. 999 line." It is an interesting pattern but rarely seen today. The company produced quite a number of pieces but apparently it was not carried on over a period of years, as most patterns were, or else was made in a limited quantity. No mention is made in any of my catalogues of pieces in color.

1. Butter dish
2. Caster set: glass standard containing three bottles
3. Cake plate on standard, 10 inch
4. Celery vase
5. Compote, 6-inch sweetmeat dish with cover
6. Cruet
7. Creamer
8. Dish, flat base, 6 inch, covered
9. Goblet
10. Salt and pepper shakers
11. Spoonholder
12. Sugar bowl
13. Syrup jug
14. Tankard pitcher, ½ gallon
15. Tumbler
16. Water pitcher

PLATE 64

1. DUNCAN. The Duncan pattern is the same as the Frosted Ribbon illustrated in *Early American Pressed Glass* but it came in other styles, without the satin, or frosted, stripe, so it should be shown in these other forms. Collectors might not recognize the glass because it appears so different without any frosted stripes. It was made by George Duncan & Sons of Pittsburgh, Pa., at the same period Three Face was being produced. In fact,

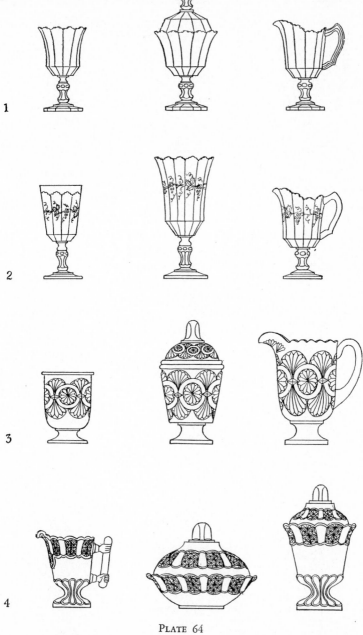

PLATE 64

1. DUNCAN spoonholder, sugar bowl, creamer.
2. DUNCAN ENGRAVED goblet, celery vase, creamer.
3. ROSETTE MEDALLION spoonholder, sugar bowl, creamer.
4. COTTAGE creamer, butter dish, sugar bowl.

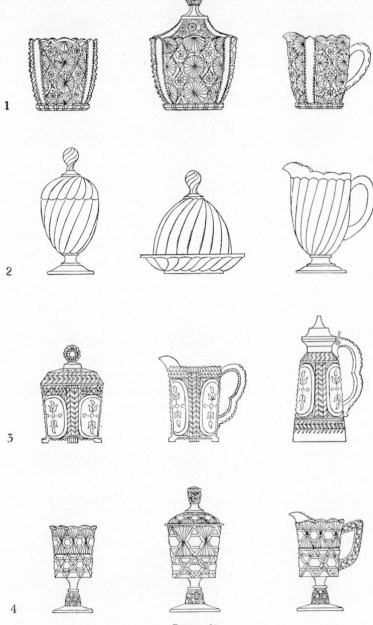

PLATE 65

1. CLOVER spoonholder, sugar bowl, creamer.
2. CYCLONE sugar bowl, butter dish, creamer.
3. WHEELING sugar bowl, creamer, syrup jug.
4. BLOCKADE spoonholder, sugar bowl, creamer.

PLATE 66

1. CORDOVA sugar bowl, creamer, butter dish.
2. DIAMOND BLOCK goblet, ice tub, finger bowl.
3. FAN AND STAR goblet, celery vase, water pitcher.
4. HOBNAIL WITH BARS spoonholder, butter dish, creamer,

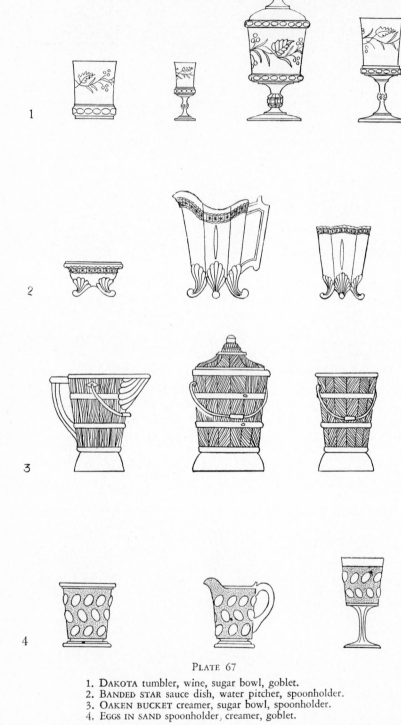

PLATE 67

1. DAKOTA tumbler, wine, sugar bowl, goblet.
2. BANDED STAR sauce dish, water pitcher, spoonholder.
3. OAKEN BUCKET creamer, sugar bowl, spoonholder.
4. EGGS IN SAND spoonholder, creamer, goblet.

PLATE 68

1. CROWN JEWEL goblet, water pitcher, salt dish.
2. DOLPHIN spoonholder, sugar bowl, creamer.
3. CLARK individual creamer, sugar bowl, salt dish.
4. STAR AND OVAL celery vase, water pitcher, sauce dish.

all the various "frosted ribbon" types pictured in this chapter are illustrated in the same catalogue as Three Face.

The Duncan was originally known as "No. 150 pattern," during the 1870's when it was being made. Line 1 on Plate 64 shows the Duncan in plain clear glass. Judging by the large number of pieces made, it must have enjoyed great popularity.

1. Bitters bottle
2. Butter dish
3. Celery vase
4. Champagne
5. Claret
6. Compotes, covered, on high standard, 6, 7, 8 and 9 inch
   a. Covered, on low foot, 7, 8, 9 and 10 inch
   b. Open, with deep bowl, on low foot, 6, 7, 8, 9 and 10 inch
   c. Open, with deep bowl, on high foot, 6, 7, 8, 9 and 10 inch
   d. Open, shallow flaring bowl, low foot, 5, 6, 7, 8 and 9 inch
7. Cordial
8. Creamer
9. Custard or sherbet cup
10. Dish, octagonal, 7 and 8 inch
11. Egg cup
12. Goblet
13. Jelly compote, 5 inch
14. Pickle jar
15. Pitcher; two sizes, quart and ½ gallon
16. Salt, footed
17. Sauce dish, flat, 4 and 4½ inch
    a. Footed, 4 and 4½ inch
18. Sherry glass
19. Spoonholder
20. Sugar bowl
21. Tumbler
22. Wine

2. DUNCAN ENGRAVED. From the original George Duncan & Sons catalogue, it is quite apparent that any of the forms listed under the Duncan pattern could be purchased engraved.

By the number of designs of engraving pictured, it is certain that Duncans did a considerable amount of work in their cutting and engraving department. Undoubtedly this glass was less costly plain, and more expensive engraved than it would be with the plain satin stripe, as in the "frosted ribbon." Another style displayed in the catalogue has a frosted panel alternating with a clear one which is cut and engraved.

No classification is being added to the Duncan Engraved, as they would be the same as the plain Duncan pattern.

3. ROSETTE MEDALLION. This pattern is somewhat similar to the one referred to as Rosettes and Palms, in the book picturing goblets by Dr. Millard. It is probably of the same period, though this was produced by the United States Glass Co. of Pittsburgh, Pa., in a large variety of tableware. It was carried for a number of years, finally winding up, along with a number of other patterns, in a five- and ten-cent assortment, under date of 1895. It was made chiefly in clear glass but I have seen a few pieces in emerald green.

1. Bowls, 6, 7 and 8 inch
    a. Covered bowls, 6, 7 and 8 inch
2. Butter dish; two styles, one plain, one with flange
3. Bread plate
4. Cake plates on standard, 8, 9, 10 and 11 inch
5. Celery vase
6. Compote, on high foot, 5, 6, 7 and 8 inch
    a. Shallow bowls, on high foot, 7, 8, 9 and 10 inch
7. Creamer
8. Dishes, oblong, 7 and 8 inch
9. Finger bowl
10. Goblet
11. Jelly compote, 4½ inch
12. Mug
13. Plate, 7 inch
    a. Bread plate
14. Pickle dish

15. Salt and pepper shakers
16. Sauce dishes, 4 and 4½ inch
17. Spoonholder
18. Sugar bowl
19. Tray, for water set
20. Tumbler
21. Water pitcher, ½ gallon
22. Wine

4. COTTAGE. The Cottage pattern was produced by Adams & Co. of Pittsburgh, Pa. It may have been made first during the 1870's as the forms are similar to those in the Wildflower, which came out during that period. There was not the demand for change in those days and patterns that proved popular were carried on for years, and various additional forms were added from time to time. There are so many pieces in the Cottage pattern that it must have been extremely popular. It should be hailed with delight by collectors today because there are plates in five sizes. The early patterns carried only a six-inch size, if any, but as time went on larger plates and more sizes came into active demand and our highly commercialized glass factories were quick to react to popular needs.

The following long list of items are enumerated in an Adams & Co. trade catalogue, largely in crystal. Some pieces may be found in amber, blue, and in crystal flashed in red.

1. Berry bowl, 10 inch
2. Butter dish, footed
    a. Butter dish with flange, flared bowl
3. Cake plate on standard, 9 and 10 inch
4. Celery vase
5. Claret
6. Compotes, covered, on high foot, 6, 7 and 8 inch
    a. Open, on high foot, 6, 7 and 8 inch
    b. Covered, on low foot, 6, 7 and 8 inch
    c. Open, on low foot, 6, 7 and 8 inch
7. Creamer
8. Custard or sherbet cup
9. Cup and saucer

10. Cruet
11. Dishes, deep oval, 7½ and 9 inch
12. Fruit bowls on high foot, 9 and 10 inch
13. Goblet (vary in size)
14. Pickle dish
15 Plates, 6, 7, 8, 9 and 10 inch
16. Sauce dish, flat, 4 inch, flared
    a. Footed, 4½ inch
    b. Berry dish, 5 inch
17. Salt shakers
18. Spoonholder
19. Sugar bowl
20. Syrup jug
21. Tray, for water set
22. Tumbler
23. Water pitchers, pint, quart, ½ gallon
24. Wine

In addition, a collector has reported an oil bottle, a champagne glass and a footed toothpick holder.

PLATE 65

1. CLOVER. It is quite likely that Richards & Hartley, of Tarentum, Pa., who named this design "Clover," made it in a full set of tableware. Unfortunately, my catalogue shows only a few pieces. It is an attractive variation of the Daisy and Button, the chief difference being that instead of the usual clear button (as in the Daisy and Button design) the button in the Clover has a fine cut design imprinted in it. This pattern was made in colors, as well as in clear glass, during the 1880's. The bowls and sauce dishes are often seen in deep emerald green.

1. Berry bowls, 8 and 10 inch
2. Butter dish
3. Creamer
4. Spoonholder
5. Sauce dish
6. Sugar bowl

2. CYCLONE. An odd page from an old trade catalogue illustrates several pieces of the Cyclone pattern, but there is no record as to which factory made it. Besides the items pictured in line 2 of Plate 65, there is shown a curious shell-shaped dish, which has a short knob stem and scalloped edge to the foot, marked "Antique Celery." It is an amusing name because the forms of the other dishes would indicate the 1890's, an era quite far from being *antique* at the time this book is being written. There is also a spiralled vase, which twists from a bulbous bowl into a rather slight stem attached to a flat foot, and this is marked "Bouquet holder." It appears to be a heavy, brilliant glass, as were many of the late patterns, even though they did not contain flint. The Cyclone probably was not made in colors.

1. Celery dish
2. Butter dish
3. Bouquet holder, 6 inch
4. Creamer
5. Goblet
6. Spoonholder
7. Sugar bowl
8. Water pitcher, ½ gallon

3. WHEELING. Line numbers do not make collectors happy, so when patterns are unknown it is necessary to do some christening. The design shown in line 3 of Plate 65 was produced by Hobbs, Brocunier & Co. of Wheeling, W. Va., and they listed it as "115 ware." The catalogue states that it "comes engraved" and "engraved in colors"—the latter having certain styles of decoration indicated by number. It should make a most attractive table setting whichever type one chooses. The items listed are all illustrated in a Hobbs, Brocunier & Co. catalogue, which is undated but appears to be of the 1880's. The pattern was made both flat and footed, the makers referring to the first as "Squat Set." The table set (sugar bowl, creamer, spoonholder and butter dish) was made without feet and with them,

as were most of the other items; one classification will be used for both.

1. Berry bowl, deep and round, 8, 9 and 10 inch
      a. Oval bowls, 7 and 8 inch
2. Butter dish, footed and flat
      a. Individual butters
3. Cake plates on standard, 9, 10 and 12 inch
4. Compote, flared, on high foot, 7, 8 and 9 inch
      a. Covered compotes on high foot, 6, 7 and 8 inch
      b. Open compotes on low foot, 7 and 8 inch
      c. Bowl, open, 6 inch
5. Creamer
6. Dishes, square and deep, 7, 8 and 9 inch
7. Finger bowl
8. Jelly compote, on foot, 6 inch
9. Pickle dish
10. Salt, oval, on four feet
       a. Salt and pepper shakers
11. Sauce dish, footed, 4 inch
       a. Flat sauce, 4½ inch
12. Spoonholder
13. Sugar bowl
14. Syrup pitcher
15. Tumbler
16. Toy tumbler
17. Tray, for water set
18. Water set with tray and bowl
19. Water pitchers; two sizes, quart and ½ gallon

4. BLOCKADE. In order to spare collectors confusion, because there are so many blocks and cubes in figured glassware, this one is being christened Blockade. It was produced by Challinor, Taylor & Co. of Tarentum, Pa., and in their catalogue it was called "No. 309 ware." The stems of the footed pieces are quite heavy and singularly different from the usual run of patterns. Perhaps some of this glass was made in color but none is mentioned in the catalogue. It appears to date in the 1880's. Probably there are many more forms than I am able to list.

1. Butter dish
2. Creamer
3. Finger bowl
4. Goblet
5. Spoonholder
6. Sugar bowl
7. Tray, for water set
8. Water pitcher; two sizes, quart and ½ gallon

PLATE 66

1. CORDOVA. The Cordova pattern was patented December 16, 1890, according to a page from a catalogue of the company that produced it. Unfortunately, the name of the factory is omitted. Among some old notes made in 1933, during a period spent in research work in the Pittsburgh area, I find only "Cordova was made in a large line, including a number of flower vases, flower baskets, etc." Apparently my time was running out and there was no way to obtain a record of all the pieces. I can vouch for the classification here and the illustrations will serve as a means of identifying the pattern.

1. Bowls, open, 6, 7, 8 and 9 inch
    a. Bowls with flared edge, 7 and 8 inch
    b. Covered bowl, not flared, 6, 7 and 8 inch
2. Butter dish
3. Cake plate on standard, 10 inch
4. Compotes, open, on high foot with flared bowl, 7, 8 and 9 inch
    a. Open, without flared bowl, on high foot, 6, 7 and 8 inch
    b. Covered compotes on high foot, 6, 7 and 8 inch
5. Celery vase
6. Creamer
7. Cruet
8. Dishes. Square almond dish
    a. Round jelly dish, with handle
    b. Olive dish
9. Finger bowl

10. Jug, ½ pint
11. Salt, individual
    a. Salt and pepper shakers
12. Sauce dishes, flat, 4 and 4½ inch
13. Spoonholder
14. Sugar bowl
15. Syrup pitcher
16. Tankard pitcher, ½ gallon
17. Tumbler
18. Water pitcher; two sizes, pint and quart

2. DIAMOND BLOCK. George Duncan & Sons of Pittsburgh, Pa., originated this pattern, and it was carried on by the United States Glass Co. when they merged in 1891, as "Pattern No. 15011." It must date in the late 1880's, judging by the style of the dishes. So far as I can learn, it was made only in clear glass.

1. Butter dish
2. Celery vase
    a. Celery tray; two styles, straight and crimped
3. Creamer
4. Finger bowl
5. Goblet
6. Ice tub
7. Plate, 6 inch
8. Sauce dish
9. Spoonholde
10. Sugar bowl
11. Tumbler
12. Wine

3. FAN AND STAR. Challinor, Taylor & Co. of Tarentum, Pa., produced this design in a fairly large line of tableware, under the title "No. 304 ware." Unfortunately, this particular Challinor catalogue is incomplete, so I cannot give a full classification. It is an attractive pattern but I cannot say whether it

was ever made in color. It appears to date in the late 1870's or 1880's.

1. Bowl, round, 6 inch
2. Butter dish
3. Celery vase
4. Compote, covered, on low foot, 7 inch
   a. Covered, on high foot
5. Creamer
6. Goblet
7. Spoonholder
8. Sugar bowl
9. Water pitcher, ½ gallon

4. HOBNAIL WITH BARS. Life would have been so much simpler for research workers during this age if glassmakers had named all their patterns. Even descriptive titles may become confusing in time.

Challinor, Taylor & Co. of Tarentum, Pa., are responsible for this barred Hobnail pattern, which they termed "No. 307 pattern." Some of the pieces illustrated by them have the bars forming a large diamond shape between the hobnails, while others, such as the berry bowl and sauce dish, have the bars forming straight panels. One might wonder if they belonged to the same set, but they apparently do because all the dishes carry the same line number. For the benefit of collectors, I can list the following pieces and hope they may find many more forms. Any odd tumbler or goblet in Hobnail would combine nicely with this set.

1. Berry bowl, 9 inch
2. Butter dish
3. Creamer
4. Sauce dish
5. Spoonholder
6. Sugar bowl

PLATE 67

1. DAKOTA. The Dakota pattern was made by Doyle & Co. of Pittsburgh, Pa. Before the original name was found in an old company catalogue it was known as "Baby Thumbprint" and "Etched Band and Baby Thumbprint." The reason for the last two descriptive names is because it was produced both plain and engraved. The illustration in line 1 of Plate 67 displays the engraved style. Another attractive form of this design is in ruby red.

There is an interesting variety of pieces of tableware for the collector to choose from, whether it be plain, engraved, or ruby The following classification may be considered quite complete because it was taken from a Doyle & Co. catalogue.

1. Berry bowls, 8 and 9 inch
2. Butter dish
3. Celery dish, oblong
4. Celery vase, tall
5. Compotes, covered, on high foot, 5, 6, 7, 8, 9 and 10 inch
6. Creamer
7. Dishes, oblong, 8, 9 and 10 inch
8. Goblet
9. Mug
10. Plate, round
11. Salt and pepper shakers
12. Sauce dishes, flat, 3½, 4 and 5 inch
    a. Footed, 3½ and 4 inch
13. Spoonholder
14. Sugar bowl
15. Tumbler
16. Water pitcher, ½ gallon

2. BANDED STAR. This pattern is rarely seen in New England. I have no record of it beyond the few pieces I purchased to use as illustrations, and a photograph of a number of pieces sent to me by a collector in Buffalo, N. Y. It is probably of mid-

western origin and would date in the 1870's and 1880's. The Boston & Sandwich Glass Co. did make some glassware with ribbed feet but the preponderance of this type came to us from the Pittsburgh area. In the chapter devoted to some unusual Sandwich dishes, with illustrations taken from a Boston & Sandwich Glass Co. catalogue, it will be noted that the feet are flipped over at the end, often leaving an opening similar to the tips of the applied handles on early creamers. The Banded Star ribbed feet are finished in a clear little ball. Probably this pattern was produced in colors but I do not recall seeing any pieces, except in clear glass.

1. Butter dish
2. Celery vase
3. Compote, covered
4. Creamer
5. Dish, covered, 4½ by 7 inches
    a. Covered dish, 6 by 9 inches
6. Jam jar
7. Salt dishes, on feet
8. Sauce dishes; two sizes, 4⅛ and 4⅝ inches
9. Spoonholder
10. Sugar bowl

3. OAKEN BUCKET. This quaint pattern appeared in the 1880's and I find it listed in this manner in an old catalogue: "Our Oaken Bucket. (Colored glass) This set is not a new one, but when the sales of such an article reach a point beyond an 800 barrel figure in a single season it would seem that the trade were not yet quite through with it. This beautiful set consists of sugar bowl, butter dish, creamer and spoonholder. Assorted in colors. Put up 24 sets in barrel. Sold only by barrel."

There were other pieces in this set, as I have found little Oaken Bucket pails, for matches, in clear glass and in colors, including amethyst. Amethyst is rarely found because, as an old glassworker assured me, the color was neither popular nor fashionable at the period when colored glassware was the fad for table use. Probably there are more forms than I can list, though this set was not produced in as wide a variety of pieces as were most of the others in this book. It was produced by Bryce Bros. of Pittsburgh, in amber, yellow, blue and clear glass. Any items in amethyst would be rare.

1. Butter dish
2. Creamer
3. Pails (small match holders, with wire handles), three sizes
4. Spoonholder
5. Sugar bowl
6. Water pitcher

4. EGGS IN SAND. The pattern illustrated in line 4 on Plate 67 has become known as Eggs in Sand, so I shall not attempt to change it. It may amuse some collectors who are familiar with the design to know that I found it listed in an old catalogue of a wholesale house as "The Bean" pattern. The cost was forty-eight cents for a dozen pieces, during the 1880's. The background of all the items are stippled, with the "bean-shaped" pieces standing out in clear relief. I have seen this glass in clear, amber and blue.

1. Butter dish
2. Creamer
3. Goblet
4. Lemonade set: tray, pitcher and six goblets
5. Platter, octagonal shape
6. Spoonholder
7. Sugar bowl
8. Tray, for water set
9. Water pitcher

PLATE 68

1. CROWN JEWEL. So far I have not found any record of where the Crown Jewel was made but doubtless it will come

to light some day. Usually a pioneer book on any subject results in a flood of new information. In my possession is a page from a catalogue illustrating it but the name of the producer is missing. The original name was Crown Jewel and since the pattern is not well known, I am giving it its original designation. By some few dealers and collectors it is known as "Chandelier." My classification will necessarily not be complete but I can say that this pattern was sold plain or engraved, and probably dates in the 1880's.

1. Berry bowl
2. Butter dish
3. Celery vase
4. Compotes, covered, on high standard
   a. Covered compotes, on low foot
   b. Square compotes, covered, on high foot
   c. Square compotes, open, on low foot
5. Finger bowl
6. Goblet
7. Salt dish, round
   a. Salt and pepper shakers
8. Sauce dish
9. Spoonholder
10. Sugar bowl
11. Sugar shaker
12. Tray, for water set, two handles
13. Water pitcher

2. DOLPHIN. Little is known about the Dolphin pattern, except that it must be of midwestern origin and apparently not much of it was made—it is so seldom seen. It may be found in clear glass or in clear glass with the dolphins frosted. This type of ware came into fashion during the early 1870's and was at the peak of its popularity during the Centennial Exhibition in Philadelphia, and into the 1880's.

Probably more forms were made than I can list, because I do not have any catalogue of the glass company covering it and have seen few pieces. Those illustrated I purchased, the spoonholder being in clear glass and the other two pieces partly frosted. Since these items are known to exist, somewhere there must be a butter dish, as well as many other forms.

1. Creamer
2. Compote, covered, on high foot
    a. Open, on high foot, 7½ inch
3. Goblet
4. Spoonholder
5. Sugar bowl
6. Water pitcher

3. CLARK. The Clark design was originally known as "No. 28 pattern" but my catalogue is not complete and so I cannot tell where it was made. It appears to be a clear glass pattern of the late 1880's or 1890's. On Plate 75 is an illustration of the water set. There may be many more forms than I can list.

1. Butter dish (individual size)
2. Caster set: these were in metal containers, and were made in 2, 3 or 4 bottle sets
3. Creamer
4. Finger bowl
5. Goblet
6. Plate, round, large size
7. Salt and pepper shakers
8. Tray, for water set
9. Tumbler
10. Vinegar bottle
11. Water pitcher

4. STAR AND OVAL. The pattern illustrated in line 4 of Plate 68, was made by the O'Hara Glass Co. of Pittsburgh, Pa., during the 1880's. It was sold both plain and engraved, the pieces pictured being engraved and copied from some of the items shown in an original old catalogue. I have not seen any of these pieces in color, but they may exist. The pattern is rarely seen, so it was probably not made in a large line of table-ware.

1. Celery vase
2. Creamer
3. Dishes, oval, 10 and 12 inch (12-inch size used as berry bowl)
4. Finger bowl
5. Pickle dish, 8 inch
6. Sauce dish, oval, 5 inch
7. Tray, for water set, two handles
8. Tumbler
9. Water pitcher

PLATE 69

1. BEATTY HONEYCOMB. In *Early American Pressed Glass* there is a Honeycomb pattern, which was produced in variations by almost every factory making tableware, both early and late. In order to differentiate this Honeycomb design, which is such an appropriate name for it, I am designating it as the Beatty Honeycomb because it was made by A. J. Beatty & Sons of Tiffin, Ohio. The forms would indicate the 1880's. My catalogue shows this Honeycomb in color, both in opalescent and in blue-opalescent. Possibly it was carried in other colors, such as rose-opalescent, but I can vouch only for those I have seen. This glass would make an interesting table setting. There are no goblets but the tumblers are most attractive.

1. Berry bowls, 8 and 9 inch
2. Butter dish
3. Celery vase
4. Cologne bottle with matching stopper, 8 oz.
5. Creamer; two sizes, one small individual
6. Cruet; two sizes, 4 oz. and 8 oz.
7. Mug
8. Puff box with cover
9. Salt and pepper shakers
10. Sauce dish, flat, 4½ inch
11. Spoonholder

PLATE 69

1. BEATTY HONEYCOMB sugar bowl, creamer, cruet.
2. BEATTY RIB water pitcher, sugar shaker, butter dish.
3. TEARDROP goblet, syrup jug, tumbler.
4. DAISY AND CUBE sugar bowl, cruet, sherbet cup.

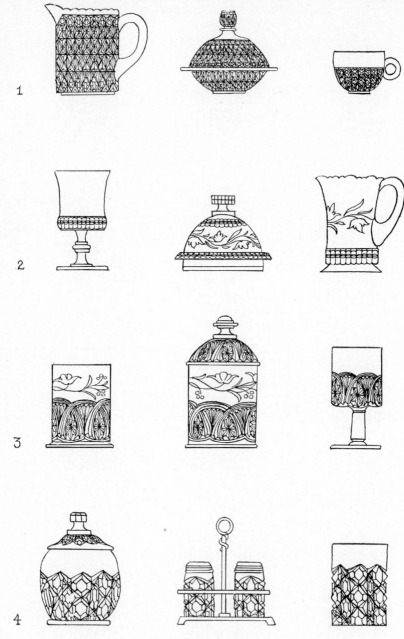

PLATE 70

1. PRESSED DIAMOND water pitcher, butter dish, sherbet cup.
2. CLIMAX goblet, butter dish, pitcher.
3. RADIANT tumbler, sugar bowl, goblet.
4. HENRIETTA sugar bowl, salt and pepper, tumbler.

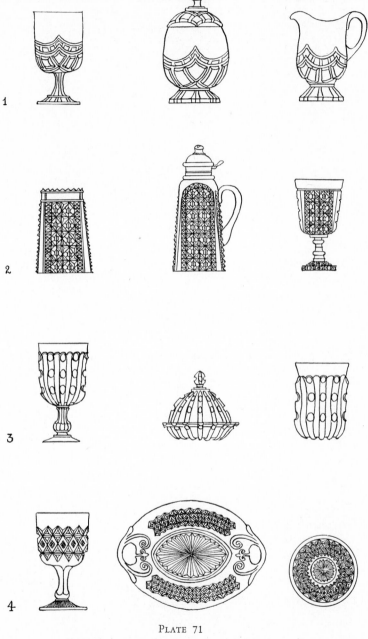

PLATE 71

1. DUNCAN BLOCK goblet, sugar bowl, creamer.
2. HEXAGONAL BLOCK pickle jar, syrup pitcher, goblet.
3. BROKEN COLUMN goblet, butter dish, tumbler.
4. PEERLESS goblet, platter, plate.

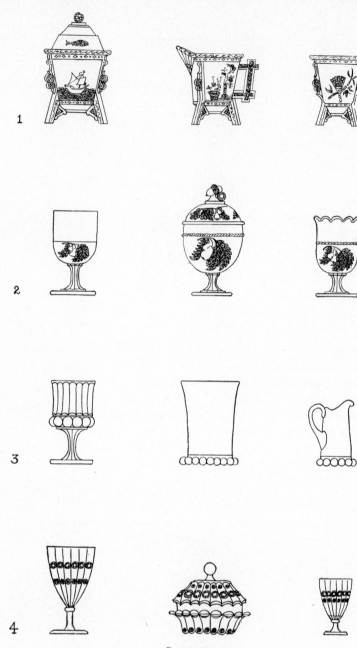

PLATE 72

1. ORIENTAL sugar bowl, creamer, spoonholder.
2. PEAR goblet, sugar bowl, spoonholder.
3. CANNON BALL goblet, ATLAS celery vase, creamer.
4. PRISCILLA goblet, butter dish, wine.

12. Sugar bowl
13. Sugar shaker
14. Toothpick or match holder
15. Tumbler
16. Water pitcher

2. BEATTY RIB. This heavily ribbed pattern also was made by A. J. Beatty & Co. of Tiffin, Ohio, probably at the same time their Honeycomb was produced. My catalogue shows the same colors—opalescent and blue-opalescent. Probably my list is not complete but I can vouch for the following, which were known originally as "No. 87 Opalescent Ware":

1. Berry bowls, 8 and 9 inch
2. Butter dish
3. Celery vase
4. Cracker jar
5. Creamer; two sizes, one individual
6. Dishes, oblong, 7 and 8 inch
7. Finger bowl
8. Lemonade (handled mug)
9. Puff box, round, covered
10. Salt and pepper shakers
    a. Individual size
    b. Larger round table salt
11. Salad bowl, large, deep, rectangular dish
12. Sauce dish, flat, $4\frac{1}{2}$ inch
13. Sugar bowl; two sizes, one individual
14. Sugar shaker
15. Toothpick or match holder, straight sides
    a. Same as above, rounded at base
16. Tumbler
17. Water pitcher, 3-pint size

3. TEARDROP. The design illustrated in line 3 of Plate 69 was made originally by Ripley & Co. of Pittsburgh, Pa., and carried on later by the United States Glass Co. after they absorbed eighteen of the older glass houses in the area in July,

1891. A large line of tableware was produced. I cannot list all of it but collectors will doubtless be able to fill in the gaps. Do not confuse it with the Crystal Wedding, shown on Plate 48. It will be noted that the loops are much smaller in the Teardrop design. Both patterns were sold plain and engraved.

1. Berry bowls
2. Butter dish
3. Cake plate on standard
4. Celery vase
5. Compotes, covered, on high foot
    a. Open, on high foot
    b. Open, on low foot
    c. Covered, on low foot
6. Creamer
7. Goblet
8. Pickle dish
9. Salt and pepper shakers
10. Sauce dishes
11. Spoonholder
12. Sugar bowl
13. Syrup pitcher
14. Tankard pitcher, ½ gallon
15. Tumbler
16. Wine

4. DAISY AND CUBE. This pattern, illustrated in the bottom row of Plate 69, is suggestive of the familiar Daisy and Button pattern. It is quite possible that it was inspired by that design. I can find no record of where it was produced, as the pages of the catalogue in my possession are unmarked, beyond calling it "600 pattern." The design is not so old that a record of it could not come to light at any time.

Many odd gadgets were made in the Daisy and Cube, one of the most unusual being a cigar lighter! The piece is footed, with a round bowl that has four tubes attached to it where it may be assumed the fluid was inserted. A wick and globe are attached rather high above it, the globe also being in the Daisy and Cube pattern. Any collector who finds one of these objects would certainly have a rarity. My list of forms is probably not complete but there are enough to enable collectors to start on their way.

1. Bitters bottle, pewter "cork and tube"
2. Cigar lighter, complete with globe
3. Cruet
4. Ice cream plate
5. Lamp, complete with globe to match
6. Oil set: tray holding cruet and salt and pepper shakers
7. Pickle and olive set: glass holder with metal handle, holding two covered jars
8. Pickle jar
9. Salt and pepper shakers
10. Sherbet cup

PLATE 70

1. PRESSED DIAMOND. Another fine cut pattern that would combine nicely with the Hourglass, was made by the Central Glass Co. of Wheeling, W. Va. That firm referred to it as "No. 775 pattern." Collectors will find the following pieces, plus others which I have probably missed, in clear glass, amber, blue and yellow.

1. Berry bowls, 5, 6, 7 and 8 inch
2. Butter dish
3. Creamer
4. Custard or sherbet cup
5. Finger bowl
6. Goblet
7. Sauce dish, 4 and 4½ inch
8. Spoonholder
9. Sugar bowl
10. Water pitcher, ½ gallon
11. Wine

2. CLIMAX. The Columbia Glass Co., of Findlay, Ohio, made this pattern, both plain and engraved. They referred to it as "No. 39 Set." The catalogue does not picture many pieces but the design was carried on by the United States Glass Co., who apparently termed it "Climax" since that name appears under a goblet in one of their later trade catalogues. It also refers to it as "Old No. J," which means the Columbia Glass Co. The goblet carries a double row of bars, one toward the top of the bowl and one at the base. I can list only a few items in this pattern but doubtless many others will come to light.

1. Butter dish
2. Creamer
3. Goblet
4. Spoonholder
5. Sugar bowl

3. RADIANT. The Columbia Glass Co. of Findlay, Ohio, also produced the Radiant pattern. That is their original name for it. It was sold plain or engraved in quite a wide variety of tableware. This firm is responsible for some excellent glassware, including the earliest and best hobnail, which they termed "Dew Drop pattern." They list the hobnail in crystal, amber and blue.

My listing of the Radiant is taken directly from their old catalogue. Colors are not mentioned. It appears to date in the late 1880's.

1. Berry bowl, 10 inch, solid glass foot
   a. Bowls, flat, $6\frac{1}{2}$, $7\frac{1}{2}$ and $8\frac{1}{2}$ inches
2. Butter dish
3. Cake plate on standard, 10 inch
4. Celery vase
5. Compotes, open, on high foot, $5\frac{1}{2}$, $6\frac{1}{2}$, $7\frac{1}{2}$ and $8\frac{1}{2}$ inches
   a. Covered, on high foot, 5, 6, 7 and 8 inch
6. Creamer
7. Goblet
8. Salt and pepper shakers

9. Sauce dish, flat, 4½ and 5½ inch
    a. Collared base, 4½ inch
10. Spoonholder
11. Sugar bowl
12. Syrup pitcher
13. Tumbler
14. Water pitchers, pint, quart and ½ gallon
15. Wine

    4. HENRIETTA. This pattern, very like the Red Block except for the shape of the blocks in the design, was made by the Columbia Glass Co. of Findlay, Ohio. It was probably put out on a competitive basis at the same period. Doyle and Co. of Pittsburgh produced the Red Block, which is fully illustrated and described in *Early American Pressed Glass*. It was originally known as the "Eva" pattern. The United States Glass Co. carried on the Eva but I do not find a record of their continuing the Henrietta, which may be the reason the latter is not found so readily today. When we do find it, it is usually in a better quality of glass and the color a clear, deeper shade of ruby. In the Red Block one often encounters pieces with the red badly worn or scratched and the shade of color sometimes varies.

    The Henrietta was made in a wide variety of tableware. The classification given here is taken directly from the Columbia Glass Co. catalogue.

1. Berry bowl, deep, 7, 8 and 9 inch
2. Butter dish
3. Cake plate on standard, 10 inch
4. Celery vase
5. Celery tray, oblong
6. Caster, with two bottles
7. Creamer, full size
    a. Individual size
8. Custard or sherbet cup and saucer
9. Dishes, oblong, 7 and 8 inch
    a. Bonbon dish, with handle
    b. Bone dish, oval
    c. Olive dish, shallow

10. Gas globe, 4 inch
11. Jar, covered, tall, marked for "confection"
12. Jelly dish, with handle, 5 inch
13. Mustard jar
14. Pickle jar, covered
15. Plate, bread, large oval
16. Rose jar, covered
17. Sauce dish, 4½ inch
18. Salt and pepper shakers
    a. Round, heavy table salt
19. Spoonholder
    a. Spoon tray, oval
20. Sugar bowl
21. Sugar shaker
22. Syrup pitcher
23. Tankard pitchers, pint and ½ gallon
24. Tumbler
25. Water pitchers, quart and ½ gallon

PLATE 71

1. DUNCAN BLOCK. In an old Duncan catalogue I find the tumbler of this pattern illustrated as "No. 326." Since the pages are merely marked "Duncan" I cannot tell whether this refers to George Duncan & Sons of Pittsburgh or to the later plant, known as Duncan & Miller Glass Co., of Washington, Pa. I believe it may have been made first in Pittsburgh, even though it could have been carried on later in Washington, Pa. There was quite a wide variety of tableware, some of which was partly in ruby red, such as the goblet, which I have seen with the portion above the design in red. Incidentally, the tumbler was made both with a plain base and with a star in the base.

My classification will not be complete but it may prove helpful to collectors of this pattern.

1. Bowls
2. Butter dish

3. Celery
4. Compotes
5. Creamer
6. Goblet
7. Sauce dish, footed
8. Spoonholder
9. Sugar bowl
10. Tumbler
11. Water pitcher

2. HEXAGONAL BLOCK. This pattern was produced by one of the factories in what was known as "the old Pittsburgh glass district." My catalogue is unmarked beyond terming this glass "No. 85 pattern." The hexagonal block, which predominates in the design, is very similar to the Henrietta pattern, made by the Columbia Glass Co. of Findlay, Ohio.

The most interesting feature of the "No. 82 pattern" is that the goblet has a square foot. This is the only American pressed glass pattern collectible in sets of glassware which has a square foot. There are some with square bases resting on feet such as the Clear Ribbon, illustrated on Plate 70 of *Early American Pressed Glass*. This latter is an entirely different type of foot. In Europe, square feet were used on many articles of glassware but it is one feature of Continental work which we never copied to any extent in this country.

Hexagonal Block may be found in clear glass and in colors, one unusual shade being an aquamarine-blue. It is unlike the blue found in most patterns of the 1870's and 1880's. There is undoubtedly a wide range of pieces to be had in this pattern but my catalogue is incomplete. I can only list those it contains, plus others I have seen.

1. Bread tray, oblong
2. Creamer
3. Compotes, square, covered, on high foot
    a. Open, on high foot.
4. Dishes, oblong, 7, 8 and 9 inch
5. Goblet

6. Pickle jar
    a. Pickle dish, oblong tray
7. Sauce dish
8. Spoonholder
9. Sugar bowl
10. Syrup pitcher
11. Water pitcher

3. BROKEN COLUMN. The Broken Column has caused considerable confusion because of the variety of names attached to it and also because of the controversy as to whether or not it was made by the Portland Glass Co. of Portland, Maine, as one writer on the subject has contended. While this design has been called Broken Column, Irish Column, Rattan and Bamboo, I have chosen the name by which it is most generally known. As to where it was made, in my possession is a catalogue of the United States Glass Co. picturing it under the title of "15021 pattern." It is also marked "Old No. E," meaning that it was originated by Richards & Hartley of Tarentum, Pa. It would be too harsh to state deliberately that the populace of Portland claim all collections of glass existing in their fair city as being necessarily products of their short-lived glass factory; all the inhabitants of that place are by no means New England die-hards.

The somewhat absurd pretensions and contentions of a few, who actually feel certain that all glass, no matter what its period, was made at Portland, make attributions exceedingly difficult for that liberal share of the population who are interested in old glass. A few amateurs take it upon themselves to claim for the Portland factory practically all glassware found in local cupboards! It is quite true that there were moldmakers who made and sold molds for glassware to anyone in the trade and that many patterns were carried by more than one factory. Even so, only the rankest novice could look at the illustration of the Broken Column butter dish on Plate 71 and not recognize from its form that it belonged to the gay nineties! Some few flat butter dishes with large dome covers may have been made in the very late 1880's, but the Portland Glass Co. closed in 1873. It seems incredible, but there are people who will not believe a catalogue picture even when they see it. They blind themselves to facts and refuse to listen. Another case in point is the Victor pattern, quite well known as Shell and Jewel. which was originated by Mr. West, of Pittsburgh, founder of the Westmoreland Glass Co. of Grapeville, Pa. Mr. West told me he brought out the pattern in 1893 and he lent me one of his catalogues to prove it. Photostats of illustrations from this cata- logue are shown on Plate 73. This design also is claimed for Portland! A further discussion of the Victor pattern will be taken up in a subsequent chapter.

The Broken Column appears in clear glass, with the bright sheen experienced collectors associate with late glass, and also in clear with the notches in the column touched in ruby red, which is extremely effective. Glassmakers used potash and arsenic to give brilliance to their wares. The classification is taken from the United States Glass Co. catalogue, as well as from actual specimens I have seen myself.

1. Berry bowl, 6, 7 and 8 inch.
2. Bowl, covered, 5, 6, 7 and 8 inch
3. Bowls, or "Nappies," 5, 6, 7, 8 and 9 inch
4. Butter dish
5. Cake plate on standard, 9 and 10 inch
6. Celery vase
    a. Boat celery
7. Claret
8. Compotes on high foot, with rounded bowls, open, 5, 6, 7 and 8 inch
    a. Open, on high foot, flared bowl, 5, 6, 7 and 8 inch
    b. Covered compotes on high foot, 5, 6, 7 and 8 inch
    c. Open, with tilted sides, known as banana stand
9. Creamer
10. Cruet
11. Custard cup and saucer
12. Cracker jar

13. Dishes, oblong, 7, 8 and 9 inch
     a. Olive dish
14. Finger bowl
15. Goblet
16. Pickle jar
17. Pickle dish
18. Plates, 5, 6, 7 and 8 inch
19. Salt and pepper shakers
20. Sauce dishes, flat, 4 and 4½ inch
     a. Berry sauce dish, 5 inch
21. Spoonholder
22. Sugar bowl
23. Sugar shaker
24. Syrup pitcher
25. Tumbler
26. Water bottle
27. Water pitcher, ½ gallon
28. Wine

4. PEERLESS. The Peerless pattern is so similar to the Hamilton design, shown in *Early American Pressed Glass,* that when the notes were being prepared for that book I mistook the 6-inch plate for Hamilton. Later I learned that 6-inch plates do not exist in the Hamilton. Peerless was made by Richards & Hartley of Tarentum, Pa. The oval platter illustrated on Plate 71 was taken from the catalogue, where it is noted as "Peerless Bread Plate." It is shown next to a large round Cupid and Venus plate.

Peerless is so beautifully pressed as to appear to be cut glass, except on close examination. The quality of the glass is brilliant and, though it does not ring when tapped, it appears to have at least a small amount of lead and flint in it. It does not have the glossy surface we associate with patterns of the late 1890's and early 1900's.

My catalogue and listing of the Peerless is not complete, so collectors will find more forms than appear in my classification. It is found in clear glass and appears to be of the late 1860's and 1870's, though it was carried on into the 1880's.

1. Butter dish
2. Creamer
3. Dishes, oval, 7, 8, 9 and 10 inch
4. Goblet
5. Plate, 6 inch
6. Platter, oval, open handles

PLATE 72

1. ORIENTAL. It is not known where the Oriental pattern was made. It could have been in Indiana or by one of the factories in the Pittsburgh glass district. Few patterns have such ornate feet, because they were too susceptible to breakage in shipping.

The sugar bowl of this set has a sailboat in one of the three panels about the bowl, a fan in the second, and a frog eying an insect, while ensconced among some tall grasses, in the third. The cover of this unusual bowl has a fish on one side (as in the illustration) and a flowerpot holding two leaning branches on the other. All the pieces have two or three intersections which divide the panels, standing out much as the grasshopper does in that pattern. Each piece of the Oriental varies, which is not only interesting but amusing. The creamer has an Oriental figure carrying a fan in one panel, an alligator envying a crane with a large fish in its bill in the second, and a flowerpot holding a plant vying with a vase of flowers in the third. The designer of this pattern must have had a busy time. The set is included in this book as a means of identification, though I have seen little of it. The three pieces illustrated are all in clear glass and appear to date in the 1880's.

2. PEAR. This design should not be confused with the Baltimore Pear. The latter is better known and was more widely distributed but is not as early or of as good quality of glass. The sugar bowl in the Pear illustrated in Plate 72 has three clusters

of stippled leaves, with two pears in each cluster, on the bowl. Above this decoration is a small cable band, such as on the Currant pattern. The lid has a knob in the form of an acorn, a motif widely used by the Boston & Sandwich Glass Co. but also utilized to a more limited extent in the midwest. The goblet has a wide clear band, with the three clusters of leaves and fruit at the lower part of the bowl, thereby losing considerable attractiveness. On the spoonholder the clear band is not quite so wide, and it has a cable band which the goblet lacks. I cannot say where this glass was produced but it appears to be of the late 1870's and 1880's. Those pieces I have seen were in clear glass.

1. Butter dish
2. Goblet
3. Spoonholder
4. Sauce dish, 4 inch
5. Sugar bowl

3. CANNON BALL. The goblet shown in line 3 of Plate 72 is known as Cannon Ball. It is the only piece I have seen in this pattern. The celery vase and creamer next to it are in the Atlas pattern (see page 72) but combine nicely. The Atlas was made both footed and with flat base, so those with the design around the base match the Cannon Ball very well, particularly as the glass is heavier than it appears to be in the drawings. There may be a full line of Cannon Ball, but it is not possible for one person to see every piece of pressed glass.

1. Cannon Ball goblet
2. Atlas celery
3. Atlas creamer

4. PRISCILLA. The Priscilla pattern was not named by me and I do not know how it has come to be so well-known by this title. None of my old glass catalogues mention it, so the place of manufacture is not known at present. It is an interesting design and one that makes a charming table setting. The glass

is panelled and has a bright sheen. The bowl of the goblet is elongated and the stem is short, as on all the stemware. Usually a goblet foot is plain, but the Priscilla is divided into nine panels, each ornamented by a circular disc, as in the upper row on the bowl. The wine glass has a more slender, tapering bowl than appears in the line drawings.

Some of the Priscilla design was made with the dots in ruby, a favored color combination in glass during the 1880's and 1890's.

Not many pieces in this pattern come to light in New England, so I was delighted when a collector sent me a list of the items in his collection. At this writing he is busily engaged overseas, in the U. S. Army.

1. Bowls
2. Butter dish
3. Cake plate on standard
4. Celery vase
5. Compotes, open, large
6. Creamer
7. Cruets
8. Cups and saucers
9. Goblet
10. Jelly compote
11. Pickle or relish dish
12. Rose bowl
13. Sauce dish
14. Spoonholder
15. Sugar bowl
16. Syrup pitcher
17. Toothpick or match holder
18. Wine

Chapter XI

SHELL AND JEWEL, OR "VICTOR"

PLATE 73

The pattern which today is rather widely known by the descriptive title of Shell and Jewel was originally named "Victor." Mr. Charles H. West, who founded the Westmoreland Glass Co. of Grapeville, Pa., told me when I called on him in Pittsburgh in 1933 that the Victor was originated by his company and that he brought it out in 1893. To prove his assertion, he lent me one of his Westmoreland catalogues, which illustrated the Victor quite fully. On Plate 73 are reproduced two pages from this catalogue.

For some curious reason, controversy raged in a certain portion of New England, because enthusiastic collectors of glass thought to have been produced by the Portland Glass Co. of Portland, Maine, were determined to claim the Shell and Jewel for their very own! Catalogue pictures in black and white failed to convince the die-hards. When they saw the actual Westmoreland Glass Co. illustrations, they said that an earlier Shell and Jewel was produced at Portland because some collector who lived there had some pieces of it! The forms tell all the story anyone needs to know. Note the banana stand on Plate 73. These were made only in the later patterns. There is not one iota of proof that the Portland Glass Co. ever made the Victor pattern and no particular reason why they should wish to claim it. The proven Portland patterns all show finer workmanship and are generally in a much better quality of glass. Moreover, Mr. West told me that he sold the "table sets," consisting of a covered sugar bowl, covered creamer, covered spoonholder and covered butter dish, to the grocery store trade, filled with pre-

Plate 73

riginal VICTOR pattern, now known as SHELL AND JEWEL, as taken from an old Westmoreland Glass Co. catalogue.

PLATE 73-A

Goblet designs collectible in sets of tableware.
Upper: Daisy and Button with Narcissus. Octagonal Daisy and Button.
Lower: Maple Leaf. Lotus.

pared mustard. I have one of these Shell and Jewel table pieces, with the dried-up mustard still in it and with the original label of the Westmoreland Specialty Co., by which name the firm was known at that time. The Victor was made in clear glass with the background of the design stippled, as well as in a rather deep blue and an iridescent green. Collectors may rest assured that the Victor was produced exclusively by Mr. West's company, twenty years after the Portland Glass Co. had closed down. But to those who have no desire to acknowledge facts, the Shell and Jewel may still be Portland glass!

1. Banana stand, 10 inch
2. Berry bowl, 8 inch
   a. Bowl, 6 inch
3. Butter dish
4. Cake plate on standard, 10 inch
5. Creamer
6. Dishes, oval, 7 and 8 inch
7. Honey dish, round, covered
8. Orange bowl, large compote on high foot
9. Sauce dish, 4½ inch
10. Spoonholder
11. Sugar bowl
12. Tray for water set, round
13. Tumbler
14. Water pitcher, ½ gallon

Chapter XII

WATER SETS

PLATES 74 AND 75

My belief that collectors would be interested to see how the glass trade illustrated water sets inspired Plates 74 and 75. They are devoted exclusively to these sets as originally shown in old catalogues of various companies.

On Plate 74, in the upper row to the left, is the Hidalgo with a water pitcher, two goblets and waste bowl, on a round tray. These waste bowls, which is the old glass factory term for them, were not usually intended as finger bowls and that is why they are so difficult to find today. Some factories did make and sell blown glass finger bowls as such, but in the older patterns they were sold exclusively with water sets, and few seem to have survived.

Next to the Hidalgo is an odd pattern which is listed as "No. 27 ware." It will be noted that the water tray is an ovoid, irregular shape. All of them had rims but some are more ornate than others. The "No. 27 ware" has the straight-sided pitcher, or that always referred to as a tankard pitcher. With it are two tumblers and a finger bowl in an extra-large size.

In the center of Plate 74 is the same "No. 27 ware, engraved," which illustrates how completely different a plain set can look when ornamented. The tray is pointed at one end, though slightly rounded, and then spreads out fanlike in shape. It is exactly the same as the set above it, except that goblets are shown instead of tumblers.

In the bottom row of Plate 74 is a Plume water set. It was advertised also for lemonade or cider! In order to embellish the water pitcher and tumblers to a greater degree, the pattern runs vertically, instead of horizontally as it does on most of this ware. The pieces in this set also come engraved. The water

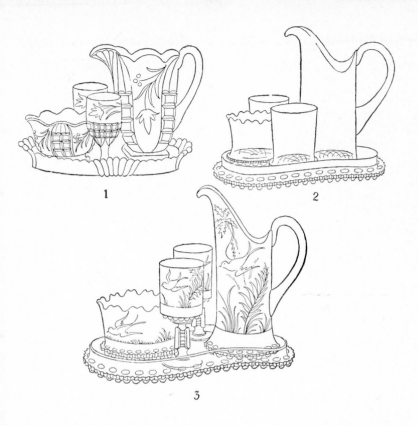

1

2

3

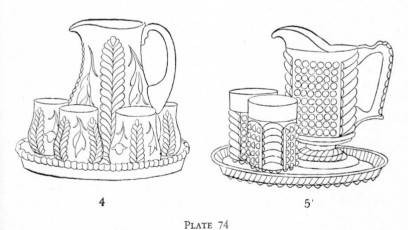

4

5'

PLATE 74

Water Sets, from Original Illustrations

1. HIDALGO   2. "NO. 27 WARE."   3. "NO. 27 WARE, ENGRAVED."
4. PLUME   5. HOBNAIL WITH BARS

PLATE 75
Water Sets, from Original Illustrations

1. SHELL AND JEWEL   2. STAR AND OVAL   3. CLARK
4. CROWN JEWEL   5. LEAF AND FLOWER

pitcher is the usual bulbous or, "belled," shape, as the glass-workers termed it, and the tumblers also are belled.

The last set on Plate 74 is a rather unusual hobnail design, with the addition of bars. It was made by Adams & Co. of Pittsburgh, who also produced the Toy Hobnail sets which are so scarce today. The buyer had his choice of a quart-size pitcher, or a half-gallon. The set is quite simple, in that it consisted of a tray, pitcher and two tumblers.

On Plate 75 in the upper row we have first the Shell and Jewel, or that which was originally known as Victor. Goblets were not made in this pattern, so the set comprises a round tray, the usual type of water pitcher, and tumblers.

Beside the Shell and Jewel is the Star and Oval set. The tray is exceedingly simple. It has handles, which is rather unusual. The pitcher is the bulbous type, and there are two tumblers and a waste bowl.

In the center of Plate 75 is the Clark pattern. This is a different style set, in that there is a tankard pitcher, a goblet, and two water tumblers. The Clark pattern is simple in design but the engraving enhances it considerably. Again we have a decidedly irregular tray.

In the lower row of Plate 75, at the left, is the Crown Jewel pattern. The tray in this set is handled and the engraved tankard pitcher has an interesting swirled handle. Besides the pitcher, there are two goblets and a waste bowl.

The last set on this page is the Leaf and Flower. The tray is of metal and there is a tankard pitcher and tumblers. This set was made in such a variety of styles and colors that it is apt to be much more attractive than it appears to be in the illustration.

Practically all of the water sets have been illustrated and described under the individual name of each pattern.

Chapter XIII

BUTTER DISHES

PLATE 76

Because there are collectors who find the accumulating of butter dishes an interesting hobby, a few unusual ones are illustrated here for their benefit. There is no intent to cover the subject thoroughly: one would never know when he had come to the end of them. They not only appear in every pressed glass pattern collectible in sets of tableware, but in a great variety of odd ones besides. Today many people utilize these novelty pieces for candy, cigarettes, or some other useful purpose.

In row 1 of Plate 76 the first butter dish is flat, with a handle, and the lid carries the face of a watch. The artist has shown a part of the cover, so the piece may be easily identified. The middle dish in the top row is in the form of a warrior's helmet. It appears in an old but unnamed trade catalogue as the "Helmet Butter" and was made in clear glass, amber and blue. An interesting item illustrated in the same catalogue and pictured on Plate 77 is termed "Spice Barrel." It is a barrel, in one of the fine cut patterns, mounted on wheels. When the cover is lifted, four compartments are found within. Some collector may come across one of these novelties but I have never seen one. They were also made in clear glass, amber and blue.

The third butter dish in the top row of Plate 76 has a stippled background and is termed "Frosted Butter" in a Bryce Bros. catalogue. A similar pattern is illustrated in *Early American Pressed Glass* as the Chain, but it has a clear background.

The first dish in line 2 of Plate 76 was made by Bryce Bros. of Pittsburgh, and they called it "Albany Butter." Next to it is the Stove butter dish. This represented a considerable amount of work for some moldmaker, since it carries a great deal of detail both inside and out. The flatiron is the knob for the cover. The stoves were made in amber, blue and clear glass. Next to the stove in line 2 is a Basket butter, another of the Bryce Bros. line. The catalogue does not state whether it was produced in colors or not.

A very curious butter dish is the first one shown on line 3 of Plate 76. This was made by Bryce Bros. and was referred to as "Shamrock Flanged Butter." It has considerable detail around the flange, as well as on the handle. The shield-shaped butter dish next to the Shamrock in line 3 was shown as the "Banner Butter" and was made by Bryce Bros. The catalogue does not mention colors, but I believe I have seen this one in different shades. There is a large shield-shaped platter similar to the butter dish and bearing a bust of Columbia in the center. I have found these in yellow, blue, clear glass and amethyst. The Swirled butter dish next to the Banner, was called "Cameo." It is better-looking than it appears in the drawing. It has a squared base and round lid. The base has a Waffle Sunburst pattern pressed into it.

In line 4 of Plate 76 the first dish was made by the United States Glass Co. of Pittsburgh and was referred to as "Tomato Butter." It is in stippled glass but I have seen these in milk-white and in opaque blue. Everything illustrated on the same page as the butter dish appears under the heading "Novelties."

The middle butter dish is listed as "Leaf Flanged Butter" and was made by Bryce Bros. of Pittsburgh. The last dish in the row is also a product of Bryce Bros. and their name for it was "Troy Butter."

There must have been a fad for odd butter dishes in the old days because I have trade catalogues which contain pages devoted exclusively to them.

On Plate 77 the first dish was made by Bryce Bros. It appears more ornate in the actual photograph than in my line drawings. It is merely called "No. 80 Flanged Butter." The middle dish in the row is decorated with flowers and is listed as "Standard Flanged Butter." I am assuming that collectors know that a flange is an outspread rim, where the cover joins the base.

These rims are generally ornamented. The third drawing in line 1 of Plate 77 is another Bryce pattern and is listed as "Charm Flanged Butter." This pattern appears in *Early American Pressed Glass* as "Panelled Forget-Me-Not."

Line 2 of Plate 77 starts with an elaborate stippled and heavily beaded dish with scalloped foot, made by Bryce Bros. and listed as "Albion Butter Footed." The same style was produced without a foot. In the middle of the same line is an oblong stippled dish, which does not appear to have been made for butter but it is termed "Avon Footed Butter." Like the Albion, it was also made flat, without a foot. It is another Bryce Bros. product. Next to it is an oval stippled dish with open handles, attached to a tray, which is seen more frequently by collectors than most of the other types. Generally it is found in clear glass, but it was also made in yellow, amber and blue. We used to think it was a honey dish, but it appears in the Bryce catalogue as "Lorne Butter." It would seem to have been named after someone.

In row 3 of Plate 77, the first butter dish is the "Maude S," named for the famous "Queen of the Turf" trotting horse during the 1880's. It was made by Ripley & Co. of Pittsburgh, Pa. Next to the Maude S, is a Bryce Bros. dish, which they termed the "Fashion Butter." It has an openwork edge. On line 4 of Plate 77 are shown the "King" and "Queen" butters and the spice barrel, mentioned in connection with the butter dishes on Plate 76.

There is a wide variety of both patterns and colors to choose from, in the hobby of butter dishes. Collectors will find special elation in amethyst and sapphire blue specimens, because both are rare. Many are simply novelties, so whether one specializes in butter dishes or not, a "Maude S" for cigarettes in a tack room or a "Stove Butter" for candy in a summer home always gives a special touch that comes as a surprise to the uninitiated.

PLATE 79

1. Goblet in a pattern which has been called "Knife and Fork." Other pieces exist to match.

2. Early flint glass water tumbler. Heavy glass, in which goblets may be found to match.

3. Early, heavy lead glass goblet, in which I have not found any other pieces.

4. A most attractive Oak Leaf Band, with medallion, goblet. So far I have not seen any matching pieces.

5. The spoonholder and sauce dish (No. 6) are in a simple beaded pattern. A goblet has been seen to match. The only other item I have encountered has been a creamer. A full set may exist but probably not much in this design was ever made.

6. Sauce dish to match above.

7. Egg cups, goblets and a sugar bowl are the only pieces I have found in this dainty Grape Band pattern. It is shown here as a means of identification because it is a pattern of merit and in an excellent quality of glass.

8. Goblet in Grape Band, to match above. Bands above and below the pattern are stippled.

9. Cheese dish in double swirled ribbon. Two panels are frosted and two clear, alternating. No other matching items have been found.

10. Creamer in an ornate draped pattern, with hollow stem. Sugar bowl to match has just recently been noted.

11. Small butter dish in an ornamented chain pattern, in which I have found no other pieces.

12. This creamer I have heard referred to as Panelled Daisy. Goblets and egg cups to match have been seen, so doubtless there may be a full set.

13. Panelled fine cut goblet, in an excellent quality of glass. The only other piece I have found is the wine glass, shown next to it.

14. Wine glass to match above.

15. Sauce dish, in pattern similar to Viking, except that there is a goat's face instead of that of the so-called Viking.

16. Beaded Star sauce dish. Probably a small line of tableware exists in this pattern, as I have seen a tumbler and creamer since these illustrations were made.

17. Beaded Star to match above, in base to sugar bowl. Cover is missing.

18. Dainty sugar bowl, having one stippled panel alternating with each clear one. The design is carried out in beading or dewdrops. So far no other pieces have been found to match.

19. Palm Leaf celery vase. There is an oriental suggestion about this, the design having three palm leaf fans, with bamboo shoots alternating with each fan. No other matching items have been seen.

PLATE 76

Butter Dishes
1. Clock, Helmet, Frosted Chain.
2. Albany, Stove, Basket Weave.
3. Shamrock, Banner, Cameo.
4. Tomato, Leaf, Troy.

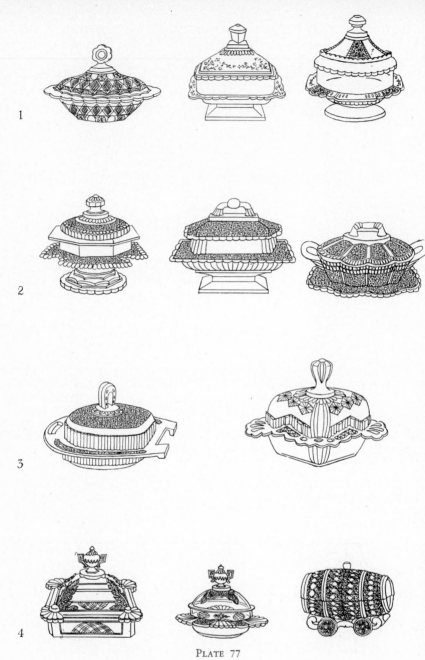

PLATE 77

Butter Dishes

1. Bryce Bros. "No. 80 Flanged Butter." Standard Flanged Butter. Charm Butter.
2. Albion. Avon. Lorne Butter Dish.
3. "Maude S." Fashion Butter Dish.
4. King. Queen. Spice barrel.

PLATE 78

1. Four Spillholders, all early lead glass types.
2. Four early lead glass drinking glasses.
3. Three early spillholders, sometimes found in color.
4. Three spillholders. These all served diverse purposes, sometimes being used for tapers to light whale oil lamps, as well as for cigars and, later on, as spoonholders.

PLATE 79
Odds and Ends, largely collectible in other forms.
(See pages 247, 248)

Chapter XIV

"OPAL WARE," OR MILK-WHITE GLASS

Though the glass known to the glassworkers years ago was then called "Opal Ware," today it is accepted as opaque-white or milk-white. The term "milk glass" is incorrect and is not to be included in the collectors' nomenclature.

The first reference I have found to this type of ware was in an old English book which stated that during the eighteenth century an attempt was made in England to produce a white glass, in imitation of china. It would cost less to make than china or porcelain and at once give the same effect. Apparently this attempt was not successful. Glass truly opal in color was made by the Boston & Sandwich Glass Co. and doubtless by many other companies, prior to the time the milk-white glass in openwork plates, compotes and table sets became commercially successful during the 1870's. The early pieces in opalescent would be such items as the lacy salts, sugar bowls, sauce dishes, and occasionally a bowl, which were produced at Sandwich during the 1840's and possibly elsewhere and earlier. The fiery opal coloring that is such a delight to collectors was produced from a deliberate mixture and not by accident.

The milk-white of the 1870's also was a deliberate mixture, the intent being to make a dense milk-white glass, even though the trade did call it "opal." The first patent referred to it as "hot-cast porcelain." By "opalescent" the trade meant a glass which was all that the term implies—a shading between opal and crystal. When milk-white turned to a delicate opalescent through no intention of the glassmakers, it was because the body of the glass burned out or "went flinty," as the glassworkers termed it, and thus it reverted more or less to its crystal, or clear, stage. This is why we see some delicate opalescent glass clear

253

at its edges. Some manufacturers used more bone ash than others to produce the transparent, or flinty, quality. An old glassworker told me that the opacity was made by the use of feldspar or fluorspar or both. Apparently there were many receipts to cover true opalescent, translucent, opaque and milk-white. I own copies of many of the Sandwich formulas but it seems doubtful that readers are interested in technicalities.

In *Early American Pressed Glass* a lengthy chapter was devoted to milk-white patterns collectible in sets, and to some of the "openwork" plates, as they were originally termed. More patterns, and more plates, all photostat reproductions of pages in old trade catalogues, are pictured here just as they were presented in the 1870's and 1880's. Animal dishes will be treated in a separate chapter.

In the upper row of Plate 80 is a beautiful all-over flower pattern, made by Challinor, Taylor & Co. of Tarentum, Pa., under the term "313 Opal Ware." The detail is so fine and the glass has such a clear bell tone when tapped that one of the most prominent collectors in our country confided in me some years ago that in his opinion it was too good to be American and was probably English.

We find the "313" pattern in milk-white, in white with the flowers painted in colors, in opaque jade green, and in opaque blue. The catalogue pictures an interesting variety of tableware, such as an eight-inch deep bowl, an eight-inch "belled" (globular) nut bowl, and an eight-inch bowl with the edges crimped. The bowl with the openwork edge in Plate 80 is listed as a salad bowl and the six-inch dish above it as a preserve dish. Besides the table set illustrated, there is a large covered cracker or biscuit jar, sauce dishes, and so on.

In the lower row of Plate 80 are some of the Flower and Panel pieces in white, which is also pictured on Plate 60 and described in Chapter X. A water pitcher in a different pattern is shown along with the Flower and Panel dishes. Goblets may be had to match the pitcher, but I have never seen any other tableware.

The "O. W." plates, as the glass manufacturers referred to those white plates with an openwork edge, did not have names but all went by line numbers. Plate 81 shows a number of patterns. The two large plates at the top of the page are in the ten-inch size. The bowls are simply referred to as "O. W. Fruit Nappy." The plain white one next to the pinwheel or swirled plate could not have been produced in quantity; they are very rare.

Popular plates for table settings are those known as "lattice-edge" some of which are shown on Plate 82. It will be noticed that the centers of the plates are decorated. My original catalogue pictures them in natural colors. The work is so skillfully and beautifully executed that one collector once wrote and asked if I did not think these plates had been sent to Bristol, England, to be hand-painted. It is possible, even today, to collect and match these plates in sets, in one style of decoration. There is one flower pattern, not illustrated, which has been a great favorite. The lattice-edged plates were made in plain milk-white and also in "Mosaic," or Marble, glass. The same style plate was produced with a closed edge. A number of them are pictured on Plate 97.

Several fruit compotes, with openwork edge, are shown in the lower row of Plate 82. While the bowls do not vary much, it will be noted that one standard has a basket weave pattern, another is fluted with a cable edge (this is the rarest type), and others have fine cut or variations of the Daisy and Button pattern. Any of these bowls, singly or in pairs, make attractive centerpieces for the table, or used on a sideboard.

PLATE 80

Milk-white glass, taken from old catalogue illustrations
1. Challinor "313 Opal Ware."
2. Flower and Panel tableware.

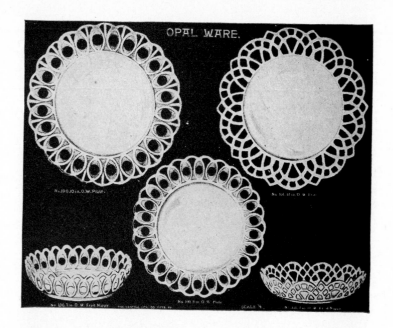

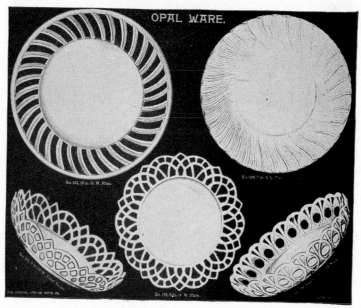

PLATE 81

1. Upper: Milk-white "Openwork" plates and bowls.
2. Lower: Milk-white plates and bowls.

PLATE 82

1. Upper: Decorated lattice-edged plates.
2. Lower: Openwork Milk-white compotes.

Chapter XV

TABLE SETTINGS

Any experienced collector appreciates the fact that not one single dish in any pattern, whether old or new, begins to portray the beauty that may be acquired by a massed effect. One tulip or one daffodil gives no impression of the delightful effect gained by a bed of them. It seems fitting, therefore, at the conclusion of chapters devoted to hundreds of forms in old glassware, that some large groups should be pictured.

Many of the patterns in this book will be a surprise, even to old-time collectors. It must be remembered that a design which may be plentiful in your locality or state may be practically unknown in other sections of the country. In New England we are likely to find old-time eastern patterns rarely encountered in Indiana, Pennsylvania or New York State. A collector buying through the mails from Minneapolis soon learns the glass patterns to expect from Massachusetts and those that will come to him from Ohio. This is in a general manner of speaking.

Of course, there will be the usual jeers from alleged experts who still think it appropriate to refer to all pressed glass as "mid-Victorian atrocities." It is undoubtedly true that many patterns shown in this book may not have high artistic or historical merit. On the other hand, it is only fair to bear in mind that neither is every piece of furniture made from designs by Sheraton or Hepplewhite a masterpiece. At all times and in all places, master craftsmen have had their off moments and the old American glassmakers were no exception. To condemn as inartistic many of our distinctly American pressed glass patterns is absurd. Study the illustrations and look not for the worst but for the best. You will find many excellent designs utterly free from European influences, which is more than can be said for most of our arts and crafts during our first century as a nation. Good designing is good designing, and all the scoffing of the uninformed and the biased cannot make it anything else. Comparatively little pressed glass dates prior to 1830, because practically all glass produced previous to that date was blown glass, as the pressing machine was in its infancy. Those who seek glass for utilitarian purposes and not to lock up in cabinets must purchase tableware dating from the 1840's. No end of these old designs are so quaint and so full of character, so overwhelmingly suggestive of bygone days and manners, that they help to produce atmosphere in the dining room as inevitably as the infinitely less subtle sideboard or chairs or panelling.

There is on record the case of a man connected with a metropolitan newspaper who knows little about old glass and apparently dislikes it to the extent that he seeks revenge on both collectors and dealers by referring to all glass produced since the mid-nineteenth century as "modern." It might be added that this is a curious attitude on the part of any editors employed by a paper which depends upon its advertisers for the existence of its page devoted to antiques! It is not really my intent to write about anything modern at present—because an excellent book entitled *Modern Fine Glass* was written several years ago.

To return to the table settings, Plate 83 pictures an interesting group in the Frosted Circle, a pattern originated by the Nickel Plate Glass Co. of Fostoria, Ohio, a factory which was later absorbed by the United States Glass Co. of Pittsburgh, Pa. It is much more attractive with the frosted finish on the circular discs. Some of this design may be found in clear glass without any satin finish. Plates, celery vases, salt and pepper shakers and finger bowls are very scarce. The covered compote is quite a rarity.

Roman Rosette is familiar to most glass collectors. Plate 84 shows an interesting group of this pattern, which is so attractive with its stippled, frosted background. The square honey dish is rare and salt and pepper shakers are difficult to find in almost any design. Roman Rosette goblets are always in demand.

It was a matter of great interest to me when a glass manufacturer told me he was going to reproduce goblets in the Beaded Grape Medallion pattern (illustrated in *Early American Pressed Glass*) and paint the cluster of grapes in red. I asked him why he did not create a new pattern, rather than copy an old one. He said the old patterns were better. I asked him if he really was acknowledging that there was not enough ingenuity left in the glass industry to originate something that would capture public interest. The reply was vague. Up to this time, and it has been over a year since our conversation took place, I have not seen or heard of any new Beaded Grape Medallion goblets, with or without red grapes.

Block with Fan plates were illustrated in *Early American Pressed Glass,* but at the time that book was written not enough other forms could be found to illustrate it adequately. On Plate 85 there is a table setting including several rarities. This pattern is shown also on Plate 41 and its history given in Chapter VIII. Since it was made by Richards & Hartley of Tarentum, Pa., collectors in the midwestern states should be able to find it fairly readily. Fortunately, nothing in this design has been reproduced.

The Currier and Ives pattern is another design more easily found in the midwest than elsewhere. It was illustrated and described in *Early American Pressed Glass* as having been produced by the Bellaire Goblet Co. of Findlay, Ohio. Some pieces, such as the water trays, cordials and decanters, are seen fairly frequently in the East, but not the other items as shown on Plate 86. It requires time and patience to acquire a set such as the one pictured, which is popular with collectors because of the plates and cups and saucers.

Curiously, the Dewdrop in Points, as shown on Plate 87, is another pattern difficult to find in New England or New York State. Mrs. Clara Edwards, who accumulated these settings, must have purchased a great deal through the mail! This is a hazardous undertaking, because so few people know how to pack glass properly. There are many casualties, whether shipped by mail or by express.

Many collectors will find the Dewdrop in Points a fascinating pattern to collect. The background is stippled and the clear pointed panels outlined in heavier beads.

There is one thing about the glass originally known as Mosaic but now generally referred to as Marble glass, and that is that collectors either like it very much or hate it. There does not seem to be any halfway measure! This ware was made in this country largely by Challinor, Taylor & Co. of Tarentum, Pa. An old-time glassworker, who was with Challinor's at the time Mosaic was being produced, told me there was difficulty in making the mixture, because the white part did not always adhere properly to the purple.

Years ago some well-meaning persons referred to this ware as "End of the Day" glass. One woman informed me that at the end of the day the workmen were allowed to have any metal remaining in the pots; they mixed up whatever was left and the result was marble glass! It is amazing how gullible people can be. I wonder if the woman who repeated this story believed that a mixture of all the ingredients left in her kitchen would produce a cake or a pie? There is just exactly as much sense to one theory as to the other. Mosaic glass was a deliberate mixture, or it would not have turned out an opaque purple and white marbelized glass. Some of it was made in England and doubtless was introduced to this country from there. Many pieces are found bearing the British registry mark. As a rule, the English pieces are darker in color and the general effect of their glass is rather different from ours.

In Plate 88 are shown various compotes and cake plates in Marble glass. In the lowest row, the two compotes at the left have a bust of a woman in the stem, supposed to be Jenny Lind, though I cannot vouch for this story. Most of the items pictured, though possibly not all of them, were made by Challinor, Taylor & Co. The scarcest piece, though not the most attractive in coloring, is the Raindrop compote, which is at the right end of the center row.

Perhaps I should say at this time that all the Marble glass pieces were collected by the late Mrs. Timothy Mojonnier of Chicago. The photographs were given to me through the courtesy of Mr. Mojonnier.

The pickle jar with fork, in the center of Plate 89, is the most unusual dish in that group. The three pieces across the lower part of the illustration are rarely encountered. The small basket with handles at the left is English. The riding boots pictured are always interesting containers for matches. It is not easy to find them complete and perfect, with the spurs.

The pair of deep bowls at the top of Plate 90 have a leaf design in the panels. Such bowls are scarce. They make a choice centerpiece for a table setting in purple. The pair of large plates in the lower part of the illustration are exceedingly rare. Dishes with crimped or fluted rims for candy or jelly and the small compotes, also with a crimped edge, are not so difficult to find. Usually they are much lighter in color than other dishes in Marble glass.

An imposing array of the much sought-after Marble glass plates is shown on Plate 91. The dish with the ring handle is most unusual and the oval platters are not plentiful. As for the goblets, they are the only ones of this particular type I have seen. It is doubtful whether they are a product of Challinor, Taylor & Co., who made the plates with the closed lattice edge, which vary in color in such an interesting manner.

When it is possible to find Marble glass goblets at all, it is usually the fluted style, as shown in the bottom row of Plate 92. These are graceful in form and there is an entire table setting to match. The celery vase in the center, between the fluted goblets, appears to be English, and most of the tumblers we find come from the same country. The leaf dish in the lower right-hand corner is rare. One would look a long time before finding one of those. The vases with the triangular foot in the second row from the top of Plate 92, as well as the three at the top, have not been identified with any particular factory. They are not like the Challinor ware, almost invariably being lighter in color. They appear to be from a different formula or mixture.

On Plate 93 is represented a varied group of Marble glass; much of it is English, a few pieces are products of Challinor, Taylor & Co., and the balance cannot be identified at this time. A typical English piece is that in the lower left-hand corner. It undoubtedly bears a British Registry mark. Challinor made the fluted creamer in the upper row, as well as the Flower and Panel spoonholder at the end of that row. The flat-sided creamer and spoonholder are American. It is not possible to state where the dark water pitcher, sugar bowl, creamer and spoonholder were produced.

A great many collectors admire purple glass and have specialized in it for years. It can be effectively used in home decoration.

PLATE 83

Table Setting in Frosted Circle.

PLATE 84

Table Setting in Roman Rosette.

PLATE 85

Table Setting in Block with Fan.

PLATE 86

Table Setting in Currier and Ives Pattern.

PLATE 87

Group of Dewdrop in Points.

Courtesy of Mr. Timothy Mojonnier

PLATE 88

Group of Purple Marble Glass

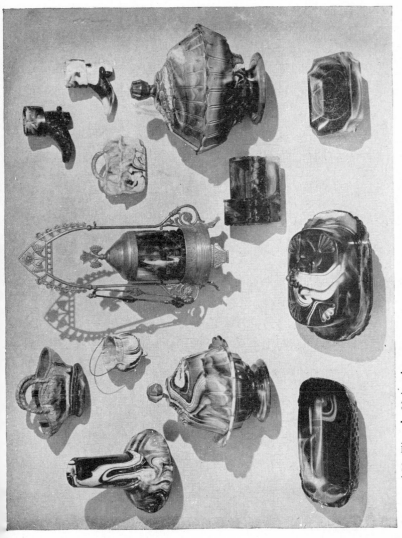

PLATE 89

Group of Purple Marble Glass.

PLATE 90

Group of Purple Marble Glass

PLATE 91

Group of Purple Marble Glass.

PLATE 92

Group of Purple Marble Glass.

PLATE 93

Group of Purple Marble Glass, including several English pieces.

Chapter XVI

FIGURED GLASS

Many times I have seen people ask, with a smirk and a quizzical look in their eye, "Where does all the old glass come from? Certainly you cannot claim all the pieces seen in all the antique shops are genuine." Those who pose this question in such a manner are almost without fail amateurs who have done little collecting themselves. Of course there are fakes in every line of "collectioning" but those who are serious, and study, soon detect the spurious.

While researching in the field of pattern glass in the Pittsburgh area during 1933, I met the presidents of many glass companies and interviewed a number of old-time glassworkers. Some of them gave me interesting stories which I jotted down for future use and others kindly handed me copies of "news and views" in the glass industry, pertaining to bygone days. Since these records will become lost in time, and represent important historical data, it seems well to save this documentary material for future generations.

Among the trade in Pittsburgh years ago there was a glass journal known as the *Commoner*. The ire of one old-time glassworker was aroused over a note that appeared in it pertaining to a pattern termed in at least one factory "Polka Dot" but widely known today as "Inverted Thumbprint." The latter is a descriptive title which came into use because the original designation was not known. As a matter of fact, several factories produced the same design under different trade names.

The article that follows is by an unknown author, so, unfortunately, proper credit cannot be given. Apparently he had served in the glass trade for many years, because most of his facts are correct. That he wrote his answer to "Mack's" note in the *Commoner* many years ago seems certain. For one thing, Deming Jarves spelled his name "Jarves" and not "Jarvis" though in early years a number of the older workers used the "i." A granddaughter of Deming Jarves explained to me that there had been considerable confusion over the spelling of the family name, but that it had finally been settled as "Jarves."

One must read the article on figured glassware with an open mind. It was written in the spirit of the times. There are a few errors but there is a great deal of value concerning locations and outputs of many glass factories in the Pittsburgh area. It is also of much interest that he speaks of "figured pressed glass" rather than pattern glass. His title is good. In speaking of the M'Kee Bros. and their "R.L." pattern, an illustration here pictures a page from a M'Kee catalogue of the 1850's and it may be seen that "R.L." means "Ribbed Leaf," now known widely by the name of Bellflower. Apparently, he knows little of the New England factories because there are records of Ashburton being made locally in the 1840's and it was still being sold into the 1880's, which is a longer period of time than he can claim for the "Diamond" (now known as Sawtooth), though Sawtooth was first made in lead glass and later continued in the cheaper lime glass.

Seasoned collectors will be very amused by the story of where much of our old glass came from. And so it goes:

"With that careless saunter and that total indifference to, and obliviousness of glass history for which he has earned a deserved reputation our good friend 'Mack' of the *Commoner* comes once again to the front with the following bunch of timothy-seed and clover blossoms dangling from his antlers:

H. S. McKee, who lately retired from the glass business, secured a patent July 30, 1878, for what he termed "Molds for decorating ware." It was simply a mold with polka dot figures cut in it. This probably was among the earliest figuring cut upon iron molds to be reproduced in glass.

"Now that is what we consider an unforgivable sin, even for a 'foot-finisher.' "

"The first pressed piece of modern glassware was a tumbler made by Deming Jarvis in Sandwich, Mass., in 1827, afterwards passed into the possession of John A. Dobson, the extensive Baltimore, Md., glass jobber, and was exhibited by Hobbs, Brockunier & Co. at the Centennial Exposition in Philadelphia in 1876.

"According to Apsley Pellatt's 'Curiosities of Glass-making,' published in England in 1849, metal plungers, (and it is reasonable to assume, metal molds, also) were then extensively used in the United States, from where the art of glass pressing had been introduced into England.

"The first flint glass works in the United States was built in 1807 by George Robinson, a carpenter, and Edward Ensell, an English glassmaker, under the name of Robinson & Ensell. Owing to disagreements the factory was bought in the following year 1808, by Messrs. Bakewell & Page, who afterwards became Bakewell, Pears & Co. Their product in the main consisted of blown and cut glassware, and the prices they obtained may be guessed at from an entry in the journal of Mr. Ferron, who visited Pittsburgh in 1817, left his order with the firm, made the following record: 'A pair of decanters, cut from a London pattern, price 8 guineas ($40).'

"The site of that historically important flint factory was at the foot of Ross Street, on the bank of the Monongahela. The first furnace contained 6 twenty-inch pots. In 1810 a 10-pot furnace replaced the original furnace, and in 1814 a second 10-pot furnace was added. The works were destroyed in the great fire of 1845, and the site was afterwards partly occupied by the depot of the B & O R.R. whose tracks and freight yards still cover the site. Bakewell, Pears & Co. afterwards rebuilt near the corner of 9th and Bingham Streets, South Side, opposite the present Ripley plant of the United States Glass Co., where they carried on business until their final retirement in 1882, after a business existence of 74 eventful years.

"In 1829 the Union Flint Glass Works were established by Hay & McCully; in 1831 the firm became Hay & Hanna; in 1839, Park & Hanna; in 1848, Hanna & Wallace, and in 1849,

Wallace, Lyon & Co. To James P. Wallace, of the latter firm, who proved himself most energetic and ambitious to improve the quality of flint glass and perfect molds and presses, is largely due the enviable reputation that Pittsburgh pressed tableware enjoyed from 1850 to the present time. In 1852 the firm name was changed to James B. Lyon & Co. and in 1875 the name was again changed to that of the O'Hara Glass Co., the officers of which were James B. Lyon, Chairman; John B. Lyon, treasurer; and Joseph Anderson, of the United States Glass Co., superintendent.

"The fact that figured pressed ware has been continuously made since 1850 is so easily established by the citation of indisputable authorities, that we propose to marshal a few.

"In 1850 Bryce, McKee & Co. built the works at 21st and Wharton Streets, South Side, which in 1852 became the property of Bryce, Richards & Co., in 1866, Bryce, Walker & Co., and from 1882 until absorbed by the United States Glass Co. [July, 1891], was operated by Bryce Brothers. They not only made figured pressed ware from the start but their famous diamond * pattern, which is still made and sold, has enjoyed the longest continuous run of any pressed figured pattern in the world.

"In 1851 the firm of Adams, Macklin & Co. started their first glass factory at the corner of Ross and Second Streets, where the late John Adams succeeded in making the first lime glass, which became a substitute for the costlier, heavy lead glass formerly used, and it may truthfully be said that to the introduction and perfection of the glass press and the use of cheap lime flint, the modern tableware industry of the United States owes more than to any other single factors which have contributed to its expansion and present importance.

"The above firm made pressed figured tumblers and tableware from the start, and in 1860 became Adams & Co., the works being located on South Tenth and Washington, now Sarah Street.

"In 1853 F & J McKee established the flint glass works at the foot of 18th Street, South Side, which afterwards became

* Now known as Sawtooth.

McKee Brothers, and where, to the writer's personal knowledge, such figured ware as R.L. tumblers, wines, eggs and nappies were pressed, beside "Star Bottom" tumblers, New York goblets, and pillared and fluted ware in car load lots. That was long before July 30th, 1878; before the war, before 'Mack' was born, perhaps or certainly before he worked in the factory or wrote nonsense for alleged glass journals.

"There are many of the glass workers still alive who gathered and pressed in that old factory, from which so many of the successful glassmakers of a later period graduated. From that old McKee factory sprang such men as William B. Schraff, the oarsman, and his brother Phillip, who became stockholders in and proprietors of the Co-operative Flint Glass Co., Beaver Falls, Pa., which was a blooming success from the first jump and is still one of the most profitable independent flint glass factories in the United States.

"In 1866 the firm of Richards & Hartley Flint Glass Co. built their works at Marion and Pride Streets (they reorganized and moved to Tarentum, Pa.) while the firm of Ripley & Co. established itself on South Tenth Street in the same year, and in 1875 D. C. Ripley and associates built their works at 9th and Bingham, George Duncan & Sons continuing to operate the Tenth Street factory on pressed tableware. Doyle & Co. built their works at 10th and Washington Streets in 1868, while the works on 18th Street, South Side, built in 1859 by Johnson, King & Co., which in 1883 became King, Son & Co., and in 1887 the King Glass Co. of which W. C. King, now with the United States Glass Co. was president, was originally started as a pressed tableware factory. Indeed, the firms of George Duncan & Sons (1875), Ripley & Co., Doyle & Co., Adams & Co. and the King Glass Co. were all of them almost exclusively engaged in making figured pressed glass and tableware from their inception, some of them fully 29 years prior to 1878, the date assigned by 'Mack' for the appearance of the polka dot pattern, alleged to have been probably among the earliest figuring cut upon iron molds to be reproduced in glass.

"The firm of Sheppard & Co., whose works occupied the site

now covered by the South Side hospital, corner 20th and Mary Streets, was built in 1863, and in 1865 became Campbell, Jones & Co., and at a later date, Jones, Cavitt & Co., made pressed figured tableware exclusively from the very start.

"But there is one other sovereign fact which should not be omitted in this connection as proving not only that figured pressed molds were in general use long prior to 1878, but that the industry had long before that date reached a point where the pressing of all kinds of glass was specialized. The Rochester Tumbler Company was organized in 1872, and rose rapidly to a specialty works, covering the entire field of pressed, plain and figured tumblers, sending its product into every city throughout the United States, and becoming one of the first American factories to reach out for and hold a profitable export trade.

"In 1856 Pittsburgh contained 33 factories, 14 of them being window glass houses, 8 were engaged in making flint glass tableware, 8 were making vials and drug ware and 2 were making black bottles. The flint glass factories made during that year 6,340 tons of flint glassware, valued at $1,147,540, and it is only a reasonable supposition that at least one or two pressed figure dishes were bundled up among that gorge of glassware. In 1865 there were 18 tableware factories in Pittsburgh, producing 4,200 tons of pressed tableware, valued at $2,000,000 and we are willing and ready to be qualified to the fact that most of it was figured pressed ware, because we made some of it ourselves.

"During the Centennial year, 1876, Pittsburgh operated 25 tableware factories, with 268 pots, producing 15,000 tons of glassware valued at $2,225,000.

"But enough we think has been shown to prove to any unprejudiced mind that, as usual, our friend of the *Commoner* does not know what he is talking about. If 'Mack' dares to provoke us a little further with his glass nonsense, we will undertake to prove that pressed figured glassware was made in American factories many years before his father dug turf in the bog of Allen, or fed the pigs of Skibereen."

Some other extremely interesting notes, which may have come

from an old scrapbook lent to a friend, should also be recorded here. I doubt if it would be possible to learn who wrote them. However, they have too much value to be passed by. Apparently it was a paper read by some member of the Glass Manufacturers' Association, telling of workmen who later became the heads of some of the leading glass factories. How those men climbed the ladder of success is a story of thrift, courage, tenacity and brains. It reads as follows:

"Between 1860 and 1870 many improvements were made in moulds and appliances for the production of pressed ware, handy levers on presses, the mould oven, the interior cooling of plungers with water, the eccentric key in place of the old lock in many places and the use of cold blast around the moulds and plungers. In fact, since that time very little improvement has been made in the methods employed in the manufacture of what is today (1890) known as pressed ware.

"I have in my possession an old account book of Bakewell, Pears & Company, covering a period from January 2, 1846, to May 1850, which contains the names of many of our friends who have since been prominent manufacturers themselves, and I doubt very much whether there is another firm that ever produced so many manufacturers. There were John Adams, William Doyle, Joseph Hale, James Reddich, Robert Bryce, John Bryce, James McDonald, John Steen, Thomas B. Atterbury, David Evans, and the first work I ever did in a glass house I did there as palot boy for Gaffer Steen in 1862. From this old book of Bakewell, Pears & Company's, it appears that John Adams, as presser, earned $1. per turn and drew wages as follows:

1846	Made	Drew
January	$ 24.17	$ 12.00
February	16.50	12.00
March	25.50	12.00
April	23.50	67.00
May	17.00	13.00
June	23.33	. . . .
July	38.33	. . . .
Total	$168.33	$116.00
Balance		52.33

119 No. 0 JUG
RUBINA VERDE

119 No. 2 JUG
RUBINA VERDE

No. 1 WATER JUG RUBINA

101 POLKA DOT CHEESE & COV. RUBINA

119 No. 5 JUG RUBINA VERDE

119 No. 4 JUG RUBINA

SET

314 No. 1 CREAM RUBINA VERDE

103 COV SPOONER

6 IN. 304 BOWL P.D.
RUBINAVERDE

308 P.D. OIL RUBINA

No. OT.
RUBINA VERDE

314 SPOON RUBINA

236 TUMBLER
RUBINA VERDE

11 COMP RUBINA

334 CELERY RUBINA

15 FINGER RUBINA

PLATE 94

An original version of the "Polka Dot" pattern, now known as Inverted Thumbprint.

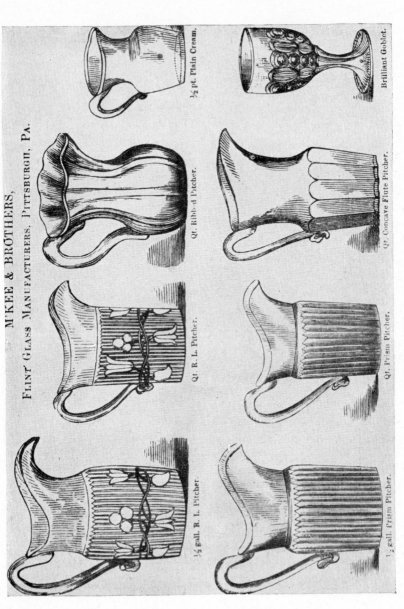

M'KEE & BROTHERS,

FLINT GLASS MANUFACTURERS, PITTSBURGH, PA.

½ pt. Plain Cream.

Brilliant Goblet.

Qt. Ribb-d Pitcher.

Qt. Concave Flute Pitcher.

Qt. R. L. Pitcher.

Qt. Prism Pitcher.

½ gall. R. L. Pitcher.

½ gall. Prism Pitcher.

PLATE 95

Original version of the "R.L." pattern, now known as Bellflower, from a M'Kee & Brothers catalogue of the 1850's.

M'KEE & BROTHERS,

FLINT GLASS MANUFACTURERS, PITTSBURGH, PA.

Eugenie Celery.

Eugenie Sugar.

Eugenie Goblet.

½ pt. Eugenie Footed Tumbler.

Eugenie Champagne.

Eugenie Wine.

Eugenie Cordial.

Eugenie Egg.

9 in. Eugenie Footed Dish and Cover.

4 in. Eugenie Footed Dish and Cover.

PLATE 96

"Figured Glass," in the Eugenie pattern, of the 1850's.

PLATE 97

View of the American Flint Glass Works, South Boston, Mass. from the Harbor during 1853.

NEW ENGLAND GLASS COMPANY'S WORKS, EAST CAMBRIDGE, MASS

PLATE 98
New England Glass Company's Works, East Cambridge, Mass. during 1851.

ADAMS & CO.

MANUF'RS

GLASS

PITTSBURGH.PA.

PLATE 99

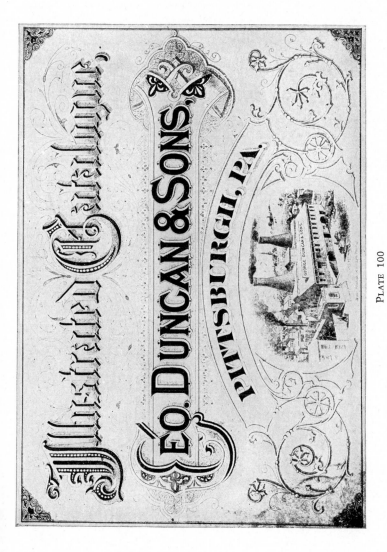

PLATE 100

Cover from illustrated catalogue of George Duncan & Sons, Pittsburgh, Pa.

PLATE 101

View of George Duncan & Sons' factory, in 1884.

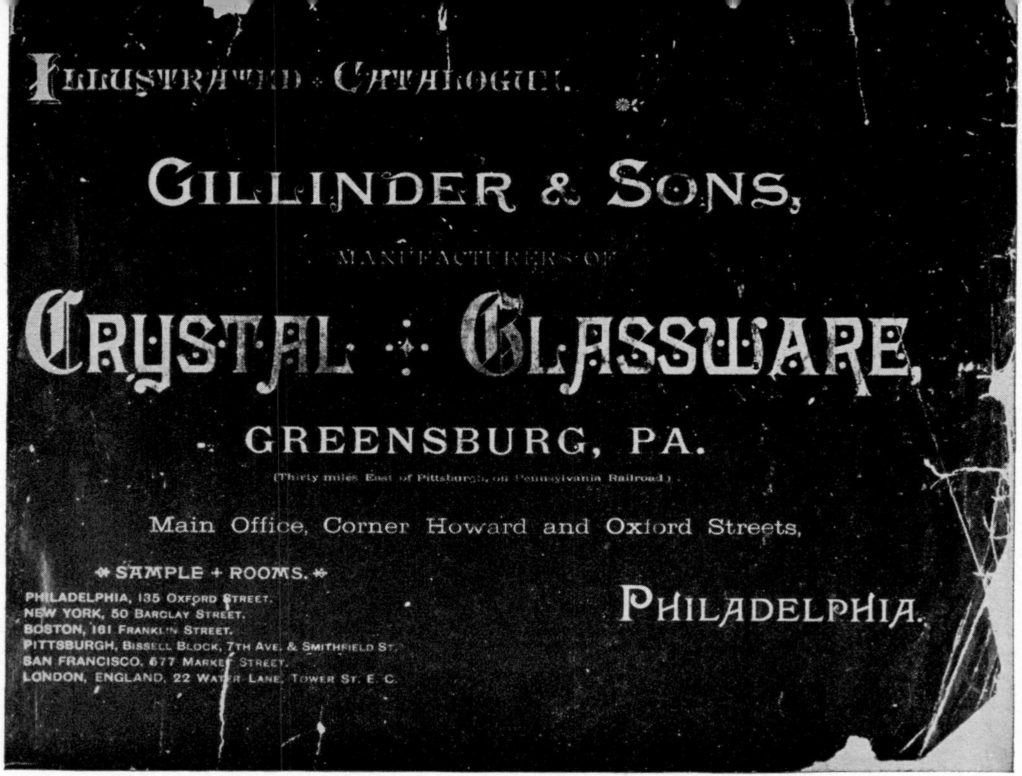

ILLUSTRATED CATALOGUE.

GILLINDER & SONS,

MANUFACTURERS OF

CRYSTAL :+: GLASSWARE,

GREENSBURG, PA.

(Thirty miles East of Pittsburgh, on Pennsylvania Railroad.)

Main Office, Corner Howard and Oxford Streets,

PHILADELPHIA.

* SAMPLE * ROOMS. *

PHILADELPHIA, 135 OXFORD STREET.
NEW YORK, 50 BARCLAY STREET.
BOSTON, 181 FRANKLIN STREET.
PITTSBURGH, BISSELL BLOCK, 7TH AVE. & SMITHFIELD ST.
SAN FRANCISCO, 677 MARKET STREET.
LONDON, ENGLAND, 22 WATER LANE, TOWER ST. E.C.

PLATE 102

Cover from Illustrated Catalogue of Gillinder & Sons, Greensburg. Pa.

"Robert Bryce was a presser and received $1. per turn. During 1846 his wages were advanced to $1.25 per turn. In 1847 they were advanced to $1.38 and so remained until June 13th, 1850.

"The most complete record of wages is that of John Steen, the excellent caster place workman of his time, and while this does not properly belong to the press branch, I hope to be pardoned for a brief digression, because of the strong light it throws on the gradual rise in wages in the flint glass industry during those early years when the pressed ware lines were making their first inroad upon the blown glass department.

"John Steen began to work for Bakewell, Pears & Company in April, 1845, at which time, it is thought, he moved from the East, fifty dollars being paid out for his moving expenses. Originally he was paid $1.87 per turn which remained unchanged during 1845, 1846, and 1847. He drew a weekly pay varying from $6. to $10. His wages were advanced to $20. per week in August, 1847. In August, 1848, to $21., September 1849 to $23., August, 1850, to $3. per turn or $24. per week continuing to 1851 when his account was transferred to another book.

"As soon as Mr. Steen's wages reached $20. per week, the charge of $6. per month for rent ceased to be recorded in the company's book, as he had evidently moved to better quarters. He also began to draw larger amounts per week, his balance vanished, he had become more liberal in his expenditures and likely more gay in his habits since he bought a decanter from the firm, paying $4. for it and drew an extra five dollars to fill it!

"While John Steen was receiving double as much as his companions, they were saving their money and nine out of the little party had factories of their own, or were partners of those that had, a few years later.

"With the exception of what was done by Bakewell, Pears & Company, James B. Lyons & Company, Wm. Phillips, John Best and John Adams in Pittsburgh, representing those well known firms with which they were connected, there was practically little headway made from 1850 to 1855 and there having been no protective duty on pressed ware previous to 1861, the development of the industry was slow, but with a 25 per cent duty the progress was rapid.

"From March, 1865 to 1866 the amount of war taxes collected from the Pittsburgh glass manufacturers was $276,364.44. This amount was derived from·a six per cent revenue tax. Of course, this included all branches.

"The Census of 1880 showed the amount of capital invested in the glassware factories of the United States to have been $6,907,378.00, and in 1890, $15,448,196.00, or an increase of 123 per cent.

"The number of presses in operation in 1880 were 522, in 1890, 804 and during the same period the number of furnaces increased from 130 to 238, an increase of 83 per cent. The number of pots from 1,247 to 2,311, an increase of 85 per cent.

	Per cent
In ten years between 1880 and 1890 there was an increase in the number of factories	71
Increase in number of furnaces	83
Increase in number of pots	85
Increase in number of employees	83
Value of product	94
Wages	125

"Having traced the industry from what must have been a few years within the time it was first accomplished to 1890, the rest may be safely left to such successors as shall enjoy the honor of entertaining future annual meetings."

Chapter XVII

VICTORIAN NOVELTIES

At the time of the Centennial Exposition in Philadelphia in 1876, we had a souvenir-loving public. The Centennial naturally prompted the making of historical and political pieces of glassware. A great many of these took the form of small, utilitarian objects, such as wall pockets for matches, toothpick holders, match holders, little mustard jars, and all sorts of small pieces which visitors to the Fair could buy and carry home to their friends. These pieces proved to be so popular that they were continued over a number of years. Today we find both men and women interested in the acquisition of these Victorian novelties. They have in their favor the fact that they are colorful and take up very little room. One does not necessarily have to collect a large number of them. A quaint little old jar for horseradish on the table, with a horse's head protruding from each side as handles, may give rise to interesting table conversation. The baskets and other pieces, used for cigarettes, fit into almost any room in a house. Because so many collectors have inquired about the history of these objects, it was decided to illustrate a number of them, while it is still possible to state accurately when and where they were produced. At least, it is possible in most cases because a large number of the pictures were taken directly from old trade catalogues. While these pieces may not seem important to some collectors today, the historical data may be considered of value in later years.

One of the old Glass Makers' Association rules was not to copy patterns or designs without permission. They also passed a resolution not to undersell their competitors.

Many of the objects pictured in the group of Victorian novelties in this chapter were made by more than one company and it seems certain that permission to copy them was not always obtained. The gypsy kettle appears in more than one pattern and with or without feet. One type, which has a flat base, is in a fine cut pattern and curves inward at the top, with a flaring edge. Patent laws are now and always have been very loose in the United States. During the 1850's the Boston & Sandwich Glass Co. was making a pattern of tableware which today is known as Ribbed Palm. M'Kee Bros. of Pittsburgh made it during the same period and called it "Sprig" pattern. One company produced it with the leaf pattern convex and the other with the leaf concave. This was one method of avoiding an accusation of plagiarism. The pattern known as Honeycomb was made over a long period of years by almost every factory producing tableware. Each one varied the form or the design enough to elude conviction of plagiarism and in each case the company called its design by a different name.

Practically all of the novelties illustrated here were produced during the 1870's and 1880's. A few were carried on longer because the United States Glass Co. of Pittsburgh absorbed eighteen of the older companies in 1891 and they continued those items which were still in demand. It is not possible for me to name all the variations of the novelties shown, or by whom they were copied. I am naming the companies known to have made them, according to old trade catalogues in my possession.

PLATE 103

1. TORCH MATCH HOLDER. Listed originally as "Liberty Torch." Produced by Bryce Bros. of Pittsburgh, Pa. Colors are not mentioned but there were probably several shades.

2. WALL BASKET. Bryce Bros. of Pittsburgh, Pa., made this as a wall pocket for matches.

3. CANNON. This unusual glass piece had an open space below the cannon for either matches or toothpicks. The makers were Bryce Bros. of Pittsburgh, Pa.

PLATE 103
Victorian Novelties.
(See pages 295, 300, 301)

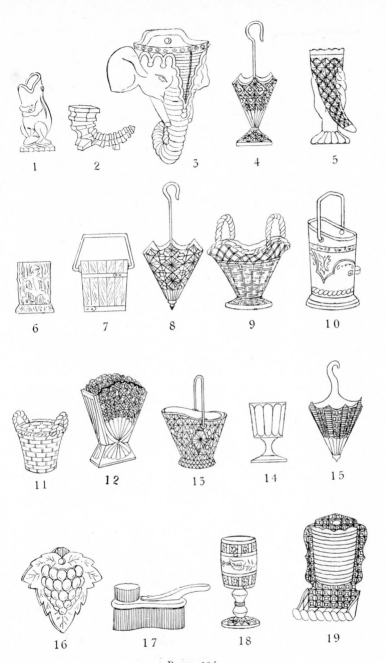

PLATE 104
Victorian Novelties.
(See pages 301, 302)

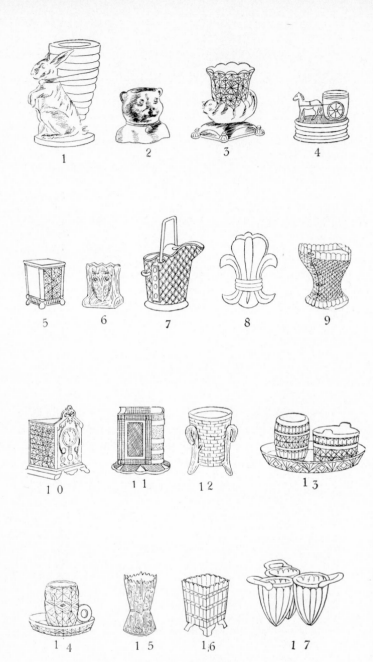

PLATE 105
Victorian Novelties.
(See pages 302, 303, 304)

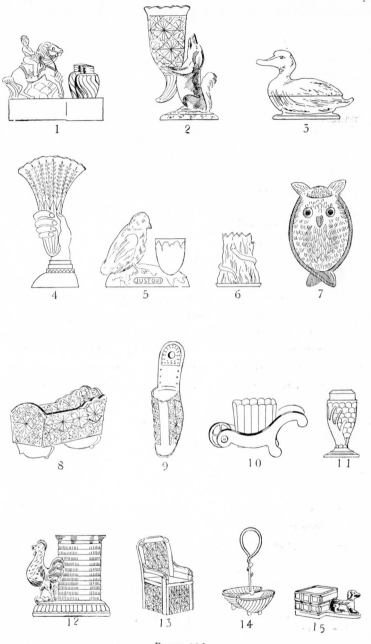

PLATE 106
Victorian Novelties.
(See pages 304, 305)

4. DOG KENNEL. Bryce Bros. of Pittsburgh, Pa., listed this as a "novelty." The roof served as a cover for a box that was intended for matches or toothpicks.

5. ICE CREAM FREEZER. This jar was so named by the makers, Bryce Bros. of Pittsburgh, Pa.

6. BIRD BASKET. Bryce Bros. made this little receptacle as a novelty, to be used for matches or toothpicks.

7. GYPSY KETTLE. These were made by Bryce Bros. of Pittsburgh, Pa., in two sizes and in several colors. They were sold either open or covered. Some of the kettles with lids were used as mustard or horseradish dishes. They had wire handles.

8. BASKET COMPOTE, with wire handle. 4½ inches. Bryce Bros. of Pittsburgh, Pa., made this to be used for any utilitarian purpose.

9. BASKET. Gillinder & Sons produced this decorated piece at Greensburg, Pa., and listed it as a basket.

10. BASKET MATCH HOLDER, produced by Gillinder & Sons at Greensburg, Pa. It is listed as "No. 10 Basket," so this form was made in at least that many varieties or sizes.

11. OBLONG BASKET, made by Gillinder & Sons of Philadelphia, Pa. Colors are not mentioned in their catalogue, but were probably made.

12. OVAL BASKET. Gillinder & Sons, Greensburg, Pa. Colors are not mentioned in the catalogue. Some basket match holders were made in purple Marble glass. Others have been seen in the same material, bearing the British registry mark.

13. TALL ROUND BASKET MATCH HOLDER. Made by Gillinder & Sons of Greensburg, Pa. It is listed as "No. 3 Basket."

14. This was produced by Bryce Bros. of Pittsburgh, Pa., as "Wicker Basket No. 2" because it had open handles instead of closed, as in No. 15, listed below.

15. Originally termed "Wicker Basket," this was made by Bryce Bros. of Pittsburgh, Pa., and carried on later by the United States Glass Co. It was listed in amber, blue and crystal.

16. PIG PAPERWEIGHT. This stippled-pig paperweight has

been reported to me, by an old glassworker, to have been made by the Bellaire Goblet Co. of Findlay, Ohio.

17. HORSERADISH JAR, made by Adams & Co. of Pittsburgh, Pa.

PLATE 104

1. FROG. Match or toothpick holder, made by the King Glass Co. of Pittsburgh, Pa., in amber, blue and crystal.

2. ODD TOOTHPICK OR MATCH HOLDER, produced by King Glass Co. in amber, blue and crystal. Same style was made covered, as an inkwell.

3. ELEPHANT. Wall-pocket match holder made by King Glass Co. in amber, blue and crystal.

4. UMBRELLA, footed. Made in clear glass and colors by Doyle & Co. of Pittsburgh, Pa. It is unusual to find this match holder footed, as more of them are found without the foot. The latter were meant to be hung up by the wire handle.

5. CORNUCOPIA. This is listed as "Medium Cornucopia" by Doyle & Co. who also made a larger size. It is similar to the Pressed Diamond pattern and may be seen in clear and colors.

6. MONKEY. Bryce Bros. of Pittsburgh, Pa., made this little holder for toothpicks, in clear glass and in colors. It is comparatively common today.

7. TOY BUCKET. The pail with wire handle was made in three sizes, in clear glass and in colors, including amethyst, though the latter is rare. Bryce Bros. of Pittsburgh, Pa., produced this style bucket.

8. UMBRELLA, WITH WIRE HANDLE, so it could be hung up. It was made by Doyle & Co. of Pittsburgh, Pa., in clear glass and in colors.

9. BASKET, footed. Bryce Bros. of Pittsburgh, Pa., made this particular style basket, in which the woven section of the form and handles varies from the others illustrated.

10. COAL HOD. Bryce Bros. of Pittsburgh, Pa., produced this novelty match holder with wire handle, in clear and in

colors. They are scarce today. Other styles in coal buckets, in a fine cut pattern, were made in amber, blue and crystal.

11. BASKET MATCH HOLDER, without a foot. Maker unknown at present.

12. FAN TOOTHPICK. Bryce Bros. of Pittsburgh, Pa., made this piece, which is usually found in color. It is rather large for a match holder but can be used for short-stemmed flowers.

13. "SKUTTLE" MATCH OR TOOTHPICK HOLDER in Daisy and Button Pattern. This was a novelty made by Adams & Co. of Pittsburgh, Pa., which may have been carried on later by the United States Glass Co. in clear and colors.

14. OPTIC is the original name for this toothpick or match holder. It was made by the King Glass Co. of Pittsburgh, Pa., in amber, blue and crystal.

15. UMBRELLA WALL POCKET. This unusual match holder, which is rarely found, was produced by the King Glass Co. of Pittsburgh, Pa., in amber, blue and crystal.

16. GRAPE WALL POCKET, for matches. The leaf is stippled and the grapes stand out in relief. This was made by the United States Glass Co. of Pittsburgh, Pa.

17. SHOE BRUSH. This was listed by the United States Glass Co. of Pittsburgh, Pa., as "Shoe Brush for Match or Picks."

18. BARREL. This was originally designed as a toothpick holder by Bryce Bros. of Pittsburgh. It may be found in clear and in colors and possibly plain, without the engraving.

19. MATCH SAFE. Under the title of "Novelties" this piece was made for matches by Bryce Bros. of Pittsburgh, Pa. It may have been a handy wall pocket but it is certainly something of a curiosity.

PLATE 105

1. RABBIT TOOTHPICK OR MATCH HOLDER. It is one of the few novelties produced by Richards & Hartley of Tarentum, Pa. Colors are not mentioned in the catalogue but may have been made.

2. DARWIN TOOTHPICK HOLDER. Someone in the Richards & Hartley Co. had a sense of humor when they named this monkey the "Darwin." The surface is stippled. Colors are not mentioned but were probably made.

3. CAT TOOTHPICK OR MATCH HOLDER. Most of these small novelties were originally intended for toothpicks but in this enlightened age are used for matches. Most collectors are familiar with the cat on a cushion, supporting a Daisy and Button receptacle. These were made in amber, blue and crystal. Blue is very scarce.

4. HORSE WITH CART MATCH HOLDER, made by the United States Glass Co. of Pittsburgh in clear and colors. This is not the type that has been reproduced.

5. MATCH BOX IN DAISY AND BUTTON. This was made by the United States Glass Co. of Pittsburgh but is seldom seen today.

6. TREE TRUNK MATCH BOX with owl's face showing in front. The United States Glass Co. of Pittsburgh made these, in clear glass and colors.

7. COAL BUCKET, made originally by Bryce Bros. of Pittsburgh and carried on for several years by the United States Glass Co. They may be found in amber, blue and crystal.

8. MATCH OR TOOTHPICK HOLDER, produced by the United States Glass Co. of Pittsburgh at the same period they were making Harrison and Cleveland campaign tumblers, "Tecumseh" Log Cabin mustard jars and hats labeled "He's all right," called the Harrison hat. Other items on the same page of the catalogue are dated 1892.

9. CORSET TOOTHPICK is the original designation of this unusual piece, which was made by the Bellaire Goblet Co. of Findlay, Ohio, and appears in one of their catalogues under date of July, 1890. This item could have been carried over from an earlier year.

10. CLOCK MATCH SAFE. Sides were in Daisy and Button pattern. No colors are mentioned but doubtless they were made.

The clock match safe was made at the same time as the above by the Bellaire Goblet Co. of Findlay, Ohio.

11. BOOK "for matches or picks," according to Adams & Co. of Pittsburgh, who made it. These are rarely seen today.

12. MATCH OR TOOTHPICK HOLDER, made in amber, blue and crystal by Bryce Bros. of Pittsburgh and later carried on for some years by the United States Glass Co.

13. SMOKER'S SET. This three-piece set was made by the United States Glass Co. of Pittsburgh. Colors are not mentioned in the old catalogue but were undoubtedly made.

14. CANDLESTICK MATCH BOX. This novelty was produced by the United States Glass Co. of Pittsburgh.

15. This dainty receptacle was labeled as a toothpick holder by the King Glass Co. of Pittsburgh. It was made in amber, blue and clear glass.

16. LONDON MATCH VASE was the original designation for this match holder. It matches a pattern collectible in sets of tableware, known today as Picket. The King Glass Co. of Pittsburgh made them in amber, blue and clear glass.

17. TRIPOD toothpick or match holder. This novelty was made by Bryce Bros. of Pittsburgh, in clear glass and colors.

PLATE 106

1. Unusual salt and pepper shakers reposing in a stand ornamented by a man on horseback. The set is in white, with frosted, or satin, finish. No record has been found as to where it was made.

2. DOG SUPPORTING CORNUCOPIA VASE. This may be found in clear glass and colors, though they are scarce. So far I have found no record of who made these.

3. DUCK PICKLE DISH, covered. Gillinder & Sons of Philadelphia picture this in a catalogue of items made during the 1870's and 1880's.

4. HAND BOUQUET HOLDER. These attractive flower vases were made by Gillinder & Sons at Greensburg, Pa.

5. CHICKEN MATCH HOLDER, marked "Just Out." It has a frosted finish. These also were a product of Gillinder & Sons at their factory in Greensburg, Pa.

6. TREE TRUNK MATCH HOLDER, with snake twined around it. These may be found in clear glass or colors. There is as yet no record of who produced it.

7. OVAL PICKLE DISH, called "Etched Pickle" by the Central Glass Co. of Wheeling, W. Va., who made it as well as other novelties in the way of covered animal dishes.

8. CRADLE in amber Daisy and Button. There is no record at this time as to where this match holder was made but it will probably be found in other colors, as well as clear glass. Rare.

9. MATCH SLIPPER, made in crystal and colors by the United States Glass Co. of Pittsburgh. It is a wall pocket. Rare in any color except yellow.

10. BARROW SALT, with revolving Britannia wheel. This interesting piece was produced by the United States Glass Co. of Pittsburgh. Colors are not mentioned but it was probably made in different shades.

11. HAND SALT SHAKER. An interesting type that is seldom found. This was made by the Central Glass Co. of Wheeling, W. Va.

12. ROOSTER MATCH OR TOOTHPICK HOLDER. This item was a product of the United States Glass Co. of Pittsburgh, Pa. Sometimes it will be found decorated with silver or gold.

13. AMBER GLASS CHAIR. A rare novelty, seldom found. I have no record of where it was made.

14. DOUBLE SALT WITH METAL HANDLE, produced by the Central Glass Co. of Wheeling, W. Va. This concern made many other novelty wares, including stoves, carriages, lanterns, etc.

15. DOG WITH CART, INDIVIDUAL SALT, originally made by the Central Glass Co. of Wheeling, W. Va. This particular salt has been widely reproduced and may be seen frequently in gift shops.

Chapter XVIII

ANIMAL DISHES

During recent years, when collectors began to specialize more than formerly, a fad started in the way of accumulating covered animal dishes. It was discovered that there existed a great variety of subjects, some of which were marked with the factory name. The value of these dishes had been underestimated, because there are rare types and rare colors. Factory-marked pieces also enhance values. Perhaps the reason there was not so much interest in these dishes at first was because the small hens and roosters were seen everywhere and, therefore, considered quite common. This can be accounted for in a story told me by Mr. West, founder and former president of the Westmoreland Glass Co. Mr. West assured me that the prosperity of his concern was due to the very large sales of the little hen dishes in the old days, filled with prepared mustard, which sold in carload lots at ten cents each! I have found one of the hen dishes with the name of the Westmoreland Specialty Co., Grapeville, Pa., still on it. These were very common in milk-white (both hens and roosters) but were more scarce in white with blue heads, in opaque blue with white heads, and in any other color would be considered a rarity. However, Mr. West's idea of chicken-covered dishes was not original. The only original part of it was in doing a mass production job—plus the mustard.

A number of factories produced all sorts of animal dishes. M'Kee Bros. of Pittsburgh and the Central Glass Co. of Wheeling, W. Va., contributed their share. Challinor, Taylor & Co. of Tarentum, Pa., made a line of their own which was continued by the United States Glass Co. of Pittsburgh, Pa. Most of the brown, or so-called "caramel" colored, animals were made at Greentown, Ind., by the Indiana Tumbler & Goblet Co.

In *Early American Pressed Glass* there are two pages of illustrations of covered dishes in milk-white, including the upright eagle, Battleship Maine, an extremely rare small hen on a nest, fish, turtle, lion, hen on a sleigh, Battleship with Uncle Sam on cover, another with Admiral Dewey, the cow mustard jar (tongue is handle for mustard spoon) an unusual fish, the ordinary five-inch hen dish, the tall upright covered owl (which may be found in milk-white, opaque blue and opaque lavender), a large round hen dish, the base of which has an openwork edge like the plates and an oval dish marked "The American Hen."

Plate 107 pictures a farmyard group, taken from an original trade catalogue of Challinor, Taylor & Co. of Tarentum, Pa. These are all in milk-white and "eyed." The same dishes were sold without eyes, but the extra labor of inserting eyes increased the cost. The workmanship displayed in all these dishes is excellent. Of all those on Plate 107, the eagle on a nest with small birds about her, is the most difficult to find. Another Challinor group shows two large milk-white roosters in the top row, the swan in the center, and a duck and hen in the lower row. These are all eyed and decorated. The swan is marked "Black Swan, Eyed," so one cannot tell whether this meant it was painted or made in black glass. One catalogue sheet shows a large milk-white rooster with red comb and another rooster the same size with the nest white but the rooster painted in natural colors. In the center is the swan, its bill yellow, neck green and body black. The nest is white. In the lower row are the duck and hen, both with the nests white and the bodies brightly decorated in natural colors.

A page from a United States Glass Co. catalogue, obviously of a later date, displays a "medium hen, decorated," a small hen, decorated, rooster, swan and duck, all decorated. The swan is in white with a red bill and red eyes, with the brim of the base painted green. There is also pictured the large turkey jam jar painted flamboyantly in bright colors, the base being green. These turkey jam jars were reproduced along about

1925 or 1926 and the market was flooded with them. The first that came out were in clear glass but they sold so well that the producers brought them out in green, amber and a salmon pink —a shade never seen in our old glass. The turkey jam jar is one of the best reproductions, as regards detail, that has appeared to torment collectors.

One can distinguish some of the animal dishes as to their respective factories, by varying details. For instance, the brim of the base of the Challinor duck dish has ridges, while the United States Glass Co. duck has a plain brim.

Both Challinor, Taylor & Co. and the United States Glass Co. advertise a "Farm Yard Assortment," made in opal, turquoise and olive green.

On Plate 108, No. 1 was listed as a "Fish Pickle" by Challinor, Taylor & Co. It is not known where the rabbit (No. 2) was made. No. 3, a lobster, No. 4, the "British Lion," and No. 5, the dove, cannot be attributed to any one factory at present. No. 6, which appears to be a robin on a nest, is a particularly decorative dish. It is somewhat larger than the preceding ones, and may be found in milk-white and opaque blue. If there are any other colors, I have not seen them. The dog and the cat (No. 7 and No. 8) are familiar to most collectors. Sometimes they are found in milk-white, often in opaque blue with white heads or vice versa, but rarely in any other colors. The turtle (No. 9) I have seen only in milk-white. They are quite scarce. The fish dish is not a great rarity. The chicken emerging from an egg (No. 11) is the only one I have seen, but I am informed it is found fairly readily in localities of the country I seldom visit. The duck (No. 12) I have and it is milk-white, with remnants of some original painted colors still clinging to its wings. One just like it is illustrated in a Gillinder & Sons catalogue, marked "Duck Pickle and Cover." I have been told that these have been copied in Europe and that they were brought into this country in large numbers just before the present war started.

On Plate 109, No. 1 is a milk-white owl pitcher (eyed) and it is an interesting piece to own. These were made in opaque blue and other colors, by Challinor, Taylor & Co. The dog dish next to it (No. 2) is in amber, with nice detail. Perhaps it was produced in other colors, also. The Bull's Head (No. 3) is an unusual dish, rarely seen today. It is listed in "opal," or milk-white. The swan next to it was made originally in opaque green, opaque blue and milk-white. These were never plentiful, and today are very scarce. The most interesting dish on Plate 109 is the eagle, with wings outspread, protecting her little birds. This is another Challinor product which was carried on by the United States Glass Co. in the same colors as the swan. The swan (No. 6), next to the eagle dish, is seldom found these days. The United States Glass Co. produced the large hen and rooster dishes, with the basket-weave nest, shown in Nos. 7 and 8. Another hen, not pictured, rests on a bowl with an openwork edge. These particular hens have been found in an opaque blue and white marbelized effect, as well as in brown and white. It is not possible to give a positive attribution to those, at present.

Plate 110 pictures a cow, covered, dish in a frosted, or satin, finish. These have also been found in milk-white, clear blue and black. The frosted dishes were not uncommon some years ago, but any of them are rare today. The robin dish in the center of the upper row has been described, as it appears on Plate 108. The frosted swan at the end of the row is unusual and rare today. Some appear marked "Pat. Applied For." They have also been seen in milk-white but I have not heard of any other colors. These are thought to be from one of the factories in the Pittsburgh glass district.

In the lower row of Plate 110 the first hen dish at the left is an unusual one. It is said to be a Flaccus hen, though not marked. There are other Flaccus animal dishes which are marked, such as the running deer, standing dog, and a rabbit sitting up, instead of reclining, as most of the animals do in this line of dishes. These specimens, which were produced by the Flaccus Company, of Wheeling, West Va., have elaborate bases depicting field and woodland scenes.

In the center of the lower row, the hand holding a dove is familiar to most collectors. The base always has an openwork edge. Sometimes the ring has a jewel and sometimes not, like the animals which come "eyed or without." The hand dish is reported to be a product of the old Atterbury Glass Co. of Pittsburgh.

The last dish in the lower row (at the right) is also said to be a robin on a nest, but it will be noted that he has a cherry in his beak. Almost all of the so-called Caramel glass animal dishes were made in Greentown, Ind., by the Indiana Tumbler & Goblet Co. This style robin dish has been found in milk-white and a clear blue. Probably other colors may be found.

An interesting, as well as rare, group of animals is shown on Plate 111. The first at the left in the upper row is a Flaccus. The ornate lower part of the dish is typical of all the dishes in this particular group. Sometimes the name may be found embossed on the base. The hen, rooster and cat in the upper row are all by M'Kee Bros. of Pittsburgh. It will be noticed that the bases are all ribbed and are identical.

In the lower row of Plate 111, the horse is a M'Kee, and may be found both marked and unmarked. Most of them are unmarked. The sheep next to it is by M'Kee also. The M'Kee dishes are generally found in milk-white and the modeling and workmanship indicate a master hand in design, as well as in cutting molds.

The dove dish next to the sheep on Plate 111 is an interesting dish, as is the frog at the end of the line. There is no accurate information about either one at present. Both are important dishes to own, as are all the Flaccus and M'Kee animals.

There is a round M'Kee dish with a bird on the cover, not illustrated, that is usually marked with an embossed "M'Kee" on the inside of the cover. This round dish may be found in clear yellow and in milk-white. It is well to watch the inside of the cover on the animal dishes.

All the dishes on Plate 112 are M'Kee products and may be found marked or unmarked. Sometimes the marks may be seen on the inside of the base. Later, all these dishes were made at Greentown, Ind. Some of them will be found in the brown caramel glass. It will be noticed that the covers of these particular dishes will fit no other bases. From the illustrations it may be seen that all bases are ribbed. Of the group, the turkey, lion, cow, squirrel and rabbit are the most scarce.

The Central Glass Co. of Wheeling, W. Va., made three sizes of the "covered egg dish," meaning the hen on the nest. They also produced the lovely frosted duck, the base of which shows cattails and water lilies, pictured on Plate 113. This one measures 8½ inches long. So far, I have heard of it only in the frosted, or satin, finish. It was probably made along in the 1880's. The duck in the center of Plate 113 is a M'Kee, and is found both marked and unmarked. More of the known M'Kee animal dishes are found unmarked than marked, so naturally the marked specimens have an enhanced value.

The third duck, or that in the bottom row, is termed by some collectors the "bobtailed duck" and is quite common. At present there is no proof as to where it was made but it appears to be a Westmoreland Glass Co. product.

One old glassworker told me that he was sent to the zoo by his superior to look over the animals and report on which he thought would make suitable subjects for dishes.

The large frosted duck at the top of Plate 114 is somewhat similar to the frosted Central Glass Co. duck shown on Plate 113. The workmanship is so excellent that it is unfortunate a positive attribution cannot be given at this time. It measures 8½ inches long.

The small milk-white duck in the center of Plate 114 is also found in an opal coloring, sometimes a fiery opalescent. It is not known where it was made. Certainly it is an interesting pose, quite different from any of the others.

The two ducks swimming across the lower row in Plate 114 appear to be the United States Glass Co. product. One is in milk-white and the other in clear glass. Both have red eyes, inserted.

In the top row of Plate 115 are pictured three of the long ducks made by the old Atterbury Glass Co. These were produced originally in milk-white, in milk-white with opaque blue heads, in milk-white with amethyst heads, and all in amethyst, the last-named color having the greatest value. Like many of the other animal dishes, they were sold "eyed or without." When they did have eyes, the milk-white usually had red eyes, the amethyst had turquoise blue, and the white with blue head was often found without any eyes. One duck has been heard of in clear green glass but I never saw it.

Unfortunately, the perpetrators of frauds saw fit to reproduce the Atterbury duck, and the new ones have been made in amethyst, in milk-white, and in any number of color combinations. It has made a difficult situation for those antique dealers who have genuine old ones of value, because they found their customers could buy more cheaply elsewhere and usually the bargain ducks turned out to be reproductions. Having studied reproductions for years, I can tell the old from the new, so if anyone has a duck about which he is in doubt, I shall be glad to write him the points of difference.

The middle duck in Plate 115 is a close-up view of the pair in Plate 114. Below it is a bottle stopper, with a duck perched atop it. These may be found in clear glass with the bill and eye painted in color. Some small animals of this type were made by the Boston & Sandwich Glass Co. but this one appears to have been made by the Westmoreland Glass Co. before Mr. West retired and the present operators took over. There is a small open duck salt, in which the detail around the eyes and bill is similar to that on the bottle stopper, which was also made some years ago by the Westmoreland Glass Co. of Grapeville, Pa. The salts have been reproduced in recent years, possibly from the original mold in clear glass, milk-white, amber, and perhaps in some other colors. They will be seen frequently in gift shops and sometimes, unfortunately, they find their way into antique shops. Very often it is difficult for

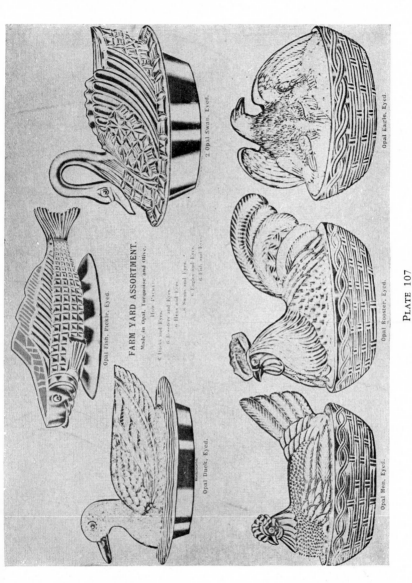

FARM YARD ASSORTMENT.
Made in Opal, Turquoise and Olive.
How Packed.
6 Ducks and Eyes.
6 Roosters and Eyes.
6 Hens and Eyes.
6 Swan and Eyes.
6 Eagles and Eyes.
6 Fish and Eyes.

Opal Fish, Pickle, Eyed.

2 Opal Swan, Eyed.

Opal Duck, Eyed.

Opal Eagle, Eyed.

Opal Rooster, Eyed.

Opal Hen, Eyed.

PLATE 107

Animal dishes, as shown in a Challinor, Taylor & Co. catalogue.

PLATE 108
Milk-white and opaque colored animal dishes.

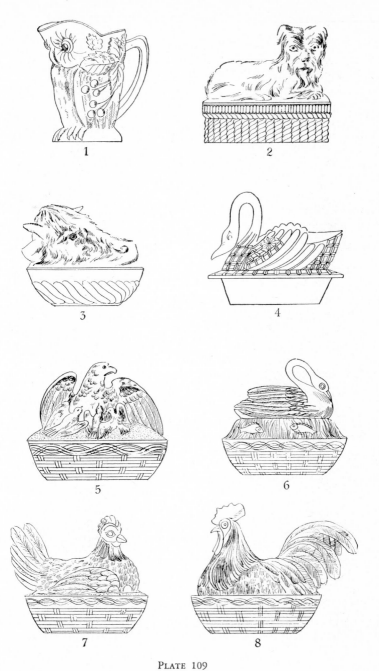

PLATE 109

Milk-white covered dishes, including an amber dog dish and owl pitcher.

PLATE 110

Animal dishes . . . . Wisconsin and Minnesota

PLATE 111

Rare animal dishes, from the M'Kee and the Flaccus factories, and a rare frog, maker unknown.

PLATE 112

Rare McKee covered dishes which may be found with the factory name, or unmarked.

Collection of Robert Van Deventer.

Three duck dishes, including one large style in a frosted finish.

PLATE 114

Three duck dishes, including a rare large one with a frosted finish.

PLATE 115

Duck dishes, plus a duck atop a bottle stopper.

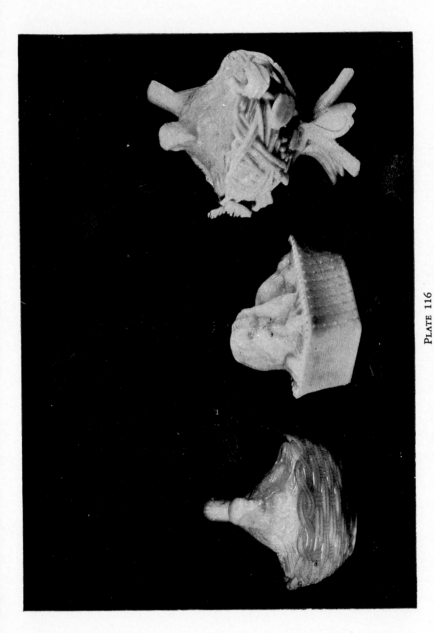

PLATE 116

Two modern Vallerysthal birds, from Alsace. A rare Spaniel made by the Boston & Sandwich Glass Co.

dealers to know whether objects they buy in good faith, usually with a plausible story thrown in for good measure, are old or new. Both dealers and collectors must study those pieces which have been copied because it is always possible to detect the spurious.

All the ducks pictured in Plates 113, 114 and 115 are from the collection of Robert Van Deventer, who would be delighted to know of any specimens he does not have. At this writing he is with an Engineering Corps in the Army of the United States.

In 1933 Mr. Fred C. Becker of Jeanette, Pa., presented me with a catalogue of the Westmoreland Glass Co. of Grapeville, Pa. It is a large and interesting catalogue. Many collectors might be shocked to see glassware which they are collecting pictured in this book, which must come under the heading of modern wares. There are copies of the "lacy Sandwich" tie-backs in the 2¼, 3 and 4½ inch sizes. The individual duck open salt is shown, as well as the covered camel dish. Reproductions of this camel have been flooding the market, so it is quite likely they were made in this country instead of being imported. I cannot vouch for this statement because I have not compared the Westmoreland camel with the more recent copies. The catalogue pictures the little "Toy Chick," which is an individual salt size. These are seen today in gift shops, in green, amber, and clear with a satin finish. The same old hen dish which Mr. West sold in carload lots along about 1892 and 1893 also is shown. Apparently he found that interest in these dishes never died out entirely.

In Plate 116 are shown two Vallerysthal specimens. Many inquiries have come in to me about animal dishes bearing this mark. Between the two Vallerysthal dishes is a rectangular covered milk-white dish with a spaniel on the cover. The dog is not in very good company: the Vallerysthal pieces are modern and the dog is one of the exceptionally few animal dishes we can positively attribute to Sandwich. Apparently it was another attempt by the Boston & Sandwich Glass Co. to meet midwestern competition. This attempt must have been short-lived because the spaniel in my collection is the only one I have ever been able to buy. The detail is excellent, with a diamond pattern in relief on both long sides of the base and a fine stippling on the ends. The spaniel looks rather sad, as most spaniels are apt to do! The white in the dish is not a dense, chalk-like white, but has a slight greenish cast to it, particularly in the cover.

The glass factory at Vallerysthal is probably the oldest in Europe and was operating almost to the day the present world conflict started. Apparently they produced a wide variety of animal dishes along about 1936 and until 1939. Some of them have "Vallerysthal" embossed in the base and others are unmarked. The bird shown at the left is in opaque blue and is marked. I purchased it in a gift shop. At one time they had very good-looking rooster dishes, fairly large, in both white and opaque blue, which also came from Vallerysthal.

An entire history of the Vallerysthal factory, which is longer than that of Baccarat in France, has no place in this chapter. For the benefit of those interested in their animal dishes, I can say that it was located in that section of Europe known as Alsace, near Marmoutier. The earliest known history of the factory begins with Charles the Bold, Duke of Burgundy, in the year 1469. He was also known as "Charles the Rash." He was continually starting wars, in an effort to enlarge his duchy. How a glass factory could flourish during such a tumultuous reign is difficult to understand. Charles had an archenemy in Louis XI (1461–1483) who was finally responsible for blasting the attempt of Charles to establish a Middle Kingdom, between France and Germany. Charles of Burgundy was finally killed in an ill-advised battle at Nancy, in 1477. Louis XI was progressive, and one of his many good deeds was to encourage Italian craftsmen to settle in France and manufacture glass.

In 1531, the first Nuremberg Glass Works was started by Venetians. By 1550 Lille, Liège, Munzthal, St. Louis, Vallerysthal and Baccarat were all under one duke. The glassworks in Vallerysthal, St. Louis and Munzthal were famous in 1580 for producing "colorless glass." These glassworks were connected with an early factory in Lille, which was known for good glass as early as 1450.

The Vallerysthal factory was under the direction of Louis René Edouard de Rohm from 1734 until 1803. Conditions must have been going from bad to worse at that period, because in 1778 the Archbishop of Strasbourg came and helped to revive the declining factories of Vallerysthal, St. Louis and Munzthal.

This résumé sketches the early history of Vallerysthal, which survived and flourished from time to time until World War II once more closed its doors.

Fragments of the beautiful large translucent jade green hen pictured on the jacket of this book have been excavated at the site of the Boston & Sandwich Glass Co. Besides the spaniel, pictured on Plate 116, it is the only covered dish which can be positively attributed to that factory at this time. There are, of course, the little Sandwich bear ointment jars found in black glass, milk-white, opaque blue and possibly other colors.

The green hen has a thick and elaborate brim where the top joins the base. This entire dish carries considerably more fine detail than is apparent in the illustration. Any specimen of this hen is rare. So far, it has been found with or without a frosted finish in yellow, translucent white, translucent blue in a variety of shades, clear glass, clear blue, and translucent green, listed in order of rarity.

Since reproductions of the turkey jam jar, Atterbury duck and Vallerysthal pieces have been mentioned, it may be well to speak of the 5-inch milk-white hen and rooster dishes, sometimes found entirely white or again with the combs painted a bright red. Large size milk-white hen and rooster dishes were on the market in 1938. Within the past two years, the Challinor duck with rippled brim has appeared in department stores, as well as the small rabbit shown in Number 2 on Plate 108.

Chapter XIX

GLASS HATS

Group I

Collectors of antiques today are generally specialists. During the early 1920's many people went in for casual purchases, which resulted in mass accumulations, rather than for industrious study and discriminating buying. Several reasons can be offered in explanation. Money was even more plentiful than it is now. Antiques of all descriptions were plentiful. House-to-house canvassing on the part of those who bought to sell to large dealers had not then depleted the countryside. Blown glass, historical flasks, cup plates, paperweights, pewter, pattern glass, and every sort of collectible could still be picked up at bargain prices. Counterfeit pieces, particularly in glass, were seldom encountered. Pattern glass was so little known that there was no standardized nomenclature and therefore prices in turn were so reasonable that there was no object in copying it. For the present, at least, the picture has changed completely and so has our latest type of collector. Today collectors appear to prefer to specialize in one or two items and enlarge their knowledge along with their purchases. I am, of course, omitting those buyers who are now furnishing their homes with what can come under no heading short of what may be termed "amazements."

Among the interesting specialties not altogether appreciated in the past are glass hats. A study of earliest types in blown glass reveals that they run the gamut from primitive styles produced by backwoods bottle houses to the sophisticated creations of such factories as the Mt. Washington Glass Co., the Boston & Sandwich Glass Co., Baccarat, and some of the finest English houses. With the perfecting of machinery for pressing glass, there followed a wide series of patterns and novelties of hats in all sorts of colors. Thus, glass hats range in rarity from unique blown forms to the common designs of the 1880's. To a student, their form is not always interesting or even good, though they vary from folk art to highly cultural styles. Artistically they are like a French rondeau in the endless variation achieved within the confines of a limited objective. A wide gap is bridged between the offhand blown hats, which represent a gratification of the creative spirit of the workman and thus, in being utterly useless, constitute the highest form of collectibles, and the commercial, utilitarian hats of later years, in the form of individual salts, toothpick holders, spoonholders and celery vases!

The hat collector not infrequently encounters a hat with a hole in the top of the crown in the middle of what appears to be a pontil break. An example is pictured in Plate 117. Many beginners believe this due to the ignorance or carelessness of the blower, or at best to be the result of an unhappy accident. A little thought on the mechanics of glass blowing will correct this misapprehension.

With the exception of some paperweights, few items in glass can be made by the blower working alone. One man must hold the pontil iron, another the blowpipe. But, after working hours, no assistant might be available or willing, in which case the blower would draw his own glass, blow and manipulate it himself. Consequently, when the piece was broken off, a hole would be found in the crown of the hat. While it must be admitted that this mars somewhat the beauty of the hat, it cannot be considered a defect. It proves the hat to be an offhand product, never made commercially, and at the present writing it also substantiates the fact that it is an old one, for this is a step the producers of copies have not as yet chosen to take.

At the upper left in Plate 117 is a cased glass clown's hat, clear blue on the outside, with an opaque white lining and embellished with an applied "rigaree" decoration in the same shade of blue. It bears the original paper label: "Clown's Hat Candle Snuffer. Made in England." A counterpart to this and other peaked hats is more often found in china.

The blown hat in the upper row next to the clown's hat in Plate 117 is brilliant aquamarine in color and has a history of being an offhand product of an early midwestern bottle factory.

Below the clown's hat is a rare witch's hat in cobalt blue. Unfortunately it was cracked while the "blow-over" was being ground off and was accordingly left unfinished. Articles blown in an open one-piece mold would necessarily have some extraneous glass left on them after being broken off the blowpipe; such articles were not transferred to the pontil iron in the making.

The hat with the hole in the crown (Plate 117) is amber in color and blown in a swirled pattern. It is distinguished by having a rather high crown. There is nothing about it to indicate any probable place of origin.

Among the rarities of interest to the advanced collector are the hats produced from medicine and pharmacy bottle molds. In Plate 118 may be seen two of these early bottles, as well as four hats. The flat hat in the upper row was produced from an eight-sided ink bottle mold. An item of this sort is called a "frigger" in the English glass houses. Our American dictionaries do not attempt an interpretation of glassblowers' terminology, though we do find the English term "friggle," meaning "to fuss," and some of the offhand pieces of glass were obviously fussy pieces to handle. The glassworker blew hats of this type in medicine or ink bottle molds and then folded over the top into the shape of a hat. This finishing was done by hand, the rim of most of the earliest hats being folded over to make a neat edge. All the hats in Plate 118 would be termed "friggers" in England. All are of aquamarine glass and all, save one, have a folded, or welted, brim. Two were perfectly shaped by expert workers; two, somewhat misshapen. The first hat in the lower row at the left has twelve panels. Behind it stands the commercial pharmacy bottle from which the hat is a rare offhand product. This middle hat in the lower row also has twelve panels and was blown in the same mold as the bottle just behind it. The third hat in the lower row is a choice example that was blown in the early patent medicine bottle which held Mrs. M. N. Gardner's Indian Balsam of Liverwort. About half the words are still legible on the hat.

In Plate 119 is a hat on a foot which appears to have begun life as a candleholder. An attempt has been made by some of our writers to christen oddities, such as this footed hat, a whimsey, but this seems an anemic expression that hardly does credit to the boldly creative imagination of the producers. "Frigger" is a more vividly descriptive term.

The first hat in the upper row of Plate 119 at the left is a cobalt blue tumbler hat; in other words, it was produced from a tumbler mold. Hats made in color from tumbler molds are rare. Next to it is an opaque black hat with a gold band. The footed hat next to it is the one previously mentioned which started out as a candleholder. The workman indulged his fancy and by tilting over the sides and folding the rim, turned out a collector's item for specialists today!

In the lower row of Plate 119 is a pressed hat, illustrating a scarcer variety of a well-known type. It differs from others in being smaller, heavier and with a thick, wide, protruding band. The different varieties of the pressed hats will be considered in detail after the blown types, which are earlier, have been covered.

In the lower row of the same illustration in the center is a small blown hat in opaque black, which came from a northern Indiana factory.

From the viewpoint of a rarity, any of the hats in Plate 120 would delight the heart of a collector. The larger one in the upper row is in a fairly deep greenish-yellow glass, an extremely rare color in early, primitive hats. It is large, as these hats go, measuring almost seven inches across the brim. The hat next to it also is in an oversize, measuring six inches across. It is a perfectly formed hat in dark olive green, which appears black when seen by reflected light. It was found in New Hampshire and accompanied with a Keene history, so it may reasonably be attributed to that factory.

At the left in the lower row of Plate 120 is a fine little hat in a light olive-green glass, perfectly formed (so many of the offhand hats were crude and irregular) and was apparently blown in the two-part mold of some unknown bottle. It measures $1\frac{1}{4}$ inches tall and $2\frac{3}{4}$ inches across the brim.

The last hat in Plate 120 is a greater rarity. It is a perfectly formed cap in a medium shade of blue, blown in the mold of a common octagonal ink bottle of the type usually found in aquamarine. This is another true "frigger" or "whimsey," whichever you prefer.

Plate 121 pictures five Saratoga blown hats. Those at the left in the upper and lower rows and that in the middle are of emerald green glass and were made at the Congressville factory, Saratoga Springs, N. Y. The one in the middle is truly remarkable for its shape and high crown. Such a hat would rarely be produced at factories where bottles were a commercial product. The two hats at the right, top and bottom rows, are called parson's hats. They are dark olive green in color and were made at the Mountain Glass Works of Oscar Granger in Saratoga.

Plate 122 illustrates six caster place hats from old bottle and window glass houses. The first in the upper row at the left is a Redwood hat in the light bluish-green characteristic of that factory, and is a well-executed and perfectly formed hat, somewhat in the shape of a derby. In the middle of the upper row is a Lockport hat (Lockport Glass Works, Lockport, N. Y.) in bottle green, which has the low crown and wide brim of a parson's hat. Next to it is an early South Jersey hat in light green. The term "caster place" is explained in descriptions of hats on Plate 133.

In the lower row of Plate 122 at the left is a little flat hat in aquamarine, from Ohio. The second is a rare and interesting hat from South Jersey in pale aquamarine. Hardly as large as a thimble, it is ¾ of an inch tall and 1⅜ inches across the widest part of the brim and is complete with pontil mark and welted edge. Definitely early, this hat is not to be confused with the late lamp-work hats which are held on and blown from a cane in front of a gas jet. Instead of a pontil mark these show a faint snip where the hat is melted off the cane or tube. The third hat in the lower row is an interesting one in almost colorless glass of surprising thickness.

The first hat at the left in the upper row of Plate 123 is blown, in clear glass, ornamented with a band of red glass around the edge of the brim and with a red glass band and bow. It is a fine and perfect hat of New England origin, standing three inches tall. In the center is a peaked Tyrolean hat in clear glass, flashed with spiral stripes in green. Such hats add an interesting touch to any collection, and they are not plentiful. It is probably of English derivation. The third hat in the upper row is blown in clear glass, partly frosted. The unfrosted part, in an elaborate design of panels enclosing floral medallions, is stained red and the pattern outlined in gold. It provides a rare and showy hat, probably of English origin, though it could be Bohemian.

In the lower row of Plate 123 are two shapes of hats in light silvery-blue glass. They were made at Millville, N. J., in the 1890's, and are from the same mold as the candleholder and hat illustrated on Plate 124, though of course they are much more unusual.

Plate 124 pictures a rather curious mixture of hats. At the left in the upper row is an Inverted Thumbprint, which is blown and has an unusual treatment of the brim. It is bent up and down in a haphazard fashion, probably to suggest a woman's hat. It is found in blue and amber, and possibly other colors. While not so charming as the Inverted Thumbprint hat just beneath it, it is far more unusual.

The middle hat in the upper row is a rare foreign hat in thick red glass of a most unusual orange and gold tone, the surface of which has been given a queer pitted appearance.

An "art" crudity, it was designed for use as a candleholder and exists also in a strange amber shade. The glass is known as Italian Jewel.

The third hat, next to the candleholder, was blown in a mold with heavy vertical ribbing. It is cobalt blue and is thought to be an unusual Millville, N. J., hat of the late 1890's.

In the lower row the first hat is the usual blown Inverted Thumbprint hat. It is most often found in a deep, rich cranberry red and is considerably more desirable in this color than in the more unusual blue, honey amber and "clear to cranberry" shaded color. This hat has not been reproduced.

The third item in the lower row of Plate 124 depicts what appears to be a wine glass or small tumbler in a rather unpleasant dark-red glass. However, it is a candleholder, originally designed for use in the churches at Millville, N. J., in the 1890's. At its left is a hat in the same glass which at first was made by the workmen for their own pleasure by simply turning out and over the top of the candleholder, to form the brim of a hat. Both hat and candleholder have been extensively and intensively reproduced. The red of this glass is attained by the use of selenium, not oxide of gold.

The first hat in the top row of Plate 125 shows a familiar pattern in the Blown Molded (by some termed "three-mold," no matter how many hinged parts there were to the mold) glass hat, of an uncommon shape. Next to it in the center is a caster place hat in a rare light olive-green color, from Pennsylvania. Next to it is an aquamarine hat with opal threads applied under the brim near the edge. This is an extremely rare detail in bottle-house hats but unfortunately the work seems to have been too much for the blower who attempted it, for the result would not be pleasing to everyone.

The first hat in the lower row at the left of Plate 125 is a sapphire blue miniature Blown Molded hat—a real rarity among hats. It was made from the little whisky-taster mold. Next to it, in the middle, is the same Blown Molded hat shown in clear glass. Both measure about $1\frac{3}{8}$ inches tall, the smallest size of the

PLATE 117

Upper: Rare clown's hat, bearing original English paper label. Offhand blown hat said to be from early Midwestern factory.

Lower: Witch's hat in cobalt blue. Amber swirled hat of a type not indicative of any particular factory.

PLATE 118

Hats blown from molds of pharmacist's bottles. Hat in upper right, blown from octagonal ink bottle mold.

PLATE 119

Upper left, blue hat from tumbler mold. Upper right, a footed hat that apparently started out as a candleholder. Between the two, a hat having a gold band and beneath it, a blown hat. The two ribbed hats are familiar to collectors, though the one at the left is scarce.

PLATE 120

Upper: Two rare over-sized blown hats.

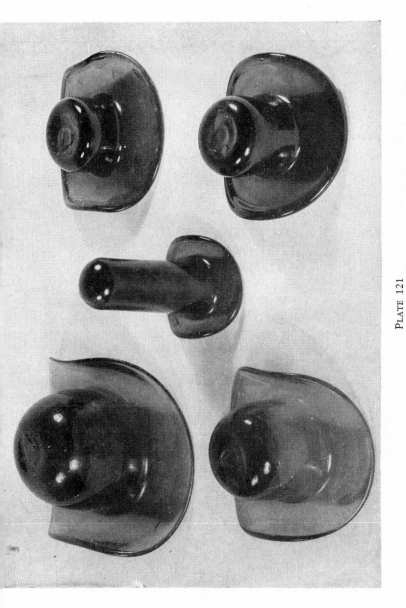

PLATE 121

Five deep green hats, from early Saratoga, N. Y., factories. The one in the middle is remarkable for high crown and shape.

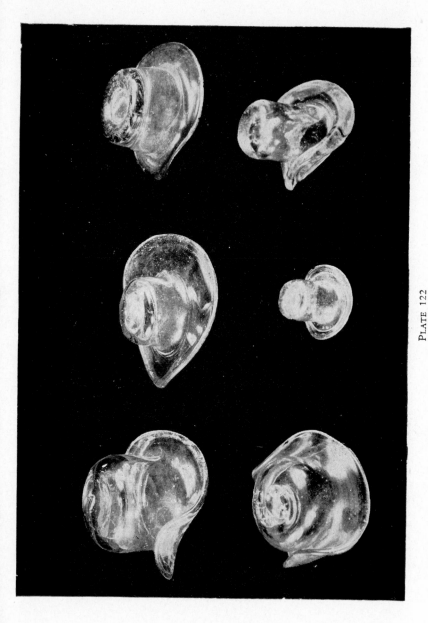

PLATE 122

Six primitive hats from old bottle or window glass factories. Represented are Redwood and Lockport, N. Y., South Jersey

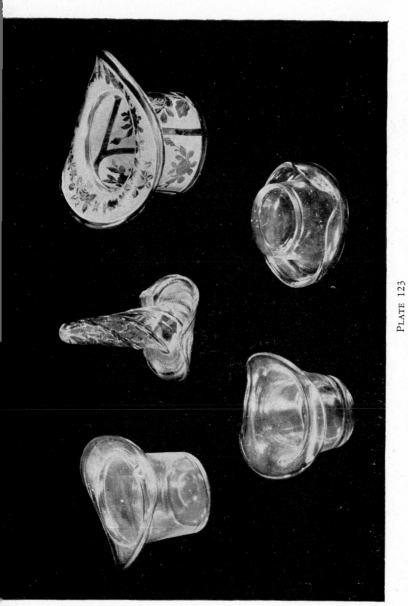

PLATE 123

Three blown hats, a decorated Tyrolean hat and a frosted type with an elaborate design of floral decorations.

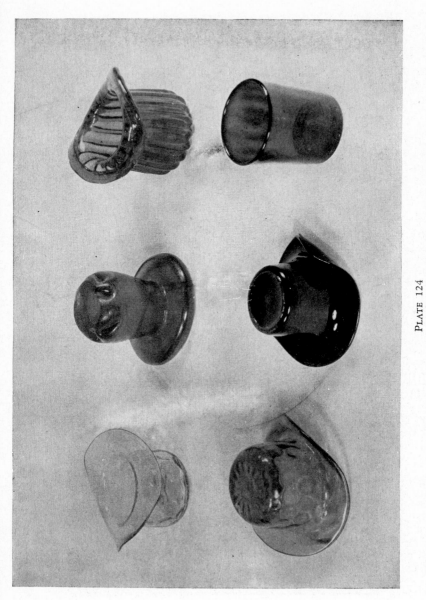

PLATE 124

Two Inverted Thumbprint hats; a heavily ribbed hat, and two candleholders. A tumbler candleholder and hat produced from the same mold are shown at the lower right.

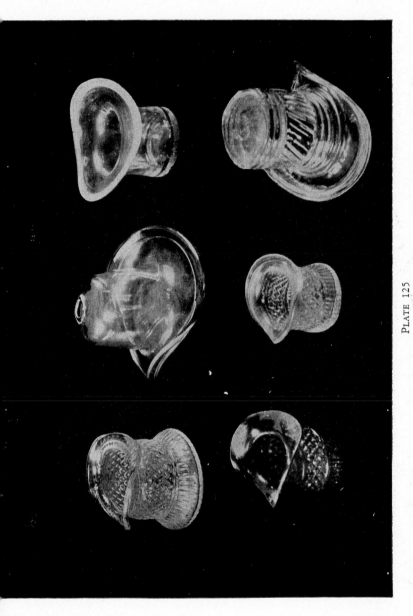

PLATE 125

Four Blown Molded hats. Two are miniatures, the rarest being in deep blue. The hat at the lower right is in an unlisted pattern. Center of upper row is a Pennsylvania olive-green hat. The one at the end next to it has an opal edge.

PLATE 126

Upper: Two blown hats with applied edge in amber.

Blown Molded hats. The last hat in the lower row (at the right) is also Blown Molded and the first recorded in this pattern. It is of a clearer, finer quality than is usual in this type of hat.

The Blown Molded hats, for the most part, were blown in molds intended for other objects; the molds most frequently employed were those of inkwells, caster bottles and tumblers. The hats were made commercially over a number of years and it is possible to accumulate quite an array of them. The largest known is in my collection, being nearly 3½ inches tall. It was made from a tumbler mold in the Sunburst with Bull's Eye pattern. The rarest colors among these hats are olive green and amber. Next in rarity is a brilliant sapphire blue, of Sandwich origin. Especially rare are those Blown Molded hats which were blown in two molds—that is, first blown in one of the Blown Molded patterns, then removed and blown in a vertical ribbed mold.

The two hats in the top row of Plate 126 are both aquamarine, with a heavy band of amber around the edge of the brim. The first one at the left is a rather large and heavy hat, measuring six inches across the brim. Both are of South Jersey origin.

Below the largest hat is one in deep olive green which has a few threads under the brim in the same color of glass.

Last on Plate 126 is an olive-green Pitkin hat, blown by the half-post method. It is one of the rarest and most desirable hats known, aside from the olive-amber Blown Molded, of which two have been found. The latter were produced from inkwell molds.

The first hat at the left on Plate 127 is olive green. The large one at the top is amber, flashed with an aquamarine band around the edge of the brim. The next large one, 3½ inches tall, is a deep-red amber. In front is a little flat hat with folded brim in a rich golden amber. Hats as small as this one, which is less than an inch high, are rare and interesting because of their diminutive size. These four caster place hats are fairly representative of the offhand products of the early bottle houses.

The smallest hat in my collection is not much over a half inch high and the crown will fit over the end of a finger, much like a thimble. It is olive green and was found in Vermont.

The first hat at the left on Plate 128 is in a medium light green and is a very early South Jersey example blown from a poor grade of silica. The second hat in the upper row is apparently from the Nailsea factory in England. It is perhaps the oldest hat in the collection and might date from late in the eighteenth century. It is blown in a deep olive-green glass, flecked with spots of opaque white. It was made in the same way as the Spatter glass hats in Indiana in the 1890's. Thus, for the hat collector, at any rate, the century begins and ends with Spatter glass.

The lower left hat in Plate 128 is a splendid example from the Ohio district, blown in a swirled pattern from a medium olive-green glass of surprising beauty and excellence. The last hat in the second row is a very early one from the Bristol district of England, blown from a heavy, thick chinalike glass. Not apparent in the illustration is the fact that it is cased, deep green on the outside and a brilliant opaque white inside.

An extremely rare hat is the first to the left on Plate 129. It was fashioned from one of the old soda water bottles in emerald green and bears, in raised letters, the words "Lancaster Glass Works, N. Y." There was an early glass factory at Lancaster, N. Y. Familiar to all collectors of historical flasks are the pint flasks, with a basket of flowers on one side and a cornucopia turned to the right on the others, lettered "Lancaster Glass Works, N. Y." The same bottle is found unlettered. The half-pints, as well as the pints, used to be found fairly frequently, in central New York State, in a brilliant emerald green. Half-pints are not seen marked; at least, I have never seen one with the factory name.

Next to the Lancaster hat, in the upper row, is an interesting crudity in hunter's green, showing a not-too-successful effort on the part of some young blower to make a tricorne hat.

It may be remarked here that the caster place hats were rather extensively reproduced in the early 1930's, usually blown in a grade of glass similar to that produced in the early bottle houses. A few types were worked to death, and most showed such poor work that they would not be worth much even if they were old. We have not had many for a few years, and they were never produced in the quantities that some would have us believe. It should be pointed out, once and for all, that anything can be reproduced, from a Rembrandt painting to a Daisy and Button hat. The collectors of Corot's landscapes did not throw up their hands and throw out their canvases when it was discovered that his paintings were easy to imitate. Men who engage in the making of reproductions are seldom the most capable sort, and a little intelligence will either circumvent them or hold them in abeyance for a few years. I predict that some of their efforts will become collector's items a generation from now.

It should be pointed out also that offhand pieces of glass have continuously been made since the very first factory went into operation, and they are still being made. An obviously new hat might have been made in 1920 with nothing behind it but the urge to create something. As a matter of fact, there is no reason why new hats (not reproductions) should not be produced. They are made for such a very short time that it is difficult to buy a new one before it goes off the market. I am referring to novelties in blown hats and not to the late copies of Daisy and Button hats which may be seen in gift shops, department stores, and even in some ten-cent stores.

To return to Plate 129, the two hats in the lower row are two caster place hats in rich golden amber, which are probably South Jersey.

The hat in the center of Plate 130 is a fine example of art glass. Embedded in the body of the glass are gold dust and larger flakes of the same metal. In this respect it represents an advance over the common Venetian technique in which gold is simply dusted or rolled on the surface. As already explained, the melting point of gold, more than 1900°, is higher than that of the glass at the time it is being blown. Glass having precious metals embedded in the body was invented by the Aurora Glass Co. of London in the latter 1860's. This company referred to it as their "metallized" glass and they sometimes coated flakes of mica with gold, silver and platinum. Sandwich took up the manufacture of this glass in our country, and in the 1880's Hobbs, Brocunier & Co. brought out their "Spangle" glass, which differs from the English and Sandwich ware in being cased, the mica flakes being spread over the exterior, and there is an interior lining of opaque white. This large hat pictured in Plate 130 measures 5 inches tall and 6½ inches across the brim, and was blown in an optic mold. Because of the presence of the gold, it is difficult to describe the color, which seems to be russet red. The hat has been attributed to Sandwich but very similar glass bearing a British registry mark is occasionally found.

The first hat to the left on the same Plate is a rare pressed hat in the familiar purple Marble glass. It is equipped with hat band and bow, and measures 3½ inches tall and 5 inches across the brim. The hat is probably English, since it is sometimes, though not always, marked with a lion rampant on a crown.

The hat on the lower right of Plate 130, is a brilliant cranberry color, with applied clear glass rim and band. It measures 2¾ inches tall and 5¾ inches across the brim.

The first hat at the left in the upper row of Plate 131 is blown in opaque blue glass, decorated with an orange enamel. This hat was blown from the same metal as the glass "friendship" mugs, and is considerably older than appears at a first glance. It occurs also with the brim turned up on one side.

Next is a cap in what is called "bubbly peat" glass, showing a mottled blue color and gold decoration. It is of English origin, and is rare. The third hat, open at the top, is pressed glass in opaque black, showing a horizontally ribbed crown with textured brim. It is one of the rarest of all pressed hats.

In the lower row of Plate 131, the first hat at the left is

blown in a brilliant maroon, said to be an offhand piece from the Union Glass Co. of Somerville, Mass. Next is a military cap in a rather dark amethyst Mexican glass. Any hat in Mexican glass is unusual, and no collector need be ashamed to possess one. There is no reason to associate it with the cheap blown Mexican pitchers, plates, etc., which are frequently seen in gift shops, department stores, and even in drugstores! The last hat in the lower row is blown in a light amethyst lead glass of fine quality, the brim turned down all around and showing six folds, to simulate a woman's hat. It is of New England origin.

The first hat in the upper row of Plate 132 is blown from a lead glass of fiery opalescent hue. It was found on Cape Cod, and is probably of about the same age as the fiery opalescent lace glass. It and the last hat in the illustration should not be confused with the later milk-white glass.

Second in the upper row is a clear glass fireman's hat with swirled opalescent stripes. It is probably a latter-day Sandwich product. The third hat was blown in an optic mold and is light blue in color with an opalescent brim.

The first hat at the left in the lower row is blown in frosted, clear glass. Next to it is a tiny hat in opaque white, rolled in gold, or gold flecked on the surface, in the Venetian manner. It stands barely 1½ inches high and measures even less across the brim. The technique of putting powdered gold on the surface of glass hats is a simple one, and factories everywhere have produced a certain amount of this ware. More than 1900° Fahrenheit are required to melt gold, and since glass at the time it is being blown is never that hot, the gold-flecking of glass on the surface is really a simpler procedure than the making of Spatter glass. For reasons of color, it is likely to be more pleasing on Venetian glass.

The last hat on Plate 132 is a fiery opalescent, deepening in intensity of color on the brim.

The first hat at the left in the upper row of Plate 133 is in emerald green. It is a curious hat, standing 6¼ inches high and was blown in the mold of some unidentified piece of hollow ware.

To the right is a large amber hat, 6¾ inches high and 9½ inches across the brim, of later Ellenville origin. Large hats from the old bottle houses are very, very rare, and the collector will do well not to let his cupidity overcome credulity and draw him into the pitfall of wishful thought. Just beneath the Ellenville hat is a very early South Jersey one in deep-red amber, an interesting crudity, long treasured, perhaps, because it was some nameless blower's "first."

The two hats just discussed are from a large family of caster place hats from the early bottle and window glass factories scattered over several states. Just why the term *caster place,* a venerable expression still in use today, is neglected by the writers on early blown glass is something of a mystery, especially since it describes so much of the New York and South Jersey production. A caster place workman is one who blows glass without the use of a mold. It is not always easy, even for an expert, to say that a certain piece was blown, or was not blown, in a mold, but for the purpose of this discussion we can call those hats caster place which were not obviously blown in a mold. Generally speaking, those blown in a mold are considered more desirable than the caster place ones. The fourth item in the illustration will be discussed later in connection with another hat.

The three hats in the upper row of Plate 134 are all in frosted opaque-white glass; all are finely decorated, and the first has an applied flower in pink glass, gold touched. The first two are rare.

The three hats in the lower row were all made by Nicholas Lutz, probably at Sandwich, for undoubtedly most of his work was done there. It must be remembered that he also worked for the Dorflingers, who claim to have brought him to this country, for a western factory as well, and for the Mt. Washington and Union factories. The first hat was almost certainly made at Sandwich, for it is in the deep-zircon blue so familiar in the

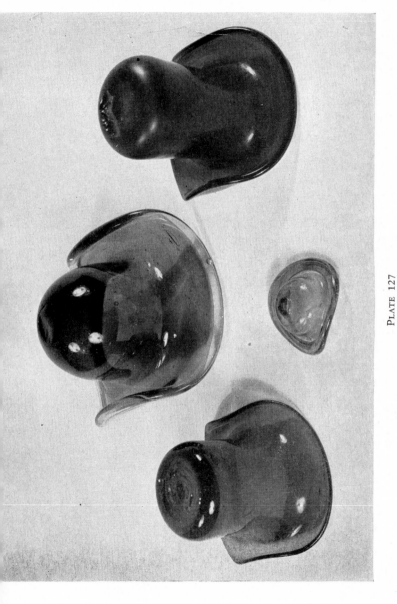

PLATE 127

Four representative types of off-hand hats, products of early bottle houses. The smallest is less than an inch high.

PLATE 128

Upper: Early South Jersey blown hat. Rare Nailsea hat.

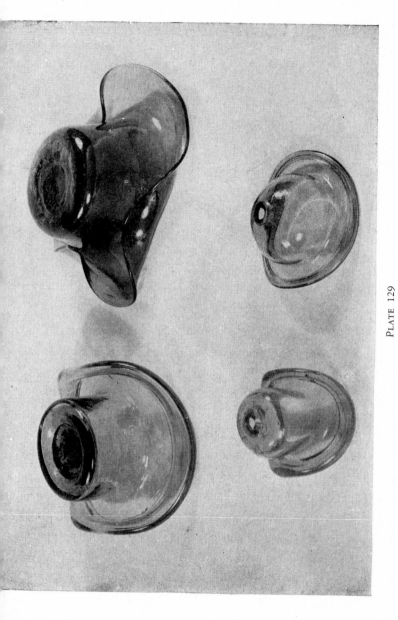

PLATE 129

Upper: Marked "Lancaster Glass Works, N. Y." hat. Rare blown tricorne by unknown maker.
Lower: Two bright golden amber hats, probably from South Jersey.

PLATE 130

1. Purple Marble glass hat. 2. Center, English hat, russet-red flecked with gold.

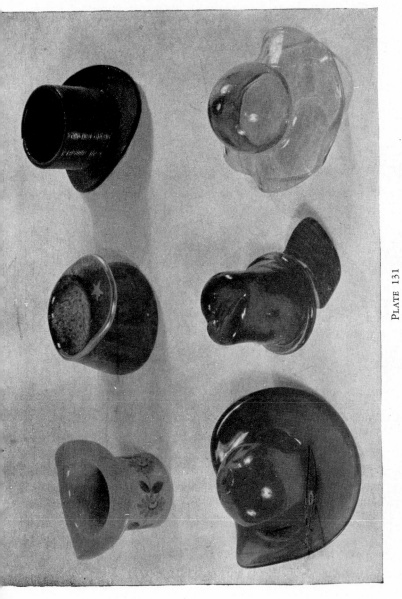

PLATE 131

A varied group, including English, one Mexican and New England hats.

PLATE 132

PLATE 133

Emerald green, amber and deep red-amber offhand blown hats.

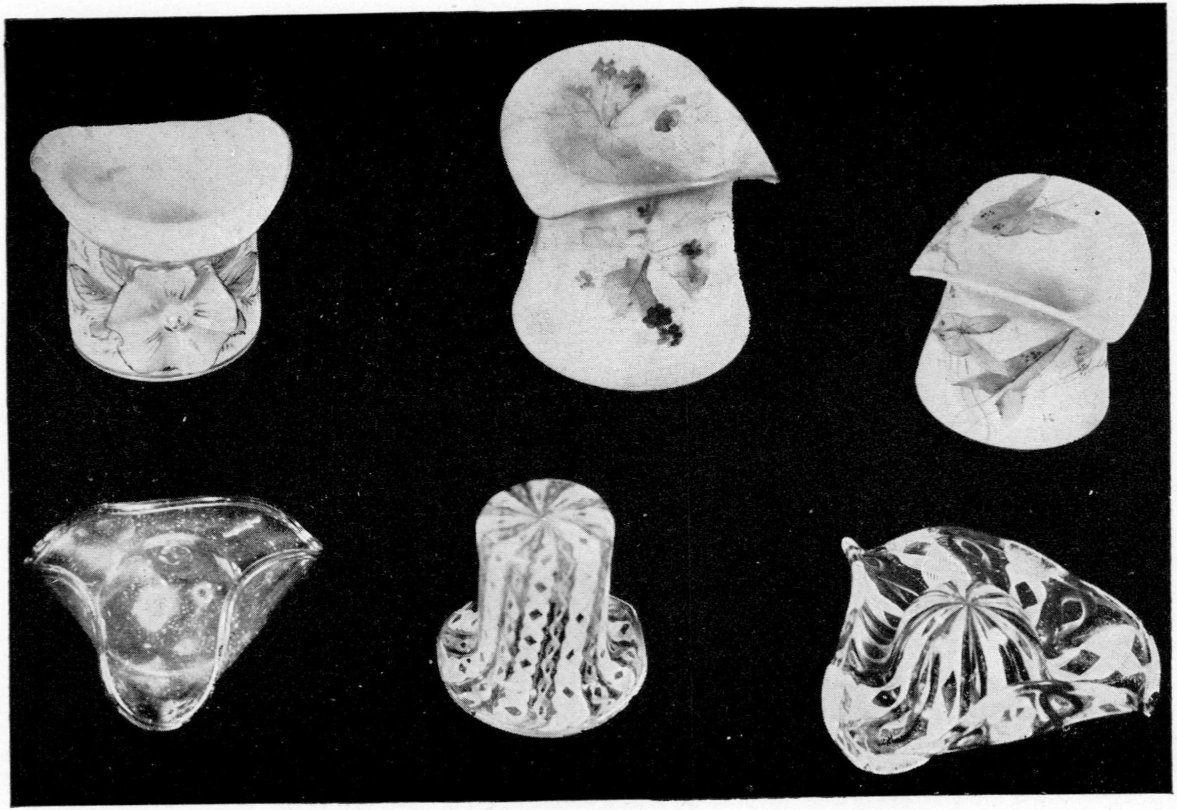

PLATE 134

Upper: Frosted opaque white hats, all finely decorated.

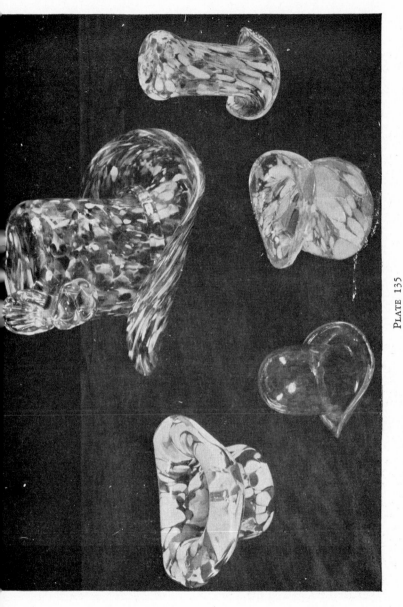

PLATE 135

A group of Spatter glass hats made in Indiana. Notable is the large one with applied cockade and band in crystal.

vases and candlesticks made there. The little top hat in the center has twisted stripes, alternately pink and white. The third hat also has twisted stripes, alternately blue and white. That these hats were not made in Italy is attested by the fact that they are lead glass, whereas the Venetian is always a lime glass. The three-cornered eighteenth century hat is the rarest shape to be found in a glass hat collection.

Spatter glass, or that which many collectors have merely designated as "Splash ware" in lieu of no name at all, has aroused the interest of many of our latter-day collectors. Plate 135 has a group of Spatter glass hats, all offhand pieces made in the 1890's in the factories of northern Indiana. Following the discovery of natural gas in that region, dozens of factories sprang up in the state, and a very large glass industry soon was established, some of which remains today.

Spatter glass may be a reaction of the blower against the insipid clear glass which so long dominated the American glass industry. The kaleidoscopic colorings enabled the blower to escape from the monotony of the clear glass he handled day after day. Spatter glass was produced by breaking pieces of various colored glass and spreading them out on the marver. The glassblower rolled his gather over the small broken colored pieces, blew it, warmed it in, and then finished the article. The result was what is here termed "Spatter" glass.

It must be admitted that it was not often completely satisfying to the aesthetic sense, but in any event it was a change— and any change is a relief. The worker may control the spatter by choosing the broken pieces in respect to color or, as is more usual, he may spread them out in haphazard fashion.

Expert glassblowers do not often make an offhand piece of Spatter glass, but the hat at the top of Plate 135 is definitely an exception, for it is indubitably a good example of the glassblower's art. The cockade and band of clear glass are applied against the colored background. The spatter is partly controlled, for a unifying color of reddish-pink glass is suffused throughout. The hat is five inches high and measures seven inches across the brim.

The other hats in Plate 135 display uncontrolled spattering of almost every color, except the one in the lower left foreground; this one is spattered only with an orange-colored glass on a clear ground. This type of ware should not be confused with Mosaic glass, which is fully illustrated in another chapter.

The first hat in the upper row of Plate 136 is an example of early midwestern technique in bottle-green glass. It was blown in the two-part mold of some early jar. The curiously hammered surface, perhaps intentionally secured, might have been caused by the use of a chilled mold. The concavity around the pontil of this hat, in early tumblers and in some early pieces of hollow ware blown in a mold, was deliberately obtained by the mold-maker to reduce suction when the piece was lifted from the mold.

The hat beside it, with its low crown, might have been made to imitate a parson or Quaker's hat, or again it might have been the intention of the blower to simulate the wide-awake hat, the headgear created and adopted by a Republican organization in 1860 but seen occasionally for several years after that date, at a time when higher-crowned hats were popular.

In the lower row, the two hats are termed "derbies" by some collectors. They are alike in having a band of glass applied around the inside of the crown at the bottom. The first, at the left, is clear with an opalescent crown, and the second is bottle green.

The first hat in the upper row of Plate 137, an oversize Quaker hat in medium amber, comes from upper New York State.

The second hat, from Pennsylvania, is rare in having its original decoration. Few of the primitive hats were decorated in the first place. The entire hat is covered with a black paint, now crazed, and the words are in yellow. The rough pontil is likewise painted, indicating that the work was done by someone without facilities. The paint is not fired on, and the hat itself is probably a memento of some forgotten firehouse.

The first hat in the lower row at the left is a small amber hat of unknown provenance, later than the others. Next is a little flat red hat, rolled in gold in the Venetian manner, barely ¼ of an inch high. It belongs with the art glass hats.

The first hat in the upper row of Plate 138 is clear glass with an applied glass berry, also clear. The glass berry, as a means toward the ornamentation of glass, has been widely used by many factories, in all countries; its use, however, as a device to hide the pontil mark is commonly accepted as a characteristic of the Mt. Washington Glass Co. in New Bedford, Mass. Next is a hat in opaque green with streaks of darker green, a rare color in glass hats. The third hat is partly amber, which merges to a rich cranberry in the brim; it was blown in a patterned mold resembling, to some extent, the Inverted Thumbprint pattern.

The first hat at the left in the lower row is a rare hat in Burmese glass, lemon yellow to pink. It is an offhand piece which might be found with either a glossy or a dull surface. The Mt. Washington people, who made this hat, probably in the 1880's, have always produced some of the finest of American glass. The next hat is partly clear, which merges to a gradually deepening wine red in the heavily folded brim.

The first hat to the left in the upper row of Plate 139 has a light-green crown with opalescent brim. The second is canary with opalescent stripes. A feature of this hat is the constricted area around the region of the hat band. The third is in clear glass, decorated with frosted stripes and polka dots all outlined in gold. The fourth is a bonnet in pellucid pink, merging to opalescence in the brim.

In the lower row the hat at the left is an interesting little thing in clear glass with a hollow brim and the crown little more than a blown bubble of glass; it is barely one inch high. Next to it is a clear glass derby with a band of opaque white around the edge of the brim.

In Plate 140 is a large hat in bluish aquamarine blown from the mold of a half-gallon fruit jar, the mold having a detachable plate on the bottom and worked with the figure 12; on the side of the crown appears the word "Ball." The hat, perfectly formed with a folded rim, was made by an experienced and capable blower. It measures 2 inches high and 9½ inches across the brim. It is of a deeper color than the modern Ball Mason glass fruit jars.

The Ball Mason hat, an excellent example of the frigger, or whimsey, already discussed, was found in Muncie, Ind., site of the large Ball factory, and hence was probably made in their factory. Other examples of the Ball hats vary in height and width, because they were finished by hand.

The next largest hat came with a Stiegel history but I cannot vouch for it. It is of a fine quality of lead glass and has a good bell tone when tapped. The third hat in Plate 140 is a frail, thin, blown, light aquamarine, shaped somewhat like the old-time fireman's helmet. Because it had the hole in the crown, as so many blown hats did, the dealer who had it thought it defective and sold it for next to nothing.

GROUP II

We are now leaving the field of the earliest blown hats and entering the period of the more sophisticated styles.

Plate 141 illustrates four threaded glass hats, all made at the Mt. Washington factory in New Bedford, Mass. All have a ground and polished pontil, and were blown in a diamond-quilted mold. The first in the upper row at the left has the brim turned up on one side and down on the other. It is about three inches high. The two in the lower row are about two inches high. The second hat in the upper row stands 3¼ inches high and measures 5¾ inches across the brim. Largest and rarest of the Mt. Washington threaded hats is the one that measures 3¾ inches high and 8¾ inches across the brim. Since they are blown hats, no two are exactly the same, but they come in two shapes and in three quite definite sizes. Their color range embraces blue, honey amber, cranberry and opalescent, which vary in intensity from pale pastel shades to the deeper tones. Rarest in color and finest of the Mt. Washington hats is the one

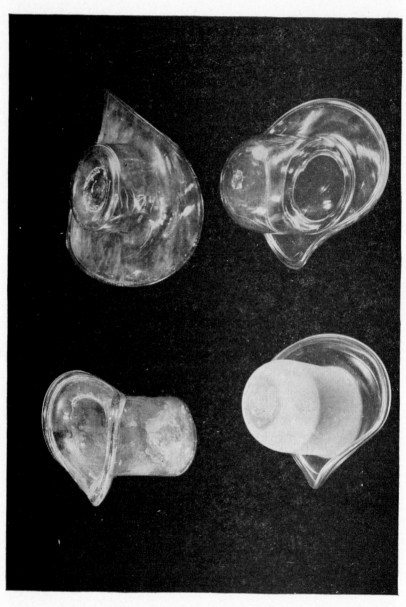

PLATE 136

Four blown hats, the one at the right in upper row being known as a Quaker hat. Those in lower row have an extra

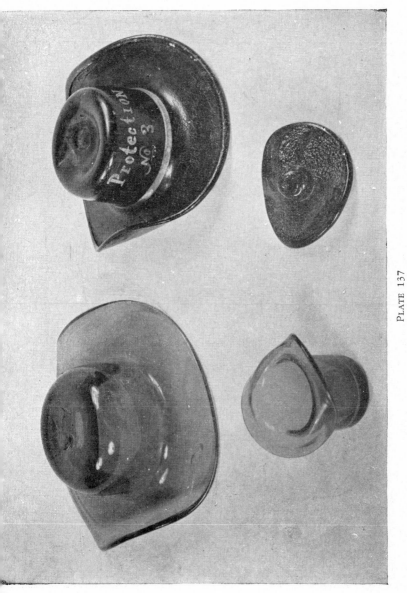

PLATE 137

Primitive hats from early glasshouses, including one that was a memento of some long forgotten firehouse.

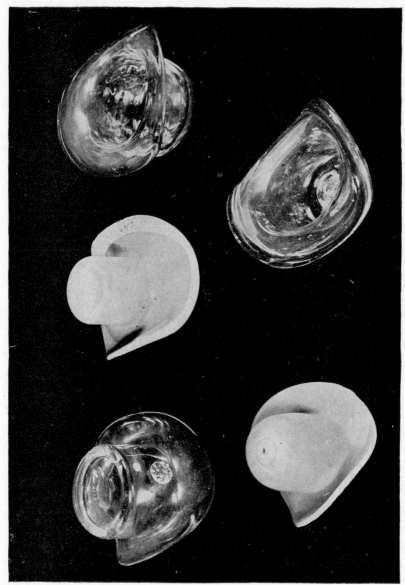

PLATE 138

PLATE 139

A group of blown hats, indicative of varied methods used by glassblowers. The hat at the lower left has a hollow brim.

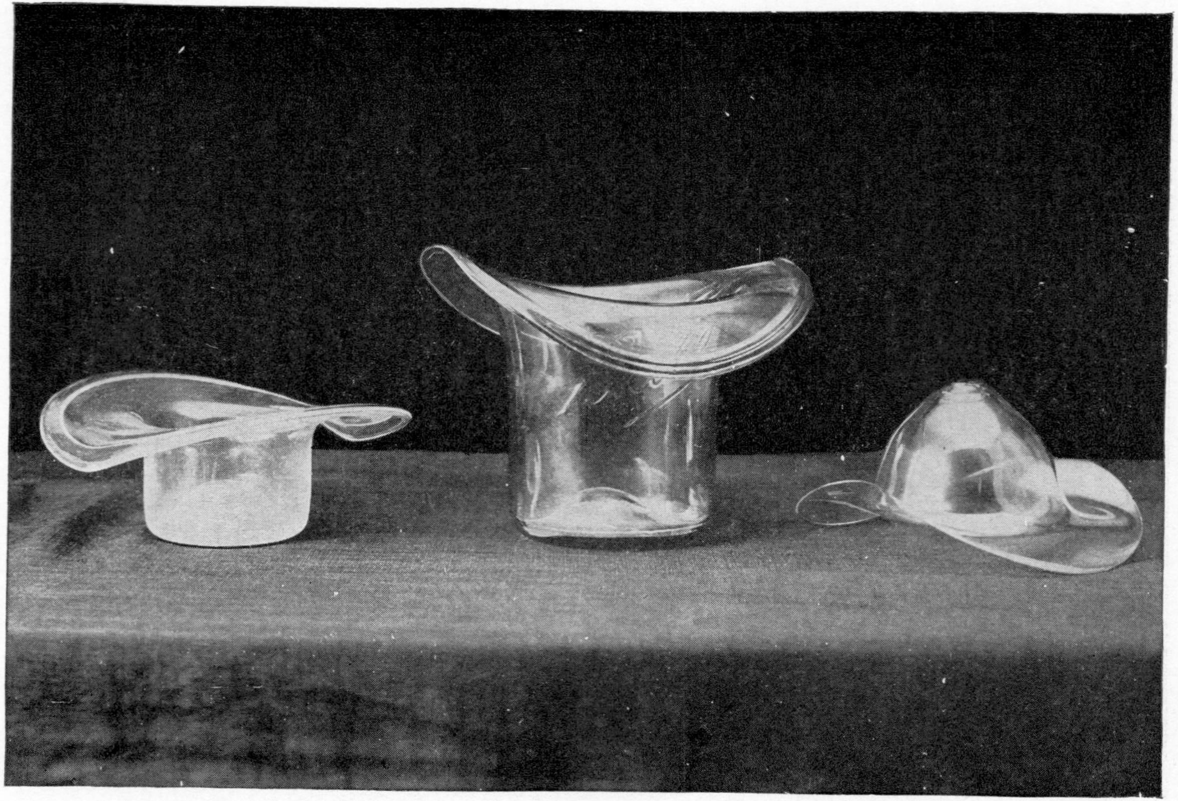

PLATE 140

illustrated on the lower right of Plate 141. It is cranberry to golden honey, wound with honey threads. The colors and the diamond quilting give it a chameleonlike quality of changing color with the angle of vision. The Mt. Washington hats in the two-inch size were made commercially for use as dessert cups. The same plates apparently did service for the matching finger bowls. These plates have, for the most part, gone with the finger bowls, with the result that a hat is rarely found with its appropriate plate.

The first hat in the upper row of Plate 142 at the left, wound with dull-pink threads, is the rarest of the threaded glass hats as regards to shape. Next to it in rarity, speaking still of shape and nothing else, is the last hat in the upper row. Some might think it a homely hat while others would cherish it. It is found in opalescent and in what might be described as a dusty pink. The pontil is not ground, and it is one of a series, like the case glass hat illustrated on Plate 143, the third in the upper row. Date and origin are unknown.

Generally speaking, the Mt. Washington threaded glass is superior to that of Sandwich, but this statement has an exception in the hats. The Sandwich threaded glass hats almost exhaust the color range of glass, and a group of them are as colorful as a garden. The five chosen for the illustration are opaque light blue wound with cranberry threads, fiery opalescent wound with pink threads, and honey color with an opalescent brim. Others are opalescent blue with clear blue threads, an olive green with rust threads, opaque light green with red threads, and many other colors and color combinations. The diamond quilting, as a rule, is not so evident in the Sandwich hats, and in some it seems to be missing altogether. The Sandwich hats have a rough pontil.

The upper row of Plate 143 shows four "case" glass hats, or those having two layers of glass. The first is lined with a brilliant deep pink. It will be noted that the second has an unusual decoration. The third hat, with crimped brim, is usually found lined in either pink or blue, but it may also be found lined with yellow or with green. Lined with either of the two last colors, it becomes a rare hat. The fourth hat may be found lined in pink or in blue. Owing to methods of manufacture, defects such as burst bubbles and uneven distribution of glass in the interior casing of these hats, are frequently encountered. Strictly speaking, they are not examples of overlay, and the glass manufacturer usually groups all such ware under the general name of "flash glass."

In the foreground are two fine and rare English hats, one in opaque white, the other in opaque blue; both are finely decorated in pure dull gold and have wreaths of roses painted in natural colors; both are inscribed in gold "To a good Boy."

Plate 144 illustrates a group of case glass hats. With the exception of the second hat in the lower row, all have a white Bristol casing lined on the inside in various shades of pink. The first at the left in the upper row is a Puritan hat, and is thin to the point of being opalescent. The second, a bonnet, has its original decoration of glass beads embedded in the enamel decoration. The third is frosted inside and out, and is a rare hat formed from a small vase. The fourth, the finest of all the case glass hats, is lined in opalescent pink and blown in a diamond-quilted mold. It is rare in that it is the only commercial cased glass hat that was blown in a mold.

The first hat at the left in the second row, is a small hat in the salt size. It is unusual in having the outside white casing folded over the inside lining of pink, to form a narrow band around the edge of the brim. Last is an unusual English hat that is triple-cased, meaning that it is clear over opaque yellow, with an opaque white lining. It has an engraved hatband.

In the upper row of Plate 145, at the left, the first hat is a bonnet in semiopaque light-blue hobnail. It is most frequently seen with handles attached, forming a small basket. The practice of omitting or attaching handles to form different pieces is not unknown in old glass and continues to the present day.

The second hat in the upper row is in a milky translucent glass with a blue stencilled decoration. It is blown, not pressed.

Next to it is a frosted clear glass hat, as are both of those in the lower row. The last hat was issued as a souvenir of the 1893 World's Fair and may be found so marked, in alloy gold of poor quality.

Plate 146 illustrates a group of six blown hats and one pressed, all in translucent glass. The first in the upper row at the left is translucent white with a band of pink glass around the edge of the brim. The second hat may be found flashed with a brim edging in red, blue, or green, listed in order of rarity. The third is a rare offhand hat in translucent lavender, an exceptionally rare color in this glass. It was apparently made by turning over the edges of a small vase. The fourth, in the shape of a parson's hat, is of fine quality and occurs in blue and in jade green.

The first hat at the left in the second row is the small salt size, in translucent jade green with a brim edge of opaque white. Second is a small white rouge pot in the shape of a woman's hat, excavated on the site of the Sandwich factory. It is a two-piece hat, one inch tall, and the lid is the same as that used for the Little Cavalier cosmetic jar (illustrated in *Sandwich Glass*). The third hat, in the small salt size, is found in blue and in white.

Some of these hats were undoubtedly made at Sandwich, but it is just as well to remember that the English factories made translucent glass of fine quality at the same time; so also did the French, though in lesser quantity and in somewhat different shades of blue. The translucent glass of those countries dates from the 1850's and 1860's. The Bohemian factories, which, since 1850 at least, have consistently copied the English products in addition to producing some characteristic glass of their own, started the production of translucent glass in the 1870's and have continued it intermittently ever since. They sent to this country shipload after shipload of the fancy decorated translucent white vases, which the decorators call Bristol, in the early 1870's. All this is written to explain the extreme difficulty of adjudicating on the origin of these hats. One can be sure only of their age and their rarity. The first hat in the upper row, and the first and second in the lower row are the rarest; the fourth hat in the upper row is perhaps the finest.

The first hat in the upper row of Plate 147 is pressed blue glass with a textured surface further ornamented with a heavy hatband and a cockade. It was originally issued with a lid in the form of a cat. It is a rare hat of English origin.

The second hat in the upper row at the right was made from an early pharmacy jar. It is opaque white and bears in molded letters on the side of the crown the words "Ung. Zinci Ox," and on the top of the crown "Whitall, Tatum Co. Phila. & N.Y." The Whitall factory has always been in Millville, N. J., but the company had business offices in the cities mentioned. The commercial pharmacy jar was equipped with a lid, and the flange on which it sat may still be seen intact under the brim.

The first hat in the lower row is an example of controlled commercial Spatter glass. How and why this glass was made is explained in connection with Plate 135. It is blue-flecked at the bottom, white-flecked at the top, on a ground of clear glass. The shape is unusual and not too pleasing, but was popular in the 1890's, and even offhand hats may be had in the same design. The commercial hat, though somewhat unusual, may be found in a wide variety of color combinations in the East.

The second in the lower row of Plate 147 is an English threaded glass hat striped in pink, blue, and green with crimped green threads. The brim is turned up on one side, down on the other, and is crimped all around. Finger bowls and plates were made to match. Threaded glass was produced by a machine, invented in England, to apply the threads. Later, it was used in a few American factories, but crimped threads are found only on English glass; at least, that is our knowledge at present. The hat shape was produced by the blower after the threads were applied.

Plate 148 features hats with metal brims. The first hat in the top row at the left has a cranberry crown and a brass brim. The second is in green transiucent glass with a thick medallion in

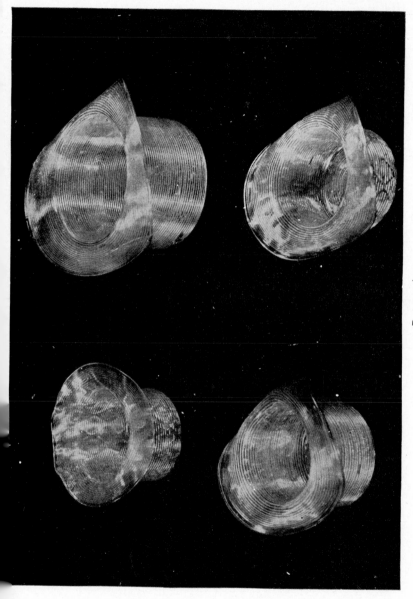

PLATE 141

Threaded glass hats, made at the Mt. Washington factory in New Bedford, Mass.

PLATE 142

Fine threaded bars probably made by Nicholas Lutz at the Boston & Sandwich Glass Co. All have rough pontil marks.

PLATE 143

Upper: Four case glass hats, or those which have two layers of glass.
Lower: Two choice English hats, both inscribed, "To a good Boy."

PLATE 144

A group of case glass hats, including a rare type blown in a diamond quilted mold. (Upper right, at end)

PLATE 145

A group of semi-opaque and milky-translucent white hats. The large one at lower left has frosted or "satin" finish.

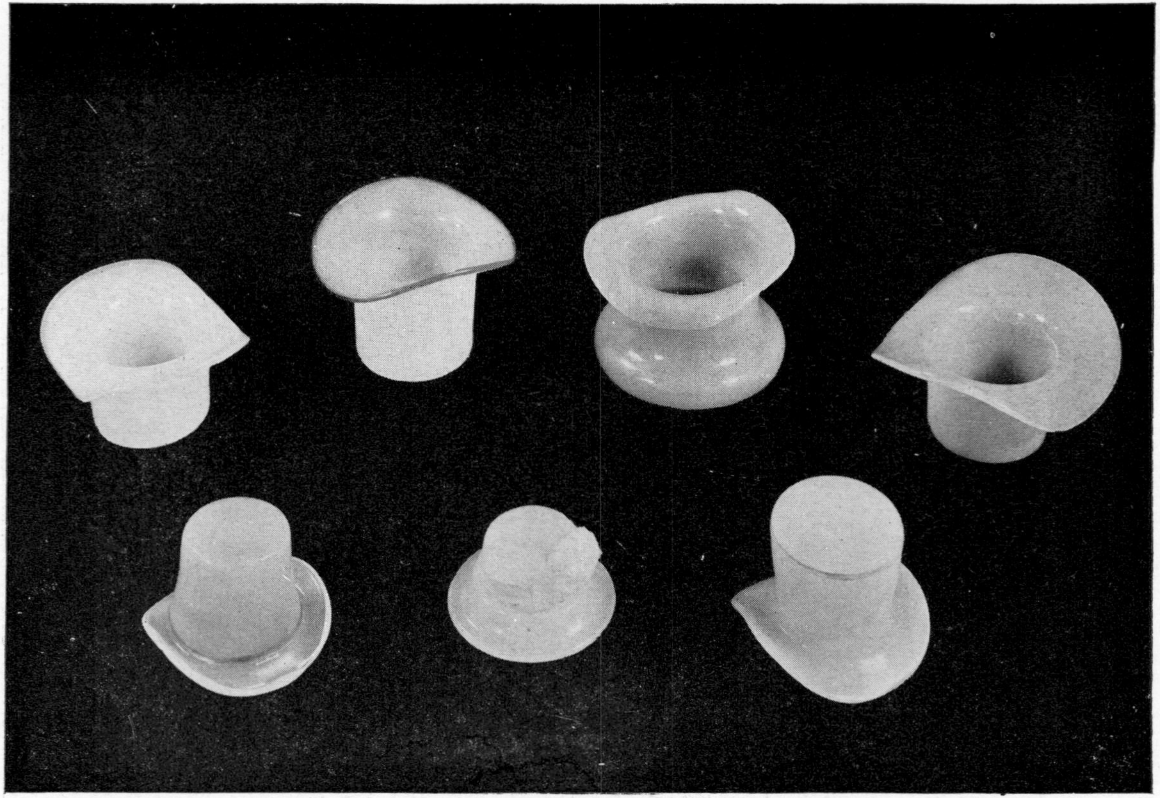

PLATE 146

A group of varied shapes and colors in translucent glass. The small hat in the center is a source mold

PLATE 147

An unusual pressed hat with cockade; a milk white hat produced from a pharmacy jar mold; a Spatter hat and an English Spatter hat which has crimped threads.

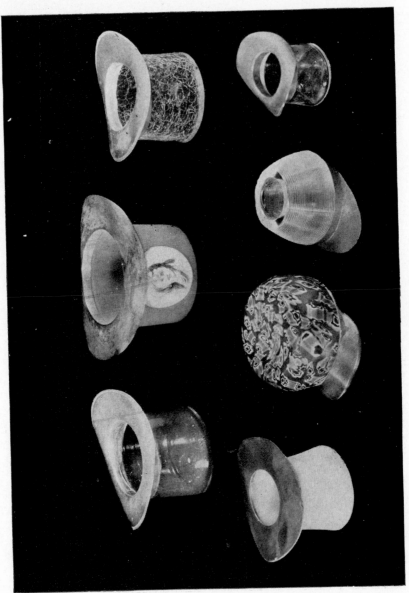

PLATE 148

A group of hats, all of which feature metal brims.

heavy white Bristol showing a painted female head; the brim is sterling silver. The crown of the third hat is in clear Crackle glass with a white metal brim.

The first hat in the lower row at the left is in opaque white with a tin brim which may be unscrewed from the threaded glass. It was originally filled with candy held within the hat by a cardboard lid on which were printed the words "Don't you want a hat full of candy?" It is one of the large family of novelty glass candy containers. It occurs also in clear glass, which was originally stained in various colors by inexpensive factory methods.

Next is a cap in Mosaic glass, made in a manner similar to that used in making Spatter glass except that paperweight cullet was used instead of ordinary colored glass. In this case the cane rests against a frosted green ground. It is fitted with a hollow sterling silver visor. The great majority of pieces in Mosaic glass were produced by the Italians who made them commercially until the present war. However, certain pieces may well have been made anywhere by one skilled in the making of Venetian glass, which, more than anything else, is a technique. It seems likely, for example, that Nicholas Lutz must have made a few pieces of this glass. Do not confuse this Mosaic with Marble glass.

Third in the lower row is a clear glass cap, open at the top, finely ribbed horizontally, with a plated metal visor. Though it must have been made commercially, and therefore in considerable quantities, it remains a scarce article.

The fourth hat has a clear glass crown fitted with brass brim. It is rare because of its small size, standing just 1½ inches high.

The first hat at the left in the top row of Plate 149 is a covered receptacle in opaque white. It is a rare hat of good quality, pressed in a diamond basket weave pattern.

The second hat, pressed in a natural basket weave pattern, is in blue translucent glass and is fitted with a metal holder presumably for flowers. The third hat, also in translucent glass and in the same pattern, shows an entirely different blue and is equipped with its original lid. The middle hat in the foreground is still another in the same pattern, this time in translucent green, and is marked "Baccarat" in molded letters on the inside of the crown. The hats illustrated represent the three sizes in which they are found, measuring, respectively, across the brim, 3½ inches, 3⅞ inches, and 4¼ inches. With the exception of the one fitted with a metal holder, they were originally furnished with lids which today are nearly always missing. They may be had in clear glass, and in translucent glass of almost unnamable soft shades and tones of blue and green. They were a commercial product of the Baccarat factory in the 1860's, and are among the finest of the pressed commercial hats.

First in the lower row at the left is a little flat hat in clear glass with its original green paint and gilt bow. The other little hat in the foreground is a straw sailor in a tiny basket weave pattern, measuring just ¾ of an inch high. Originally, perhaps, sold as a salt, it is sometimes recovered by collectors in sets, and comes in blue, amber, canary, and clear, of about equal rarity, with the exception of the last, which is quite rare. It appears in a catalogue of Geo. Duncan & Sons.

The first hat on Plate 150 is of the bonnet type in frosted clear glass and is engraved with the words "Hang Up Your Hat." To do this, ribbon or fancy cord would have to be fastened to each of two protruding glass knobs, and the hat might be filled with flowers. While the idea is interesting, the result is marred by inferior work.

The hat in the upper right, in amber hobnail, is a lamp shade, or possibly a shade for some lighting fixture, in the perfect form of a hat. It is large, measuring seven inches high and nine inches across the brim, and is in sparkling, brilliant glass.

The picture in the lower right shows a clear glass hat with a double crown. It is an oversize hat, four inches high and seven inches across the brim. Little is known about it beyond the fact it was found in the middle west.

The first hat at the left in the upper row of Plate 151 is in an iridescent glass called Taffeta; it is found in blue and in gold-iridescent colors, and has the brim turned up on one side and down on the other. Quality was sacrificed to cheapness during the vogue of this glass, which was about the turn of the century, and it is usually dismissed as a cheap and vulgar imitation of Tiffany, but a hat in this glass is not common, and happy indeed is the collector of animal-covered dishes who can bring home a hen in Taffeta glass.

The middle hat in the upper row is a tumbler hat in light opaque green. It is a comparatively late hat, but any hat in opaque green is a rarity, and very, very few collections can boast of even one. Another, and much finer, hat in opaque green may be seen on Plate 138.

The third hat in the upper row began life as a wine glass. Before the glass had cooled, however, the workman folded over the bowl to form what is now a perfect hat atop a pedestal. Such a thing is called a "frigger" in the glasshouses of England. It is easy to opine that there would be several friggers in any large hat collection; with the exception of some tumbler hats which were made commercially, they are among the most desirable of all hats. The most eagerly sought after, perhaps, are the hats made from the very early medicine and pharmacy bottles. These are *known* rarities, but the serious collector will soon discover that it is not impossible to discover an *unknown* rarity, one that at less cost will give him equal satisfaction.

The first hat in the lower row of Plate 151 is a decorated fedora in milky-translucent glass. These hats were issued as souvenirs, and may sometimes be found bearing various dates ranging from 1886 to 1897, which may be taken as their period of manufacture. They are found in milky-translucent, clear, opaque white, and red stained; they have not been reproduced and are considerably more pleasing if their original decoration is intact.

The last hat in the lower row of Plate 151 is a clear glass bonnet, engraved and gold-filled. Originally expensive, today worth very little, this hat is an example of a type of decorated glass most frequently found in the larger and more opulent cities.

The first hat at the left of the upper row on Plate 152 is a clear fireman's hat blown with a hollow knob, the end of which was knocked off so that the hat might be used as a funnel in canning juices. The third hat in the same row has a solid knob, and is an example of the later type of offhand hats. Both these hats were made by Theodore Peters in the Graham glass factory in Evansville, Ind., about the year 1900.

The middle hat in the same row, of somewhat earlier eastern origin, is characterized by two knobs atop the crown. Hats may be found with three or four knobs similarly placed, following the fantasy of the workman.

The first hat in the lower row is a clear tumbler hat of choicer quality. It is lead glass, perfectly shaped with folded brim, and shows a pattern reminiscent of cut glass. Carloads of pressed glass made to imitate the popular and high-priced cut ware were sold as *cut glass* in the late 1890's and the early years of the present century. It is not always easy to distinguish between the two (to the novice it is impossible), and the unscrupulous found thousands of victims. This practice, plus the cost of the genuine, sounded the death knell of cut glass, though cut and engraved goblets, chiefly light cut, have always been made in bewildering and tiresome thousands of patterns.

The last hat in the lower row is a tumbler hat in the Colonial pattern. This was an early Sandwich design which may have been copied by other factories. It is a rarity, of course, but cannot be said to be as desirable as a Bellflower hat. The value of a pattern glass hat is determined by the collectors of that pattern, not by the hat collector. Very few collect the Colonial pattern, many collect Bellflower; hence the difference in the desirability of the hats!

GROUP III

It does not require much time for the novice who begins specializing in the collecting of hats to learn that the blown ones are more easily found than the pressed varieties. Even among a selection of five hundred hats, it is difficult to find enough

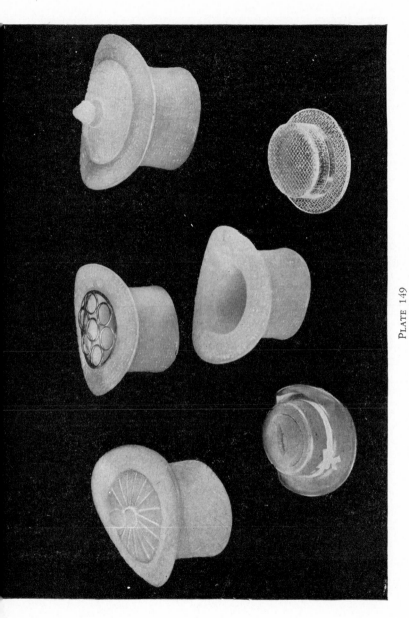

PLATE 149

Four translucent hats, found in numerous shades of color, which were made at Baccarat during the 1860's. The sailor hat at the right was intended as a salt dish and may be found in sets, in color.

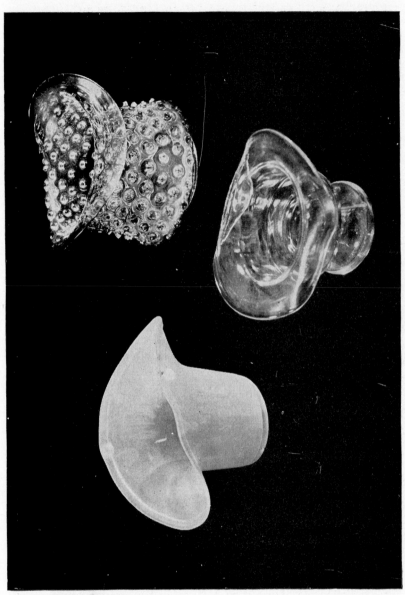

PLATE 150

A white frosted bonnet, marked "Hang up your hat." 2. An interesting amber hobnail

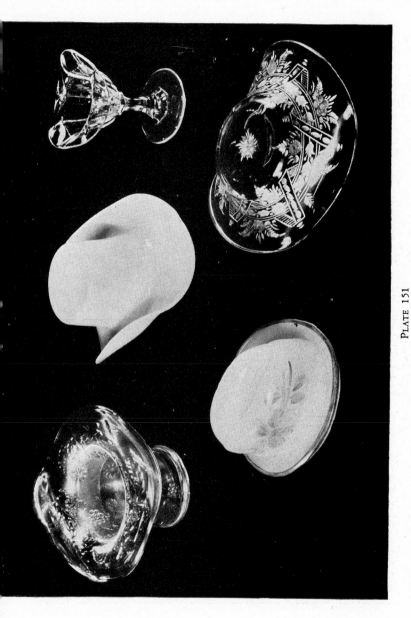

PLATE 151

A varied group, including a gold-iridescent; an opaque blue tumbler hat; a wine glass turned into a hat; a fedora and a bonnet.

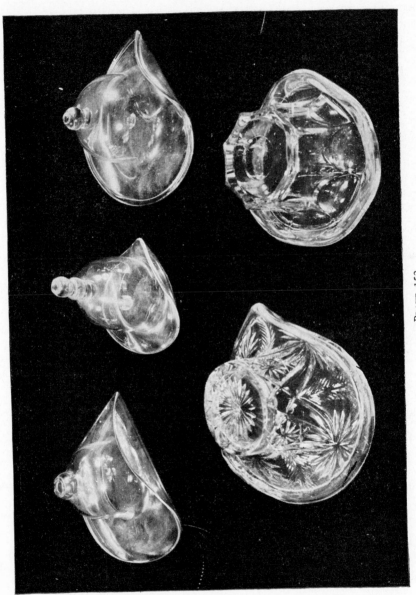

PLATE 152

Upper: Three blown hats, with open, closed and double knob finials.

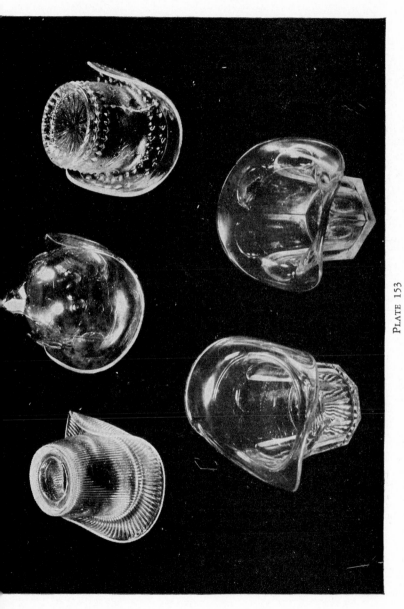

PLATE 153

Four hats produced from tumbler molds and a cherry pattern hat, made from a goblet mold.

pressed varieties to make an interesting story. While most of the hats pictured in this chapter are blown, it is not possible to cover the subject and at the same time ignore pressed types, particularly those used for souvenirs and for advertising various products. Most of the commercial glass hats of the 1880's and 1890's were made for use as toothpick holders. The practice of picking the teeth, now hardly a subject of polite conversation, is really an old and honorable custom. As far back at least as the days of Queen Elizabeth, every perfumed and beruffled courtier carried a golden toothpick set with precious stones, and teeth were industriously and ostentatiously picked! Even in Victorian times, toothpicks in carved bone and ivory were not uncommon; those fashioned from a quill and folding ones were manufactured commercially. It is only in comparatively recent times that shame has come to wait upon necessity and decrees privacy for an act that once was fashionable. There is no good reason to disbelieve that the Blown Molded ("three mold") hats were anything but toothpick holders.

Among the rarities in glass hats most eagerly sought by collectors are the tumbler hats. In Plate 153, all those shown are "tumbler" hats and all are in clear glass. By *tumbler* hats is meant those produced from water tumbler molds, the tops being folded down and finished by hand, thus utilizing one mold for two purposes.

The first hat in the lower row at the left is panelled, with a rayed base. It may be regarded as typical of the dozens of late tumbler hats found in western Pennsylvania and the middle west. The second hat in the lower row (at the left) is a very early blown tumbler hat, probably produced in the Bakewell factory in Pittsburgh. This is the same type of tumbler that is found in vivid colors, such as amber, sapphire blue, etc., in many collections of blown glass.

The first hat in the upper row of Plate 153 at the left is the Fine Rib pattern, which was produced in tableware during the 1850's and 1860's and possibly earlier by the New England Glass Co. It is lead glass of good quality.

The hat in the middle was fashioned from the bowl of a goblet while the glass was still hot. It is in the Cherry pattern, made by Bakewell, Pears & Co. of Pittsburgh during the 1870's. Such a hat may well be unique, as it was not a commercial product and appears to be a capricious piece of work done by some workman after hours. It will be noted that the knob on the crown is the stem of the goblet, where it has been clipped short. The third hat, in the Stippled Forget-me-not pattern, may have been produced commercially; if so, it is the rarest of the commercial pattern glass hats, if we neglect the rare colors in Daisy and Button. Some collectors might call it the finest of the pressed tumbler hats, which taken as a group are not particularly pleasing in design. The few known hats in Stippled Forget-me-not are nearly always found in the middle west.

Pattern glass hats from tumbler molds are known in the Colonial (Plate 152), Fine Rib, Bellflower, Bull's Eye, Hamilton, Ribbed Ivy. Of those listed, the rarest would be the Bull's Eye, Ribbed Ivy and Bellflower, though *any* of them will prove to be elusive enough when one searches for them!

Among the hats to be listed as both amusing and sheer curiosities today are the souvenir and advertising hats. There are cup plates which specialists cherish, bearing the names of advertising concerns, and no collection of any sort is complete without some of these forms, in the event that they exist. Any marked piece of either glass or china carries a special appeal to its owner, whether it be early or late.

In Plate 154 is shown a group of scarce souvenir hats. The striped glass one at the left in the upper row has incised on the brim the words, "Pan-American, 1901." It is in canary yellow with opalescent stripes to the right, and may be found in blue also. At first glance it resembles a modern hat produced by Fenton, but by running the fingers over the crown one can detect that the stripes are raised, whereas in the modern hat the surface is smooth. The old one may be found, and usually is, without the incised words.

The middle hat in the upper row (Plate 154) is clear to opalescent and was blown in an optic mold; that is, the inside shows vertical fluting whereas the outside is plain and smooth. The effect was obtained by blowing the hat in two molds. It was first blown in a mold with heavy vertical ribbing. Withdrawn, it was then blown in a "paste" mold—that is, a perfectly plain one, showing no pattern on the outside while retaining it on the inside. The optic mold is an old one and is still in use today.

The top of the crown of the hat just described is decorated with a transfer outline of a buffalo and on the side in old English letters "P A E 1901" (Pan-American Exposition). This second souvenir hat is unusual and rarely found today.

The third hat in the top row is in frosted glass and bears on the brim in molded letters the words "Worlds Columbia Exposition, 1893," and on the inside of the crown "Libbey Glass Co., Toledo, Ohio." More often it is discovered without this marking. On the Exposition grounds it was sold along with the Cabbage Leaf pattern and so may possibly have been intended to go with that design of tableware. It is in the form of a slouch hat of the type that fishermen affect. Besides being produced in frosted, or "satin," finish, it was also made in clear glass.

The first hat in the second, or lower, row at the left is a variant of the Daisy and Button in clear glass, and advertises on the clear brim the Goettler Hat Co., 1260 South Broadway, 60th Anniversary. The small hat in the middle is in clear glass with a queer surface finish cheaply decorated in blue paint and asks you to "Tip Your Hat at Asbury Park." The third and largest hat in the lower row is filled with seashells, one of which bears the name of Revere Beach, near Boston.

Plate 155 shows another group of advertising and souvenir hats. The first at the left in the upper row is a blue ribbed one with molded letters on the plain brim, reading: "The Bazar [*sic.*] Canton, Ohio, G. W. Warner." When these hats were made, the mold was so constructed that the top plate was detachable; thus the name of another firm could be substituted without remaking the entire mold.

The next hat, in the center of the upper row, is a red-stained fedora and advertises the Vermont State Fair. The third in that row is an amber ribbed one advertising "Bostick the Tailor, Noble Block, Wichita."

The first hat in the lower row at the left (Plate 155) is a blue cube pattern, bearing the molded letters "W. V. Rieger, 802 Main St., Kansas City."

In the center is a rather large yachting cap, stained in an amethyst color. It was issued as a souvenir or to be used as a "favor" at parties, particularly in the Middle West. Not unusual in clear, it is difficult to find in opaque white and rare in any other color. The last hat, a favor or souvenir item, was sold from coast to coast. The one illustrated is marked "Souvenir of Holyoke, Mass."

The first hat in the top row of Plate 156 at the left is blown in a good quality of clear glass decorated sparingly with light copper wheel engraving in the form of lines and crossed arrows. By some it is said to be Irish glass, but it is usually found in New England. It seems to be a companion hat to the third one in the same row, which is partly frosted and with different engraving. The middle hat in the top row features heavy vertical ribbing with curved lines on the brim. It is a well-designed hat, bearing a British registry serial number on the inside top of the crown. The early triangular registry mark was discontinued by London in 1883, after which a serial number was used. This hat is found in clear and opaque black, and possibly in other colors.

The first item in the second row, at the left, is a toy tumbler or whiskey glass made at Sandwich in their usual gamut of colors. The last hat in the same row is a frigger made from the commercial toy tumbler. Needless to say, the hat, though in clear glass, is a genuine rarity. The middle hat in the same row is a much later hat made from a midwestern wine glass.

The first hat in the top row of Plate 157, at the left, shows the well-known Thousand Eye hat which forms part of the extensive table service produced by Adams & Co. in Pittsburgh and by Richards & Hartley in Tarentum, Pa., in the 1870's and early 1880's. It is found in clear, amber, blue, and canary, listed in order of rarity. It has not been reproduced.

The second hat in the upper row illustrates the one known as the Raindrop hat. It is found in amber, canary, blue, and emerald green, listed in order of rarity. If clear ones were ever made, they must be quite scarce. It has not been reproduced.

The last hat in the top row is the Cube pattern hat. It is found in amber, canary, blue, clear, emerald green, and lime green, listed in order of rarity. It has not been reproduced.

It must be remembered that rarity alone does not determine the desirability of a hat. All the hats hitherto illustrated were designed for use as toothpick or match holders.

The first hat in the lower row at the left illustrates the Daisy and Button salt size hat. In addition to the fairly exact American reproduction, the Japanese produced a blown Daisy and Button hat in this size, and the French one with a heavy plain brim. Both these latter, however, are much rarer than the genuine original, though I do not know who would want them.

The middle item in the lower row is a salt in the form of a jockey cap. Fairly unusual in amber and blue, it is doubly so in canary and green.

The last item in the bottom row is the Daisy and Button bandmaster's cap. Never reproduced, it is found in clear, amber, canary and blue, of about equal rarity.

Plate 158 shows a variety of hats in the Daisy and Button pattern. In the upper row the first one is in frosted clear glass with red buttons; the second is similar but with blue buttons; while the third has a clear crown with red brim. In the lower row the first hat is a Daisy and Button tumbler hat. The second, with a fan top, is really not a hat, but is often found in hat collections. The third hat is clear with an amber hatband. The color in four of these hats is obtained by the use of stain that is afterward baked or fired on in a kiln. So intense is the heat that the stain almost becomes a part of the glass, and will withstand all ordinary use. The stain on these hats is in almost perfect condition after many years.

The Daisy and Button hat in the toothpick holder size may be found in blue, clear, amber, canary, raisin amethyst, smoke, clear with amber hatband, clear with red buttons, canary opalescent, clear with blue buttons, strawberry, and opalescent blue—carefully listed in ascending order of rarity. Queer omissions from this color scheme are red, green, and all the opaque colors, which seem never to have been made in the original, though reproductions have supplied our lack in this respect.

The Daisy and Button tumbler hat may be found in blue, clear, amber, canary, green, all of about equal rarity except the last which is unusual indeed, for it is the only green Daisy and Button hat. To date the Daisy and Button tumbler hat has never been reproduced. Not illustrated is the small tumbler Daisy and Button hat made from a wine glass, which is also quite unusual.

The fan-top toothpick holder may be found in cobalt blue, amber, canary, clear and light blue, named in order of rarity. It has been reproduced for use as an ash tray with two grooves in the fan top to receive a cigarette, with the result that the reproductions need deceive no one.

The smallest, or salt size, Daisy and Button hat is found in clear, amber, canary, blue of equal rarity and apparently in no other colors, though it has been reproduced in these and other colors including a cheap amberina.

The two largest sizes in this pattern, designed for use as spoonholders and as celery holders, are found in the same colors as the salt size. In the celery holder size, which is five inches tall, the rarest seems to be the clear, and the most beautiful the blue, which is in a lovely shade.

The Daisy and Button pattern is said by glassmen to have been created by the designers for cut glass, who gave it the name Russian Diamond, by which name it is still known to some glass cutters. The pattern was extremely expensive to cut. It was impossible, of course, to cut the hats as we know them, for the cutting wheel could not get under the brim. The manufacturers of pressed glass marketed it under several different trade names.

Almost every factory producing tableware made Daisy and Button, each one varying the design somewhat so that we distinguish them today by descriptive titles, such as Daisy and Button with Crossbar; Panelled Daisy and Button; Daisy and Button with Thumbprint, and so on. These variations apply to the tableware and not to the hats. A set of the hats in the four sizes in which they were made is illustrated in a Geo. Duncan & Sons catalogue, so this company may have been the originators of the design here.

On Plate 159 the first hat at the left in the upper row is in the familiar Diamond pattern with English hobnail brim; the third hat in the same row has both the brim and the crown in the Diamond pattern. This hat may be found in cobalt blue, clear, amber and light blue, listed in ascending order of rarity; only the last is unusual. To date this hat has not been reproduced, though six years ago a so-called English hobnail hat was produced in a variety of colors.

More recent than these two is the middle hat in the top row which was issued as a souvenir. It is found in cobalt blue, emerald green, clear, opaque white, light green, light blue, and frosted cobalt blue, listed in ascending order of rarity; none is very unusual. This hat has never been reproduced. Some years ago a hat having a brim identical with this one, but with a ribbed crown similar to the ones illustrated on the next Plate, was produced in rather limited quantities, and was promptly reproduced by the Japanese, who may be said to have achieved the dubious honor of reproducing a reproduction.

The first hat in the lower row is in the Daisy and Star pattern, which differs from the Daisy and Button hat in having four-pointed stars between the daisies instead of buttons. It comes in more brilliant, more definite colors than its predecessor, and may be found in amber, blue, canary, pale blue, clear, lime green, apple green, and emerald green, listed in order of rarity.

The middle hat in the lower row of Plate 159 illustrates an opalescent blue Daisy and Button hat. The last hat in this row might be called the "flattened hobnail" hat for want of a better

name, since a hat pictured on Plate 157 is almost universally
referred to as the Raindrop hat. In raised letters around the
hatband, it is marked with the words "Pat. Appld. For" and is
found in canary, amber, blue, and apple green. If clear ones
were made, they must be quite rare. Any hat in this pattern is
unusual, the apple green especially so. Though by no means so
fine a hat as the Thousand Eye, with which it is sometimes confused, it is still a more unusual hat, especially in the East. It is
most frequently found in Indiana. It has not been reproduced.

The first hat in the upper row of Plate 160 at the left illustrates what is usually referred to as the Finecut hat, though it is
not the Fine Cut pattern. It is found in clear, amber, canary,
blue and opaque white of about equal rarity. None is very
unusual. The brim of this hat may be found with a slight variation of pattern, of no great importance. There are no reproductions of it, so far.

The last hat in the upper row illustrates a Cube hat with
plain, heavy brim, sometimes referred to as the Block hat. In
clear it is the commonest of all the Cube hats; in frosted opaque
white it is unusual; in blue, illustrated on Plate 155, and in any
other color it is rare. It has not been reproduced.

The two hats in the lower row illustrate one variety of the
horizontally ribbed hat—the first with ribbed brim, the second
with plain brim. The plain brim apparently is found only in
opaque white. It is furnished with a hatband and bow, and is
further embellished on the top of the crown with a circle inside
an oval. It is found in clear, amber, canary, blue, opaque white
with plain brim, opaque white with ribbed brim, frosted opaque
white, opaque blue, opaque black, green and opalescent blue,
of about equal rarity with the exception of the last, which is
unusual. As such it has not been reproduced, though a similar
hat has been brought out.

The middle hat in Plate 160 also is a horizontally ribbed hat,
but has no bow on the hatband and no circle within the oval
on top of the crown. It is found in clear, amber, canary, blue,
and green, the colors all light. None is unusual. It was fre-

PLATE 155

A group of advertising and souvenir hats.

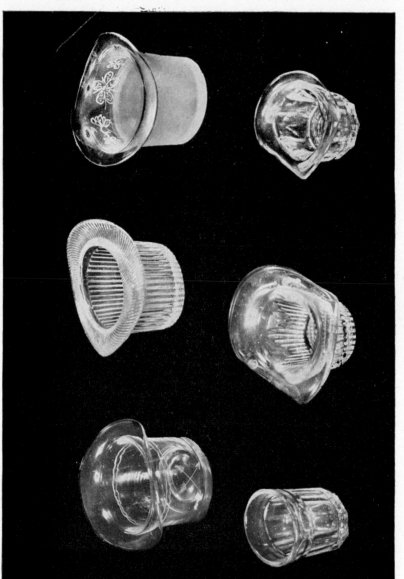

PLATE 156

Upper: Two engraved and an unusual ribbed hat.

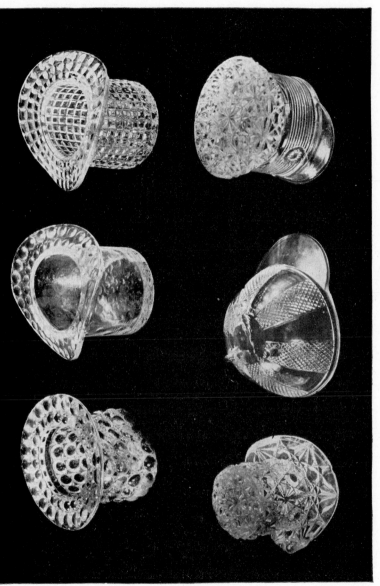

PLATE 157

Upper: Thousand Eye, Raindrop, Cube.
Lower: Daisy and Button salt size hat; Jockey's cap; Bandmaster's hat.

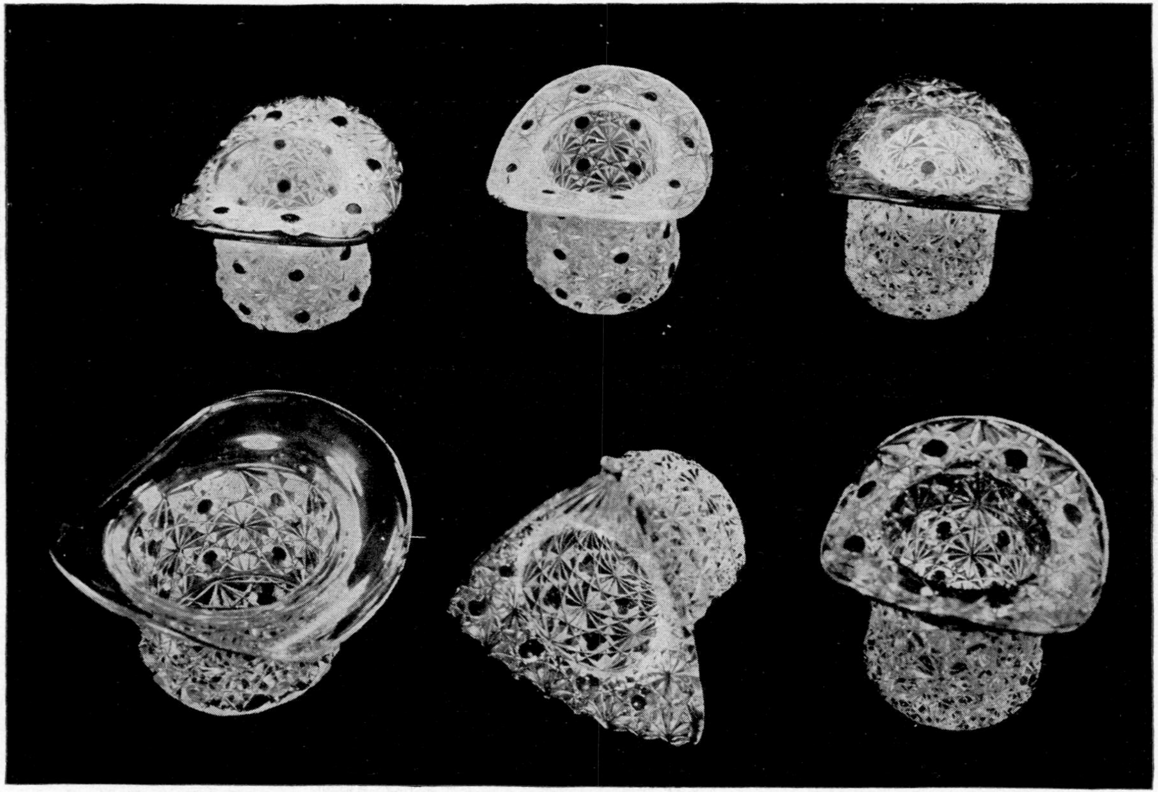

PLATE 158

A variety of Daisy and Button hats with the buttons decorated in color. A fan-shaped toothpick holder and Daisy and

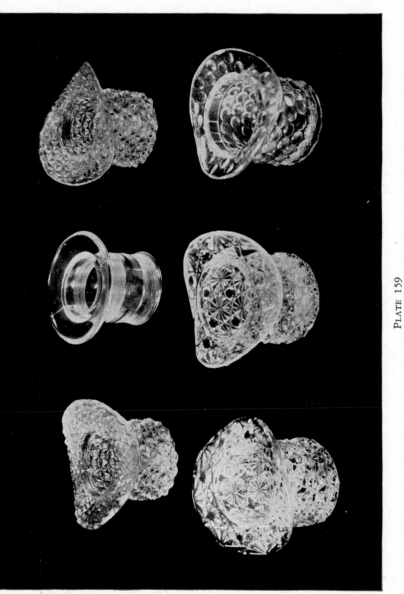

PLATE 159

UPPER: Two Diamond pattern hats with English hobnail brim; in the center a simply ribbed hat.
LOWER: Daisy and Star; opalescent-blue Daisy and Button; Raindrop pattern.

PLATE 160

Upper: Milk-white Finecut hat; Cube pattern.

PLATE 161

Celery vase size, ribbed hat. Three foreign hats, used as a vase, a wine glass and a cordial, according to size.

quently used as an advertising hat, and may be had with a metal collar around the crown engraved with the name of a business or product. This hat has not been reproduced.

The first hat in the upper row of Plate 161, at the left, is the largest, or celery size, horizontally ribbed hat, five inches tall. It is found in clear, amber, blue, canary, and green. It is unusual in canary and rare in green.

The other three pictures show three sizes of a rare foreign hat, the largest of which was sold as a vase, the smallest as a cordial and the middle-sized one as a wine glass. The largest, five inches tall, is cranberry; the smallest, 2¼ inches tall, is blue; the other is green. This rare hat was reproduced in Czechoslovakia and imported into the United States in 1938 in clear glass. The reproductions themselves are now rare. In this connection, it is well to point out that any foreign hat is rare. Importers often receive less than a dozen, and a gross is practically an unheard-of quantity except in the very cheapest ware, and not so much of that is imported, for they encounter the American manufacturer on his own ground.

GROUP IV

The first and fourth hats in the upper row of Plate 162 are clowns' hats with applied rigaree decoration, bearing the original paper label: "Clown's Hat Candle Snuffer, Made in England." One is pink to opalescent, the other green to opalescent. Between these are two fine hats in a rich opaque pink elaborately decorated in pure dull gold. They are really "flash," or case, glass in that they have a casing of clear glass over the opaque pink. Opaque glass always lacks clarity, and usually brilliance. Thus the outside casing of clear glass, which seems to serve no practical purpose, imparts to the completed work a brilliance it would not otherwise possess. Because of the transparency of the outside clear glass, the gold decoration seems to stand out and apart from the hat itself.

In the lower row are two rare hats decorated in silver deposit.

The first, in light blue, simulates a woman's hat with flowers and bow. The second, in opaque black, features a rococo decoration of interlocking scrolls.

The first hat in the top row of Plate 163 is stained a red amethyst, which is cut through to the clear glass in a Thumbprint pattern. Next is a cobalt-blue bonnet with an engraved and gold-filled band and bow. The third hat is overlay glass with a heavy sterling silver brim. The outside red glass is cut through to clear in a pattern resembling the Pineapple. In its fine quality of metal, the glass resembles that of Dorflinger; however, it bears the original paper label of the Belgian factory of Val St. Lambert, for a century or more a leading producer of fine glass.

The first hat in the lower row is also overlay glass, and has a sterling silver hatband on which is incised: "Columbian Exposition." The outside blue is partly cut to clear, partly stone engraved. Next is a triple-cased English hat, pink spatter over clear over an opaque-white lining. The hat is cut in a pattern of double lines and Thumbprint. Last is a fine hat, red over white Bristol, cut through in a Fan and Thumbprint pattern.

On Plate 164, the first two hats in the upper row and the first in the second row are a puzzle to those sufficiently versed in the mechanics of glass manufacture to realize the impossibility of stone-engraving such a small delicate pattern, and the prohibitive expense of doing it with the copper wheel. In reality, they are acid engraved in the following manner. The pattern was cut on a metal plate and transferred to the glass by means of tissue paper and asphaltum. Following the removal of the paper, the hats were given an acid bath, which ate the pattern into the glass around the asphaltum. The hats were then painted solidly with gold; a delicate wiping with a cloth left the gold only in the acid engraving. The hat was then fired in a kiln and thus completed. The hat in the middle of the upper row is inscribed "Father's napkin," indicating its use. It is difficult to imagine how either of these hats, with pure gold filling, could at any time have been sold for less than ten dollars, which may account for their rarity. The first hat in the lower row is enamel-filled.

The third and last hat in the top row is opaque black decorated with an arabesque pattern in gold.

The second hat in the lower row is a tiny woman's hat in clear glass with a red bow and ribbon. It is an example of lamp work—that is, it was made from glass tubes and rods in front of a gas jet. Lamp work, an old and honorable art, is the basic work of many paperweights, and is the method employed in making the excellent collection in the Peabody Museum at Harvard. In modern times, however, the art has been degraded into the making of inexpensive novelties. Most common of the lamp-work hats are those which appear to be knitted glass. Formerly these were made by itinerant lamp workers, often on exhibition at Fairs. They have been sparingly reproduced in modern times.

The third hat in the lower row, also quite small, is in opaque white with a green crown; around the brim appear the words "Tipped the World Round," acid-engraved and gold-filled.

The fourth hat in the lower row is an extremely rare overlay hat, green cut to clear, with a layer of opaque white on top of the crown delicately painted with an intricate floral design.

Plate 165 shows a group of paperweight hats. The first in the top row is a bubble-ball hat weight, part clear, part gold ruby. It is $3\frac{1}{2}$ inches tall, and the glass in the crown is very thick, measuring three inches wide and two inches thick.

Next is shown a paperweight of various colors and five large teardrops supporting a hat in clear glass. This hat weight is a northern Indiana product of the 1890's. The third is a bubble-ball weight in light blue supporting a hat in the same glass. The hats atop these weights are a survival of the shot cups used before the advent of blotting paper.

The hat at the bottom is a small derby with a solid crown centering a single flower. Considered as weights, these hats do not show fine workmanship, but they are an important item in a hat collection because of their extreme rarity.

The middle hat in the top row of Plate 166 is spattered only with particles of blue so fine that a delicate mottling is the result and appears as if it might have been sprayed on. Not very evident from the illustration is the fact that it is a policeman's hat.

The first hat in the lower row at the left is mottled only with pink; the companion hat on the lower right, only with blue. The small piece between these two is a jockey's cap in a pepper and salt effect of various colors.

The first hat in the upper row at the left is in blue translucent glass; the companion hat on the right, in translucent pink; the brims, which appear to be handmade, are of sterling silver. The glass of these two hats and the cap is probably foreign, but the silverwork is most likely American. The glass of the cameo scent bottles, for example, is English, but the silverwork is nearly always American, and so marked. The foreign glass manufacturer can compete with the American manufacturer in the United States, but the foreign silversmith is apparently not able to do so, for foreign silver, excepting the antique, is rare in American stores.

The first hat in the top row of Plate 167 is a rare offhand English hat blown in opaque-white Bristol. Not evident in the picture is the unusual brim treatment. It is thin to the point of danger, and gives off a high ringing sound when tapped, showing high molecular tension.

The second hat is cased in white over clear, cut through in a wreath and daisy design, and further embellished with an old-fashioned floral medallion of many colors and great complexity. Just beneath it is a derby showing similar treatment; both hats are probably of Bohemian origin.

The third hat in the upper row is an English Bristol one painted reddish purple on the inside and decorated with a band of roses in fine natural colors; the heavy glass has a chinalike quality. The fourth hat, like the first, is offhand Bristol with a high crown giving it the shape of a helmet. The gilded metal boss hides the hole made in breaking the glass from a blowpipe instead of a pontil iron.

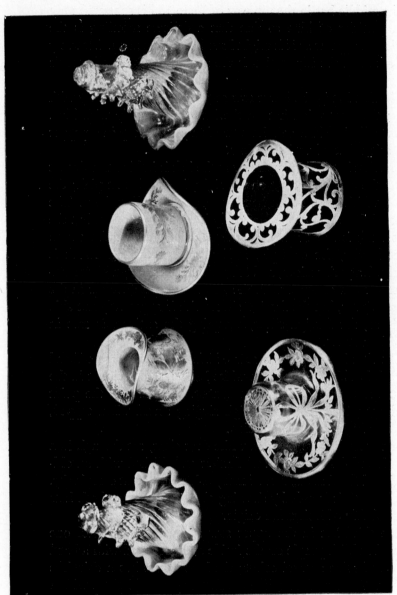

PLATE 162

Upper: Two clown hat candle snuffers, made in England.
Center: Two opalescent hats, decorated in gold.

PLATE 163

A group of cut and engraved hats, some in overlay glass. One bears the label of the Belgian factory of Val St. Lambert.

PLATE 164

Art glass hats of various styles, several of which were expensive types to produce.

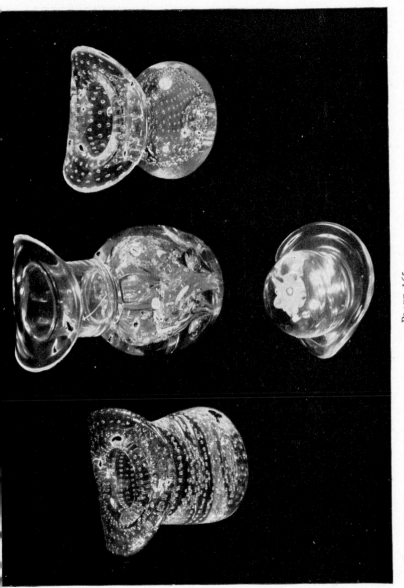

PLATE 165

A group of paperweight hats.

PLATE 166

Four hats spattered or flecked in color. Two translucent colored glass hats,

PLATE 167

Group of choice Bristol and Bohemian hats.

PLATE 168

A varied group, including cut, engraved, pressed and blown glass hats.

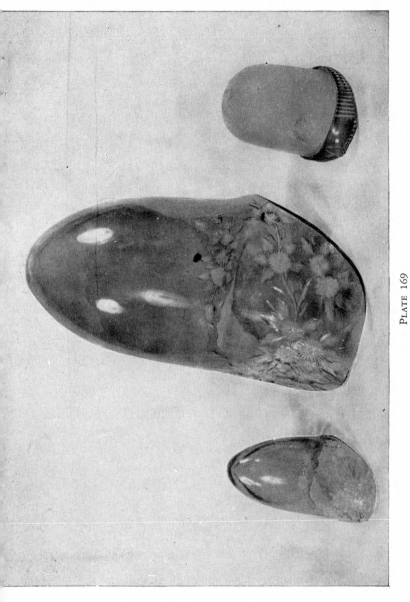

PLATE 169

Three unusual pitcher hats. Two are in overlay glass, and were made by Dorflingers for the Vanderbilt-Fair wedding.

The second hat in the bottom row is a typical example of the commercial Bristol hats, decorated, as it is, by means of a transfer print of a Dutch windmill. The other hats on Plate 167 were entirely hand done without the use of a transfer.

The first hat in the top row of Plate 168 at the left is a clear cut-glass hat, cut in a pattern known to glass cutters as the pinwheel, with a "glorious" star cut on the base. This should not be confused with the pressed glass pattern of the same name, to which it bears no resemblance. It is one of the elaborately over-cut patterns popular at the close of the last century, and is of interest chiefly because of its rarity. Any cut-glass hat is rare, which is remarkable if we stop to consider the erstwhile prominence of the industry. In the year 1900 there were more than three thousand glass cutters in Brooklyn alone. Today these are very, very few. One of the largest of the Brooklyn firms was owned by a Mr. Schotton, who employed several hundred cutters, and to whom the Union Glass Co. alone sold more than $50,000 worth of blanks a year. The discovery in England of a method of acid polishing glass gave greater impetus to the industry.

The middle hat is blue, mirrored on the inside and further embellished by four cut stars. Third in the upper row is a clear glass hat with an amber brim, pressed in a pattern to simulate cut glass. This hat is in the toothpick holder size, smaller than the one previously illustrated.

The first hat in the lower row is clear merging to a pellucid chartreuse. It is also found in clear to blue, and is blown in an optic mold with a flat ground base. It is a small and unusual hat. The next hat is a small straw sailor in a light canary with engraved hatband, engraved with wreaths and interlocked hearts with piercing arrow, all gold-filled.

The last hat in the lower row at the right is blown in what appears to be an "art" amber color, made by the Union Glass Co. and marketed under the name of "gold glass." It was made in this century, and hence is not very old, but the hat is of considerable interest in that it is a rare offhand product in a glass in which hats were never made commercially.

Plate 169 illustrates three pitcher hats. Originally designed for use as pitchers on a silver base or in a silver liner, they are sometimes found in large hat collections because their form instantly suggests a helmet or a London bobby's hat.

The first two are overlay glass, one green cut to clear, the larger a brilliant light gold ruby also cut to clear, in a floral pattern. They were originally made for the Vanderbilt-Fair wedding, a social event in the early years of the present century, and were salvaged from the old Dorflinger showroom when it was moved from downtown New York. The largest helmet, nine inches tall, bears the original Dorflinger paper label, and is a fine example of the glassmaker's art. Not everything that the Dorflinger people made is fine by any means, but in their happier moments, and for those who cared to pay for it, they made overlay as fine as any ever produced in America, though not, perhaps, equalling the superb excellence of English mid-nineteenth century overlay.

The third helmet is frosted clear glass with a band of cut ruby around the base.

GROUP V

The first two hats at the left on Plate 170 show two sizes of a rather elaborately patterned hat that in some ways resembles a crown. Both sizes seem to have been made only in clear and in a greenish canary, the latter originally decorated rather profusely in alloy gold. Variants of the small size may be found in clear glass; all are old.

The second hat in the top row, in clear glass, is decorated with copper wheel engraving and the words "Pass the Hat." It is rarely found with the engraving, and does not instantly reveal itself as a hat. It was originally issued as a lining for a silver container, designed perhaps as a mayonnaise or sauce boat. It is of New England origin.

The second hat in the lower row shows a clear glass cap with cut edges and elaborate copper wheel engraving in a vintage design. It is a rare piece of English or Bohemian origin. Copper wheel engraving is the oldest and still the most expensive thing that can be done to glass. The light, surface engraving, however, such as is found on this cap, is not costly, and the deep carving done by the copper wheel, in which the design seems to stand out in bas-relief, is not to be found on hats.

The first hat in the upper row on Plate 171 is a two-piece fedora in a rather deep hard blue. On the right is the same hat with the lid removed. Undoubtedly manufactured for some specific use, it is difficult today to surmise what that use might have been. Two-piece novelties were often put out as manufacturers' receptacles to contain sundry products, but such containers must be cheaper than this hat could have been. It is found in clear, amber, blue and canary, all rare. This hat I discovered pictured in a Gillinder & Sons catalogue of the 1880's, simply marked "Hat and Cover." It appeared on a page devoted to novelties, and was made at Greensburg, Pa.

In the middle of Plate 171 is a poke hat in cobalt blue showing a feather, gold-filled, a kind of Simple Simon affair by some called a Tyrolean hat. In front of it is a policeman's hat, also in cobalt blue, decorated with a band and a wreath, engraved and gold-filled. The engraved number "79" was a former characteristic of the actual hats. To the right is a cut-glass hat, cut in a pattern known to glass cutters as the six-side pattern. This hat, also in cobalt blue, is a minor achievement in the art of cutting glass. In ordinary practice, the object to be cut is held *over* the wheel, and the worker looks *through* the glass at the particular spot he is cutting. This, of course, would be impossible in dark-colored glass, as in the case of this hat. Accordingly, he would have to hold the hat *under* the wheel, working blind to a certain extent, in the manner of a copper wheel engraver who always holds the object to be cut under his wheel. These three hats, all in cobalt-blue glass of fine quality, were made at the Union Glass Co. in Somerville, Mass., out of the same glass that appears in the blue linings of silver salts.

At the bottom left of Plate 171 is a hat, mottled green, in bubbly peat glass, a rare hat of English origin.

The first hat in the top row of Plate 172, at the left, is a curiously molded small hat with a parrot sitting on the brim. Apparently it was made only in milk-white.

The second picture shows a clear bottle hat. It was made in two parts, the bottom part being pressed and joined to the crown while the glass was still hot. This was an original and interesting idea, but the result is marred by a poor quality of metal and by inferior workmanship. It is an unusual hat. The third hat is small and blown in opaque white, from northern Indiana.

The fourth picture shows a top hat with a narrow brim and a hatband in opaque white. The decoration, factory work of poor quality, was evidently put on "cold pack"—that is, not fired in the kiln—or else the enamels were not the special type required for glass- and chinawork. While it is a pressed commercial hat, the narrow brim makes it a fairly interesting one.

The first hat in the lower row is an oblong pressed hat in opaque white showing no pattern. Rather a plain hat, it is still a very rare one of foreign origin. Next is a small jockey's cap in clear glass.

The last hat in the lower row of Plate 172 shows heavy horizontal ribbing with a plain brim, and is found only in the salt size in clear, amber, blue and canary. Not a very impressive hat, it is still rather unusual in any color.

The large hat on Plate 173 has three wide folds in the brim. It is sometimes called the Dolly Varden hat, perhaps because of its resemblance to a woman's wide-brimmed hat. The one illustrated is clear to opalescent, and it may be had in blue—a typical example of the late cheap ware sold in the early years of the present century.

The first hat on Plate 173 has a heavy naturalistic hatband but otherwise shows no pattern. It is common in green, fairly unusual in amber, and rare in pink. In fact, any pink glass hat is rare. It has been sparingly reproduced in opaque black, and possibly in other colors. Originally it was made by the old Westmoreland Glass Co., before that firm changed hands.

The two hats at the bottom show two varieties of the straw sailor hat. The one at the left seems to have been made only in opaque white; the other is found in opaque white and clear, often crudely decorated. The opaque white of this hat will vary from an off-custard color to a very vague pink—the latter color induced, perhaps, by long exposure to the sun. They were produced by M'Kee & Brothers, Pittsburgh, Pa.

The first hat in the upper row of Plate 174, in deep rich cranberry, was blown in a diamond-quilted mold; the same mold, in fact, as was used for the cased glass hat, the fourth on Plate 144. The diamond quilting is quite small, and is not to be confused with the larger diamond quilting used on a group of hats made some six or seven years ago.

Second is a covered receptable in the shape of a crown resting on a cushion in brilliant blue translucent glass. In quality of metal and in fineness of mold work, this must be adjudged a piece of unusual merit. The British registry mark on the bottom indicates that it was registered in the Patent Office January 14, 1865.

The third hat in the upper row, also English, is opaque mandarin red flashed in a casing of clear glass to give it brilliance. It has a black hatband and has, on the brim, gold letters which read "Compliments of the Season." It is a rare hat, issued originally for the Christmas gift buyers.

The first hat in the lower row, in cranberry glass of English or Bohemian origin, has enamelled scrolls in what seems to be an attempt to reproduce Roman gold, familiar to the collectors of Worcester china. The second hat is early amberina, blown in what may best be described as a diamond quilted pattern. It was made by the Libbey Glass Co. in Cambridge, Mass., probably in the 1880's. A later version of this same hat in the cheaper amberina was sold as a souvenir of the Columbian Exposition, and may be found so marked. It is of interest in showing that some amberina, at least of this quality, was made after Libbey had moved his factory to Ohio.

The third hat is a Beau Brummel in cranberry glass of indifferent quality.

The first picture on Plate 175 shows a covered tumbler in the form of a laughing face in a rare frosted lemon color, the lid of which is a separate and perfect cap. This item is part of a drinking set consisting of six such tumblers and a central bottle in the shape of a man in golfing clothes, marked "The Jolly Golfer." Just beneath the covered tumbler is the same cap in frosted cobalt blue; turned the other way, it served as a coaster to hold the tumbler. This cap is unusual, and a complete set is rare.

The second hat in the upper row is a crown in Tiffany-type glass. It is cased, white on the inside, yellow on the outside.

The third hat is opaque black with six large dents in the crown, the lid of which is in the shape of a baby in frosted opaque white. The hat is not hard to find but the baby lid is unusual. A counterpart to both hat and lid exists in china in two or three sizes, and it is interesting to speculate as to which was the original. The black base to this hat may be found without the dents in the crown.

The large middle hat in the second row is a sombrero in selenium red glass, of Millville origin, about 1900.

The third hat in the lower row is an offhand piece in a rare glass of orange-red color with a red agate glass crown.

First in the upper row of Plate 176 is a large hat in the shape of a German field helmet in pink and white cased glass. It is decorated with glass acorns and has painted oak leaves outlined in gold. It is five inches tall and almost ten inches across the brim. To the right is a hat in clear overshot glass with a metal brim. Issued originally as a drinking set, the six holes in the brim held six small cups, and a bottle stood in the crown of the hat.

The first hat in the lower row at the left is clear glass with a frosted brim. It measures six inches across the brim, which is solid glass an inch or more in thickness, thus giving the hat considerable weight for its size. Next to it is a still larger hat in frosted clear glass, measuring more than ten inches across the brim, which in this case is hollow. This hat was found in the bins of the Union Glass Co., where apparently it had been forgotten. These hats illustrate a special technique, which is best explained by a careful study of the broken specimen illustrated in the bottom row of Plate 133. The hollow brim is shown, plus the fact that the hat was blown off the blowpipe, without the use of a pontil. Thus no pontil mark is seen on the finished hat. The blow-over, shown just under the brim, was later cut off, and the hat was thus completed.

The first item on Plate 177 is a tobacco jar in the form of a Negro head, the lid of which is a perfect straw sailor hat. The jar is opaque white; the hat lid is opalescent white. They are usually so found, but this apparent discrepancy caused little trouble, because the jar was entirely painted in lifelike colors. The hat measures five inches across the long way, and is much rarer than the straw sailors depicted on Plate 173.

The second large hat in the upper row at the right shows a hat in the spoonholder size pressed in a pattern to resemble cut glass. It is clear glass with an amber brim. It is a fairly late hat of foreign origin, but is rare with an amber brim.

The other three on Plate 177 are campaign hats. The middle one is the familiar Uncle Sam hat; this was never rare and has been made less so by reproduction. Originally it seems to have been made only in opaque white, but the new ones were made in colors as well, though not many colored ones have been made, and they are rarer than the old ones. They were first issued during the campaign of McKinley and Roosevelt; they were issued again when Taft and Sherman won the Presidency, and in each case were fitted with a slotted metal lid on which was pasted a paper label bearing the portraits of the candidates. Those bearing the portraits of the Democratic nominees are much scarcer.

The second hat in the bottom row at the right is variously stained in amethyst, blue, and amber colors cut through to clear in copper wheel engraving in a design of American flags on the crown and arabesque tracing on the brim. Around the hatband are cut the words "Bryan and Free Silver." This hat, so extremely rare, was probably designed on special order, for some Democratic club.

The first hat in the lower row at the left was produced in a finely stippled mold and bears in raised letters the words "The Same Old Hat" on one side of the crown, and on the other "He's All Right." This second phrase, a line from a popular song, is said to refer to Grover Cleveland, and the first phrase, "The Same Old Hat," to be an allusion to his first term as President. This hat is found in clear glass of poor quality and in milk-white of fine quality. The milk-white, of course, makes apparent the excellent design. This hat was produced by the United States Glass Co. of Pittsburgh, Pa. Why it should be referred to in the catalogue as a "Harrison Hat" is a mystery, unless it was used for the same Presidential campaign.

All of the hats pictured in this chapter are from the collection of Mr. Hobart Hollis.

PLATE 170

Two pattern glass hats and two engraved styles.

PLATE 171

An unusual two-piece hat; a Tyrolean hat; two cut and engraved hats and a mottled English model.

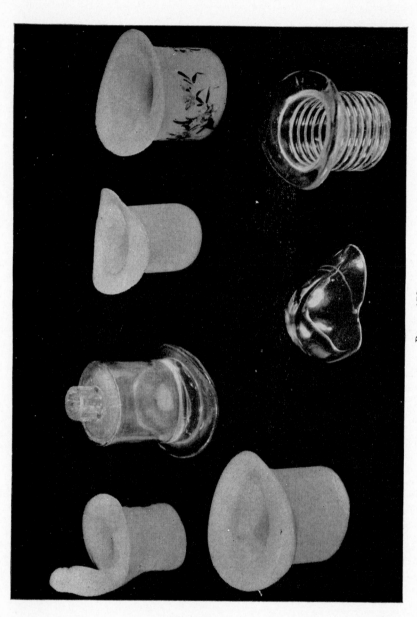

PLATE 172

At the left, a parrot perched on the brim of a Milk-white hat. A bottle hat. Three in Milk-white, a jockey's cap and a

PLATE 173

A plain hat with ribbed band; a tilted bonnet; a decorated white hat and two sailors which vary in detail.

PLATE 174

A varied group, including an English crown in opaque glass, a choice diamond-quilted amberina bar and other novelties

PLATE 175

Unusual two piece hat, in form of man's head with separate cap. Crown in ware similar to Tiffany's FAVRILE ware; black glass hat with parian baby lid and two blown hats.

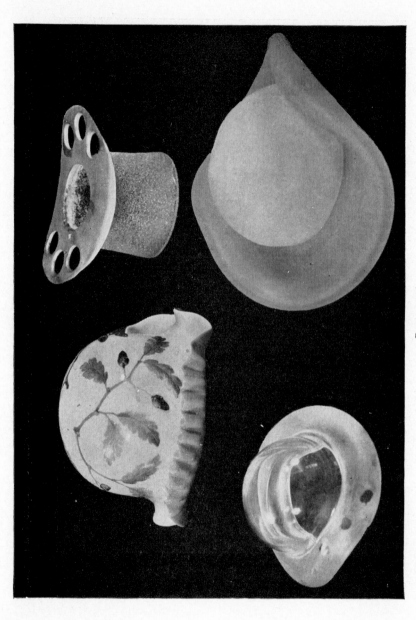

PLATE 176

Large decorated and crimped hat similar in shape to German field helmet. Overshot glass hat with metal rim. Two blown

PLATE 177

"Darky," two piece hat. Only one style of sailor will fit the head. In the center, "Uncle Sam" painted hat. An unusual pressed hat with amber brim and two souvenir hats.

Chapter XX

GLASS SLIPPERS, SHOES AND BOOTS

Apparently novelties in the form of little slippers and boots were made in many countries, both in glass and in china, over a long period of years. Just what material was used for the first of these interesting objects has not been established, but I am inclined to believe that the earliest may have been of blown glass.

There is a tradition that blown glass boots were made in England during the reign of George III in derision and ridicule of the Earl of Bute. While the former was still Prince of Wales, John Stuart, Earl of Bute, acquired great influence over him and, indeed, put into the head of that misguided and obstinate monarch the exaggerated idea of the powers of kingship which some years later was to cost him thirteen American colonies. After George became king, his friend and confidant was raised to a position of importance, first becoming one of the principal Secretaries of State and then Prime Minister. He lasted about a year in the latter post. His private life was above reproach, but he was probably one of the worst public servants England has ever known. His policy was one of royal absolution and his levying of excessively high taxes met with no favor in England. So great was his unpopularity with the people that in 1763 he was practically forced to resign as Prime Minster. It is quite possible that the slang phrase "boot him out" may have originated at that time.

There is an obvious difference between a slipper and a boot. According to the dictionary a boot is "a covering, usually of leather, for the foot and more or less of the leg." In the United

States, the word "boot" is distinctively applied to the form reaching at least well up on the leg. Otherwise, both here and in England, "boot" is a term generally used for any high-cut shoe. Thus, a baby's shoe is referred to as a bootee. A slipper, of course, is a low shoe easily slipped on or off the foot.

It has been my good fortune to have photographed the large and varied collection of nearly five hundred glass slippers and boots belonging to Mrs. Lloyd B. Wilson, of Washington, D. C., for use in this chapter. Mrs. Wilson has been a discriminating and avid collector.

From the examples shown here, one may gain an excellent idea of the variety and scope of this phase of collecting. On Plate 178 we see three boots blown in bottle form, and a fourth delicately swirled and in the shape of a rummer. The latter was a favorite in early days at hunt clubs. The glass boots with the loopings in white or color are in a Nailsea type, so all three pictured may be of Continental origin. The rummer in boot form with delicate spiral swirling may date from the time of George III.

On Plate 179 may be seen rarities in a group of boots, which may possibly have been made for drinking glasses or loving cups at hunt clubs. The largest boot in the collection measures $10\frac{1}{4}$ inches high by $6\frac{1}{4}$ inches in foot length. These have been found only in crystal. The largest shoe bottle is pictured in the same illustration. It is an elaborate frosted and clear high button shoe, resting on a hassock. Its total height is 12 inches. It is of French origin, being marked Deposé on the base. The style would denote the time of our Philadelphia Centennial in 1876 though it embodies the characteristics of what most people invariably associate in their minds with Victorianism. Next to it is a clear glass high button shoe, the engraved top flared and open, to form a flower vase or a drinking glass. The shoe rests on a round base. Because pictures are deceptive and collectors like accurate details, I am going to give dimensions in many cases. This shoe is $7\frac{1}{4}$ inches high and 4 inches across the base. Next to the largest man's boot, which incidentally is one of a pair, is a heavier crystal boot, though the lines are similar. It is 7¾ inches high and the foot is 5 inches long. There is an engraved mark on the base, which must signify the factory but it is unlike any other such mark I have seen. It would doubtless be difficult to find anyone today who could identify it. The smallest boot on Plate 179 is in a clear cranberry color, such as was used in several of our New England factories. This one is 6¼ inches high by 4¼ inches in length of foot.

Plate 180 pictures a varied group, from a shoe bottle to blown rummers and slippers. In the foreground is a dainty little slipper, decorated in a delicate pattern. The sapphire-blue swirled rummer and the crystal one near it appear to be among the earliest and best types in the collection, though I have been told similar glasses were made by the Corning Glass Works, of Corning, N. Y. The sapphire-blue plain boot between the two swirled glasses could have been produced almost anywhere but looks as if it might be of English origin. The shoe bottle with the metal cap is interesting and the clear boot, engraved about the top, is a choice piece. The great difficulty is in attempting to make attributions, when such boots as the one in clear glass and that in milk-white next to it could have been produced by an American or a foreign workman, at any one of a large number of factories, over a period of years. Glassblowers can make the same style boots today and it would be more difficult to tell them from old ones than it is in the later pressed glass varieties. The three earliest boot glasses pictured usually date from 1790 to 1810. They were imported from England.

In the center of Plate 181 is an amber boot, 6 inches high, engraved in the characteristic Bohemian Vintage pattern. This is marked "Teplitz 1840." Next to it at the right are three choice Bristol-type slippers. I say "Bristol type" because an illustrated catalogue of the Boston & Sandwich Glass Co. pictures such a quantity of finely decorated wares that slippers could well have been included in their line. There was a time when all such painted articles were lumped under the heading of "Bristol," just as all glass in this country was "Stiegel" or "Sandwich."

To return to the slippers, one is plain green with a white lining; one is rose, painted with colored flowers and the third is opaque lavender, enameled in white. Not illustrated is a slipper in orange decorated with flowers, and another in white also decorated with flowers and the edge striped in gold. All measure about 6¾ inches long.

Boots were produced in Spatter glass, in much the same manner as were the hats, except that they were usually more elaborately decorated. On Plate 181, at the left, are three case glass shoes, having applied glass or "rigaree" decoration in crystal against the colored background. Two are in Spatter glass and one is in a plain rose color. These could well have been made by Hobbs, Brocunier & Co. of Wheeling, W. Va., who turned out many novelties during the 1880's, but some of this type are known to have been produced in Indiana.

On Plate 182 may be seen three perfume bottles in the shape of Dutch slippers and also four slipper and shoe bottles. The Dutch slippers may be encountered frequently, though seldom in the tiny size pictured. In Holland, years ago, blue china Dutch shoes filled with eau de cologne were seen in all shops carrying novelties for sale. The Dutch slippers are blown glass perfumes, similar in style to our Blown Molded glass except that the patterns of decoration are entirely different. The largest one illustrated is 3¼ inches long. The other two are about 3 inches long. Most of the Dutch shoes do not measure over 4½ inches long. Generally there are flowers on the vamp, but the styles vary.

The shoes on Plate 182 are an interesting group. The first at the left may have been an ink bottle. It is very rough and sharp where the cork fits in. It is plain aquamarine, 4 inches long and 1½ inches high. Next to it is a long, flat high shoe, laced up the front. This one is 3¼ inches high, the foot 4 inches long. The cork is missing. It also appears to have been an ink bottle. The shoe next to it has more detail. It is laced up the front and has a scalloped edge adorning the top. Probably the stopper is not original though it appears to be. This shoe bottle is also 3¼ inches high, the foot 2 inches long. In general style it suggests a perfume bottle. The last shoe in the row has ribs about the top which do not show in the illustration, and two flowers on the vamp. It is 3¾ inches high, the foot 3 inches long.

Among the rarest novelties in slippers are the little thimble holders. Four are pictured on Plate 183. They are exceedingly scarce today, doubtless owing to their diminutive size, thereby causing them to be easily lost or overlooked. Two are slippers, in shape similar to our modern "mules." They measure 2¼ inches in over-all length. They were made for the Pan-American Exposition at Buffalo, N. Y., in 1901 and have been found in several colors. The little blue high shoe has white enameled lacings. The very dark one is in a deep amethyst, with frosted, or satin, finish. The detail is exceptionally fine. It is an oxford style, with four lacings. One wonders whether it could not have held a tiny scent or perfume bottle, rather than a thimble. Possibly they were made and sold both ways. These so-called thimble holders have been found in blue, with white enamel lacings; lemon color; amber; honey amber with no decoration; in crystal with a flower in white, besides the amethyst oxford style and blue high shoe. The high shoe is the smallest of all, being only 1½ inches high and the same in length.

In the upper row of Plate 183 is a cut scent bottle with original stopper, 2½ inches long. Next to it is a crystal blown perfume without a cork or stopper, 3¾ inches high. Alongside it is a clear blue slipper, shaped like the thimble holders. This is 3¾ inches over-all length. An unusual boot completes this page. It is a translucent white, decorated in gold, of the Bristol type. This is 3 inches high.

The boots in pairs, meaning a right and a left, were made in some patterns and one such pair in a frosted, or satin, finish may be seen at the left of Plate 184. Each boot stands on an oval base and is 3¾ inches high. These are scarce but well worth searching for because they make such interesting containers for matches. The story accompanying these boots is that they were made at the Mt. Washington Glass Co. of New Bedford, Mass., as a gift to the wife of one of the company officials, for her new baby, by one of the glassworkers. It is said that this was the only pair of the kind made and that they were produced in 1883. I cannot vouch for this story. If it is true, then the mold for the boots must have been destroyed. It will be interesting to learn whether any others like them ever come to light.

An indication of the popularity of blown glass boots in Europe is shown by the two pictured in the center of Plate 184. One carries a view in the city of Hamburg and is further embellished with gold decoration. The similar boot beside it is plain, with no decoration, but would appear to have been produced by the same company. The leg in the latter bulges outward, instead of being straight.

The two slippers at the right of the boots are both rarities. One is frosted and very nicely cut; the other is of heavy glass with a small applied decoration. All the slippers display an interesting variation in the style of the heels. The last one described has a high "spike" heel. The over-all length of this slipper is 7½ inches. The other frosted slipper on Plate 184 is attractive because of its simplicity.

Of interest to collectors will be the pair of Continental lacy boots shown on Plate 185. The workmanship is unlike anything the Boston & Sandwich Glass Co. ever turned out. These boots could have been made in France, Belgium or England. They are the only pair of lacy boots known in this country at this time.

An unusual slipper of the type to delight the heart of any collector is that in the lower right-hand corner. It is threaded and has a decorative applied rigaree band about the top; it rests on a mirror. Choice specimens such as this, which have an appeal that reaches others besides specialists in boots and slippers, always spur a collector on.

Above the threaded slipper is a painted slipper with a white lining. The decoration is exceptionally attractive. It could have been done at Sandwich or by the New England Glass Co.

PLATE 178

Boot 9¾ inches high, with enameled loopings. Two smaller Nailsea type, with white loopings through the glass. Early English blown boot drinking glass, in swirled pattern.

PLATE 179

From the right, cranberry colored boot. Two clear glass blown boots, the taller being the largest in the collection. Woman's shoe drinking glass and frosted shoe resting on hassock, in form of bottle.

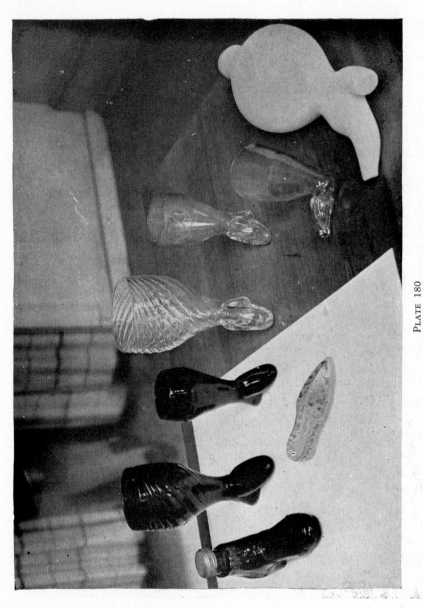

PLATE 180

Two shoe bottles, five boot drinking glasses and a decorated slipper. Boots blown in the swirled pattern have been made in America, as well as in Europe.

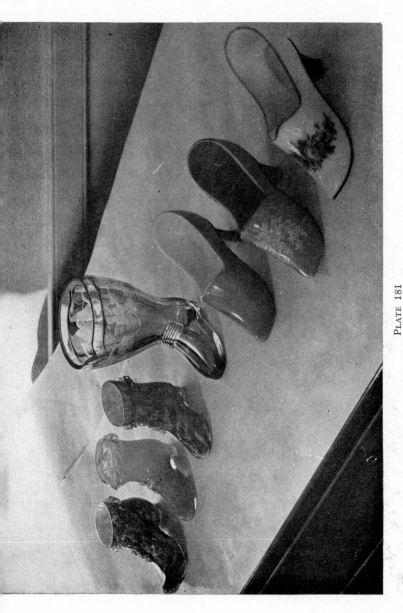

PLATE 181

One painted, one enameled and one plain Dutch slipper. Amber boot drinking glass, cut in Vintage pattern. Three case glass shoes, two being in Spatter glass and one plain blue, decorated in crystal.

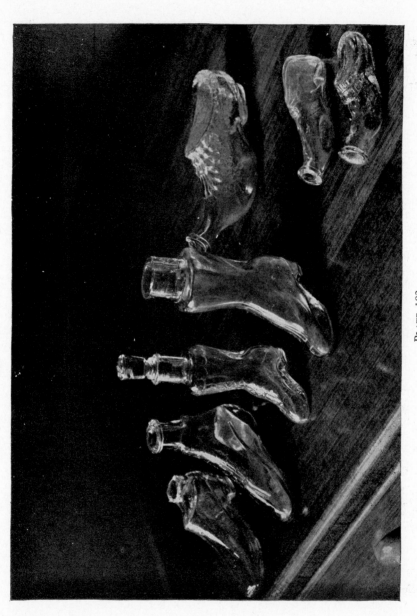

PLATE 182

Three blown glass Dutch slipper bottles in a type made in many sizes. Three high shoe bottles and a smaller one,
which may have been used for ink.

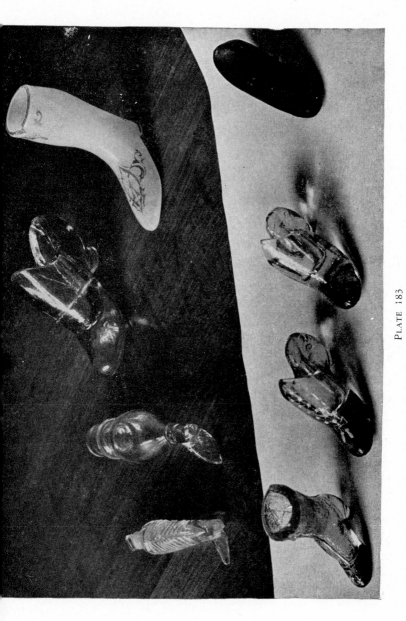

PLATE 183

Upper: Cut glass scent bottle; blown shoe bottle; heavy glass slipper; translucent white boot decorated in gold.
Lower: Four rare miniature slipper thimble holders and a miniature shoe.

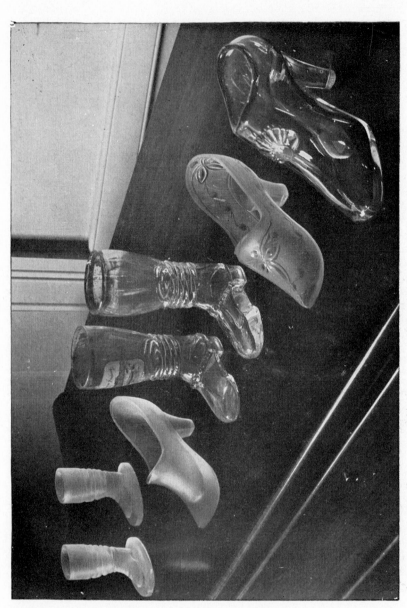

PLATE 184

Right, heavy crystal high slipper with applied decoration. Frosted and cut slipper. Pair of tall boots, one enameled with

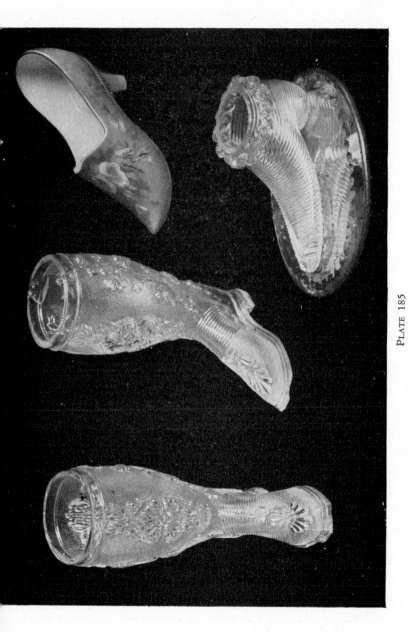

PLATE 185

Pair of lacy boots which are probably French. Decorated slipper in Bristol style. Rare threaded glass slipper mounted on a mirror.

Plate 186 shows a varied group. The large boot at the left is blown in cranberry color, and has a clear glass applied heel. It is obviously a vase, heavy and well balanced. The other large boot at the right is a deep ruby red, and might be Bohemian glass. It is a curiosity, in that it has a heel of wood covered with kid, which covers the pontil mark. The band at the top and the decoration on the sides and front are in silver. The three clear, small boots are all English drinking glasses, supposedly made about 1800. The first one with the cut design is slightly later.

The large slipper in the center of Plate 186 is Venetian. It was brought directly from that country some years ago, so there seems little doubt of its origin. The general coloring is blue, with the flowers mostly in red and the heel in gold. The threaded slipper and lacy boots are repetitions of those shown in a close-up view on Plate 185.

A really handsome slipper is the largest in the group on Plate 187. It must have been an expensive one to produce because there is a considerable amount of work involved in making one so heavily decorated in silver. Beneath the filigree casing there is a lining in blown glass. It was purchased in Holland. Beside it to the right is a colored Spatter glass shoe with applied crystal decoration. This is case glass and probably a product of one of the Indiana factories, though Hobbs, Brocunier and Co. of Wheeling, W. Va., were large producers of novelties during the 1880's. In front of the Spatter glass shoe is one in opaque white, with colored flower and leaf applied on the vamp as well as about the top. An unusual swirled case glass slipper with a turned-up toe is at the lower left. This is in color, with an applied leaf across the front and a rigaree band at the top. Such a slipper in a swirled pattern is more rare than the Spatter types.

Next to the shoe with the silver deposit, at the left, is another attractive painted slipper, with a white lining. This was made by the New England Glass Co., and bears a paper label on the base, marked: "Patented N. E. G. Co., March 23, 1875." The figured shoe resting on a round base with a scalloped edge in the foreground is a rarity found lately by Mrs. Wilson. The larger figured slipper at the right, with an applied ribbon, also is a rarity. It is a blown piece, in a diamond quilted pattern. There is a little hand-pressed berry on the front, typical of the Mt. Washington Glass Co.

Plate 188 illustrates an assortment of boots, shoes and a slipper. The boot with the strap, first at the left, has a figured pattern on the foot and plain solid glass heel. This type is scarce. Next to it is a baby's shoe with the tongue hanging out. These are rare today. They were made by the Bellaire Goblet Co. of Findlay, Ohio. One is pictured in a Bellaire Goblet Co. catalogue; apparently the shoes were not made in large quantities, because they are so scarce today. The one pictured is in amber. Next to the little shoe is a baby's bootee, which has been found in several colors, including opaque light blue, apple green, amber, clear blue and crystal. The detail is so fine and lacy that when collectors first discovered it, it was immediately attributed to Sandwich. However, it appears in an old trade catalogue of the King Glass Co. of Pittsburgh, Pa. They are a little-known company but in their day turned out quantities of novelties. The items on the page where the baby's shoe is pictured, are listed in crystal, amber and blue, but apparently the line was so popular that other colors were included. These are 2¼ inches high.

In the center of Plate 188 is a Daisy and Button slipper mounted on a tray. The tray is what we know today as Fish scale, though it was made originally by Bryce Bros. of Pittsburgh who termed it the "Coral" pattern. An entire table setting was produced in the Coral. The slipper, when mounted on a tray, was listed by Bryce Bros. as an ash tray. The same type slipper was made without the tray. The ash trays were made in blue, amber, yellow and crystal.

The maker of the boot to the right of the Coral, or Fish scale, ash tray is unknown. The one pictured is in opaque light blue, in a rather elaborate pattern of conventionalized leaves.

There are probably other opaque shades in this same boot, but any are rare. It stands 3 inches high.

Next to it is a man's plain amber boot with a satin finish. Nothing is known about it, but the satin finish would indicate a possible date of manufacture at the time when satin glass was so popular in the 1870's and 1880's. At the right end is a plain amber boot, without a satin finish. It has a band of horizontal ribs as decoration just above the instep.

Many of the somewhat later novelties are pictured on Plate 189. Beside the large buttoned shoe in the center is a pair of salt and pepper shakers with pewter tops. These fairly scarce items are seen in crystal as well as with a frosted finish. They were probably made at the time of the Centennial in Philadelphia. I have heard that similar boots were produced having screw tops and a handle in addition, and that they were sold filled with candy. Another style had a pewter top with a lid designed to be used as a mustard jar.

The high shoe in the center is of clear glass and has buttons, with a scalloped edge, like many old-fashioned high shoes. It is 4¼ inches high and was undoubtedly designed for a flower holder.

The three slippers on Plate 189 show how they were utilized as containers for perfume bottles. The smallest slipper is in a cube pattern and holds two orange-colored scent or perfume bottles, which the owner cannot guarantee are the original bottles. They could be. This particular type of slipper is later than some of the others and has been rather widely reproduced. The slipper is 3 inches long and 1½ inches high.

Next to it, at the right end, is another perfume bottle in a rather short, stubby slipper which is in color, while the bottle is crystal. At the left end of Plate 189 is another perfume bottle in a different shaped Daisy and Button slipper. In an old catalogue it was amusing to find these listed as "Our Exquisite Odor Stand."

The tall boots on Plate 190 are from Germany and were doubtless filled with beer at one time. One bears an inscription which, translated, reads "Good Thirst." These are not very old. At the right of the smaller boot is an interesting shoe bottle with metal stopper, which is equipped with metal roller skates. In these maidless days such a gadget might be welcome at times—it could be sent spinning across a table! This sugges-tion may not be welcomed by mothers who are laboring over their children's table manners.

There are two figured glass high shoes in the center of Plate 190 both attached to bases and containing perfume bottles with the original stoppers. Both are in fine cut patterns, one show-ing buttons reaching to the top. In the foreground is an un-usual frosted glass baby's shoe, as well as a clear glass Dutch shoe. Behind them appear a frosted, or satin, glass boot and an exceptional clear glass shoe.

The round flat piece on Plate 191 is a wall plaque in blue, with two receptacles for matches. The match holders are in the form of slippers, which are stippled. The background of the plaque is in a pressed Cube pattern. It is 4¼ inches in diameter. This piece has been noted in amber and in milk-white. Prob-ably one exists in yellow.

The large slipper in the center is in a blue fine cut or dia-mond block pattern, with a decorative bow. It will be noted that it has a band of vertical ribbing about the top, which is an unusual feature. It also has a wide, clear sole, visible across the toe, and a Cuban heel. It is 7¼ inches long and 3½ inches high. Duplicates of this slipper are rare, so it may be Continental.

The first slipper at the left on Plate 191 has a pincushion container, instead of perfume bottles. It is clear glass painted black and has a flat bow with short ribbon streamers. The heel, which is clear, and the sole are both solid, thick glass. This novelty was probably put out for Christmas sales, or possibly at the time of the Centennial in 1876, though it appears to be of a later date.

Next to the pincushion slipper is another clear glass one, sans the cushion, which has been stained in red. The heel is clear, solid glass.

The wall pocket for matches at the left of the large slipper is in the form of a boot and may be found in crystal and in colors. It is not particularly rare. The little Daisy slipper at the right-hand end of the row is an individual salt. These were made in clear and in colors. Considering the fact that they were a novelty of the 1870's and 1880's, they are now quite difficult to find. These are 3¼ inches long and 1½ inches high. There is a fine mesh on the sole of this particular type and the heel is solid.

The two slippers at the left on Plate 192 are alike, except that one is clear and the other stippled. The stippled slipper has a large Cuban heel. Its only decoration is a small bow Though they appear very small in the picture, they are 4½ inches long and a little over 2½ inches high. The one next to it answers the same description, except that the surface is bright and clear, without stippling.

The baby's moccasin has been found only in clear and in frosted glass, so far. It is an extremely difficult item to find. In height it measures 2¼ inches and is 4¼ inches long. Next to the moccasin is the heaviest slipper in the collection. It is plain solid heavy glass, blue in color. Others have been seen in clear glass, milk-white, light green and emerald green. It measures 6½ inches long by 3½ inches high. The slipper beside it is similar, except that it has a row of beading along the edge and is cut in, in front, instead of being rounded. On the end, or the first slipper at the right, is a yellow wall pocket for matches. It is in the Daisy and Button pattern, with a wide panel dividing the design. It is 6¼ inches long and has a double row of dewdrops around the heel. There is a fine Diamond Quilted design over all the sole. This "Match slipper" was produced by the United States Glass Co. of Pittsburgh in crystal and colors, though it is rare except in yellow.

In the center of Plate 193 is a pair of high shoe flower holders. There are not many shoes, boots or slippers which were made in "left and rights" but here is a pair in blue. They are mounted on a scalloped base, marked "B & H." They are button shoes, as may be seen in the illustration, and are 5¼ inches high by 3 inches across the base. The pattern is a star design, which we lump under the heading of "fine cut" because there are so many variations.

To the right of these high shoes is a man's boot in blue, with heavy horizontal ribbing on the heel. The vamp is stippled and the back of the boot clear. This is an unusual collector's piece, seldom encountered. It is 3 inches high and 3¾ inches long. Lately a duplicate has been found in dark amethyst.

At the right end of Plate 193 is a funny little ragged shoe, with small toes protruding through the end. It has been found in opaque lavender, and in milk-white decorated in gold. Probably these were produced about the time of the Pan-American Exposition held in Buffalo, N. Y. They are 2 inches high. At the left end of the row in Plate 193 are two dark glass slippers with Cuban heels. When held to a strong light, the one next to the high shoe is a deep amethyst but the other has been painted. It will be noted that the heel is of clear glass. The slipper with the high vamp, next to the boot, is stippled in front and back and has a row of small hobnails decorating the sole. This is thought to be of English origin, though it is not marked. It is 4½ inches long. The end slipper at the left is flashed in red, with a hollow toe. It is plain except for a scalloped border near the edge and there are double lines panelling the vamp. It is 4½ inches long and 2½ inches high. The edge of the opening is sometimes gilded.

In the center of Plate 194 is a pair of heavy amber slippers with pointed toes turning up like Chinese shoes. They have a small bow in front and a row of beading may be discerned forming a border along the edge. As an unusual feature, the back edge is adorned with one large and four small scallops. These have Cuban heels. They measure 6½ inches long and 3½ inches high. At the right are two shoes on skates which vary in detail, though they are both in a fine diamond mesh. The one at the end flares at the top, is larger around, and has a scalloped edge. The shoe section is meant to simulate alli-

PLATE 186

Two extra large boots and three small ones which were probably drinking glasses. Rare slipper in foreground with

PLATE 187

Elaborate slipper with heavy silver deposit decoration. Two Spatter shoes, one swirled, both with applied decoration in crystal. White shoe with applied decoration in color. Small Daisy boot on standard. Painted Bristol type slipper and a rare figured glass slipper with bow, at the right.

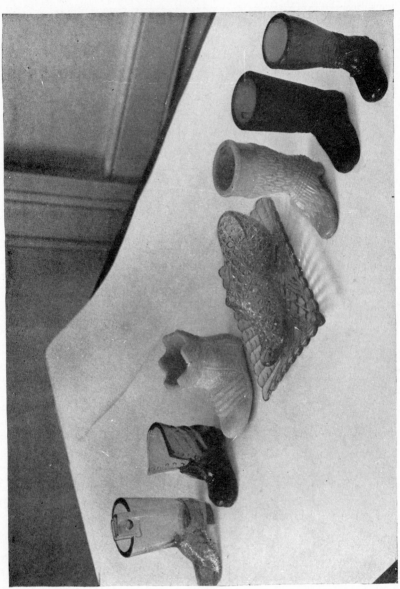

PLATE 188

Center, Daisy and Button slipper mounted on Fishscale tray, which was an ash tray. Four unusual boots, a child's shoe

PLATE 189

Three slippers which held perfume bottles. Two different styles in salt shakers and an unusual crystal high shoe.

PLATE 190

A varied assortment, including two high boots, two ladies' shoes holding perfume bottles, a boot salt shaker, baby's shoe

PLATE 191

Center, rare large slipper with flat bow. Two styles in wall pockets for matches; salt size slipper and a slipper containing a pin cushion.

PLATE 192

Wall pocket for matches; four styles in ladies' slippers and a baby's moccasin.

PLATE 193

Pair of ladies' shoe bouquet holders, a man's boot, a child's shabby shoe and two styles of ladies' slippers.

gator but the toe is plain. There is a single row of beading around the vamp. The sole is covered with a fine diamond pattern. This shoe is 4 inches high and 3 inches in length. The other shoe on skates is in amber, the edge is plain instead of being scalloped, and the pattern of the shoe extends the full length, rather than having a plain toe. It is 4¼ inches high and 3 inches in over-all length.

At the left end of Plate 194 are two round covered boots on round bases. These are said to have been vaseline jars, but one was for ink. There are two varieties. One is blue with a fine cut pattern under the base. It has a six-pointed ornament on the cover. The base is 3 inches in diameter and it is 2¾ inches high. The other jar is amber, slightly smaller, and the cover has a circle of fine Cane design. It is 2¾ inches high and 3 inches in diameter.

The round jar with the star-ornamented cover is illustrated in a Butler Bros. catalogue of the 1880's as "Our 'funny' ink stand." The advertisement reads that it was made in an artistic manner and put up in assorted colors—at ten cents! These jars were also sold without the covers, for matches.

The "three-way" shoes back of the jars are in a dense amber, and I have been told that they were made by the Bellaire Goblet Co. of Findlay, Ohio. I cannot vouch for this but the Bellaire Co. did produce many novelties. The base is stippled and the piece is very heavy. It is 4½ inches high and is known in clear glass, as well as amber.

In the center of Plate 195 is a tiny slipper in a small alligator pattern, mounted on a round base. The slipper may have held a perfume bottle at one time. The base is ornamented with sprays of flowers on top and vertical ribbing about the edge. This is a rare slipper and so far has been found only in clear glass. It is 3¼ inches high and 3¾ inches in diameter.

The large slipper to the left of the little one on a base is a brilliant clear glass, with plain square toe and vamp but the sides and back are decorated in quite an elaborate Sunburst pattern, with Bull's Eye center; a row of hobnails forms a border about the edge and there is a flat bow in front. It measures 7½ inches long and 3¼ inches high. This is one of the most attractive of the pressed glass slippers. A mate has been found in a brilliant sapphire blue, so other colors may exist.

The first shoe at the left on Plate 195 is in frosted glass, ribbed all over, and has a little tassel hanging down in front. There is a hobnail in each flute around the scalloped top. It may be found in clear glass or frosted, 4¼ inches high and 3¾ inches long.

To the right of the small slipper on the base is a large one that is not Daisy and Button but a fine cut pattern, which connects small parts so that they make up a large diamond. It has a plain, clear panel above the heel and a small flat bow in front. This is a rare, as well as an attractive, slipper. While it appears to be American, a similar style with minor variations has been found in amber, bearing a British mark—"Registered 64088." Next to it is a frosted, or satin, slipper with a large bow in front and a slightly turned-up pointed toe. On the vamp is painted "World's Fair '93." Embossed above the heel is "World's Fair—1893." The base is marked "Libbey Glass Co., Toledo, Ohio." There do not seem to be quite so many souvenir slippers as hats, perhaps because the shape of a hat lends itself better for advertising purposes.

There is an interesting group on Plate 196. Probably the rarest is the shoe in a Cane pattern in the foreground. It has five large hobnails as buttons, up both sides of the front. The vamp and toe are plain. Only three of these have been found, one in crystal, one blue, and one amber. It is 4¼ inches long and 2¾ inches high.

Beside this unusual shoe is a pair of baby shoes. In a catalogue of the King Glass Co. of Pittsburgh, Pa., I find this listed as a "Double shoe." It was made in crystal, amber and blue. Opaque blue is a rarity.

In the back row of Plate 196 is a baby's bootee with a ribbed vamp; two flowers aid in embellishing the ribbon bow. Most of the bootee is made up of a fine diamond pattern. It has a hollow toe and the balance of the sole is smooth. It may be found in clear glass and in colors. The one pictured is a clear deep apple green. It is 2¼ inches high and 4¼ inches over-all length.

At the right of the bootee is another in the Daisy and Button pattern. The shoe is open but there is a rosette with ribbon on each side and three spots for lacing, also on each side. This bootee holds a perfume bottle. The heel is ribbed but the balance of the sole is plain. A small, clear perfume bottle fits inside, which is also in the shape of a shoe. Whether it is original or not, I can not tell, but since many of the shoes and slippers held bottles, it is reasonable to suppose that it may be. The bootee is marked "Pat. Oct. 19, '86." It is 4¼ inches long and 2 inches high.

The Chinese shoe on the toboggan was made by Bryce Bros. of Pittsburgh, Pa., and is pictured on a page showing numerous novelties. Both shoe and toboggan were made and sold separately. The toboggan and slipper shown on Plate 196 also contains a perfume bottle.

The last item on Plate 196 is an amethyst Daisy and Button slipper, with ribbed toe and a panel of horizontal ribbing over the heel. This type has not been reproduced. It was made by Bryce Bros. of Pittsburgh, who list it simply as a "Large slipper." It is 7¼ inches long and 1¾ inches high. There are many variations and sizes and colors in the Daisy and Button slipper, only a few of which have been reproduced.

On Plate 197 in the center is a curious yellow Daisy and Button slipper with a chassis like a dachshund! Certainly it is an odd-looking object but in its day it had a utilitarian value. It was designed as a spoonholder! It measures 7¼ inches long and 2½ inches high. Probably it was also made in crystal and other colors.

The usual type of Daisy and Button slipper is next to the spoonholder, at the right. It has a smooth sole and plain toe and heel. This style was produced by Bryce Bros. of Pittsburgh in clear glass, in colors, and in clear flashed in color. Possibly other factories made them but in order to avoid plagiarism, it seems the others would have made variations—and they doubtless did. This slipper measures 4⅝ inches long and 1¼ inches high.

The Daisy and Button slipper on skates, to the left of the spoonholder, was produced by the United States Glass Co. of Pittsburgh in crystal and in colors. As will be noted, it is high in front, the toe is plain, and there is a plain panel the length of the center. There is also a plain band around the top. It is 5¼ inches long and 3¼ inches high.

The first slipper at the left on Plate 197 is in a Finecut or Diamond Block pattern, on skates. The front of the shoe is opened into a V and then filled in. The toe is plain and the slipper has eyelets to lace up the V. It is in blue but doubtless may be found in crystal and other colors. It is 5½ inches long and 3½ inches high.

The man's boot in the background is the same one shown in a close-up view on Plate 193.

At the right end of Plate 197 is a large amber Daisy and Button slipper, which displays careless workmanship as it is rather crude. The plain toe turns up somewhat and the sole is covered with a diamond mesh pattern. The vamp is cut in slightly and the heel is plain solid glass. This slipper is 5¼ inches long and 3¼ inches high.

An unusual high shoe that will seldom be encountered is the large one, partly buttoned, at the left end of Plate 198. It is blue and stippled. Curiously, it has a stippled, scalloped rim which extends out, both in front and at the back. These rims could be dangerously susceptible to nicks and breakage, which may be the reason why not so many of these elaborate shoes were made. It has a rather low Cuban heel, not stippled. It is 5 inches high and 4½ inches in foot length.

In the center of Plate 198 is a blue high shoe, with horizontal ribbing all over and a tassel hanging down in front. It has a solid Cuban heel and a hollow space under the foot. Another shoe like it in milk-white is pictured on Plate 200. It will be

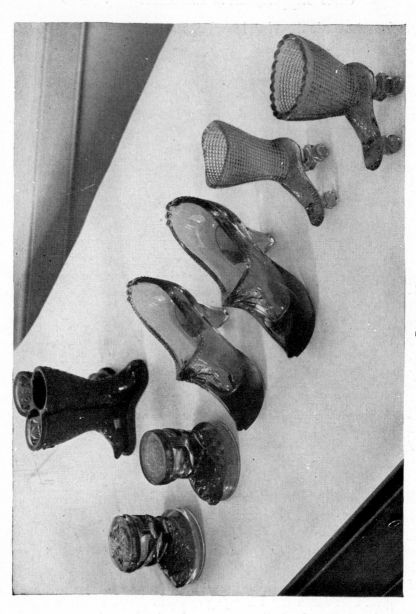

PLATE 194

Two different shoes on skates; pair of large slippers in a rare pattern; two shoe jars, one style of which was used for

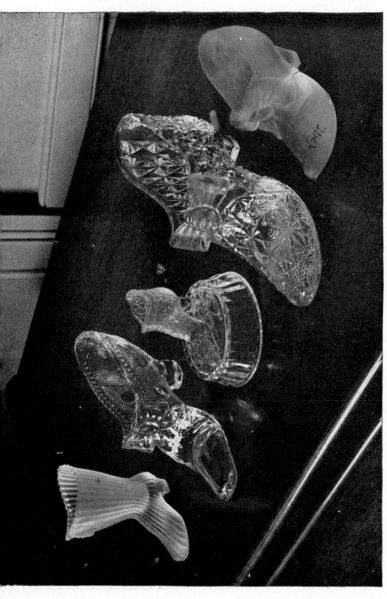

PLATE 195

A frosted slipper advertising the World's Fair; a large diamond pattern slipper; small slipper mounted on round base; a rare slipper with Sunburst pattern decorating the sides and a ribbed, frosted shoe.

PLATE 196

Baby's double shoe; two baby shoes, one holding a perfume bottle; shoe on a toboggan, holding a perfume bottle; rare

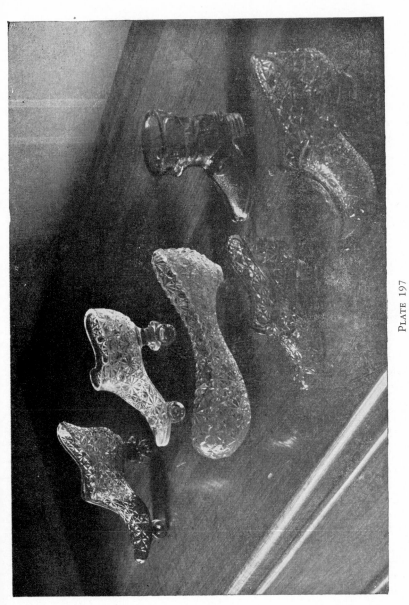

PLATE 197

Five styles in Daisy and Button slippers. The large one was a spoonholder. Unusual type man's boot in background.

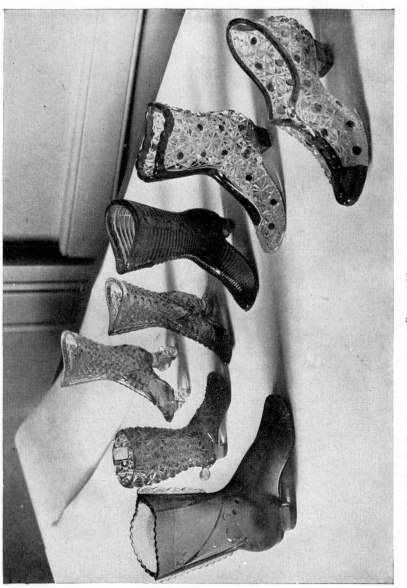

PLATE 198

Daisy and Button shoe and a slipper decorated in red; a ribbed high shoe; two diamond pattern shoes, one on skates; rare Daisy and Button boot with spur; rare frosted high shoe partly buttoned

PLATE 199

Group of Milk-white slippers with various styles of decoration. Frosted slipper in original metal holder and a frosted boot salt shaker.

PLATE 200

Group of Milk-white slippers; a pair of black boots bottle and a frosted shoe bottle.

noticed that both button up the side. This shoe is 4¼ inches high and 3¾ inches long. An unusual feature is that these shoes may be found in pairs—a left and a right. They are most scarce in milk-white and emerald green but have been found in clear glass, amber, and a peacock blue.

To the right of the horizontally ribbed shoe may be seen a Daisy and Button shoe and slipper, both decorated in red. The shoe is clear glass, with the buttons flashed in red and the heel and band about the top and down the front also in red. The shades of color vary, the bright ruby red generally being considered the most desirable. The shoe is 4¼ inches high and the foot is the same length. These were produced by George Duncan & Sons of Pittsburgh, Pa., in large, medium and individual (salt) sizes, in clear glass and a varied assortment of colors.

The slipper next to the shoe is decorated in a similar manner. There is somewhat more red on it as the plain toe also is colored.

The rarest Daisy and Button piece among the boots, shoes and slippers is the blue high boot with spur, shown next to the partly buttoned high shoe. Lucky the collector who comes across one of these! It is 3¾ inches high, with plain sole, vamp and heel. One has been found in clear glass and another in amber.

There are two remaining shoes on Plate 198, one being on skates and the other with the heel resting on a round plate. The shoe on skates is amber, in a small diamond block pattern. In the scalloped edge on one side is a patent date of December, 1886. It is 4½ inches high. There is no record at present of who made it, but Bryce Bros. of Pittsburgh produced the one similar to it, which is alongside. It is a smaller shoe, 4 inches high, and in the same pattern. It bears the same patent date. The heel rests on a round plate that is marked "Trademark T H." The Bryce catalogue lists this as "Small Boot. Right & Lefts." Probably it was made in clear glass and the usual line of colors.

Plate 199 begins at the left end with a boot salt shaker having a frosted finish. Incidentally, there are two variations in these boots. One type has a rayed base and the other is more shell-shaped, with wide flutes over the shield on the front. They measure 3¼ inches high.

Next to the boot salt shaker is a small pair of milk-white slippers, having a bow on the front of each. There is a round depression in the article attached to the slippers, as if it were designed for a salt dish. It does not appear to have any great age, so is doubtless a late novelty. Duplicates may be found in clear glass.

The third piece from the left of Plate 199 is a milk-white baby's shoe with two openings on each side for lacing. These openings are really open! A bow decorates the front of the shoe. So far this shoe has been found only in milk-white. It is 2¼ inches high and 4¼ long.

Next to the baby's shoe is a large milk-white slipper, so white that it looks almost like alabaster. The vamp is decorated with roses in color. There is a large flat bow with long streamers. This slipper is marked on the base "National Export Exposition, Philadelphia, 1899."

To the left of the frosted slipper in the metal container is another in milk-white, which laces up the front and has an added decoration in the way of a scalloped piece on the toe. This is 5½ inches long and 2½ high.

The slipper in the metal holder was a Centennial specialty of Gillinder & Sons of Philadelphia and may be found so marked. Probably they were sold as souvenirs at the Exposition. It has a square toe and is decorated with quite a large bow with the ends streaming. These may be found in crystal, in milk-white and in frosted glass. There may be a wide range of colors but I have seen only one in amber. They were made in several sizes and those marked are lettered "Gillinder & Sons, Centennial Exhibition." The most common size is 5 inches long and 2½ high. They have a solid heel and a hollow depression under the foot. Others have a hollow heel and are hollow the full length of the foot but this does not show unless the slipper is turned over. A crystal slipper of Gillinder's, in the same style but unmarked, may be found 4¾ inches long and 2¾ high.

To the left of the Gillinder slipper in the holder is an attractive milk-white one with a bow in front and a conventional design in relief, not colored, all about it. The edge of the top has a border of small beads or hobnails. This is a rare slipper, seldom encountered. It is 4½ inches long and 2½ high.

The first slipper at the right is light opaque blue with a poppy decoration in relief. It is laced up the front and gilded, as well as along the upper edge. The same slipper may be found in milk-white with gold decoration and in amber, slightly opalescent, almost like the so-called "Caramel" glass, of which so many were made in Indiana.

Plate 200 starts at the left with a shoe bottle that laces up the front and has a metal screw top. It is a frosted glass, and it will be noted that one toe is out of the shoe! It is something of a curiosity but not particularly attractive. It may be found in a dense amethyst and possibly other colors. There is one story to the effect that this was called the "Depression" shoe bottle, put out during the depression of 1893 and said to have been given away at Christmas filled with whiskey, by hotels. We wonder! If so, I have not heard of anything like it happening since and we have had a depression outranking the doings of 1893.

Next to this Depression shoe is a milk-white high-cut slipper with a small bow in front. There are flowers raised in relief as a decoration but they are not painted. A scalloped band ornaments the edge.

In the center of Plate 200 is a scarce milk-white lamp which has a pair of boots mounted on the round base, the boots being painted black. It is 4 inches high and 3½ inches in diameter. The chimney and globe are missing.

To the left of the boots is a milk-white heavy slipper with a greenish tint to the white. It has three flowers in relief; these had once been decorated in color which has mostly washed off. It has a crude gold decoration about the top and the bow knot. There is not much to recommend a slipper of this kind, except that it is something different.

The high shoe back of the painted boots was described in connection with the illustrations on Plate 198.

To the right of the black-painted boots is a milk-white Gillinder & Sons slipper, like the one illustrated in the holder on Plate 199. The first slipper at the right is a heavy one in milk-white, with a Cuban heel. It is very simply decorated with a beaded band. It appears to be of a later style than most of those pictured.

Many collectors will be interested in the shoe hand lamp, complete with wick and chimney, shown in the background of Plate 203. A close-up view appears in Plate 204. The base of the lamp is marked "Pat'd June 30, 1869." The collar of the lamp has still another patent mark: "Pat'd Dec. 10, 1867, Venus." Just what the "Venus" is for must be left to conjecture. Certainly the lamp is a pleasing novelty. Apparently the lamps were not produced in quantity, because they are scarce. Perhaps they are more plentiful in other localities. As this goes to press, another such lamp has been found in olive green. Two more lamps have been reported, one marked on the collar, "Pat. April 19, 1875," and the other, "Pat. Mar. 21, 1875." The patent marks must refer to the collars, or else more than one firm produced the shoe lamp.

The large Daisy and Button boot at the left on Plate 203 is in clear glass with the toe, heel, spur and band across the instep and top all flashed in amber. So far I have seen exactly two of these and both were imperfect. The boot was made in crystal and possibly in colors but any of them are rare. Beside the boot is an extra-large Daisy and Button slipper with ribbed toe and ribbed panel above the heel. This slipper was made by Bryce Bros. of Pittsburgh, Pa., and the buttons are in amber. The one next to it, in crystal, is flashed with red. The tall plain boots are thought to be Bohemian glass, but they are a type that could have been made here. Between the boots is an extra-large blown glass Dutch shoe, with a stopper that probably is not the original. This is the largest of these Dutch shoes found to date. It is a French wine bottle marked "Deposé" on the base. In the foreground is an amber slipper wall pocket.

The first slipper at the left in Plate 202 is pictured as a "Chinese shoe" in a Bryce Bros. of Pittsburgh catalogue. These shoes were so popular that they were carried on by the United States Glass Co. after they absorbed some eighteen older glass factories in July of 1891. The Chinese shoe was produced in crystal and in colors, made in two sizes, one wider than the other.

The Puss in Boots slipper is familiar to most collectors. This variety is in the Daisy pattern (no button) with an alligator toe. It was made in crystal and in colors, and measures 5½ inches long by 2½ inches deep. The slipper pictured in Plate 202 is in a deep blue. It was made originally by Bryce Bros. of Pittsburgh, Pa., and continued by the United States Glass Co.

Beside the Puss in Boots slipper to the right is one in a large clear pressed Diamond pattern with a flat bow. The toe is slightly squared. In detail it is somewhat similar to some of the Daisy and Button slippers. It has a small clear toe, the flat bow is stippled, and the ribbon ends hang down almost to the sole. It has a clear Cuban heel. All the balance of the slipper is covered with the Diamond design. A similar slipper may be found, with a trifle thinner bow, bearing a British Registry mark. Next to the pressed Diamond slipper with the flat bow, to the right, is a fine cut slipper that is fairly common today. The slipper laces to a V at the top; the toe is plain and tilts upward at quite an angle. This slipper is fairly common, even today, and collectors will find it in crystal, yellow, amber and blue. Any other color would be rare. It is 5¾ inches long.

The high-cut slipper next to it is an emerald green Cane pattern with a fine mesh on the sole. There is a plain panel that runs from the toe up the front of the slipper. This type was made in crystal and colors by the United States Glass Co. It is

4 inches long and 2 inches high. Probably some other firm produced this slipper first and the United States Glass Co. carried it on.

The first slipper on skates at the right in Plate 202 is in the Daisy and Button pattern. It was made in crystal and colors by the United States Glass Co. of Pittsburgh, but this does not mean that some other factory may not have made a similar slipper, with some slight variation. This one has a mesh on the sole, a plain toe, and a plain panel that runs from the toe to the top of the slipper. Around the edge of the top is a border formed of scallops. This little slipper is 3¾ inches long and the same in height.

A black glass boot, similar in quality to the black glass plates with openwork border, and a "Mosaic," or purple Marble, glass boot are shown at the left in Plate 201. Both have spurs and I might add that it is difficult to find these boots with the spurs intact. The black glass is more scarce than the Marble glass. The boot is also rare in opaque purple. It makes an attractive holder for matches or cigarettes.

Next to the boots is an amethyst high shoe in the Cane pattern. It is mounted on a scrolled base that is lettered "Bouquet holder. Pat. applied for." It stands 5½ inches high. As may be noted in the picture, the shoe is laced up the front, as many old-fashioned shoes were.

Beside the amethyst high shoe are three sizes in Daisy and Button slippers and three variations. The smallest beside the shoe is in amethyst. It has a panel of horizontal ribbing above the clear solid heel and a plain toe which tilts upward, though not so much as the Chinese shoe. The medium-sized Daisy and Button is practically the same, though the toe is more square and does not turn up so much. The next largest style, as seen in the first slipper at the right, was probably made by several factories. Some have four (closed) depressions for lacing, some five and others six. That with six depressions was made in three sizes by George Duncan & Sons of Pittsburgh, Pa. The same shaped slipper in the smallest size is illustrated in a Bryce Bros.

catalogue. I am leaving out of consideration those rare extra-large slippers, which are 11½ inches long. There is a 4¾-inch Daisy and Button slipper, wider than most, gilded on the toe, in the front panel and on the heel, which is 2¾ inches wide. The heel too is wider than the more common types. This slipper is marked "Pat. Oct. 19, 1886."

Four approximate sizes may be singled out in the Daisy and Button slipper. The first is 4¾ inches long and 2¾ inches high; the second is 4¼ inches long and 2¼ inches high; the third is 3¾ inches long and 2¼ inches high; the fourth, and rarest, is 11½ inches long by 4¼ inches wide and 2½ inches deep. The last named are pictured on Plate 206.

There have been many reproductions of Daisy and Button slippers. Among the first to come out was one in amethyst 4¾ inches long, measuring underneath the base. It has a solid heel and a deep hollow under the foot. The pattern is rather dull and the buttons have what can best be described as a "crinkly" appearance. They are not soft and glossy, with a fair amount of sheen to them, as in the old. Collectors also have seen many of the shoes on skates in gift shops, one of the favorite colors being a salmon pink, which was never used originally. This shoe has a scalloped edge, fine mesh below, and an imitation of the alligator section in the foot. The toe and vamp are clear. By clear, in this case, I mean smooth. Some of these find their way into antique shops but they are so obviously new that no experienced collector would be deceived.

The Puss in Boots slipper has been copied, as well as the plain little wrinkled boot shown on Plate 190 in frosted glass. There is no harm in the reproductions when sold as new, at not over twenty-five cents.

There is quite a varied group on Plate 204. The first slipper at the left is painted with flowers and could be American or Continental. The milk-white Daisy and Button is the usual type, discussed in connection with Plate 201. Such a milk-white baby's bootee as that in the foreground is unusual and rare.

Collectors do not see many of the shallow, odd-shaped Daisy
and Button slippers, as the third from the left. It was produced
by Bryce Bros. of Pittsburgh, Pa., in clear and colors, and they
termed it a "Sandal." The United States Glass Co. continued
these in later years.

Next to the sandal, at the right, is a more elaborate form of
the pressed Diamond slipper, with a flat bow. The first slipper
at the right is finely painted and bears an initial. This slipper
was purchased with a history attached to it. It was made, so
the story goes, by the New England Glass Co. while William
L. Libbey was the agent and his son, Edward D. Libbey, also
was employed there. A member of the Libbey family gave a
party and every lady received a slipper as a favor, filled with
flowers and having her initial on it. The slipper was obtained
from one of the guests at this party, which took place before the
Libbeys moved to Toledo, Ohio. The previous owner claimed
it was made during the late 1870's. Without this personal history it would be hazardous to state definitely whether this slipper was produced by Sandwich, by the New England Glass Co.,
or in Europe.

Plate 205 pictures an unusual assortment. The crystal slipper
at the left carries a British Registry mark. Not many of them
are found in this country, though I came across one in peacock
green. It bears the same registry number—87058. There is a
flat bow, the vamp is ribbed horizontally and the sides vertically. A row of small beads forms a border at the upper edge.
Both the small Cuban heel and the balance of the slipper are
hollow underneath. It is 4¾ inches long. One has been seen
in sapphire blue with a tiny sea lion stamped in the heel.

Next to the English slipper is a large heavy crystal slipper
with an applied heel. There is no opening except for the rough
hole which may be seen in the illustration. It bears a Dorflinger
paper label which illustrates on it a decanter, goblet and wine
glass. It may have been intended for wine, and a cork used
as a stopper. An interesting contrast is the fragile, pointed
slipper next to it. The glass is blown exceedingly thin. This

is a type that could have been produced many years ago, or made by one of the glassworkers blowing glass at the New York World's Fair!

In the center of Plate 205 is a large milk-white, two-part slipper. It hitches together in the center, and out of five hundred slippers it is the only one I have ever seen made in two parts. It might have been made at the turn of the century. It has a bow embossed in front, a gilded Cuban heel, but most of the rest of the gold decoration has worn off. It is 8 inches long and 5 inches high. Whatever inspired this creation is a mystery, though it is said to have been intended as a trinket box.

Next to the milk-white shoe at the right is a stippled high shoe. It buttons on both sides of the front and there is a border of scallops about the top. The toe is clear and so is the Cuban heel. It is a rare shoe; the only one like it in the collection. The height is 4¼ inches by 3¼ inches over-all length of the foot.

The first slipper at the right on Plate 205 is said to have been brought from Sweden. It is a brilliant, clear crystal, finely stippled except for the flat bow and clear toe. This is 4¾ inches long.

The largest glass shoes known are those pictured on Plate 206. It will be noted that one has the Daisy and Button pattern all over, including the sole and heel. The other has plain sides, with design only on the sole and heel. Of the two, the latter is the more rare, even though it is not the more attractive. The one with the all-over design is in yellow; that with the plain sides is in apple green. They measure 11½ inches long, 4¼ inches wide, and 2½ inches deep. It is not known at present which factory made this largest size. They could not have been produced in quantity, since they are exceedingly rare today.

All of the illustrations in this chapter are from the collection of Mrs. Lloyd B. Wilson.

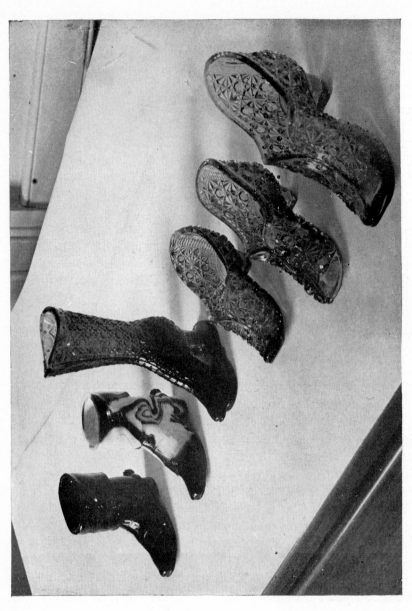

PLATE 201

Three usual types in Daisy and Button slippers. Amethyst shoe on scrolled standard. A purple Marble glass and a black

PLATE 202

Slippers in Daisy and Button, Cane and Finecut patterns which are most frequently encountered.

PLATE 203

Pair of blown boots with applied decoration. Blown glass Dutch shoe bottle. Wall pocket; two Daisy and
Button slippers; a rare shoe long and a rare boot in clear glass dashed in amber.

Courtesy of Mrs. F. H. Mann.

PLATE 204

Rare shoe hand lamp, with applied handle, made in the 1860's.
Top: A varied group, including two choice painted slippers, a rare Milk-white baby
bootee and Milk-white Daisy and Button slipper, as well as a "sandal" in the same
pattern. Attractive colored slipper with flat bow and a similar one in crystal.

PLATE 205

Right, stippled slipper from Sweden; rare stippled high shoe; Milk-white two-part slipper; fragile blown glass pointed slipper; large, crude heavy slipper with applied heel. English slipper bearing British reviewe mark.

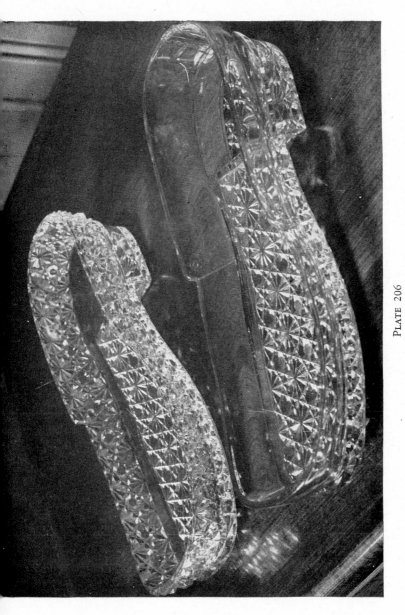

PLATE 206

Largest known Daisy and Button slippers in two different styles and colors. 11½ inches long.

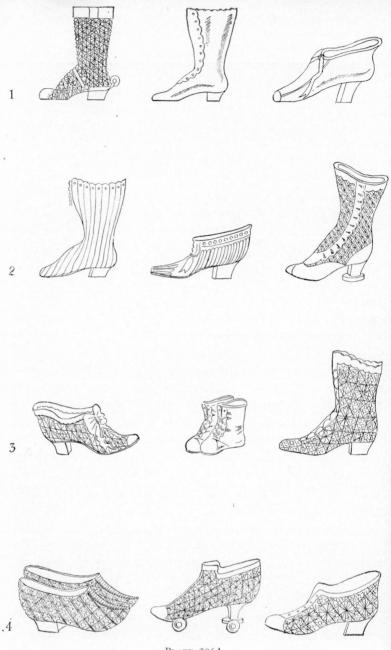

PLATE 206A

1. Large Daisy and Button boot with spur; Frosted glass shoe made by Gillinder & sons, Philadelphia; Frosted slipper by Gillinder & Sons.
2. Ribbed shoe by Gillinder & Sons (frosted); English slipper; Shoe by Bryce Bros.
3. Slipper by King Glass Co., Pittsburgh; Double baby shoes by King Glass Co.; High shoe by unknown maker.
4. Double Chinese shoes by Bryce Bros.; Slipper on skates by the United States Glass Co.; Daisy and Button slipper by Doyle & Co.

Chapter XXI

VICTORIAN VASES

In considering between four and five hundred pairs of vases, it seems reasonable to assume that the easiest and simplest method of reference for the collector is to catalogue them according to Plate numbers, particularly since there are usually anywhere from ten to fourteen vases in each illustration. Single specimens are used except on Plate 207, in order to cover all the forms, though the vases pictured in this chapter were all collected in *pairs*. After each five illustrations will be found the text describing each vase.

In this collection there are overlay vases, painted and enamelled vases, rose bowls and vases in satin glass and with applied decoration. There are all the types of Victorian vases in the line of art glass that the average collector would buy. It would not be humanly possible to list, describe and classify all the vases produced both here and abroad, in even one decade. No attempt is being made to enter the field of ceramics, where there are no end of museum pieces. They are of an earlier era. These are for the most part everyday vases, just as pattern glass is a utilitarian, everyday glass to use, even though some of it is rare and costly. Some collectors buy a pair or even several pairs of vases for home decoration, while others concentrate on them, just as others do in all manner of objects, from postage stamps and coins to sugar bowls and paper-weights. Fortunately, all collectors do not enjoy the same hobby.

Probably the most costly wares represented in this chapter are the overlay vases. These are *plated,* or made in two or three layers of glass, with the design cut through so that the color practically dominates the piece. Three pairs are pictured on Plate 207. These are white on the outside, cut through to rose pink, emerald green or turquoise. There are no end of combinations of color. In my collection is one in ruby red cut to crystal, and a pair in white cut to amber. Of all the colors, the white cut to turquoise blue seems to be the most beautiful.

Some opaque white vases were left with their natural or glossy finish, while others were dipped in hydrofluoric acid which leaves a soft, dull, satinlike surface. Another method of achieving the soft surface is by sanding, a process too intricate to interest the average collector. The sanded surface leaves a different feel than the acid bath achieves. Decoration could be applied to any of the surfaces described. Some were painted, some enamelled, and others had a combination of both. When the body of a vase is in one color and the edge in another it merely means that the workman had subjected the edge to a reheating and this second heating changed the color.

Among the most popular of collectibles is satin glass. Many types are pictured here in plain color, shaded, and patterned. Some are painted or enamelled. Plate 215 pictures some of the most attractive styles, with the exception of the reproduction, which is placed there as a warning to the unwary. Fortunately, little satin glass has been copied.

For those interested in collecting little night lamps, two of the most attractive types are shown in the lower row of Plate 217.

On Plate 219, in the upper row, is a ruby-red vase, enamelled in white, showing a child and some flowers and leaves. In New England these are referred to as "Mary Gregory" vases. Upon inquiry in the village of Sandwich, Mass., I was told by a woman whose relatives worked at the Boston & Sandwich Glass Co. that a person named Mary Gregory did work in the decorating department. Whether the rest of the story is a myth or not apparently cannot be proved now. The legend is that a Mary Gregory, who was a spinster, was so fond of children that she devoted most of her time to painting them. It is true that many objects in various colors may be found in New England enamelled with either a boy or a girl, and they have a striking similarity. The Mary Gregory children do not resemble those we find on vases and other ornamental pieces imported from Bohemia. Undoubtedly figures of children were painted or enamelled on pieces from other countries but they still do not look like those which apparently came from the Sandwich factory on Cape Cod.

Collectors of bells may like the one shown in the center of the lower row on Plate 219. It has a milk-white handle, a cranberry-red bell, and a white clapper. An interesting series of bells can be had in glass.

For those who concentrate on rose bowls, Plates 220 and 221 show familiar types. Between the two bowls on Plate 221 is a shaded-red basket, with a twisted, crystal thorn handle. This is from the collection of Mr. George Tilden. There are almost as many varieties of baskets as there are hats and slippers, but space does not permit picturing all specialties in detail.

It would seem to me that more collectors would specialize in that attractive form of art glass shown on Plate 222. There was a time when objects with applied glass decoration in the form of flowers, leaves, cherries, etc., were highly regarded. They represent a phase in American glassmaking that has been underestimated. The objects are colorful and at the same time represent skillful workmanship.

Plate 234 illustrates two vases, at the left end of the upper row, which have been casually cast into the lap of the *Bristol* family. So much of this glass, having a similar decoration, has been found in this country that it seems perfectly certain a good share of it was made and decorated here. Wines in various sizes and shapes, tumblers and handled mugs are frequently seen and always decorated with roses. Let us hope that at some not too distant date someone may be able to throw light on these attractive pieces.

In the lower row of Plate 234 is a vase decorated with birds. It is certain that many of these finely decorated wares were done in New York City, because more of them are found there than elsewhere. Just as blanks were made of many pieces in

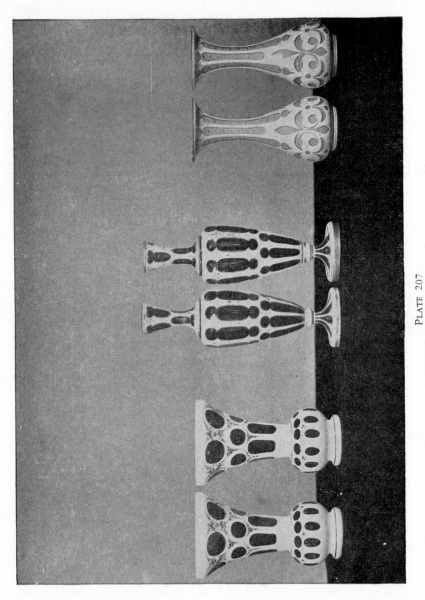

PLATE 207

Three pairs of Overlay vases. White cut to rose. White to emerald green. White to turquoise blue.

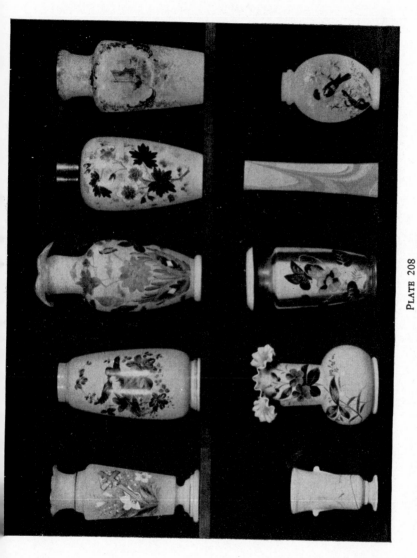

PLATE 208

Various styles of painted and enameled Victorian vases. Two in the lower row are in Marble glass.

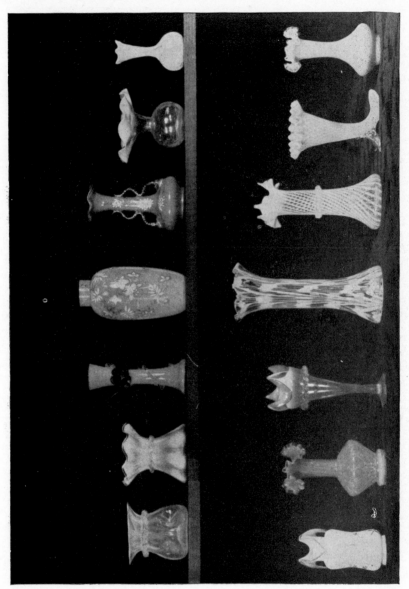

PLATE 209

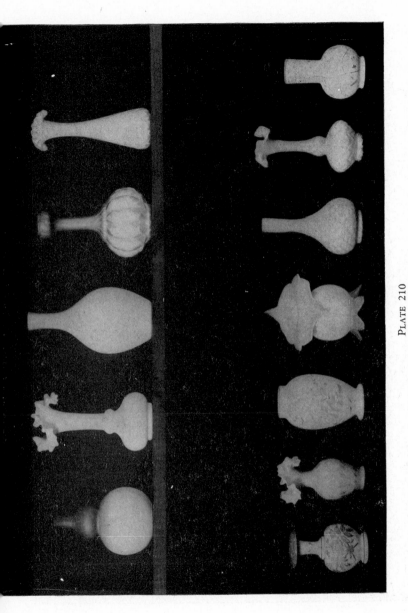

PLATE 210

Satin glass vases in Polka Dot, Herringbone, and Diamond Quilted patterns. A few others are plain or decorated.

PLATE 211

glass and sent to another factory to be cut, so were vases of this type made by the Mt. Washington Glass Co. or elsewhere and sent to some skilled decorator for the final work. I have seen a Burmese vase painted with birds like the white one with the sanded finish which is the third from the left on Plate 234.

Any other necessary detail pertaining to the vases will be found in the text following each group of the illustrations. Vases are all from the collection of Mr. Russell Neilson.

PLATE 207

Left. Pair of overlay vases in case glass, cut from white to rose red. Parts of the white section are decorated with flowers and a vine-line tracery in gold and colors.

Center. Superb pair of overlay vases, in white cut to emerald green. There is a small amount of gold tracery on the white.

Right. Pair of choice overlay vases in white, cut to turquoise blue.

Overlay vases were produced in Bohemia, in England, in France and various other places on the Continent, as well as in America. It is difficult to distinguish our overlay. For the most part, we made lamp bowls and vases while the Europeans produced ornamental objects in the way of urns, elaborate drinking glasses, and all sorts of ornamental objects. Some overlay "lamp bowls" produced by the Boston & Sandwich Glass Co. may be identified from old trade catalogues of the company. The type of vases, bowls, lusters, etc., that we know were a commercial product from the 1840's.

PLATE 208

Upper row, left to right.

1. White vase with sanded finish. Decorated with white flowers, green leaves and three gold stripes, painted on. Not a case glass. Shallow scalloped edge. 11 inches.

2. Blue-gray opalescent. Bird painted in natural colors, against green foliage. 11 inches.

3. Opaque cream, washed in blue about top. Decorated with pink flowers and colored leaves. Bird on branch. Rather long neck and edge folded down, forming two large scallops. 13 inches.

4. Opaque cream vase, washed in brown forming band around top. Pink and white flowers with deep-green leaves. 11 inches.

5. Soft opaque jade green. Medallion encloses water scene, with sailboat, glossy surface, not case glass. 11 inches.

Lower row, left to right.

1. Light-brown and white marbelized vase. There are six graduated raised panels on one side. 6¼ inches.

2. Deep opaque cream vase with glossy surface. Brown flowers and green leaves. Elaborately fluted edge.

3. Glossy-surfaced white vase with brilliant wide orange stripes. Butterfly, flower and leaf decoration. Band of orange color around the neck.

4. Unusual square gray and white thick marbelized glass. 9¾ inches.

5. Translucent white vase with glossy finish. Sides are flattened and decorated with bird in high relief, painted in yellow with brown head, wings and tail. Bird rests on branch with pink flowers and green leaves. 7¼ inches.

PLATE 209

Upper row, left to right.

1. Yellow vase with opalescent edge. Applied ornamental band about neck. 4 inches.

2. Green-opalescent vase with plain scalloped edge. Applied ornamental band in green, about the neck. 4½ inches.

3. Green bud vase, with applied crimped crystal ornamentation in a swirl, with bright-colored flower.

4. Blue-opalescent vase with delicate enamelled decoration in

color, showing flowers and leaves. This vase is also found in a lavender-opalescent glass. 7¼ inches.

5. Lavender-opalescent ornamental vase. Handles in crystal with gold decoration. White flowers and gold leaves enamelled on both sides. 6½ inches.

6. Green vase, with flaring, scalloped edge in a deeper green. Opalescent under rim. 4¼ inches.

7. Small blue-opalescent vase, having splashes of pink, yellow and a few gold flecks. Produced in similar manner to Spatter glass. 4½ inches.

Lower row, left to right.

1. Heavy blue-opalescent vase, enamelled with small flowers. Tilted top is in deep blue, with four petals having applied clear yellow edge. 5¾ inches.

2. Pink-opalescent vase, blown with loops in lower part of bowl, running into panels which join into the fluted neck. Frilled or fluted edge, with yellow applied band. This same vase comes in yellow-opalescent with bright blue applied band. 6¾ inches.

3. Yellow vase, with applied crimped band. Top has four opaque-pink petal edges, tilted downward.

4. Clear blown vase with loopings in opalescent. 9¾ inches.

5. Clear glass vase, with opalescent stripes. Clear applied band in ribbon candy style. Opalescent frilled edge. 8¼ inches.

6. Pink-opalescent Diamond Quilted (indented diamonds) vase, supported by two vaseline colored applied glass leaves, as feet. 6 inches.

7. Powder-blue swirled vase in case glass. White lining extends to frilled top, which is edged in band of clear glass.

PLATE 210

Upper row, left to right.

1. Shaded glass vase, in deep brown at the neck, shading to light brown in the bowl. Same shaped vase is found in shaded

blue. Both are case glass, and may be products of Hobbs, Brocunier & Co. of Wheeling, W. Va., as the midwestern factories produced more case glass than New England. This ware dates from the 1880's.

2. Deep-rose-colored vase with unusually large frilled edge, which shades to a lighter color at the base. The same shaped vase was made in blue. This is not case glass and not Peach-blow, which will be described and pictured in another chapter.

3. Case glass vase in unusual shade of robin's-egg blue. It shades softly to a lighter color toward the base. This is a rare color in satin glass.

4. Rose satin glass vase, having melon-shaped fluted bowl. This is a beautiful piece, with a Diamond pattern against the background. Case glass. 7 inches.

5. Choice vase in cased satin glass. Blue, with delicately fluted edge. Herringbone pattern, which does not show well in the illustration. 7¼ inches.

Lower row, left to right.

1. Blue vase with exquisite detail. The bent-over edge carries the same design as is found on one vase from Wanamaker collection. The rolled edge is blue with red vine. The bowl is almost white and has an enamelled decoration of flowers and leaves. Mate to this vase has rim in deep rose and bowl in faintly light pink. 5 inches.

2. Unusually small satin glass vase with heavy frilled top. Case glass, white lining. Deep blue with polka-dot pattern. Same vase may be found in light brown. 5¼ inches.

3. Plain white satin glass, with enamelled decoration in delicate colors. 5¼ inches.

4. White satin bowl with a bright yellow collar. Six frosted leaves serve as feet. 6 inches.

5. Jade-green case glass, in a heavily ribbed Diamond Quilted pattern. Soft satin finish. Workmanship slightly crude. 6¼ inches.

6. Yellow satin glass vase in Herringbone pattern. Case glass; white lining to frilled edge. 6½ inches.

7. Soft white satin glass vase, with same enamelled decoration as on No. 3. 5 inches.

PLATE 211

Upper row, left to right.

1. Plain opalescent vase with small frilled edge. 5½ inches.

2. Powder-blue vase painted with daisies having yellowish-green leaves. Elaborately frilled edge. 5¾ inches.

3. Thick blue-gray-opalescent vase. Bowl was washed in color which is partly worn off. Glossy surface. 7½ inches.

4. Large caramel, or deep coffee-colored, vase having decoration of white flowers and colored leaves. 10 inches.

5. Opaque yellow vase with glossy finish. White enamelled flowers, light green leaves striped in brown. Frilled edge in amber. 8¼ inches.

6. Green Diamond Quilted vase, shading to much lighter color at base. Diamonds are so expanded they almost disappear. Base is square. 8 inches.

7. Amethyst vase, shading to nearly clear at base. Enamelled lily in creamy yellow with green leaves. Frilled edge. 4¼ inches.

Lower row, left to right.

1. Amber lightly fluted or ribbed vase, with folded rim and foot. Light shade. 6 inches.

2. Shaded vase; clear at top, to light amber and then to amethyst. Diamond Quilted pattern. Decorated with enamelled red flower and white leaves. 5¼ inches.

3. Light amber swirled vase with enamelled flowers and leaves in color. 4 inches.

4. Shallow bowl in red, shading to amber at base. No pattern. Scalloped edge. 2¾ inches high, 5 inches diameter.

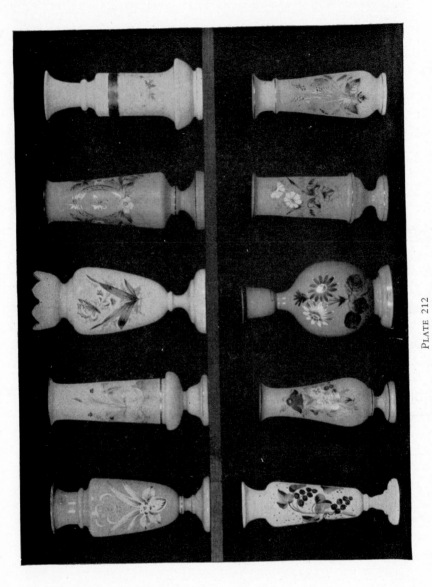

PLATE 212

Large-sized and enameled vases

PLATE 213

Upper: Group of square vases.
Lower: Varied group of Victorian vases.

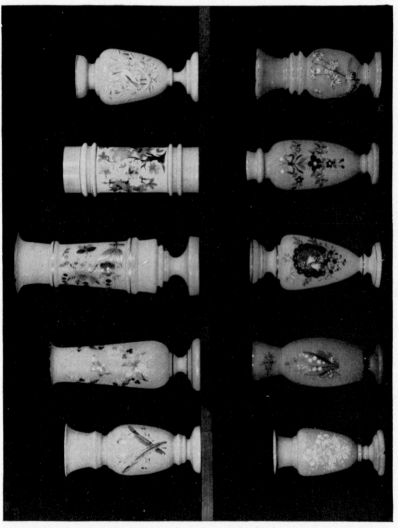

PLATE 214

Various shapes in painted and enameled vases.

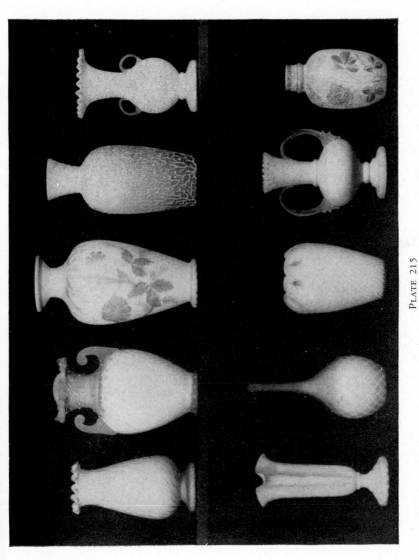

PLATE 215

Choice group of decorated and patterned satin glass vases. One at upper right end is a reproduction of satin glass.

PLATE 216

5. Emerald-green vase with flowers and leaves in silver deposit. 4½ inches.

6. Sapphire-blue vase with applied spiral of opaque white. 3 inches.

7. Shaded vase, in amethyst at the top, to clear at base. Enamelled lily of the valley in white with gold leaves. Edge is formed in three scallops. 7 inches.

PLATE 212

Upper row, left to right.

1. Light-brown vase with flowers and leaves in white enamel, with some color. 11 inches.

2. White vase, sanded finish with painted and enamelled design in color. Conventional pattern in gold. 11 inches.

3. Opaque blue vase with flattened sides. Design of painted and enamelled flowers and a large butterfly. Leaves are in gold. 12 inches.

4. Deep-blue vase with sanded finish. Flower decoration and horseshoe-shaped ornament in center, enclosing a butterfly. Rare color. 11 inches.

5. Opaque blue vase with faded gold conventional design and gold band decorated with red berries and black leaves.

Lower row, left to right.

1. White vase with soft sanded finish. Decoration of large spray of red currants and green leaves. An unusual design. 10¾ inches.

2. Jade-green vase, with sanded finish. Decorated with white flowers, red poppy and gold leaves. 9¼ inches.

3. Light-brown rounded bowl with heavy enamelled decoration of daisies and leaves. 10½ inches.

4. Jade-green vase with sanded finish. Decorated with spray of white flowers, green and gold leaves and red berries. 9½ inches.

5. White vase with sanded finish. Decoration of spray of

leaves and berries, mostly in gold. There are a few red and blue berries to lend color. 9¼ inches.

PLATE 213

Upper row, left to right.

1. Light-brown square vase, with glossy surface. Decorated with forget-me-nots, yellow and brown leaves, and some gold. 7¾ inches.

2. Deep-blue square base, with sanded finish. Decorated with design having a bird on branch of leaves with berries, the bird being done in colors and the rest in gold. 10¼ inches.

3. Pink vase with sanded finish. Enamelled decoration of white flowers, gold leaves and wheat. Bee hovering over flowers. All four sides are decorated. 12¼ inches high, 4 inches across.

4. White vase with sanded finish. Heavy enamelled decoration of flowers in conventional design. Sprays glittering with beads on sides and blue spray on back panel. 10¼ inches.

5. Heavy opaque blue vase with white-enamelled design of boy with butterfly net. Sprays of leaves on other three panels. All the other vases are footed, except this one. It is a style that could have been made by the Boston & Sandwich Glass Co.

Lower row, left to right.

1. Rare type of vase in opaque white. The bowl has expanded heavy ribs in blue. Neck shows nothing except blue ribs. This is a case glass with white lining. Frilled top is edged in clear glass. 9¼ inches.

2. Opaque blue vase, having enamelled flowers in color and painted green, gold and brown leaves. Frilled edge. 10 inches.

3. Opalescent-lavender vase with brown decorated bands, alternating with gold ones. 11 inches.

4. Pale opaque green vase, with design of red strawberries and green leaves. Shallow scalloped edge, striped in gold. 9½ inches.

5. Rose-pink Spatter glass vase, with splashes of white and pink. The coloring in this vase was controlled by the workman; in other words, it is not an indiscriminate mass of color. Frilled top, edged with crystal band. 8¾ inches.

PLATE 214

Upper row, left to right.

1. Opaque lavender vase, decorated with flowers and leaves in green and yellow. Glossy surface. 9½ inches.

2. Jade-green vase with sanded finish. Decoration of wreath of flowers, leaves and red berries, enclosing a butterfly. 10½ inches.

3. White vase with sanded finish, adorned with bright-colored spray of red flowers and berries, blue flowers and berries with gold leaves and a butterfly. 12⅝ inches.

4. Bristol type vase with glossy surface. Light-brown band around the top and the base. Center has white flowers, bird and butterfly in a design suggestive of Chinese style.

5. Gray vase with flattened sides. Design shows heron and fish in natural colors, surrounded by bright blue leaves and flowers. Glossy surface. 8½ inches.

Lower row, left to right.

1. Creamy-brown opaque vase with glossy surface. Decoration consists of spray of white-enamelled leaves and flowers. 7¾ inches.

2. Pink vase with sanded finish, having spray of white lily of the valley against green leaves and blue flowers. Another spray of flowers decorated the neck. This is in a combination of enamelled and painted work. 9¼ inches.

3. White vase with sanded finish. Vivid gold decoration with blue bellflowers and brown leaves. Gold stripes add to decoration. 9¼ inches.

4. Gray-blue-opalescent vase, decorated with red and blue flowers and a gold bowknot. 9½ inches.

5. White sanded vase. Top and base washed in blue. White bowl has delicate design of bird in natural colors, butterfly, forget-me-nots and leaves. 8¾ inches.

PLATE 215

Upper row, left to right.

1. Light-brown satin case glass vase. Elongated polka-dot design. Frosted, applied edge to frilled top. Shape of vase suggests old-time lamp chimneys. Same vase is found in blue. 8¼ inches.

2. Delicate shaded yellow satin glass vase, in case glass. This came from Wanamaker collection. The handles are frosted and ribbed and there is a frosted edge at the top. Decoration is in enamel with vivid blue dots. The body has a large, irregular diamond pattern. About the foot is an unusual vinelike tracery in rose-colored enamel. 9¾ inches.

3. Light-blue satin case glass vase, in small Diamond pattern. Gold enamel decoration of flowers with a bird. Very beautiful. 11¼ inches.

4. Shaded vase, light at top to deep rose at base. The type of decoration has been known as Coralene, and is said to have been made at Sandwich. The process of making it is unknown at present. The seaweed design is in a sparkling yellow and apparently is applied by hand to the finished vase. Some crude imitations of this fine workmanship are not uncommon. 10½ inches.

5. Reproduction of a blue satin glass vase. It is of a very thin case glass, so thin the blue can be seen through it. Note the small handles. This is not an exact copy of any known old satin vase. The market has been flooded with the copies, particularly in Pennsylvania, in various colors.

Lower row, left to right.

1. Blue satin vase, shaded slightly lighter at the base. Square in shape, with the panels indented. Diamond pattern. Case

glass with white lining. An unusually lovely vase, which may also be found in shaded rose. 8¾ inches.

2. Rose satin glass vase, in Diamond pattern. Case glass. Deep rose in the neck, shading to a light color in the bowl. Graceful shape for this type, which has not been popular with collectors. 9½ inches.

3. Blue satin glass vase, having a design showing a diamond within a diamond. Frills at top indented so closely that they make opening quite small. Case glass. Blue is slightly shaded. A lovely and unusual vase. 7 inches high, 3¼ inches diameter.

4. Deep opaque rose satin glass, not cased. Frosted thorn handle and frosted applied edge. 7 inches.

5. Plain rose satin glass, with fine workmanship displayed in design of enamelled roses which are outlined in gold. This pair of vases comes in a left and a right. 8½ inches.

PLATE 216

Upper row, left to right.

1. Sapphire-blue vase flecked in silver. In England this was first termed "Metallized Glass." The process of inserting the silver flakes of mica is discussed in the chapter on glass hats. 8½ inches.

2. Amethyst vase with fine enamelled decoration. Bird in flight (heron) and green leaves. Edge is striped in gold, as are the stems of the leaves. 10 inches.

3. Brilliant sapphire-blue vase. Enamelled conventional design with flowers. Fluted top. 11 inches.

4. Ruby-red vase. Delicate design of frosted panels. Conventional border in brownish-yellow enamel. 10 inches.

5. Vivid sapphire-blue vase in an unusual shape. Decoration of white flowers and gold leaves.

Lower row, left to right.

1. Amethyst vase with enamelled decoration of bellflowers and forget-me-nots. 6½ inches.

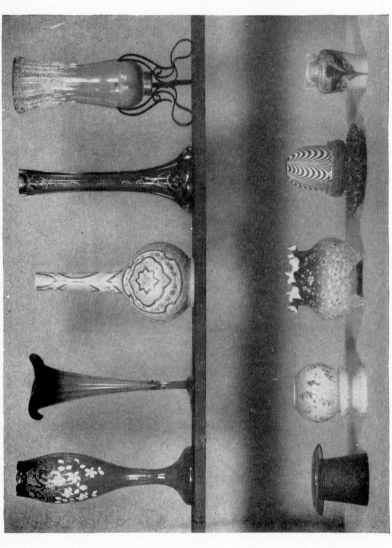

PLATE 217

Upper: Late Victorian vases except second from left, which is a New England Amberina vase. The same shape is found both in Peachblow and Burmese.

Lower: A hat; a satin glass enameled night lamp; an enameled vase; Night lamp with rose and white shade;

PLATE 218

Upper: Group of black glass enameled vases.
Lower: Varied group of Victorian pieces.

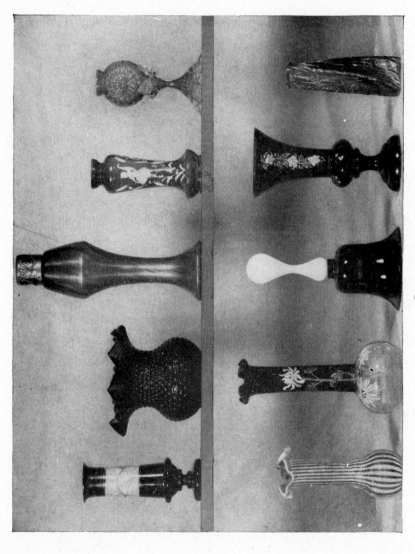

PLATE 219

Group of decorative art ware of the 1880's including a glass bell in the center of the lower row.

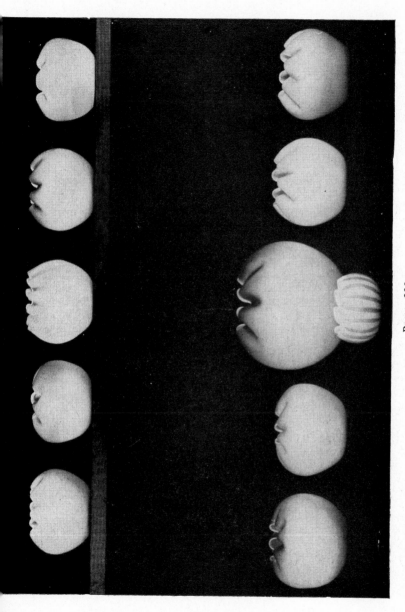

PLATE 220

Group of satin glass rose bowls. Little 2 inch bowl in striped satin glass in foreground has been found only in blue.

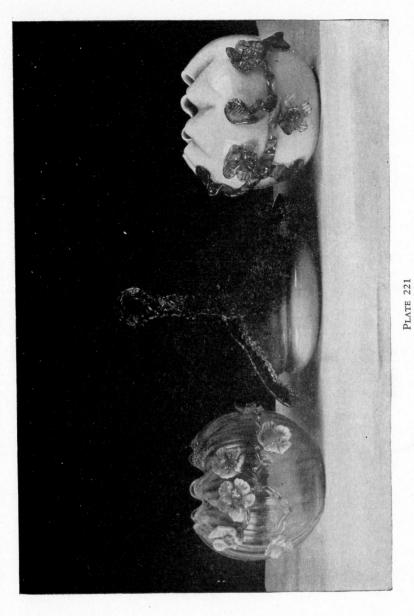

PLATE 221

Two rose bowls with applied glass leaves and flowers in color. Center, Victorian basket in shaded red with thorn handle.

2. Amethyst art glass vase, encrusted in silver and threads of glass which are melted into the surface. 6½ inches.

3. Cranberry-colored vase with blue swirls through the glass. Fluted edge.

4. Bluish-purple bulb vase. Early type. 8½ inches.

5. Rose-red swirled vase. 6¾ inches high, 3¾ inches diameter.

6. Amethyst vase with white-enamelled flower decoration. 5½ inches.

7. Small amethyst vase with frilled edge. Bowl enamelled with white flowers and leaves.

PLATE 217

Upper row, left to right.

1. Emerald-green vase with enamelled decoration of white flowers. Conventional design in brownish gold. 12¾ inches.

2. Amberina vase in the typical and best-known New England type. It is found in a wide variety of sizes, from small to large. Same shaped vase was also made in New England, both in Burmese and in Peachblow. 11¾ inches.

3. Opaque white vase, enamelled and painted to simulate Persian art ware. In coloring it is rose pink and blue, outlined in black. There are many small colored flowers and leaves. 12 inches.

4. Late type of Victorian vase in emerald green. Gold enamelled decoration. 12½ inches.

5. Peacock blue-green vase with frosted icicles. Vase is supported by copper holder. 12¾ inches.

Lower row, left to right.

1. Ruby hat, 4 inches high, 5 inches across. These have been made in a variety of sizes, some with the brim turned down more than others.

2. Delicate shade of pink, satin glass night lamp. Back-

ground has herringbone pattern. Enamelled decoration of birds and leaves in color. A choice lamp.

3. Typical Victorian-style flower holder of the 1880's. Shaded rose pink with white lining. Enamelled with blue and white flowers having gold stems. Four crystal feet. Frilled top.

4. Night lamp. Rose with white loops through the glass. Crystal holder marked "Trade mark. Cricklite. Clarke's Patent." Center has figure of fairy holding wand.

5. Late Victorian art glass. Slightly iridescent. Bright colors in blue, red, green, etc. 4¾ inches.

PLATE 218

Upper row, left to right.

1. Black glass vase, which shows purple through a strong light. Enamelled with spray of blue and white leaves and flowers. 6¾ inches.

2. Black glass, painted and enamelled with spray of pink flowers and colored leaves.

3. Black glass, enamelled with spray of blue flowers and red and white butterfly. Frilled edge. 8½ inches.

4. Mary Gregory type of vase, showing girl pouring water into dish. Mary Gregory is said to be have worked in the decorating department of the Boston & Sandwich Glass Co. and to have painted children almost exclusively. Vase is in copper holder. 11¼ inches.

5. Black glass, with small spray of painted and enamelled flowers. White daisies with green and brown leaves, and small pink flowers. 9 inches.

6. Black glass vase, enamelled with design of flowers, leaves and a butterfly in color. 6½ inches.

7. Black glass vase, with spray of flowers and leaves, all in silver. 6¼ inches.

Lower row, left to right.

1. Tiny black vase with frilled edge. Enamelled decora-

tion of white flowers with red centers, and green leaves. 3½ inches.

2. Unusual square black marble glass match or flower holder. 4 inches.

3. Blown bud vase with frilled edge. 8 inches.

4. Large black vase with enamelled decoration of flowers, leaves and bird, in color. 10¼ inches.

5. Bud vase, panelled, with heavy enamelled decoration of flowers and leaves in natural colors. 6¾ inches.

6. Black glass vase with frilled edge. No decoration. 5¾ inches.

7. Black vase with iridescent coloring. This comes under the heading of art ware. 3¼ inches.

PLATE 219

Upper row, left to right.

1. Clear ruby-red vase, having frosted band decorated with green oak leaves and acorns. 7½ inches.

2. Ruby-red vase, with fluted top edged in gold. Very small indented thumbprints, like honeycomb. 6 inches high, 7¼ inches across.

3. Rose-red vase slightly swirled, art glass. Ornate open-work brass collar. 12 inches.

4. Ruby-red Mary Gregory (previously described) type vase, with enamelled decoration of girl, in white. The detail is well-executed. 7¼ inches.

5. Ornate rose-red decorative vase. Bowl has swirls on sides, pinwheel decoration on flattened sides. Bowl of vase is enclosed in five crystal leaves. The stem is ruby and the vase stands on six clear glass leaves.

Lower row, left to right.

1. Rose-colored vase with opalescent stripes. Unusual shaped fluted top.

2. Cranberry-colored top, clear bowl enamelled with chrys-

anthemums. There is one pink and one yellow flower. Decoration is well done. 10¼ inches.

3. Glass bell, of the 1880's. Milk-white handle, ruby bell, white clapper which is set in plaster of Paris. Probably midwestern.

4. Ruby vase, enamelled in the Vintage pattern in white. 9½ inches.

5. Art glass. Iridescent coloring. Square in shape, with a swirled design. 7½ inches.

PLATE 220

Upper row, left to right.

1. Shaded yellow satin glass rose bowl. 3½ inches.

2. Pink shaded to blue, but color does not continue to base. 3¼ inches.

3. Shaded light blue. 3½ inches.

4. Shaded deep rose red. 3½ inches.

5. New England Peachblow, in coloring. Color reaches nearly to base. 3¼ inches.

Lower row, left to right.

1. Shaded-pink rose bowl.

2. Shaded blue at top, nearly white at base. 3½ inches.

3. Rose-shaded large bowl, nearly white at base. 5¾ inches. This bowl is also found in shaded blue to white and in yellow to white.

4. Shaded-red rose bowl. 3½ inches.

5. Blue-shaded bowl, quite light in color at base. 4 inches.

6. Small blue satin striped rose bowl, in foreground. These bowls vary in coloring. One style alternates dull-surfaced stripe with satin stripe. So far this size and type has been found only in blue.

Rose bowls vary greatly in coloring. A rare shade is a lavender-blue, almost a violet color. The red bowls run to about five different shades. Blue also varies considerably. Probably light-brown satin glass bowls exist but they are difficult to find.

PLATE 221

Left. Greenish-yellow rose bowl, with yellow-opalescent stripes. Pink flowers in applied glass adorn the front. 5¾ inches high.

Center. Victorian basket in shaded red, with crystal border added to crimped edge. Clear glass twisted thorn handle.

Right. Cream opaque rose bowl with applied pink glass flowers and amber leaves and stem. 6 inches high.

PLATE 222

Upper row, left to right.

1. Translucent opaque white ewer, which has opal coloring when held to the light. Applied leaf decoration, frilled edge in applied light-blue glass and blue applied handle. Glossy surface. 4¾ inches.

2. Rare brilliant emerald-green case glass vase. White lining with red stripe on inside of scalloped edge. Large applied flower decoration, with two leaves, on bowl of vase, all in deep green. Applied handles. 6¾ inches.

3. Opaque cream-white vase. Applied light-green leaves on lower part of bowl of vase, and light-green handles. Applied colored glass flower above the leaves. Pointed edge was reheated, causing the color to change to deep rose pink. 9¼ inches.

4. Shaded rose-pink vase having ribbed pattern through the glass. Applied crystal band winds spirally about the vase, the band being pinched and crimped in the process of making, so that these portions extend outward as a further embellishment or ornamentation. 7 inches.

5. Opaque white case glass vase, with blue lining. Exceptionally heavy. Pink and white applied flowers, with amber leaves. Blue frilled top.

PLATE 222

Group of vases, all of which are adorned with flowers and leaves applied to the bowls in varied color

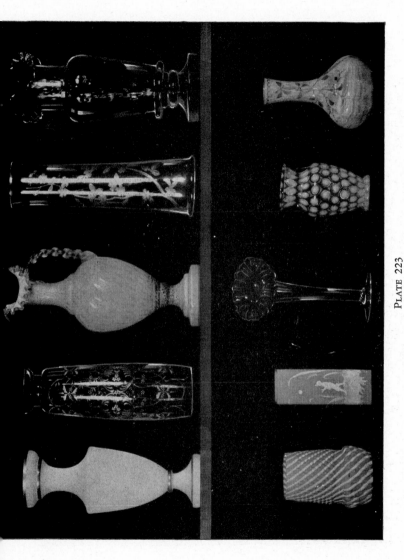

PLATE 223

Various types of Victorian vases, including an unusually large satin glass ewer in Polka Dot pattern.

PLATE 224

Group composed largely of Silvered glass vases.

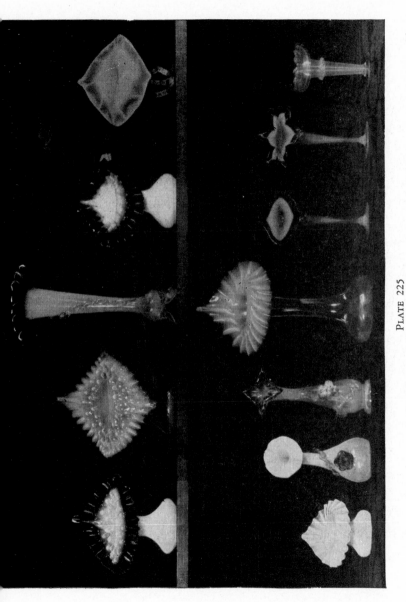

PLATE 225

Group of novelty vases, popular during the 1870's and 1880's.

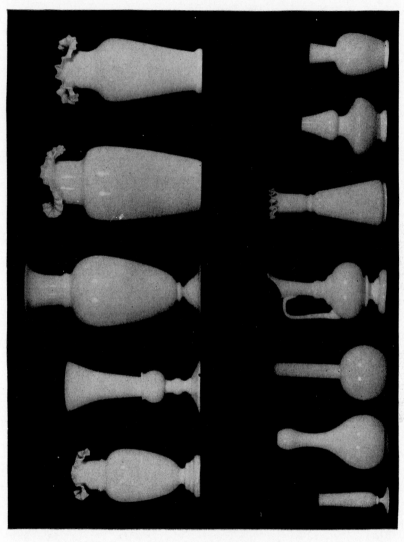

Lower row, left to right.

1. Translucent opal thick glass vase, decorated with deep-pink flower, amber stem and blue outstanding leaf. 3¾ inches.

2. Translucent opaque white vase, with melon-shaped ribbed bowl. Applied small red and opaque white apples, with amber leaf and stem. Amber applied rim. 5 inches.

3. Shaded case glass vase, in deep rose shading to light color toward base. Elaborate applied decoration on both sides of one pink and white flower and bud and leaf. Amber leaves and amber thorn handles. White lining. Frilled top, edged in clear amber. 9 inches.

4. Translucent white vase, with opal tints. One applied light-amber leaf and stem with an additional two green leaves and red cherry. Frilled top edged in amber. 5¼ inches.

5. Ewer in glossy white translucent glass. Amber band and stem, pink and white flower with amber center in flower. Three green leaves. Frilled top edged in bright, clear amber. 4¾ inches. These vases come in a right and left, thus forming a pair.

PLATE 223

Upper row, left to right.

1. White vase with sanded finish. Gold stripes about the base and edge. 13 inches.

2. Amethyst vase with delicate gold and white decorations all over bowl. 13 inches.

3. Unusually large satin glass ewer in shaded pink with frosted white crimped handle. Frilled top edged in frosted white. Elongated polka-dot pattern. Case glass, with white lining. 14¼ inches.

4. Sapphire-blue vase with slight iridescent coloring. Elaborate design of leaves and flowers in gold.

5. Brilliant cranberry-red vase, with panels showing faintly. Elaborately frilled edge. 14 inches.

Lower row, left to right.

1. Green satin panelled vase with blue stripes running diagonally through it. $6\frac{1}{2}$ inches high, $3\frac{1}{4}$ inches diameter.

2. Square opaque blue vase, with enamelled decoration of boy playing with ball.

3. Cranberry-red vase, so dark it barely shows in illustration. In shape it is similar to the Amberina vase shown on Plate 217, except that the top of the back stands up and the front edge tilts downward, and the edge is frilled. The vase is washed or flashed with color on the inside and fluted. The foot is clear. $10\frac{1}{2}$ inches.

4. Unusual blue Inverted Thumbprint vase, with blue-opalescent dots. Fine gold tracery around all the thumb-spots. $6\frac{1}{2}$ inches.

5. Unusual lemon marbelized case glass vase, decorated with enamelled pink and white flowers, with gold leaves. $8\frac{1}{4}$ inches.

PLATE 224

Upper row, left to right.

1. Blue Mercury glass vase, with dull finish. Decorated band about the bowl and foot. Balance of vase lightly painted with flowers and leaves, in white. 12 inches.

2. Vivid bright lavender vase, not as deep as purple. Decorated with lavender and white band of leaves around the bowl. $10\frac{1}{4}$ inches.

3. Bright silvered glass vase with elaborate painted design in white. Gold lining. 8 inches.

4. Rare brilliant sapphire-blue vase, with festoons in the glass but no painted decoration.

5. Large bright silvered glass vase, fluted in panels and painted with white leaves, green leaves, dark-blue flowers and others in rose red.

Lower row, left to right.

1. Tiny silvered vase, painted with white leaves in band around the bowl. 3¼ inches.

2. Plain silvered glass. 4¼ inches.

3. Bright silvered glass, decorated with a rose and leaves, in center of front. 6 inches.

4. Bright silvered glass, having bouquet of flowers in natural colors with green leaves. Striped in white. Vivid colors. 7¼ inches.

5. Square art glass vase in deep green with iridescent bands heated into the glass, irregularly. 10¼ inches.

6. Gold Mercury glass vase, painted with white flower and leaves. Decoration quite worn and faded. 8½ inches.

7. Silvered vase painted with white leaves which are rather faded. 7½ inches.

8. Silvered wine glass, decorated with yellow rose tinged with red, and green leaves. 3½ inches.

9. Plain silvered individual salt. 1¾ inches.

Some of the old glass factories referred to the vases just described as "Silvered glass." The Boston & Sandwich Glass Co. made a good deal of it, as did many other factories. At one time collectors referred to this type of ware as "Mercury glass." The clear vase, or any other object, was blown and finished and later the workman blew the nitrate of silver inside the vase from the open pontil on the base, until it was thoroughly coated. Then he sealed the base. The method of producing these vases is really a silver nitrate process, the nitrate of silver coming in any color. It was important that the base be sealed properly because the silver became badly discolored when exposed to the air for any length of time. After the inside of the vase had been completed and the base sealed, any form of painted decoration could be added to the exterior. Vases are found most commonly but other objects were made, such as salts, wines, sugar bowls, etc.

PLATE 225

Upper row, left to right.

1. Light opal vase, with shaded-red frilled edge, which is tilted to a point at the back and dips downward in front. Blown hollow dots in open face of vase. 7½ inches.

2. Light-green vase, with small raised Diamond pattern in bowl. Shaded rose-pink frilled edge having blown hollow dots just inside the frilled edge. Opalescent color in tilted portion. 8¾ inches.

3. Opal vase. Deep-red frilled edge tilted downward in points. Light-green applied spirals in crystal wind about vase. Five green leaves form feet. 11¼ inches.

4. Opaque white with shaded opaque red frilled edge. Hollow dots on face, inside rounded frill. 7¼ inches.

5. Green-opalescent vase, with few ribs on tilted portion to add to ornamentation. Front plain, tilted to a point back and front. Base stippled green with three green logs supporting vase. Base is round. 6¾ inches.

Lower row, left to right.

1. Small cased white vase with jade-green frilled edge, which is pointed at top and rounded in front. 4½ inches.

2. Translucent bluish-opal with unusual opening tilted forward to form an eight-petalled flower. Applied green spiral with single applied rose-red flower on bowl. 7½ inches.

3. Fluted vase in nearly clear glass shading to green at the foot. Red frilled top forming points. Light-green applied stem and leaf with rose and white flower. 8¾ inches.

4. Very pale-green glass vase with rose-opalescent frilled edge. Pointed in back and rounded in front. 12 inches.

5. Numbers 5 and 6 were purchased as a pair. Both have clear yellow stems and feet, and rose-colored tops. One top is pointed front and back and the other top is formed into a six-petalled flower. 7¼ inches.

6. Described above.

7. Rare Sandwich Lutz type of threaded glass. Clear glass threaded vase, frilled at back and plain in front. Single applied ribbon of glass about the bowl and clear foot. 4¾ inches.

PLATE 226

Upper row, left to right.
1. Opaque white, fairly thin glass vase with frilled edge, which is tipped downward to form three scallops.
2. Early white vase, with bowl and stem fused into foot, which is cupped. In the pair, one is slightly taller than the other. Rare. 9¼ inches.
3. White vase with rather rough surface which might signify poor iron in the mold from which it was made. Vase is fused in two parts, with cupped foot. 12¼ inches.
4. White vase of particularly fine quality and texture. Glossy surface. Frilled edge tilted down on three sides. 11 inches.
5. Very similar to above, glossy surface. 10 inches.

Lower left to right.
1. Plain opal bud vase. 5 inches.
2. White vase, slightly opal. 8 inches.
3. Slightly opal white vase, with plain long neck. 8¾ inches.
4. White ewer, with perfectly plain dense-white, long-pointed spout. 8¾ inches.
5. White vase in a graceful form. Frilled edge at top. 8¼ inches.
6. White vase, slightly opal, in odd shape. 6¼ inches.
7. Plain, simple white vase in dense white. 5¾ inches.

PLATE 227

Upper row, left to right.
1. Heavy cream-white glass, decorated with seaweed in orange. The seaweed was painted on after the vase was completed. 5¼ inches.

PLATE 227

Varied group of cut-glass vases including Satin-glass, Mary-Gregory type and Spangled glass

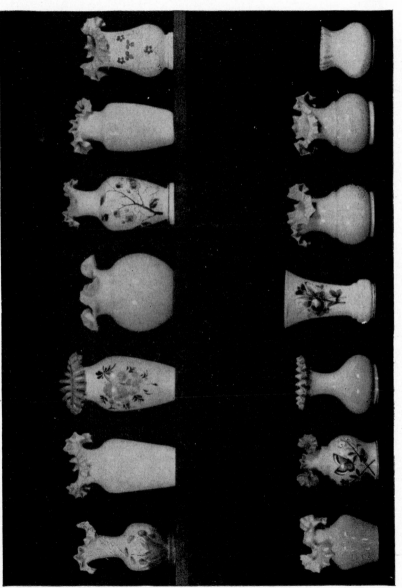

PLATE 228

Varied group of opaque vases, with and without decoration.

PLATE 229
Group of large decorated vases.

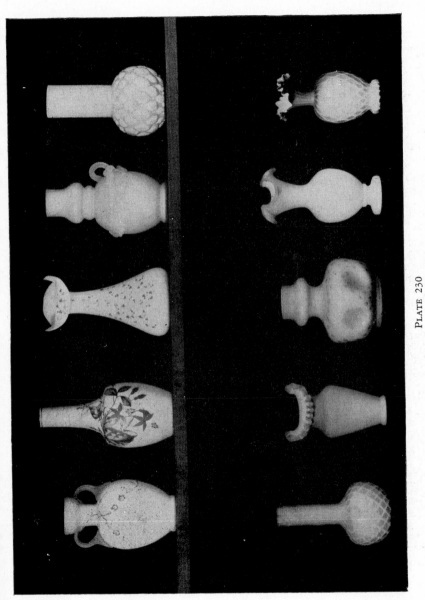

PLATE 230

Varied group of plain and decorated Satin glass vases.

PLATE 231

Group of large vases, ranging from 10 to 15 inches in height.

2. Vase in imitation of tortoise. Deep-claret color with darker spirals alternating with opalescent and white spirals. Square top pulled in to form four rounded corners. Clear white thread on top edge. 6¼ inches.

3. Vase with melonlike flutes. Delicate yellow in color with stripes having flecks of white alternating with stripes flecked with silver mica. Whole effect is a silver color. 6½ inches.

4. Opaque cream-white vase with small frilled edge. Bowl washed in light blue, and decorated with flowers and leaves in deep blue, outlined in gold, sanded like the seaweed. Glossy surface. 8¾ inches.

5. Powder-blue vase with grapes and leaves in white enamel. May be American imitation of more expensive cameo glass. 7 inches.

6. Same as No. 3, except blue with white flecks. Two sides indented like old-time pinch bottles. 6½ inches.

7. Exceptionally heavy white vase, in tortoise effect. Cloudy red and yellow intermingled in bowl. 6 inches.

Lower row, left to right.

1. Case glass in deep rose pink with pink mica stars. Could have been made by Hobbs, Brocunier & Co. of Wheeling, W. Va., or Boston & Sandwich Glass Co.

2. Case glass in yellow with white lining. Melon-shaped bowl. Shall amount of mica flecks through the glass. Frilled top is edged in clear yellow. 9½ inches.

3. Delicate satin glass vase in light blue, filled with flecks of silver mica. Top is tilted down to form three wide scallops or petals. 8¾ inches.

4. Deep-rose case glass. Surface is splashed in red with some silver mica flecks. Hobbs, Brocunier & Co. of Wheeling, W. Va., invented this type of novelty, and termed it "Spangled ware." 8½ inches.

5. Case glass vase similar to above. Light blue, flecked with silver mica, deep red and lemon yellow. 7 inches.

PLATE 228

Upper row, left to right.

1. Creamy-opaque vase with frilled top. Lower part painted in orange color and decorated with large blue berries and leaves. 6½ inches.

2. Opaque blue vase with glossy surface. Choice shade of color. Plain, with elaborately frilled edge. 7¼ inches.

3. Shaded pink-opalescent vase with frilled edge in a deep rose pink. Painted with flowers which are beaded, and green leaves. 7½ inches.

4. Opaque white vase with glossy surface and no decoration. Frilled top has been washed in a deep rose. 6½ inches high, 5¼ across.

5. Shaded pink vase, deep in color at top and lighter at base. Glossy surface. Painted flowers in brown, yellow and blue. 7¼ inches.

6. Opaque blue vase with frilled edge, similar to No. 2.

7. Translucent pink-opalescent vase in translucent glass. Deep-pink frills. Decorated with spray of deep-rose flowers, green leaves and gold and white stems. 6 inches.

Lower row, left to right.

1. Jade-green translucent glass, slightly opalescent, glossy surface. Frilled top, striped in gold on edge. 5 inches.

2. Cream-white opalescent glass. Rose frills with edge striped in gold. Decorated with colored flowers, green leaves and large butterfly. Glossy surface. 5¼ inches.

3. Translucent blue, very slightly opal. Frilled edge striped in gold. No decoration. Glossy surface. 5 inches.

4. Heavy opaque-cream vase, decorated with brightly colored flowers, including red rose, poppy, blue flowers and green leaves. Striped in gold. 6 inches.

5 and 6. Opaque blue vase with glossy surface. Some decoration but badly worn. Frilled tilted edges. This same vase may be found in light brown. Two sizes: 5¼ and 5½ inches.

7. Delicate shaded-pink vase, without decoration. Crimped top. Glossy surface. 3½ inches.

PLATE 229

Upper row, left to right.

1. White vase with sanded finish. Sections are washed in bands of blue and white. Scattered decoration of red berries, and a conventional band about the center. 12 inches.

2. White vase with sanded finish. Bands of gold about foot and knob in stem. Spray of flowers and leaves in blue and gold. Beautifully decorated. 13 inches.

3. White footed vase with sanded finish. Bowl is decorated with flowers and leaves. Gold stripes about stem and foot.

4. Brilliant emerald-green vase, with four sides indented. Sprays of leaves and flowers enamelled in gold. Edge has four tilted petals. 11½ inches.

5. Deep-rose vase, with sanded finish. Elaborate design of pink enamelled flowers and gray painted leaves outlined in pink. Pink is predominating color in the vase. Frilled edge shading to delicate pink. 11½ inches.

Lower row, left to right.

1. Opaque blue vase with rather crude decoration of spray of white berries with green leaves. Frilled edge. 10¼ inches.

2. Unusual vase in robin's-egg blue, with scattered flecks melted into the surface. Shallow scalloped edge. 10 inches.

3. White vase with sanded finish. Decorated with spray of white flowers and blue ribbon against gold background. 10½ inches.

4. Sapphire-blue vase, with painted splashes of color to simulate Spatter glass. 9¾ inches.

5. Shaded-blue case glass vase, with white lining. Thin, small drape pattern in the glass in panels. Frilled top, edged in amber shading to yellow. Top is flattened on two sides and pointed in center. 9½ inches.

PLATE 230

Upper row, left to right.

1. Shaded light-blue satin glass vase, enamelled with apple blossoms. Case glass. Frosted ribbed handles. 6¾ inches.

2. Yellow satin glass vase, with enamelled fuchsias and green leaves. 8¼ inches.

3. Yellow satin glass vase in unusual shape. Delicate painted design. Exceptional shape to edge, which is tilted upward at back and sides and downward in front. 8 inches. Same vase may be found in blue.

4. Yellow satin glass vase with almost invisible diamond quilting. Frosted handle which is nearly dwarfed by frosted applied leaf across front of vase. 7¾ inches.

5. Deep-blue satin vase, with Diamond pattern bowl tufted like a quilt. Same vase may be found in deep pink. 7½ inches.

Lower row, left to right.

1. Blue satin vase in diamond quilted pattern. Case glass. Same may be found in orange-red and probably other colors. 7 inches.

2. Shaded-blue satin case glass vase. Plain with no decoration except elaborately frilled top which has an applied rim of frosted glass. Mate to this vase may be found in tangerine-yellow shading to white at base. 6 inches.

3. Deep-blue satin glass vase in polka-dot pattern. Six deep indentations in bowl. 6½ inches.

4. Bright yellow plain satin vase shaded to lighter color at base. Case glass, with white lining. Four-petal edge. 7¼ inches.

5. Deep rose-pink satin case glass vase, with white lining. Rose color shades to lighter tone at base. Diamond quilted pattern. 6¼ inches.

PLATE 231

Upper row, left to right.

1. Jade-green tall vase, decorated with gold ivy leaves. Sanded finish. 13½ inches.

2. Blue-green vase, painted and enamelled in conventional design. Medallion in center encloses red and blue flowers, with green leaves. 13½ inches.

3. Rose-pink vase with sanded finish. Foot, in white, is fused to bowl. Bowl is decorated with wreath of delicate leaves about center of bowl. Gold dots with white centers above and below the design. 15 inches.

4. Opaque lavender vase with glossy surface, decorated with large white flower and bud, green leaves and spray of red flowers having white centers. 13 inches.

5. White vase with sanded finish. Scalloped edge striped in gold. Same vase may be found in opaque jade green. 12½ inches.

Lower row, left to right.

1. Cream-opalescent vase in an unusual shape. Decorated with large pink, blue and white flowers with green leaves. Frilled edge. 10½ inches.

2. Left and right ewers in this pair. They are white at the top, shading to deep brown. Brown handle. Bowl decorated with pink and white flowers having dark-blue centers. There is also a bird and leaves in gold. 10 inches.

3. White vase, with slightly glossy finish. Decorated with leaves outlined in pink enamel, partly filled in gold. There are also white flowers. Elaborate design. 10½ inches.

4. White satin glass ewer with a fluted bowl. Pointed lip. Deep-green handle. Bowl is washed in green and lightly decorated.

5. Opaque blue vase with slightly glossy surface. No decoration. Attractively frilled edge. 10 inches.

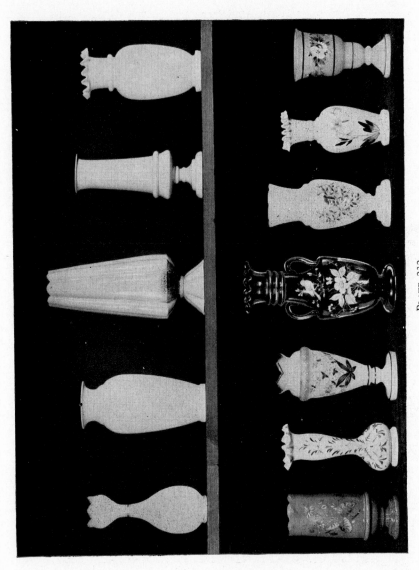

PLATE 232

Group of vases in plain opaque colors and others with painted and enameled decoration.

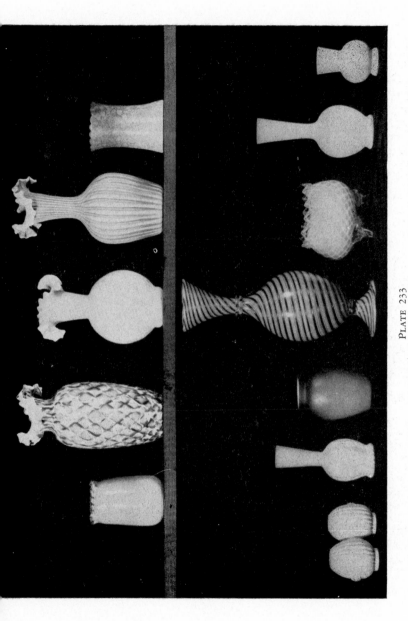

PLATE 233

Interesting group of varied types, including Agata vase (right end, upper row) a Nicholas Lutz Sandwich glass striped vase (center, lower row) and several Mt. Washington, New Bedford, Mass. pieces.

PLATE 234

Groups of painted and enameled vases of Victorian era.

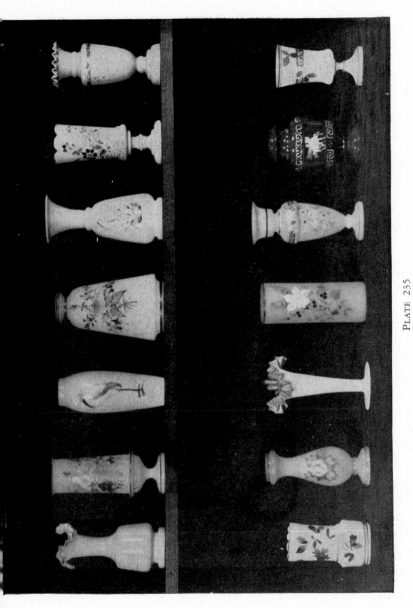

PLATE 235

Group of painted and enameled Victorian vases.

PLATE 236

Upper: Group of decorated Victorian vases.

PLATE 232

Upper row, left to right.

1. White vase with sanded finish. No decoration except gold stripe about neck and on pointed edge. 8¼ inches.

2. Opaque plain jade-green vase, without decoration. 8½ inches.

3. Heavy paneled deep green vase, in imitation of pottery. 10¾ inches.

4. Opaque lavender vase, without decoration. 8½ inches.

5. Soft translucent greenish-opal vase. No decoration. Frilled edge. 8 inches.

Lower row, left to right.

1. Opaque light-brown vase, with floral decoration lightly applied in gold. 7½ inches.

2. Opaque light-green vase with glossy surface. Painted and enamelled decoration of flowers and leaves in blue, brown and gold. Frilled edge. 7¾ inches.

3. White vase with sanded finish. Delicate but rather elaborate design of flowers and leaves, which are painted and enamelled, mostly in gold. A few very small blue flowers add color. 8 inches.

4. Light-amethyst vase with green handles. Bird and flower decoration in natural colors. Frilled edge. 10 inches.

5. White vase with sanded finish. Decoration consists of a birdhouse, set in bower of green leaves, with bird emerging from it. Design is painted and enamelled. 8¼ inches.

6. Translucent opaque blue vase, having rather crude decoration of colored pink flower and greenish-brown leaves. Small frilled top. 7¼ inches.

7. Jade-green opaque vase, slightly translucent. Glossy finish. Band of flowers in bright colors about bowl including morning-glory, daisy and fuchsias. 6½ inches.

PLATE 233

Upper row, left to right.

1. Opaque vase with crimped top which may be found in following colors: Deep pink; pink shading to white. Both have applied edge in clear glass. Some show opalescent coloring when held to the light.

2. Choice, unusual Diamond Quilted vase. Ridges in quilting show plainly. Deep rose, splashed in white, with satin finish. Case glass, white lining. Frilled edge. 9 inches.

3. Blue satin glass vase, having pattern of elongated loops in bright satin. Frilled top. This is a scarce pattern. 7¾ inches.

4. Rare, rose satin vase with heavy ribs. Lighter shade of color between ribs. Case glass with white lining which extends to the frilled edge. 9¼ inches.

5. Agata vase, made by the New England Glass Co. at Cambridge, Mass. This ware always has a glossy surface, colored somewhat like Peachblow but with a mottled surface in an irregular design showing slight iridescence. It was not a success commercially, so not a great deal of it was made, and for this reason it is scarce today.

Lower row, left to right.

1. Double flower holders, joined together. Satin glass in jade green with a "strawberry" on each side, meaning a small round rosette with indentations in surface. This ornament was largely used in this country by the Mt. Washington Glass Co. of New Bedford, Mass. 3 inches.

2. Satin glass vase, in irregular Diamond pattern. Case glass. May be found in varying shades of blue. Some have vertical ribs in neck and others are swirled. 6 inches.

3. Rose-red vase, slightly shaded. No pattern. Case glass. 4¾ inches.

4. Striped vase, a type made by Nicholas Lutz at Sandwich. Broad gold stripe alternating with deep-blue and white. Folded

rim on foot. Double crystal ring applied around neck. 11½ inches.

5. Satin glass vase in so-called "Mother of Pearl," because of its sheen and coloring. Diamond pattern. Three crystal applied feet. Scroll about brim. Frosted "strawberry" ornament underneath base. Coloring is light blue, pink and yellow against Diamond pattern background. Probably made at Mt. Washington Glass Co. at New Bedford, Mass., during the 1880's. 4¼ inches.

6. Greenish-yellow satin glass vase with irregular small dots in pattern. 7¼ inches.

7. Light-brown case glass vase in satin glass. Small Diamond pattern. 4½ inches.

PLATE 234

Upper row, left to right.

1. Opalescent vase, painted rose and red flowers with green leaves. Three orange stripes. Thin scalloped edge with gold stripe. This same style of decoration is found on wines, mugs and tumblers. For years it has been attributed to Bristol, but undoubtedly much of it was made in this country. 6¼ inches.

2. Same type as above, though the glass is more opaque and thicker. Decorated with roses in blue, alternating with smaller pink flowers. Blue and pink flowers about bowl. Three gold stripes. Scalloped edge. 7 inches.

3. Fairly deep-blue vase with opalescent tint. Decorated with few small sprays of flowers and leaves in gold. Said to be a Pittsburgh type. Wide scalloped edge. 9¾ inches.

4. Gray-blue translucent glass vase with delicate painted conventional design in gold, enclosing a blue vase containing pink roses. Pink bird on each side of conventional ornament. 10 inches high, 5 inches diameter.

5. Opaque blue vase, in deep shade of color. Somewhat crude conventional design in brown-orange, with baskets of

flowers alternating. Similar to some Pennsylvania Dutch designs. 8½ inches.

6. Early Victorian vase in thick opaque white glass. Delicate conventional design in light colors. Bee with wings closed on one side and open on the reverse. Top folded over and striped in gold.

7. Opaque blue vase, with violet tint to glass. Delicate enamelled design in white with a few small gold flowers. 7 inches.

Lower row, left to right.

1. This is really a jar rather than a vase. May be found with cover. Fine white-enamelled decoration with small amount of gold. Could be Bristol. 7 inches.

2. Glossy opaque white vase decorated with a rose alternating with a pansy. Small scattered sprays of blue flowers. Very deep-green color in leaves. 8¾ inches high, 4½ inches diameter.

3. Opaque white vase with fairly rough sanded finish. Decorated with birds in vivid colors. No two birds alike on either vase in the pair. Similar bird decoration may be found on some Burmese vases. 9 inches.

4. Translucent white vase with glossy surface. Three medallions of roses are enclosed in conventional style, striped in blue. Conventional ornament above and below, between the medallions. Plain edge striped in gold. Red and green vine with leaves, about foot. 10 inches high, 6 inches diameter.

5. Glossy opaque white vase, washed in deep green in band about top and base. Painted and enamelled decoration in colored leaves, which are striped in gold. 9 inches.

6. White vase with sanded finish. Upper part washed in light brown. Arches painted and enamelled in burnt orange and gold. Green medallions. Festoon of leaves in red and brown.

7. Small blue-opalescent vase with delicate tracery of gold about the bowl and neck. Scalloped edge. 6¼ inches.

PLATE 235

Upper row, left to right.

1. Soft jade-green color, glossy surface. No decoration. Frilled edge. 7 inches.

2. White vase with sanded finish. Bird and flowers painted in natural colors. Small amount of gold enamel. These vases are found in a right and a left.

3. White vase with sanded finish, case glass, white lining. Vase washed in deep gray shading to a lighter tone. Decoration consists of a large stork painted in gray. 7 inches.

4. White vase with sanded finish. Excellent quality. Decorated with large red flower and other smaller flowers and leaves in natural colors. One spray with red flowers on reverse of vase. 7 inches.

5. Opaque bluish-opalescent vase, with crane or heron in color, standing in marshes. Long red bill, red legs. 7½ inches.

6. Opaque blue vase with glossy finish. Spray of red and white flowers decorate bowl. Shallow scalloped edge. Striped in gold. 6⅞ inches.

7. Light-brown vase with glossy finish. Rather crude decoration of a few red dots; gold band above also contains red dots. 6¾ inches.

Lower row, left to right.

1. Opaque light greenish-cream colored vase, with flower and leaf decoration, rather crudely executed. 5¼ inches.

2. Fairly deep-blue vase with sanded finish. Conventional design, painted and enamelled. 6¼ inches.

3. Interesting vase, made in two parts, the foot being fused to the stem. Early type showing rather crude workmanship. Opal-white, with glossy surface. Mustard-colored lining and frill. 6½ inches.

4. Pink vase with sanded finish. Painted decoration of white flower, and berries and leaves. 6½ inches.

5. White vase with sanded finish. Spray of painted flowers

and enamelled leaves. Conventional gold band dotted in white enamel, above and below flowers. 7 inches.

6. Terra Cotta vase, glossy surface with white-enamelled boy and horse. Greek key below figures and rococo design above. This is an imitation of real Terra Cotta. 6¼ inches.

7. White vase with sanded finish. Gold band decoration with red beads, pink flowers and gold leaves. 6½ inches.

PLATE 236

Upper row, left to right.

1. Thick opaque white vase, washed in light brown and painted with winter scene, all in deep brown. Snow is not painted but is the untouched white glass. 6¼ inches.

2. White vase, washed in yellow at the top and in pink toward the center. Painted decoration of large flower, brown and green leaves. 7¼ inches.

3. White vase, washed in shaded light gray. Decorated with purple tulip with green leaves. 8 inches.

4. Thick glass vase, having a design in purple grapes and green leaves in relief, which are painted. Scalloped edge. Appears to be a late type. 8½ inches.

5. White vase, washed in a delicate green. Painted bird in white with brown breast and wings. Green leaves. Gold stripes about top and base. Pair in right and left. 8¼ inches. Signed "Smith Bros."

6. Opaque white vase with sanded finish. Hand-painted with yellow background on one side, lavender on reverse, with roses and leaves against this background. 7½ inches.

7. Glossy vase in light brown shading to orange. Painted with strawberries, leaves, and flowers in blue. Unevenly frilled top. 6¾ inches.

Lower row, left to right.

1. Dense white vase, flaring slightly at the top. Very plain. 4½ inches.

2. Melon-ribbed vase, plain neck. White, slightly opalescent. 5¼ inches.

3. Opal vase, perfectly plain. 6¼ inches.

4. Dense white vase, having large roses and leaves in heavy relief. A glassworker told me these were originally pickle jars, as were those in the grape pattern, and were made with heavy design because it could be done cheaply and imperfections in surface would not show. Cloth was tied over top when jar was used for pickles. 7 inches.

5. Dense white vase with large, rounded bowl. 7 inches.

6. Opalescent vase with frilled edge bending downward on two sides. Balance of vase is plain. 5¾ inches.

7. Opalescent vase, footed, plain, with no design. 5 inches.

Chapter XXII

PEACHBLOW, BURMESE AND OTHER
SHADED GLASS

About fifteen years ago, collectors susceptible to color became attracted to Peachblow glass, without really knowing a great deal about it. It was my good fortune to unearth information concerning its history, while doing research work in the Pittsburgh area, in 1933. My first article telling the story appeared that same year. Subsequently, in 1934 and 1935, two other writers added technical details.

It is my belief that the first Peachblow vase, under that name, may have been inspired by an episode that occurred at the auction sale of Mary J. Morgan's collection of Chinese and Japanese porcelains in New York City on March 8, 1886. At least the incidents are well worth recording. One obtains an interesting view of the times from contemporary accounts of this event. For example, considerable newspaper space is devoted to a bidding duel between Charles A. Dana, once famous editor of the New York *Sun,* and Charles Crocker, the California railroad millionaire. The two were competing for a Buddhist Communion Service. The report described the wild excitement as the price climbed, in five-dollar advances, until it reached $310, at which staggering figure "the millions of the Golden State captured the sacred prize!"

The highest price paid at the Morgan sale was $18,000 for an "Ovoid Peachblow vase, 8 inches high." Another of the same shape and size, but darker in color, brought only $6,000. Other Peachblow pieces sold as follows: ovoid vase, 8½ inches high, $1,200; amphora-shaped vase, 6 inches high, $1,150;

ovoid vase, 8¼ inches high, $1,000; semiglobular bottle vase, $675; rouge box, $375.

The New York *Times* for March 9, 1886, remarked: "The greatest excitement of the sale was when the famous $18,000 Peachblow vase was set on the table, covered with a spread of old gold cloth. To any but a connoisseur it appeared to be a very common bit of plain porcelain. Ovoid in shape, it had a slender neck spreading at the top. It was eight inches in height and three inches in diameter. I Wang-Ye, a Chinese Mandarin Prince, once owned it. That was one point in its favor. It was made in the Tang-He period, somewhere between 1661 and 1722, and that was another point. It was these features that set collectors raving; and the experts among them say it was the finest specimen of its class in existence. A sharp rivalry for its possession was anticipated; but the price it brought exceeded all anticipations."

The sensation created was even more general than that which followed the sale of the Reifsnysder highboy for $33,000 in 1929. For months people talked about nothing else. The cheeks of lovely ladies must be Peachblow or nothing. The comic weeklies were full of Peachblow jokes. A Kentucky correspondent sent me a copy of the *Western Farmers Almanac* for 1887. I quote from it: " 'A Peachblow vase was knocked down for $18,000,' read Mrs. Diggory. 'My gracious alive! Why, I would have knocked it down for 75¢, if I didn't have to pay for it in case it broke when it fell.' "

On March 24, 1886, the New York *Times* sprang a second sensation by declaring that the "Peachblow family was not recognized in China as a standard or a desirable color. The vase (that brought the record price) is not perfect, there being a number of spots near the base which are off color. . . . It is not a Peachblow color at all, as Peachblow is understood in China, but an entirely different and darker shade of red. The vase was never in the collection of Prince I Wang-Ye, who is called a 'Mandarin Prince.' There are, in China, Mandarins, who are government officials, and Princes, who are of Royal

Blood. But a Mandarin doesn't become a Prince except in art sale catalogues." There followed a long tale to the effect that the vase in question had been bought in China from a curio dealer for the equivalent of $200 American money, and that it had been marked up to $2,000 and sold to Mrs. Morgan for $12,000 by a clerk who misread the price tag.

Several of the Morgan pieces came from the Prince of Ye's collection, which was second only to that in the Imperial Palace. That famous vase did not. The Prince for many years was in favor with the reigning family and amassed a vast fortune, which after the Chinese fashion he invested in porcelains, bronzes, ivories, jades, and other articles loved by Chinese collectors. On the death of his emperor, however, he lost favor and received the "white silken cord," signifying the privilege of hanging himself instead of being beheaded by the public executioner. The *Times* reporter continued: "The 'Peachblow family' exists only in the brain of American dealers and collectors, who have invented such names as, 'Ashes of Roses,' 'Manchu ware,' 'Ovoid Shape' and a hundred others that have no corresponding names in China or Japan. Aside from the ridiculous prices paid for some of the crushed strawberry or, so-called, Peachblow pieces, I don't think the prices at the sale were exorbitant."

But these shattering observations could not kill the public interest in Peachblow vases. For one person who read them and smiled, thousands quite overlooked them, and remembered only the fact that $18,000 had been paid for one eight-inch vase. What did this vase look like that made it worth such a fortune? The belief that it must be beautiful, as well as rare, was so general that all the glass houses must have had the same idea, along about the same time—to capitalize the magic name.

As a matter of fact, our glassmakers did not follow the Chinese models very closely, though some of the Oriental forms were imitated. Incidentally, the porcelain of this type which has been exhibited at the Metropolitan Museum of Art is today known as "Peachbloom Glaze." Its color, instead of suggesting peach blossoms, more closely resembles crushed strawberries mixed with cream. It differs from other reds, like *sang de boeuf,* for example, in that it is not crackled, although occasional specimens of crackled Peachbloom have been found. The discolorations in places where the red color—from an oxide of copper—has been burnt in the heating are a kind of sage green such as one might find here and there on a copper roof. The "Peachbloom Glaze" is found in the interior of the necks of the vases.

Peachblow glass, therefore, cannot be said to be "true Peachblow" merely because the color goes through from outside to inside, or because it shades to a red from white as in Cambridge, or from yellow as in the Wheeling variety. These variations and the diversity of forms catalogued afford sufficient evidence that the chief concern of the glassmakers during the 1880's was to capitalize the sensational publicity attached to the name "Peachblow." They had been making and selling colored ware. A self-selling term like "Peachblow" was a special gift from Providence.

A comparison of the forms made by the New England Glass Co. and by Hobbs, Brocunier & Co. will tell more clearly than words their essential differences in color and design. Copies in glass of the famous $18,000 Morgan vase were made and sold by the Wheeling concern, as shown on Plate 237. At the same time, the firm was more concerned with commercial than with artistic success, its real business being to supply the demand for colored tableware. Below the vase in Plate 237 are shown a Wheeling Peachblow finger bowl, whisky tumbler, and sherbet cup! The illustrations are taken from a Hobbs, Brocunier & Co. catalogue. They were a mass production concern who catered to the people in the West. Old Pittsburgh glassmen have assured me that Hobbs, Brocunier & Co. grasped the sales value of the Peachblow name well in advance of the Eastern makers, and that the Wheeling Peachblow was first on the market. Their memories may be at fault. At all events, I have found a

Fac-simile—Morgan ($18000) Vase and Stand

PLATE 237

Glass vase produced by Hobbs, Brocunier & Co. in imitation of the famous Morgan porcelain piece, though it is not precisely the color of the original.

Wheeling Peachblow finger bowl, whisky tumbler and sherbet cup.

PLATE 238

Wheeling Peachblow vases in Oriental forms.
Wheeling Peachblow butter dish, spoonholder, water pitcher, creamer,
and sugar bowl.

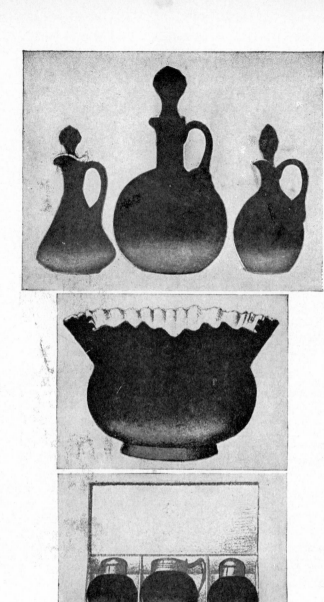

PLATE 239

Wheeling Peachblow cruets and a decanter. Also a gas shade and a
gift box containing salt, pepper and mustard pot.

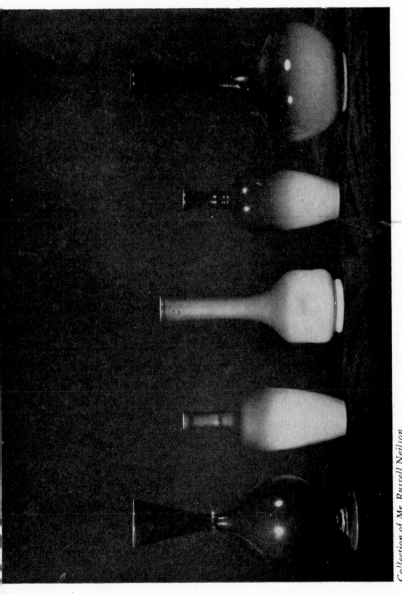

PLATE 240

Wheeling Peachblow vases, showing both glossy and dull surfaces.

PLATE 241
New England Glass Company Peachblow vases.

record showing the ware was listed and sold as "Peachblow glass" as early as 1886, so it is entirely possible it was being made before that date.

Of course, none of the glass factories at which Peachblow was produced adhered either to the shapes or to the purposes of the Peachblow porcelains in the Morgan, Altman, Havemeyer, and other collections. Hobbs, Brocunier & Co., according to their contemporary catalogue, made salts, pepper shakers, mustard jars, gas shades, tankard pitchers in several styles, as well as several sizes of tumblers, including one whisky, handled tumblers, champagnes, water tumblers, sherbet or custard cups, finger bowls, twenty styles of vases, sugar bowls, creamers, spoonholders, butter dishes, five sizes of pitchers, water bottles, decanters, celery vases, molasses jugs, sugar sifters, oil and vinegar cruets. Such forms as those listed above are far removed from China or the vase in the Morgan collection, which was not glass, but porcelain!

Let us consider the known manufacturers of Peachblow. These are recorded as the Mt. Washington Glass Co. of New Bedford, Mass., and the New England Glass Co. of Cambridge, Mass., representing the East, and Hobbs, Brocunier & Co. of Wheeling, W. Va., who represented the Pittsburgh district. So far as is known, no one can definitely prove which of these concerns first made Peachblow. In the East, of course, you will find those who insist the Cambridge or the Mt. Washington Co. product is not alone the first but the only "true Peachblow." Others award both seniority and exclusive genuineness to Wheeling, because of its alleged closer resemblance to the porcelain from which both color and name were derived. As has already been pointed out, it seems certain the name came into prominence shortly after the furor caused by the $18,000 sale of the Morgan vase.

Since the Hobbs, Brocunier & Co. version of the vase that commercialized Peachblow has been pictured first, let us proceed with the differences between the various companies' products.

Hobbs Peachblow can always be identified because it is a rather deep rose red at the top, shading to a yellowish tint at the base. The Hobbs ware was always a case glass, or that which was "plated" and had a white lining. When this glass was produced, all of it had a glossy surface. A bath in hydrofluoric acid left it with a soft, dull, "satin" finish. While the Hobbs Co. made it both ways, more of their Peachblow may be found with the glossy surface than with the acid-treated finish. Now for the forms produced at Wheeling. Plate 238 pictures some vases which display a decidedly Oriental influence. Below the vases are shown some of the utilitarian pieces. Hobbs, Brocunier & Co. were definitely appealing to the masses with a highly commercialized line. Plate 239 illustrates more Wheeling objects, all taken from one of their old trade catalogues. William Leighton, Jr., whose name was so prominently connected with the Hobbs firm, is said to be responsible for their Peachblow. It will be remembered that he took out the patent, under date of February 1, 1870, on the milk-white Blackberry pattern, so he must have been an enterprising, progressive person. Plate 240 illustrates other Hobbs Peachblow vases, with the exception of the one at the left end, which cannot be positively identified. Three of the vases have a glossy surface and two have been given a bath in acid. One vase (second from left) is the same as the one in the standard, shown on Plate 237. It is difficult to find that particular Peachblow vase today, complete with the amber dolphin holder.

Each of the three companies mentioned had their own method of production of this glass, and their own names for it. Plate 241 pictures three New England Peachblow vases. In the ware made by the New England Glass Co., the color pervades the body of the glass, and the inside of any of their objects is the same as the outside. One such vase as illustrated on Plate 241 was found bearing a triangular label on the base reading, "N.E.G.W. Wild Rose—patented March 2, 1886." This would indicate that the original name of the New England Glass Co. product was not Peachblow. A collector wrote me that she has a dish marked, "Patented Mt. W. G. Co. Peach Blow, Dec. 15, '85." I have found no record of a patent taken out by Hobbs, Brocunier & Co. on this ware, though the trade catalogue illustration on Plate 237 proves they were marketing a "Peach Blow Vase" in 1886.

The New England Glass Co. did not produce as wide a line as did Hobbs, Brocunier & Co. It must be remembered that the New England and Wheeling concerns each appealed to a different class of buyers. New England catered to a smaller and more refined clientele, while the Wheeling makers, with an eye to volume, sold to the masses in the South, in the West, and in Canada. The vases in Plate 241 display the delicate and restrained influence associated with the Boston of the 1880's. Their wares were more in the nature of "art glass," and little tableware was made beyond water pitchers and tumblers. Their pitchers were very similar in shape to the Hobbs, Brocunier & Co. pitcher, shown on Plate 238, except that the New England ware did not have a white lining. It is not my desire to attempt to impress anyone with my knowledge of glass by resorting to lengthy discussions of the technical details of producing the similar Peachblow wares, because it is my belief that the content of the formulas used is of no particular interest to the average reader. Indeed, whether a product contains oxide of uranium or fluorspar or feldspar means nothing to dealers and would not concern more than one out of a thousand collectors. In my possession are some very old formula books giving the needed contents for various colored mixtures but they are not deemed of enough general interest to be added here. It *is* of interest that more of the New England Peachblow may be found with the velvetlike surface obtained by subjecting it to an acid bath than with the natural finish. Collectors seem to prefer the dull finish. Typical Cambridge (N. E. Glass Co.) pieces shade from a deep rose red at the top to white at the base.

Though the Mt. Washington Glass Co. at New Bedford, Mass., were among the first to experiment with Peachblow, their ware differs in coloring and is least known to collectors.

In fact, when a piece is found it is sometimes viewed as a curiosity. In coloring, it varies greatly. Some is a delicate pink shading to yellow. Others show pastel colorings, with a light rose pink shading to pale blue and violet. Though they utilized the term "Peachblow," their ware is least like that collectors know as Peachblow. The colorings of the ware produced by Hobbs, Brocunier & Co., the New England Glass Co. and the Mt. Washington Glass Co. all differ, yet collectors lump it all under one heading today.

The Mt. Washington Glass Co. Burmese glass is better known than their Peachblow. Plate 242 pictures three of their vases. These are all large, running from 8½ inches to nearly 14 inches in height. The shading in color varies. Some are a lemon yellow at the base shading to a deep pink or rose at the top. Others are much lighter in tone. Now and then there will be found a piece that is almost an orange color, instead of lemon yellow. The New Bedford Co. obtained a patent on this glass and named it "Burmese," December 15, 1885. Like the Peachblow, it is found both with the dull and with the glossy surface, though more of it was apparently finished with the acid treatment. To most collectors the soft, dull finish is an added attraction. The output of the Mt. Washington Glass Co. in Burmese was similar to their Peachblow. Tall vases were made, similar to the one at the left end of Plate 242, but with the top crimped and tilted upward at the back and down in front, somewhat like some of those shown in the chapter devoted to vases. They did not make as many utilitarian objects but rather leaned toward the art types. I have seen little match holders which appear to have started out as a hat, but the top is formed in a tricorne. Burmese was made over a period of only five or six years. By that time, the New England factories had given way to midwestern competition.

An interesting object produced by the Mt. Washington Glass Co. is illustrated on Plate 243. It does not appear to be a commercial piece and certainly had little utility value. It will be noted that the top is fastened with a "strawberry," a mark of many Mt. Washington pieces. Of course, this tiny ornamental berry was used both here and abroad, but not to such a great extent in this country as in Europe.

Amberina is so well-known as not to require a long discussion here. For the benefit of the novice, it is a shaded glass (not opaque) red at the top and gradually running into amber toward the base. A typical New England Amberina vase is pictured in the upper row of Plate 217. It became highly commercialized after it was first made in New England, dating from approximately 1883. The midwestern factories were quick to take up this novelty and were soon producing table sets in Inverted Thumbprint and other patterns. Again it was a case of the midwest doing a mass production job against the more conservative line produced in New England. Some of the earliest and best Amberina is said to have been produced by the old Flint Glass factory at South Boston, who made a Diamond Quilted pattern, with a fine bell tone when tapped. They were careful workmen, who polished the pontil marks on such pieces as water tumblers, bowls, etc. Other factories also produced the Diamond Quilted, or "Venetian diamond" as it was known then. In the last stages of the long run of popularity of Amberina, it was made in the Daisy and Button pattern.

Agata was produced by the New England Glass Co. but was not a commercial success, so it was short-lived. A vase is pictured on Plate 233. It is a light-colored, opaque rose color with a mottled, glossy surface. In point of beauty, there is not much to recommend it. Little of it is found, even at its birthplace in New England. I have seen small vases, tumblers, pitchers, and bowls with frilled edges.

Novelty wares were produced in almost unlimited quantities in the midwest, particularly by Hobbs, Brocunier & Co. of Wheeling, W. Va. Frilled and ripple-edged bowls in attractive forms were made by the Hobbs concern. A page from a Hobbs catalogue picturing these bowls is shown on Plate 244. The frilled bowls were named "Richelieu" and were made in pink, turquoise, ruby and canary, edged in another color. The

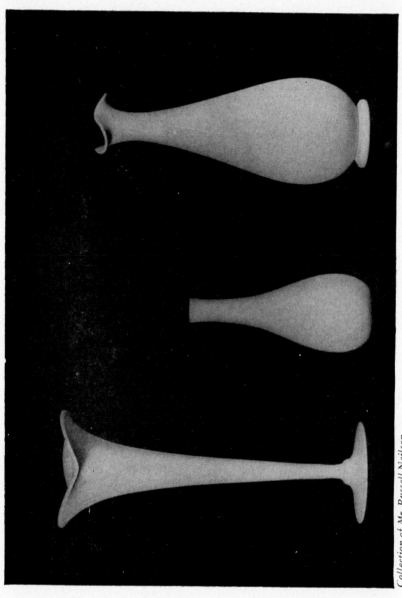

PLATE 242

Mt. Washington Glass Company Burmese vases.

PLATE 243
Mt. Washington Glass Company art object, produced at the same period as the Burmese.

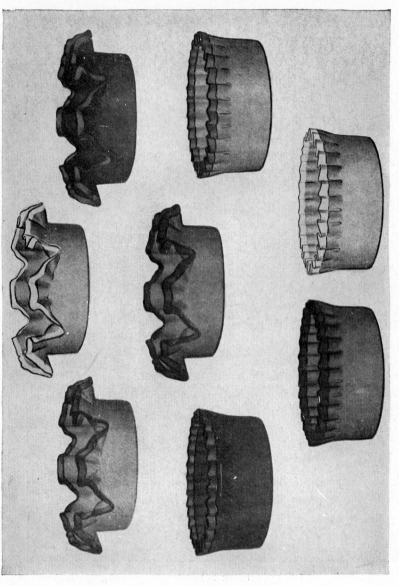

PLATE 244

Bowls in opaque glass with applied edges in different colors, as taken from a catalogue of Hobbs, Brocunier & Co., Wheeling, West Virginia.

No. 207 Tumblers 6 colors in box.

PLATE 245

Box of tumblers as pictured by Hobbs, Brocunier & Co.

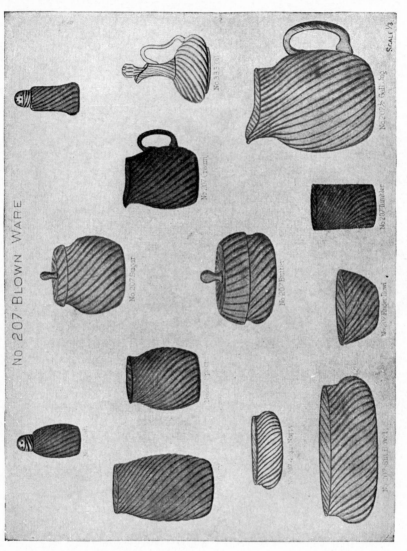

PLATE 246

Blown ware in opaque colored glass, produced by Hobbs, Brocunier & Co.

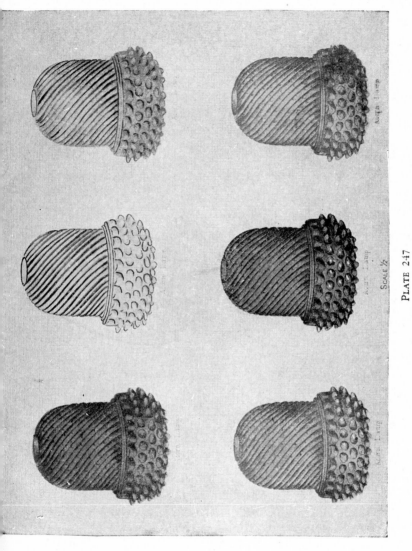

PLATE 247

Group of "Acorn" lamps, produced by Hobbs, Brocunier & Co.

ripple-edged bowls, in the lower part of the picture, are attractive in ruby, canary, pink and turquoise, all with applied edges in either a color or a frosted glass.

Plate 245 illustrates how Hobbs, Brocunier & Co. put up novelty tumblers in fancy boxes, designed to catch the eye of the trade. These glasses are swirled, with a soft acid finish, and were made in various colors.

Blown glass tableware was produced in the same pattern as the tumblers, in various shades. A page picturing some of the articles as presented by Hobbs, Brocunier & Co. is shown on Plate 246. In catalogues of the late 1880's we find another novelty ware which was known to the trade as "Venetian." It was produced in various colors, with an opaque Diamond pattern displayed against the plain colored background. A vase which has a swirl instead of the Diamond pattern, in the type of glassware I have mentioned, is shown at the lower left end of Plate 223. Practically all the shaded opaque glass and the novelty wares with a satin finish were at the height of their popularity during the 1880's.

A fad with some collectors has been collecting old-time night lamps. A group produced by Hobbs and termed "Acorn lamps" is shown on Plate 247. There is a wide range of these novelties. Plate 217 pictures an attractive and interesting type, a Fairy lamp with a trade mark of a figure of a fairy holding a wand. It is marked "Trade Mark. Cricklite. Clarke's Patent." The base is in crystal but the globes are found in various colors. Probably as beautiful a lamp of this kind as any collector could find is in enamelled satin glass, and shown in the lower row of Plate 217.

An original sketch of a decorative lamp submitted by a designer for the Mt. Washington Glass Co. of New Bedford, Mass., during the 1880's is pictured on Plate 248. A number of original drawings were given to me while in Pittsburgh as being the handwork of Deming Jarves of Sandwich, Mass., but on close examination of all of them I found one stamped with the name of the Mt. Washington Glass Co. and dated. There were two separate groups, so possibly Mr. Jarves did do some of them. Nearly all the sketches were of vases which appear to have been drawn for the New Bedford firm. If not, then possibly the artist was doing free-lance work. Three reproductions of the vases from the original sketches are shown here and they bear unmistakable characteristics of Mt. Washington products. The fourth has a Diamond pattern and is decorated, so this appears to have been a satin glass vase.

These drawings were given to me with the assurance that they were made by Deming Jarves, and had been presented by the superintendent of the Mt. Washington Glass Co. to Mr. Ruben Haley at New Bedford in 1893.

Collectors' hobbies are endless these days but so long as they afford mental relaxation, as well as the joy of the chase, the pleasure they afford the owner can be just as endless.

PLATE 248

Facsimile of an original drawing of an art glass lamp, submitted to the
Mt. Washington Glass Co. of New Bedford, Mass.

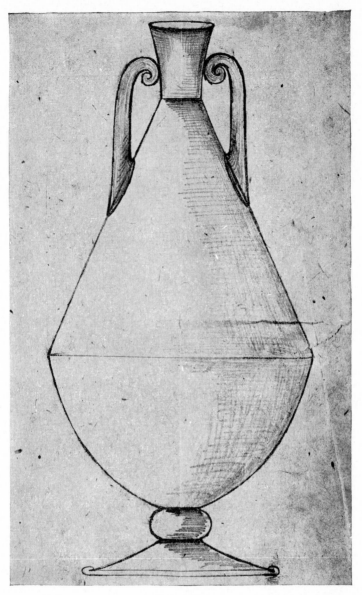

PLATE 249
Copy of an original drawing for a vase, for the Mt. Washington Glass Co.

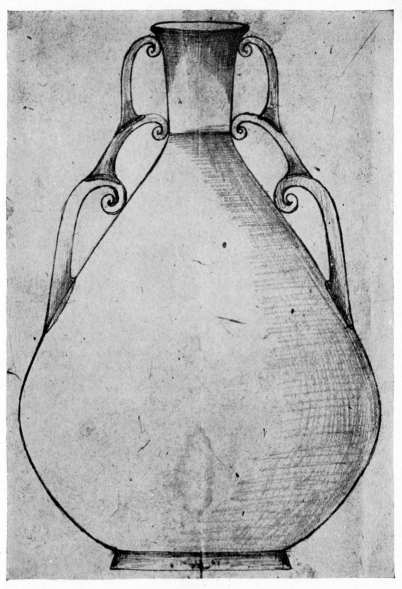

PLATE 250
Copy of an original drawing for a vase, for the Mt. Washington Glass Co.

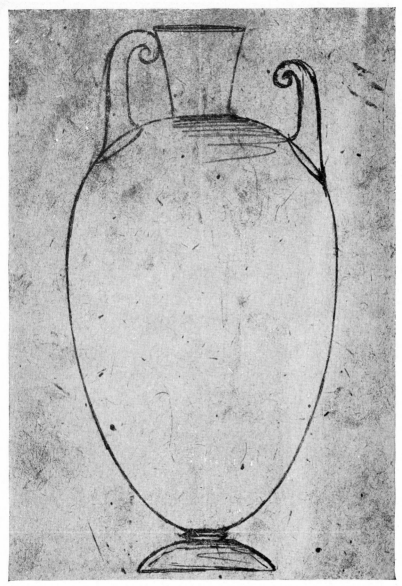

PLATE 251

Copy of an original drawing for a vase, for the Mt. Washington Glass Co.

PLATE 252

Copy of an original drawing for a decorated Satin glass vase.

Chapter XXIII

SANDWICH ENGRAVED, CUT, AND DECORATED GLASS

Of all the old wares ever produced in the United States, none is so well-known as Sandwich glass. Ever since antique shops sprang up in every state, uninformed tourists still pick up any piece of glass and ask, "Is this Sandwich?" The Sandwich tradition will never die. More special articles and more books have been written about it than about any other American glass factory. Any time any light could be thrown on the activities of the company, a new Sandwich article instantly appeared.

It is, therefore, a curious commentary on the capriciousness of human events that three years after the appearance of my book, *Sandwich Glass,* and fifty-three years after the closing of that factory, there should be delivered into my hands all the records, letters and other material devoted to the Boston & Sandwich Glass Co., which were deemed by its executives of enough importance to be preserved. Included in this mass of Sandwich documents are the records of every meeting from the day of incorporation until operations ceased, the books recording transfer of stock and a wealth of correspondence.

Among the notes in the old ledger, which date from 1826, are many references to the cutting, engraving, and decorating departments. From time to time the space was enlarged, which could only indicate that the volume of sales was great enough to warrant larger quarters. Indeed, the cutting and engraving departments of the Boston & Sandwich Glass Co. were important adjuncts of the factory. In the late 1860's and early 1870's as many as fifty of the best glass cutters in the country worked in the cutting shop, as did a number of engravers.

Many special orders were executed in addition to their regular commercial output. The finest of flint glass stem ware blown at Sandwich, often engraved with the initials of the owner, may still be found in many New England homes.

Collectors today would find amusing an article which appeared in the now defunct Boston *Transcript,* under date of July 3, 1925, in regard to Sandwich glass. Under the heading "Designs of Victorian Era" the writer stated: "That period of the stilted, the bizarre and the ugly which we are accustomed to call the Victorian era drew on and its standards of decoration caught up the Sandwich factory together with all other makers of household goods or decorations and swept them along into artistic darkness but financial brilliance. The book of designs used in the Sandwich factory which I discovered is unfortunately of the Victorian period." At another point (the reporter being quoted has never been a collector and his actual knowledge of antiques must be considered superficial) he rambles on: "Unfortunately this book of designs represents the artistic decadence of the Sandwich factory. The objects here pictured may be classed as antiques only by courtesy, because they were made considerably less than a hundred years ago, and one hundred years seems to have been informally adopted generally as marking the age limit of an antique."

This article appeared nearly twenty years ago, so the author of it should be mellowing but at this writing he still rants on tirelessly and tiresomely that the age of a true antique has been established at the year 1830. Progress is being made! An antique must now be 145 years old!

The illustrations in this chapter, with one exception, are taken from a catalogue of the Boston & Sandwich Glass Co.; it is undated but apparently pictures wares they produced over a period of years. There was not the demand for incessant change in the old days, so articles could be and were carried on for many years and they still found a ready market. There was good and bad taste in the past and we still have good and bad taste, so my readers can judge for themselves whether the articles pictured, from the 1870's and some, perhaps, from the 1880's, deserve being relegated to the dark ages of artistic decadence.

On Plate 253 is a dolphin epergne. The stem that holds the upper engraved flower holder is of spun glass. Try to find one today! Beside the epergne are two classical figures with a frosted, or satin, finish supporting bowls, one of which is cut and the other appears to be engraved. All three pieces undoubtedly date in the 1870's and are exceedingly rare today. Candlesticks also were made in a similar style to the stems supporting the bowls, but try to find any of them! They were produced in color and one or two pairs appeared in a collection sold at the Parke-Bernet Galleries a few years ago; they brought a high figure. In fact, the bidding on these "decadent" objects became almost as spirited as at the sale of the Morgan "Peachblow" vase.

Plate 254 pictures blown pieces delicately engraved. Many such dishes may be found in the cupboards of New England homes today, where they are treasured. It will be noted that there are compotes, open and covered; a covered cheese dish; pitchers in tankard and bulbous styles; decanters, a "water bottle and tumble-up," and one lone goblet.

For years many collectors attributed vases with ribbed, crystal turned-up feet as midwestern. Those pictured on Plate 255 are not a style we usually associate with Sandwich. Midwestern competition was cutting in on New England trade during the 1870's, and by 1888 had forced practically all of them out of business. There were three large factories operating in the East as against some twenty or more in the West, so the odds were too greatly against them. These vases undoubtedly represent an attempt to keep in stride, by making the same sort of novelty wares the Pittsburgh district was finding so profitable. Certainly the New England companies did not come to any "financial brilliance." On the contrary, they went down and out.

On Plate 256 we find other forms of cut and engraved wares,

PLATE 253

Dolphin epergne and two frosted glass classical figures supporting bowls which are engraved. Taken from a
Boston & Sandwich Glass Co. sales catalogue of the 1870's.

PLATE 254

Cut and engraved ware, as shown in a Boston & Sandwich Glass Co. catalogue.

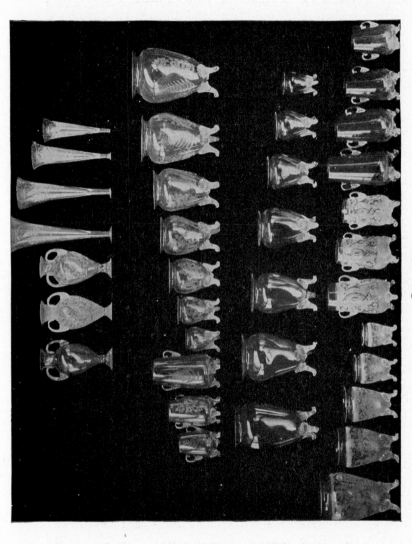

PLATE 255

Vases produced by the Boston & Sandwich Glass Co. to meet midwestern competition.

PLATE 256

Delicate blown, cut ware produced by the Boston & Sandwich Glass Co.

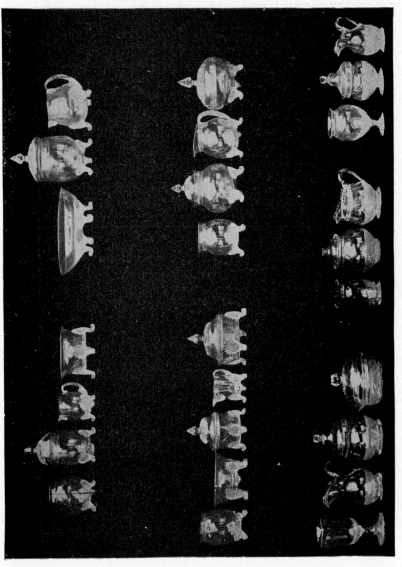

PLATE 257

Tableware with applied ribbed feet, produced by the Boston & Sandwich Glass Co.

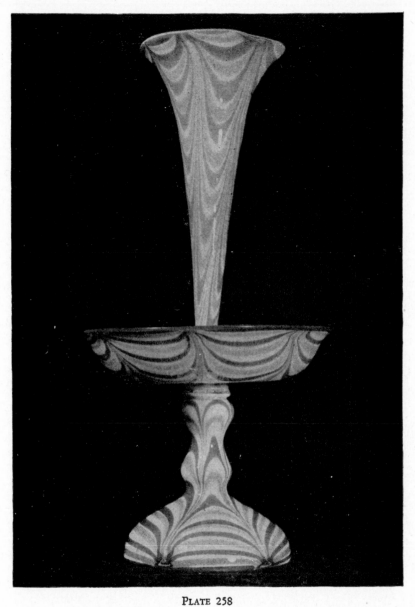

PLATE 258

Epergne in Milk-white with red and blue loopings, produced during the period of
Nicholas Lutz' stay at Sandwich.

PLATE 259

This type of glassware is not usually associated with Sandwich but as documented by old catalogues, was made there in large quantities. It was probably inspired by contemporary English glass.

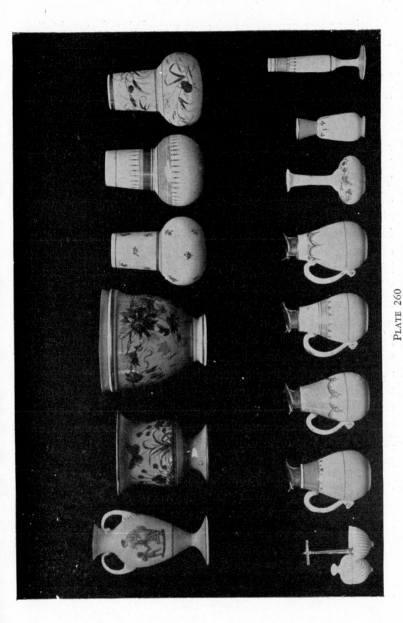

PLATE 260

Page from an old Sandwich Glass Co. catalogue. The water bottles with inverted tumblers seen at the upper right were known as "water bottles with tumble-ups."

this time more compotes and stem ware being featured. Certainly the fragile beauty of these pieces cannot be denied.

Some of the plainer footed tableware is illustrated on Plate 257. It is quite likely that the bowls of many of these pieces may have been made in color, and the feet applied in crystal.

During the period Nicholas Lutz was associated with Sandwich, many artistic articles were made, which could easily be attributed to a man born in St. Louis, Lorraine, France, and who had served his apprenticeship at the local glass factory (Cris Talleries de St. Louis). He was a master workman in all lines of glassmaking but specialized in fancy colored glass. He was also noted for his threaded glass (some of his hats are pictured in the chapter devoted to that subject), flasks, paperweights, etc. The epergne pictured on Plate 258 is undoubtedly some of his work. It is in red, white and blue. The background is white, with red and blue loopings through the glass. Flasks may be encountered in the same colorings.

There is not room in this volume to picture all the decorative glassware produced at Sandwich. There are many ornamental epergnes, some decorated with cutting or engraving; dolphins supporting fish bowls, the globes being either plain or engraved with fish and seaweed; candlesticks; and an almost endless amount of cut and engraved ware of all sorts. Many people consider the latter tiresome but some of the delicate and beautifully executed wares could hardly be considered so by any real glass enthusiast.

The painted and decorated wares are probably the least known of all the Sandwich products. Just one of my catalogues pictures fourteen full pages. There are tall round vases decorated with flowers, butterflies, birds and conventional designs. There are epergnes, flowerpots, light globes and all manner of articles. The fact that this department at Sandwich has been so neglected by writers on the subject caused me to decide to illustrate two pages showing some of the objects.

Plate 259 pictures three styles in epergnes in the upper row, as well as two well-decorated vases. In the lower row at the left are three vases, each treated in a different manner. The first vase is in opaque white. The second, exactly like it, has the background painted and the white flowers stand out in relief. The third vase, still in the same pattern, has the background in the natural opaque white and the flowers painted. The other three vases in the lower row represent different types, and varied forms of decoration.

On Plate 260 there are three water bottles and tumblers at the right in the upper row, which the trade referred to as "water bottle and tumble-ups." The three vases next to them are typical of the latter part of the Victorian era. In the lower row are four syrup jugs, three vases and a table accessory which may be assumed to have served for salt, pepper and mustard.

If other New England factories turned out as much decorated ware as did the Boston & Sandwich Glass Co., then no piece can positively be attributed to any one factory without documentary evidence to prove its birthplace.

No mortal can hope to live long enough to list and authenticate all the blown, cut, engraved, and decorated pieces made at Sandwich. All that it appears feasible to do is to point out some of the most interesting types, which have been neglected up to this time.

Chapter XXIV

DEVELOPMENT OF ETCHED GLASS

The story of the development and progress of etching on glass will not be of interest to all my readers but certain facts are recorded here for the benefit of those who enjoy historical and technical details.

Etching glass by placing it over a bath of fluorspar and sulphuric acid was known in Nuremberg in 1670. Panes of window glass are in existence dating from that year showing raised writing and ornamentation, the background being etched away. The earliest method of applying the design was undoubtedly painting it by hand. Improvements on this method date back to the middle of the nineteenth century when hydrofluoric acid began to be manufactured as a commercial article; the composition of substances resisting its action was studied, and methods of applying them were developed in many ways. The chief use of hydrofluoric acid until 1853 was for etching off groundlaying in glass painting or in removing the ruby or yellow coatings of flashed glass. Owing to the harmful action of the acid on the skin, a Swedish chemist named Berzelius recommended the use of ammonium fluoride (modern white acid) as a harmless substitute. A mixture of wax and turpentine or gutta percha was used to protect the surface not to be etched.

The printing process in etching was not known until 1853, when C. Breese, of London, patented a process of printing a negative on paper with printing ink and transferring this to glass to be etched. Specimens of this work were exhibited at the Paris Exposition in 1855. In 1857 a patent was granted to Benjamin Richardson, of the Wordsley Flint Glass Works, near Stourbridge, England, "for the invention of improvements in manufacturing and ornamenting articles of flint glass." His process consisted in coating the articles to be etched with a composition containing gutta percha or India rubber dissolved in turpentine, and to this solution was added beeswax and tallow. The articles were then dipped into a bath composed of fluoric and sulphuric acids. The first printing in the Stour-bridge district was done by Henry G. Richardson in the year 1855. Glass plates were used and made in a very crude manner. The pattern was etched on sheet glass, the glass cemented onto stone, and the prints taken from the pattern on the glass. Soon after this it was found that lithographers' stones and copper and steel plates were more suitable. The St. Louis Company of France was undoubtedly the first to develop the commercial side of the art. They were engaged in etching in 1850 and in 1870 employed a considerable force making etched goods, for the home and foreign markets. The plates used were first made on stone, but this was eventually replaced by copper and steel. The methods employed were crude and slow. From two to three weeks were required to make a plate and from twenty-four to forty-eight hours to etch it. Patterns etched on the clear glass remained in the acid bath from three to four hours; those etched on ground glass, about half an hour.

The well-known Baccarat Company of France, in the early seventies, exported etched globes to this country in considerable numbers. The shapes were on simple lines limited principally to the round globe, shallow bowl and the deep scalloped cut top tulip form, all having 2½-inch holders for gas and "the Moehring" globe with openings top and bottom, for oil lamps. The etched designs were remarkable for their excellence, consisting of Roman and Greek allegorical figures, examples of Renaissance and realistic landscape designs of such artistic merit that many of them were later reproduced by American manufacturers. The style of work was what was then termed "deep or bright etched," the figures in clear on a roughed background.

The method was to etch the pattern deep on the clear glass, afterward grinding or roughing on a lathe with a wire brush or flat hard metal. In this way the sharpness of the etched lines was reduced, giving a roundness to the figures which stood out in bold relief. Many of the patterns were rendered more pronounced by being in colors; the figures in some instances were filled in with an amber enamel and in others raised as the blue, green and pink flash had been etched away, leaving the colored figures in relief. Up to 1870 or 1871 no etching had been attempted in this country, but about this time one William G. Webb, of Wordsley, England, assigned to William Langdon Libbey, of New Bedford, Mass., a patent for a new and useful improvement in the mode of ornamenting and etching glass. Mr. Libbey in turn assigned the patent to the Mt. Washington Glass Company, that company subsequently disposing of its rights to Samuel R. Bowie, also of New Bedford.

In 1876, James Corbett, who had been in the employ of the Mt. Washington Glass Company, interested the E. P. Gleason Manufacturing Company in the etching of glass and, together with Marshall W. Gleason, established a department of their own. Mr. Corbett remained with the company for only a short period, but Mr. E. P. Gleason, foreseeing great possibilities in the business, decided to continue it. The company started with steel plates, reproducing many of the Baccarat patterns. It attempted to follow the Baccarat method of etching the pattern on clear glass, but finding the process slow and expensive, decided to rough the glass first, and then etch through the ground surface. The business rapidly increased and Mr. Bowie, on account of the competition, threatened suit for infringement of the Webb patent. Eventually the E. P. Gleason Manufacturing Company purchased the patent.

In 1878 the firm of McFadden & Hatton of New York started etching in a small way. The E. P. Gleason Manufacturing Company brought suit for infringement of its patent, but before the case could be tried the defendants discontinued that branch of their business. At about the same time the Boston & Sandwich Glass Company of Sandwich, Mass., started in the etching line, catering chiefly to the Boston trade.

In 1880 Tietz & Stenger took up etching in Philadelphia, continuing until 1883, when they were succeeded by W. H. Buckner & Company. In 1884 H. J. Merchant, of the same city, attempted to do some etching, but did not remain long in the business. Meanwhile, the business of the E. P. Gleason Company had grown to such an extent that it became necessary to look for enlarged quarters. In January, 1883, the J. B. Seibel Company, which had operated the old Dorflinger plant at Greenpoint, Brooklyn, was purchased, and in July of the same year the etching department was transferred to that place.

Gillinder & Sons used white acid for roughing as early as 1873. At the Centennial Exhibition held in Philadelphia in 1876 they exhibited paperweights and other articles finished in this manner.

From an insignificant beginning in 1871 the etching on glass in this country became a thriving industry. Modern laborsaving methods were adopted so that, by 1904, plates which in the earlier days took from two to three weeks to complete were being made in the same number of days. The sand-blast process of grinding long ago supplanted the old style of lathe roughing. The process of printing and the printing ink were greatly improved, as well as the method for the removal of the printing paper. The price of acid was cheapened 80 per cent and the cost of washing and handling the product reduced to a minimum. The technical development in etching glass may not have reached its end.

There is another style of etching known as "Needle Etching" which is done on a machine by scratching with a needle through a coating of wax and etching the tracery. The inventive genius of Guillot was essential in bringing this branch of etching to great industrial importance through the machine named after him. France and Germany took up this work almost simultaneously.

The first English machine was made in 1855 in a very primitive way by one James Smith, an engineer in the employ of W. H. Richardson, of Wordsley, being constructed out of an old lathe which had been used for turning gun butts. The St. Louis Company, of France, started with one machine in the fall of 1873. In November, 1874, it had three machines in operation and in 1890 fourteen machines were running day and night.

In the early seventies William L. Libbey, of the New England Glass Company, sent his son, Edward D. Libbey, to Wordsley, England, to learn the process of needle etching and on his return that branch of decorative glassware was introduced to the New England Glass Works, resulting in a very successful business in etched tableware.

In 1877 Geo. Duncan & Sons, of Pittsburgh, and the Central Glass Company, of Wheeling, W. Va., started in this line of work. The first-named company abandoned etching after a short time, but the Central Glass Company continued it for many years.

By 1905, the article to be etched was first immersed in wax, then the design was put on by needles, mechanically tracing the required design on the wax, after which it was ready for the acid. The work was being turned out more rapidly here than in the old country. In the factories on the Continent, the wax or paint was applied in a cold state with brushes. That took a day to dry. The second day it could be marked on the machine and made ready to be etched on the third day. In our home factories the paint, or wax, is put on hot, the articles being dipped in it. In one hour after dipping it could be worked on the machine and etched. Very often the plain ware sent to the workrooms in the morning was finished and in the cars on the way to the customer in the afternoon. The mixing of the acid required considerable care, particularly where lime glass was used. The foreign-made goods in needle etching, being of lead glass, showed up well since the articles could be left in the acid bath for a longer period.

Etching must be recognized, besides cutting and engraving, as the most appropriate means of embellishing glass. Like the other two processes, but unlike enamel painting and gilding, it adds no foreign material to the glass. Its place among the crafts of decorative glass is most legitimate. Its product is noble whether simple or elaborate, moderate in price or costly. The strong point of advantage of etching over its associates among the arts of glass decorating is that it makes possible a mechanical reproduction of patterns, bringing an article of high artistic merit to a democratic plane of wide distribution, without confining itself to cheap goods. A low-priced etched pattern may be of infinitely higher artistic merit than a cheap hand-engraved one.

Index